ITALIAN ARCHITECTURE

1750–1914

ITALIAN ARCHITECTURE

1750–1914

CARROLL L. V. MEEKS

NEW HAVEN AND LONDON: YALE UNIVERSITY PRESS, 1966

Copyright © 1966 by Yale University.
Designed by John O. C. McCrillis,
set in Times Roman type by
Connecticut Printers, Inc., Hartford, Connecticut,
and printed in the United States of America by
The Meriden Gravure Co., Meriden, Connecticut.
Distributed in Canada by McGill University Press.

Library of Congress catalog card number: 65–22334

Shakespearean fish swam the sea, far away from land:
Romantic fish swam in nets coming to the hand;
What are all those fish that lie gasping on the strand?

YEATS—*Three Movements*

Dedicated to

CAROL SILVESTER MEEKS AND

DOUGLAS AND SUSAN SCOTT RICHARDSON

without whose skills, patience, and enthusiasm

this book would have been greatly delayed

Contents

Preface

This book is addressed to those English-speaking persons who, although knowl-edgeable about the architecture of the last two centuries in its more familiar manifestations, are less cognizant of the Italian parallels. It is not intended to be encyclopedic, since such information is available in quantity in a recent work by Emilio Lavagnino, *L'Arte moderna,* Turin, 1956, and a new edition, 1961, both in two volumes. There are also some biographical studies of the prominent Italian architects of the period. The Bibliography refers to biographical sketches, some of which give lists of works.

In more positive terms this is an essay on the art of architecture as it appears to have been conceived and followed in Italy from 1750 to 1914, organized by the examination of its theory and of its significant episodes.

In the architectural history of the western world during the eighteenth cen-tury there are as many interesting problems as in that of the nineteenth, such as: which countries led in the architectural revolution; whence arose the new the-ories; what were the contacts among the innovators; what, if any, were the common denominators of their programs; which are the key works; when does Palladianism become Neo-Palladianism; and what positive program was offered by the opponents of the late Baroque? Answers to some of these are indicated in this book.

As in the nineteenth century, an astounding diversity of points of view existed simultaneously.[1] It included those who merely sought something novel; those Venetians and Englishmen who chose to follow Palladio; those who wished to re-establish architecture on a rational basis, such as Lodoli, Laugier, and Memmo; those who modified that rigorist position to tolerate some ornament, such as Algarotti and Milizia; those who admired antiquity so fanatically that they aspired to rival it, such as the Grecians led by Winckelmann, the Romans by Piranesi, and the Medievalists by Walpole and Goethe. In addition there also existed what we might call cults, as of those who sought for simplicity and purity in the idealized primitive or in mysterious Egypt, or those who were briefly titillated by the exoticisms of the Near and Far East, such as Sir William Cham-bers. Gradually a nationalistic theory spread which dictated the use of styles from each nation's most glorious moments in the past—medieval in some coun-tries, Renaissance in others. In Italy the *Cinquecento* was one of the basemarks throughout the period under review.

1. See Henry A. Millon, *Baroque and Rococo Architecture* (New York, 1961).

The diversity of vocabulary is easily observable but the motivations and moods require more subtle analysis. It is easy enough to tag a fluted baseless Doric column as "Greek Revival" or the presence of a low dome on a low drum as inspired by the Pantheon.[2] But with Palladianism we have more difficulties; at Vicenza is it merely continuing tradition, whereas at the York Assembly Rooms of 1730 is Lord Burlington being Neo-Palladian? What makes it one or the other? Is it the introduction of classical elements as recorded in Palladio's works or the absence of Palladio's own "Liberté qui va jusqu'à l'audace . . . une originalité d'expression d'une fraîcheur étonnante"?[3]

What lay behind these variations on familiar themes, which are never exact replications? The answer lies in the artistic nature of architecture—that is, its forms are not used merely to show familiarity with an authority or model but to express emotional or intellectual ideas which it is the critics' obligation to recover, either directly from the documents of the period or indirectly by intuition. Suddenly, it had become respectable to have "a degrading thirst after outrageous stimulation."[4] This makes the recovery of such alien ideas difficult for us. As Mérimée and Saint-Beuve said of Stendhal, "it needs a special sensitivity and long practice to love and understand form and color. . . . It is only fair to add that there is no language with which to express the subtleties of form or the variety of the effects of color. For want of ability to express what one feels, one describes other sensations which everybody can understand." This situation often gives rise to the sentimental criticism which became so common in the nineteenth century and made possible the attitude ascribed to Canova by Mérimée, who said "he was far more concerned with the thought he might conjure up in a cultivated mind than with the impression he might create on an eye which loved and understood form."[5] The critic or historian of architecture must try to follow the example recently set by some critics of painting, and must seek to understand the conceptual and expressive content of buildings of other times as their makers understood it. The critic should rely less confidently on subjective interpretations.

Until the mid-eighteenth century the range of expression had been relatively confined by the traditional vocabulary; there was at hand a repertory of orders, moldings, pediments, vaults, and domes augmented by surface treatments such as rustication, paneling, and sculptural accessories. Within these limits a considerable range of expression was possible. At times invention was carried to

2. See Chapter 2, "The Pantheon as a Paradigm."

3. Gino Chierici, *Palladio* (Turin, 1952), Introduction, p. 3.

4. Wordsworth quoted in Edgar Wind, "Critique of Connoisseurship," *Listener, 64* (Dec. 1, 1960), 976.

5. Jean Dutourd, *The Man of Sensibility,* Eng. trans., Robin Chancellor (New York, 1961), pp. 64–67.

the point of fantasy. In very broad terms Alberti and Guarini made use of the same vocabulary. Construction was restricted to masonry in one form or another, employed at times with great audacity.

The birth of a new style may be said to require the happy conjunction of four factors: a new intellectual view of the world, a new aesthetic doctrine, a new vocabulary of form, and a new structural system. If this rule is rigorously applied, it will seem to break on the fourth factor, since history reveals many more styles than it does structural systems. On the other hand, the Rationalists did not create a new style because they did not formulate a positive aesthetic canon.[6] In other words, any three of the four factors may produce a new style. In the case of the Renaissance there was the new humanist philosophy, the anti-Gothic aesthetic, and a mixed antique-modern vocabulary. With the Art Nouveau there was a new vocabulary, a new aesthetic, the potential of the new material—reinforced concrete—more exploited as form than as construction, and an increased use of metal, but not a generally accepted new world view. The Romantics had a new world view and in many instances made use of non-current, though not new, vocabularies. But for the most part they did not have much interest in new materials, although they did have a number of new aesthetic principles. As is well known, the gradual introduction of metallic structure into architecture during the nineteenth century did not immediately produce a new style. Likewise, the Impressionist aesthetic cannot be shown to have had any significant architectural parallel until the Art Nouveau, which recently has been granted the status of an architectural style, but was contemporary with Post-Impressionism and other later aesthetic movements.[7]

To the American or British historian, the architecture of their countries during the years 1750–1914 has become entangled with irrelevant factors, such as historic events or traditional derision, which make it difficult to judge the buildings as works of art. The greater the time interval, however, the greater objectivity is possible, and in the case of a country more remote from the historian's personal associations, such as Italy, English-speaking historians can aspire to a still greater degree of objectivity. Nevertheless, little attention has been paid to these relatively recent Italian monuments, so overpowering has been the universal admiration for the monuments of more remote ages. Yet Italy, as we will attempt to demonstrate, continued to exercise a major rôle in architecture throughout the eighteenth century.

In the eighteenth century "Italy was still the unrivalled school for architects; her ancient monuments and those of the great masters of the Renaissance were

6. Emil Kaufmann, *Architecture in the Age of Reason* (Cambridge, Mass., 1955), p. 99.
7. Henry-Russell Hitchcock, "Architecture," in Peter Selz and Mildred Constantine, eds., *Art Nouveau* (New York, 1959), pp. 123 ff.

still the inexhaustible source of inspiration."[8] Italian authorities tend to be little impressed by the rôle of Italy at this time, although Italian influence continued through important treatises and the work of Italian architects practicing in France, Germany, Russia, and England.[9] Furthermore, important architects and their patrons from the rest of Europe were constantly coming and going through Italy (see Appendix B). Were the new styles of the eighteenth century therefore created by Italians, French, or British?

The problem of priorities is particularly confused in Venice. There, the strength of the Palladian tradition makes it very hard to know "what is Palladian and what is already a little Neoclassical."[10] On this point Emil Kaufmann has contributed subtle formal analyses. We can almost but not quite accept his conclusion that in the late eighteenth century Italy and France changed rôles. Italian architects had striven with a certain frenzy to attain the unattainable (they had not attempted to be rigorists), and "about 1800 Italian architecture fell into a state of exhaustion, into the stage of lethargic classicism."[11] One can question this opinion since it is colored by Kaufmann's interest in "the architecture of revolution" in contrast to which Neoclassicism may seem "lethargic," whereas the "frenzy" may well have combined with Napoleonic programs to produce the major Italian works of Neoclassicism in the nineteenth century. A good deal depends, as in the laboratory, on what you are looking for.

There is much against giving Italy the highest rank as a creative center in the eighteenth century. As Wittkower states: the dominant terms of the Late Baroque were not Italian in origin; aesthetics as an autonomous discipline was German; the nature of genius was defined in England; the science of connoisseurship was also English (Jonathan Richardson); there were no collectors outside France so discriminating as Mariette; the theory of art was finding expression in English and French treatises; and Algarotti, the most prominent Italian critic of his day, can be accused of merely rehashing old classical theory.[12] A further point of Wittkower's is harder to substantiate—that foreign treatises were being translated into Italian. One of these was Sir Joshua Reynolds' *Discourses,* of which Italian translations appeared in 1778 and 1787, but were there many other important translations? See Appendix A.

Nevertheless, as demonstrated in Chapter One and Appendix B, there is evidence to support the contention that Italy was the meeting place in which the germinal ideas of the mid-century were exchanged and nourished. To Rome in

8. Wolfgang Herrmann, *Laugier and Eighteenth-Century French Theory* (London, 1962), p. 167.

9. Henry-Russell Hitchcock, *Architecture: Nineteenth and Twentieth Centuries* (2nd ed. Baltimore, 1963), p. 14.

10. Nello Tarchiani, *L'Architettura italiana dell'ottocento* (Florence, 1937), p. 7.

11. Kaufmann, *Age of Reason,* p. 122.

12. Rudolf Wittkower, *Art and Architecture in Italy* (Baltimore, 1958), p. 239.

particular came crowds of eager students and patrons, to see its buildings of all periods, encouraged by the antiquarian interests of the Papal Court and the presence of Neoclassically minded artists like Mengs (who began his Roman visits in 1741 and continued them until his death in 1779), Piranesi, Clérisseau, and others.

Thus Rome functioned as a forum, not only sending her visitors away with new ideas but receiving some as well, since the idea of reusing medieval styles may well have been introduced to the Italians by their visitors from England and France. In those two countries Gothic had been revived more freely and spectacularly at an earlier date. This interest in medievalism would be reinforced in Italian minds by those Italians who made trips northward.

In dealing with the complexities of Italian architecture it is customary to treat each province separately in accordance with political, linguistic, and other factors which have given rise to the belief that even today Italy is not so much a nation as a union of states. As one moves nearer to our own day this factor seems to have less and less importance in architectural matters. It is of more consequence that the principal architects moved around freely, not only in Italy but throughout Europe. They studied under masters in regions other than those in which they were born, and in the academies at Milan, Parma, Bologna, and Rome under famous professors. Ultimately they were likely to become professors themselves and to teach students drawn from all parts of Italy. Increased ease of travel, especially in the long era of tranquility during the second half of the eighteenth century, scholarships, and the flow of printed material made it feasible for architects and patrons to keep abreast of new developments wherever they occurred.

It would be highly desirable to have numerous statements from the architects or patrons as to their specific aims. Some are available, but, alas, architects are not very reliable about their aesthetic intentions. Often the most original seem to be the most inarticulate. Very few communicate as well with words as with bricks. An only too common practice is to repeat the traditional platitudes about simplicity, truth, economy, nature, beauty, or proportion with little or no reference to their own way of working. To take only one famous case, the lawgiver Palladio: it is well known that he broke all his own rules and perpetrated all the "errors and abuses" which he decried at the end of Book One.[13] Sir William Chambers, another respected figure, was inconsistent in the same way. As Kaufmann says, "Discrepancies between the works and the words of architects are rather the rule."[14] The qualities mentioned above, such as truth and beauty and fidelity to the principles of nature or of the antique, are common denomi-

13. Palladio, *I Quattro Libri dell' architettura* . . . (4 vols. in one, separately paged. Venice, 1570), *1*, 51–52.
14. Kaufmann, *Age of Reason,* p. 109.

nators of architectural theories and, according to architects, of their works. One cannot find any serious advocate of license, extravagance, the unnatural, or the ugly. Yet all of these qualities can be found in prominent buildings. However diverse the pleas, all lawyers take oaths on the same Bible. All architects believe in "beauty" and "reason," although their creations may seem to others to lack both. Hence, as with science, we must often seek out hypotheses and their subsequent experimental applications without the guidance of appropriate theoretical principles. A new movement in architecture is not just the brain child of a philosopher but the work of one or more architects exploiting a new concept more or less fully. Both are necessary just as they are in science, even though the methods of the two worlds are not necessarily parallel. In another sense, too, we are involved like Darwin "in looking at whole classes of facts from a new point of view."[15] The intention here is not to pass judgment on these works, but to recognize and if possible to illuminate the qualities put into these works by their builders, to respond to the values detectable therein, and thus perhaps to assist the reader's appreciation of them.[16] In order to achieve such an aim it is necessary to pay attention to the content and imagery in use at the time of conception, to discover the associations attributed by the artist to his subject. This, it has been said, is the central problem of art history, which includes architecture in its important aspect as art. The emphasis, then, must be on the ideas, feelings, and moods which the architects were attempting to express through their formal, derivative, and eclectic vocabularies, by their use of masses, volumes, planes, and ornament.[17] We must be alert to the whole range of expression through character, images, and symbols—however farfetched they may seem to us today—since these were not motivated by self-expression for its own sake but formed an intelligible system of communication from artist to public, which we must attempt to read again.

The following chapters will apply this method to such Italian manifestations of Eclecticism as Romanticism, Neo-Palladianism, Neoclassicism, Academicism, Medievalism, the *Stile Umberto,* and the Italian equivalent of the Art Nouveau —the *Stile Floreale,* which with Futurism flowered toward the close of the optimistic nineteenth-century world which ended in 1914.

15. A. C. Crombie, "The Private and Public Faces of Darwin," *Listener, 62* (Dec. 3, 1959), 978.

16. Paraphrased from Hilary Corke, "A Very Good Critic," *Encounter, 13* (Sept. 1959), 78, a review of Helen Gardner, *The Business of Criticism* (London, Oxford University Press, 1959).

17. Michael Kitson, "Baroque Conceptions of Art," *Encounter, 12* (April 1959), 49.

Acknowledgments

The research for this book was begun on a Fulbright Fellowship and continued with a Grant-in-Aid from the American Council of Learned Societies, supplemented by other grants and generous treatment from Yale University.

In Europe, several directors and their wives and the staff of the American Academy in Rome extended many gracious courtesies.

Among my colleagues I wish particularly to thank George Kubler and Sumner Crosby for helpful suggestions and valuable advice. Others who rendered aid in various ways include George Hamilton, Christopher Tunnard, William MacDonald, John Hoag, Spiro Kostof, John Jacobus, Guelfo Frulla, Adolf Placzek, Henry-Russell Hitchcock, Henry Millon, Richard Carrott, George Hersey, and Hellmut Wohl.

An enormous amount of indispensable aid has kindly been supplied by Vivian Penney, John Cameron, Helen Searing, Shirley Davenport, Gail Swerling, Patty Mittelstadt, Marion Card Donnelly, David Merrill, Amy Vandersaal, Samuel Roberson, Mary Lowe, David Coffin, Leonard P. Perfido, David Hamilton, John Rohsenow, Milton Carrigan, Arthur Hacker, Steven Ocko, Earl Gruber, Douglas Richardson, Douglas Lewis, M. L. Hadzi, David Summers, Angus MacDonald, Lewis Bryden, and Arnold Cuthbert Harrison.

My wife and daughters have labored loyally in the office, at home or abroad, typing, filing, or checking, and thus making possible a fuller and more accurate text.

Many others have helped in various ways, particularly the officers and staff of the Yale University Press, and I wish that it were possible to thank each of them here by name and to recount their kindnesses.

The editors of the following publications have politely permitted me to reproduce here material which had previously appeared in their journals: *Art Bulletin, Perspecta, The Journal of the Society of Architectural Historians, Architectural History,* and *The Art Quarterly*.

C. L. V. M.

New Haven
January 1964

List of Illustrations

1

Architectural Ideas of the Eighteenth Century

Introduction

Romanticism

Range of Feeling: The Heroic, the Hallucinatory; Morbidity, Sublimity, Nobility, Dorism, Horror, and Gaiety

The Critical Decades: The 1740s and 1750s

The Rôle of Italy

Concurrency of Systems

The Older Architectural Systems
  Renaissance
  Baroque and Late Baroque
  Neo-Palladianism

The Newer Architectural Systems
  Eclecticism; Gothic, Egyptian, Neoclassic
  The Picturesque; Gardens
  Purists, Rationalists, Rigorists, Revolutionaries, and Pure Geometry
  The Revolutionary System
  Symbolism, Allegory, and Iconology
  Scenography
  Character

Conclusion: The Longevity of These Systems

1

Architectural Ideas of the Eighteenth Century

Introduction

A century and a half ago three predominant attitudes toward architecture were observable: that of the Eclectics, who made use of past styles, such as the Neo-Palladians, the Neo-Goths, and the Neoclassicists; that of the Purists, Rationalists, and *Rigoristi,* who sought to establish new simplified architectural rules from the basic essentials of function, material, and geometric form; and that of the "Revolutionary Architects," as Emil Kaufmann called them, whose main motivation was the discovery and application of a new "revolutionary" system of composition.[1] All of these were Romantics, in that through the manipulation of symbols and associations they intended to give their buildings an emotional or didactic significance.

This classification, roughly parallel to the one which Kaufmann offered, is an arbitrary one since the groups cannot be kept separate.[2] One man often held more than one of these attitudes. Nevertheless, such a framework enables us to understand the period a little better than would a bare catalogue of men or buildings, and all of them have in common the Romantic point of view.

Romanticism

Romanticism has as many roots and branches as love, and as with love not all of them are acknowledged and respected. The architecture of the western world from 1750 on seems to be impossibly varied and chaotic, yet all of it is romantic in one way or another, from the fantasies of Picturesque Eclecticism to the severest rationalism. Even the geometrical mountains of a Boullée are sentimental in inspiration. Of all the apparently contradictory manifestations,

---

1. Emil Kaufmann, "Three Revolutionary Architects, Boullée, Ledoux, and Lequeu," *Transactions of the American Philosophical Society,* new series, *42,* part 3 (Philadelphia, 1952), passim.
2. Emil Kaufmann, *Architecture in the Age of Reason,* p. 142.

Neoclassicism is one of the most incongruous and persistent. The common denominator of all the aspects of Romantic architecture was the point of view which saw architecture primarily as a vehicle for the expression of a non-architectural idea or feeling. Romantic architecture was made to carry a diversified freight of associations, ideals, moods, symbols, and allusions. It was not expected to limit itself to the traditional aesthetic subtleties of line, form, space, or proportion. The beholder was expected to "read" a building as though it were a poem or a novel and to bring to his reading either a goodly store of learning or some slight practice in reacting to moods and symbols.

Emotional demands rather than their formal expression are the easily recognized attributes of Romanticism. Fiske Kimball, essaying to define it in 1944, emphasized the former and sketched in one or two of the latter, such as irregularity, the increasing scope of eclecticism, and—what he considered the deepest current—the demand for originality. He attributed the movement to English origins.[3] More than a decade later Summerson asserted that the priorities were shared by Rome and Paris, which is also Hitchcock's view.[4] None of them, however, lays as much stress on the Italian rôle as the evidence would seem to merit.

The heightening and intensifying of emotional effects occurred simultaneously in other arts and became a cult of sensation. The emotions of the time craved material to feed on and relished those impossible landscapes, those towering castles, those reconstructions of the antique and the remote. Those who could built exotic villas, traveled, or bought pictures and prints. Everyone read the Gothic novels and the poems, and yearned for more intense experiences.

Edmund Burke's *A Philosophical Enquiry into the Origin of Our Ideas of the Sublime and Beautiful* of 1757 was to be the major English contribution to the theory of Romanticism, since it enlarged the range of possible reactions to works of art from ideal beauty alone to include a range of sensations such as awe, thus opening the gates for the heroic, the gay, the melancholic, the pathetic, and ultimately the picturesque, the rustic, and the irregular.[5] These latter enlargements were by Sir Uvedale Price and Richard Payne Knight and fitted in well with the English landscape theory of William Kent and Humphry Repton. Support for them was to be found in such high quarters as Sir Joshua Reynolds' *Discourses* of 1769–91.[6]

3. Fiske Kimball, "Romantic Classicism in Architecture," *Gazette des Beaux-Arts,* series 6, *25* (1944), 95–112.

4. Sir John Summerson, *Architecture in Britain 1530–1830* (1st ed. Baltimore, 1954), p. 248; (4th ed., 1963), p. 246; and Henry-Russell Hitchcock, *Architecture: Nineteenth and Twentieth Centuries* (1st ed. Baltimore, 1958), p. xxi.

5. Edmund Burke, *A Philosophical Enquiry into the Origin of Our Ideas of the Sublime and Beautiful* (London, 1757).

6. Sir Joshua Reynolds, *Discourses* (London, 1791). His views were also echoed by Robert Adam, *The Works in Architecture of Robert and James Adam* (3 vols. London, 1773–1822).

Simultaneously a new intellectual attitude was developing which would upset the old versions of such concepts as authority, man, nature, or liberty. The authority of the Establishment was repudiated, but man continued to seek external guidance of some kind. In the late eighteenth century he found his absolutes in the cult of the hero, the idolatry of a nation, and the worship of genius. Newton, Frederick the Great, Voltaire, and Napoleon were admired as supermen. The Enlightenment, which had joined a common faith, a common language, and the free exchange of ideas, was replaced by a narrower concept of race, blood, and fatherland. Competition came to be more valued than cooperation. The authority of the academies with their rules and formulae was swept away in favor of the less tangible, more flexible mystical belief in individual genius. It was no longer possible to believe as Shaftesbury had that "the Whole [is] a system complete, according to one simple, consistent, and uniform design."[7] It followed that architecture was no longer to be practiced following accepted rules, but as a medium for self-expression. The theory arose that architecture was capable of mirroring many moods. This was pronounced in such terms as "l'architecture parlante," or "an architecture of expression," all linked with the new emphasis on man as an emotional rather than a primarily intellectual being. Rousseau supplied the keys: the emphasis on the differences between individuals, the uniqueness of each man, and, above all, the intrinsic rights of the great passions. Such ideas culminate in the belief that ultimate truth is not external but is embodied in the experiences of the naked passive self.[8] Emotions, as Kenneth Clark says, even become an end in themselves to be deliberately cultivated.[9] Lord Byron, for example, noted in his journal, "the great object is sensation—to feel that we exist, even though in pain."[10]

Such views implied that architecture could become genuinely democratic. Since emotions were common to all men, an architecture which expressed moods would speak a universal language. The training in scale, proportion, and rules which were traditionally necessary for the appreciation of architecture would no longer be required for its enjoyment. This implication was never fully realized.

Nature, which for some centuries had been regarded as a friendly force subject to the same universal laws as man himself and reflecting directly the Divine Wisdom, became an inimical, incomprehensible power. She ceased to be thought of as orderly and predictable, but instead became capricious and irrational,

7. The Earl of Shaftesbury, *The Moralists* . . . , as quoted by Wylie Sypher, *Rococo to Cubism* (New York, 1960), p. 37.

8. Geoffrey Grigson, "The Romantics in London," *Encounter, 13* (Sept. 1959), 54.

9. Sir Kenneth Clark, "Introduction" in: The Arts Council of Great Britain, *The Romantic Movement* (London, 1959), p. 19. See also p. 409.

10. *Lord Byron's Journals,* as quoted by J. Donald Adams, *New York Times Book Review* (Jan. 15, 1961), p. 2.

though the idea that she was on the whole benevolent, ineffably wise, and the fountainhead of all knowledge survived.

So it was that some could still look to Nature for a new code of architectural laws while others sought to emulate her untamed moods, ranging from the pastoral to the sublime. While Cordemoy in 1706 found the qualities natural to architecture to be rational ones like clarity, truth, and suitability to function, Algarotti, writing in the '50s, found that Nature was occasionally extravagant, such as in providing male animals with breasts.[11] At about the same time Piranesi was agreeing with Ovid that "Nature renews herself constantly to produce new out of old," but in practice he seemed to demonstrate that man was puny in the face of Nature, who would in time conquer everything as she had reduced the monuments of Rome to ruin.[12] Milizia found the avenues and the canals of the Baroque unnatural and admired the naturalness of the English school of landscape architecture. There were many followers of Rousseau's rhapsodies who found everything in unspoiled Nature perfect. So we can agree with Fiske Kimball when he said that to many Romanticism meant the worship of Nature, but we must do so with the caution that Nature had many faces. Kenneth Clark is illuminating when he says that the revolutionaries sought only to return to the simplicity of Nature but in fact "endow us with a far richer and more complex response to life and art by extending the dimension of time, by accepting the continuance of change, and by encouraging us to explore the recesses of our hearts."[13]

There were some oddities about this new faith in Nature. The highly artificial, codified gestures used in the theatre to express the emotions were held to derive from natural expression. The anthropological evidence to the contrary was not yet adduced.[14] The next century would see a much more profound and subjective interpretation of Nature. Baudelaire said that "the whole visible universe is but a storehouse of images and signs to which the imagination will give a relative place and value; it is a sort of pasture which the imagination must digest and transform."[15] Wilde would be able to say that "Nature . . . is our creation. It is in our brain that she quickens to life."[16] Frank Lloyd Wright's worship of Nature in its pastoral and organic aspects is typical of the old Romanticism. Today, in spite of our, for the most part uncritical, acceptance of the old attitude, there are some who can say, like Gio Ponti, "Nature is cruel. Architecture had better stick to geometry."[17]

11. Conte Francesco Algarotti, *Saggio sopra l'architettura* (Milan, 1831), p. 14.
12. Giovanni Battista Piranesi, *Della Magnificenza . . .* (Rome, 1761), p. 31.
13. Clark, *The Romantic Movement,* p. 20.
14. Wylie Sypher, *Four Stages of Renaissance Style* (Garden City, N.Y., 1955), pp. 274 ff.
15. Sypher, *Rococo,* p. 125.
16. Ibid., p. 223.
17. Gio Ponti, *In Praise of Architecture* (New York, 1960), p. 185.

As has been said above, the new concepts meant the overthrow of all traditional architectural rules. Piranesi had taught Robert Adam that the only valid criteria were taste and feeling.[18] Thus Adam was able to say of the orders:

> The rules and orders of architecture, are so generally known, and may be found in so many books, that it would be tedious, and even absurd, to treat of them in this work. We beg leave, however, to observe that among architects destitute of genius and incapable of venturing into the great line of their art, the attention paid to those rules and proportions is frequently minute and frivolous. The great masters of antiquity were not so rigidly scrupulous, they varied the proportions as the general spirit of their composition required, clearly perceiving, that however necessary these rules may be to form the taste and to correct the licentiousness of the scholar they often cramp the genius and circumscribe the ideas of the master.[19]
>
> In the first place, we acknowledge only three orders; the Doric, the Ionic, and the Corinthian: for as to the Tuscan, it is, in fact, no more than a bad and imperfect Doric; and the Composite, or Roman order, in our opinion, is a very disagreeable and awkward mixture of the Corinthian and Ionic, without either grace or beauty. We do not, however, mean to condemn the composing of capitals; a liberty which has often been taken by the antients [sic] with great success; and in a former part of this work, we have exhibited an attempt of our own in this way. . . .[20]

The giving way to one's emotions has never been considered good form by Anglo-Saxon peoples while it is freely indulged in the Latin countries. Hence the new liberalism of the English-speaking world was thoroughly supported by the Italians. The prejudice against the expression of feeling is so bred into modern man that his criticism is affected by it. He finds it uncomfortable to recognize that it exists, and generally cannot approve of any very striking expression of the heart. Geoffrey Grigson demonstrated this in his criticism of the recent exhibition "Romanticism in Painting."[21] Unlike Sir Kenneth Clark's magnificently wholehearted appreciation of Romanticism as seen in the same exhibition, Grigson attacked it for being restless, grandiose, brash, smooth, hard, vapid, and obvious, in other words, for not being classical. Some of his terms are merely the Romantic goals reversed. Frequently his objections are based on the childishness or naïveté of expression, even while tolerating the importance of the expression of moods such as melancholy, joy, ecstasy, morbidity, terror and

18. Sir John Summerson, *Architecture in Britain* (4th ed. Baltimore, 1963), p. 261.
19. Robert Adam, *Works in Architecture 1*, no. 1 (London, 1773), 6–7.
20. Ibid., *1*, no. 2 (1774), 4–5.
21. Grigson, "The Romantics in London," *Encounter, 13* (Sept. 1959), 54–56.

revolt. "Childishness" of expression is an inherent factor in Romanticism. As Philip Toynbee has said, a sophisticated allegory is an impossibility.[22]

The full freedom of expression, the wild flinging-around of the emotions, finds an outlet more readily in the other arts than in architecture, since the architect's medium is a relatively recalcitrant one. The taste of the late eighteenth century is linked with that of its past. What was present but rarely dominant in the Baroque became overwhelming in the next centuries. The ecstasy of Bernini's St. Teresa becomes the sentimentality of Canova's *Penitent Magdalene*. There was a lowering of levels in order to reach a wider audience. By the mid-nineteenth century homes and picture galleries filled their walls with scenes of cows grazing quietly in lush meadows, peasant youths and maidens, beggars, dogs, and deathbed scenes, all calculated to appeal to an easy, obvious, and superficial sentimentality. The appeal formerly made to the trained eye may have been latent, but "character" and "naturalness" were essentials. Thus the arts of the nineteenth century continued to stress narrative and sentiment more than "beauty," and communication tended to become more important than form and technique.

The intellectual content which is the raw material of art also changed. The legend of St. Ursula or the apotheosis of the Virgin were vehicles for aesthetic invention, but beggar girls and grazing cows were used primarily to evoke a mood. Sir Joshua Reynolds, among others, extended this concept to architecture. He said that buildings should no longer be like pictures, but should convey a moral or stimulate a sentiment.[23]

Range of Feeling: The Heroic, the Hallucinatory; Morbidity, Sublimity, Nobility, Dorism, Horror, and Gaiety

The feelings or moods of the eighteenth and nineteenth centuries expressed in architecture vary widely: from those associated with the most violent activity to those connected with the quietest resignation. Not, as Grigson implied, that the change is from one extreme in 1750 to the other in 1850, but rather that all types of expression come at once.[24] A kind of contemplative eroticism crops up again and again as it had in Bronzino, now in Canova and Baudelaire.

The Architecture of Revolution was largely hallucinatory. The drawing boards were covered with utterly unreal projects—Gilly's tombs, Soane's bridges, Antolini's forum (Figure 32), Cagnola's palaces. The range of passion could have a negative side in its melancholy, morbid, crepuscular aspects.

22. Philip Toynbee, review of Saul Bellow's *Henderson the Rain King, Encounter, 13* (Sept. 1959), 70.

23. Kaufmann, *Age of Reason*, p. 141.

24. Grigson, *Encounter, 13* (Sept. 1959), 54–56.

Or it could be stoic, solemn, and forbidding. Many of these moods were intro-
verted; Mario Praz, who is particularly alert at discerning morbidity, has reviewed some of its forms in his *Gusto neoclassico*. He sees sadism in Piranesi, for
example, in his engraving of the construction of the Tomb of Caecilia Metella,[25]
where the violence and energy of the clamps are, as Marinai said, "like a surgeon
dissecting a corpse."[26] The sense of torment flows out from many of the prints,
not just the *Carceri*. Sometimes the Piranesian mood is funereal as in the *Piazzale* and the *Appian Way*. There was the mood of despair or, as Summerson said,
"melancholy restraint."[26a] In comparison with the mighty achievements of the
past, eighteenth-century man's efforts are felt to be ineffectual. Men who admired heroes of antiquity, the stoics, the men of Plutarch, were themselves often
listless, irresolute, and drugged. The virility and courage which they admired so
much in others they tended to reduce to a softened Alexandrian grace. The preoccupation with death, graves, and above all monuments, was persistent.

If it becomes the business of architecture to communicate moods, sentiments,
and feelings such as these, some language for doing so must be at hand. This may
include the association of the most direct kind of signs and symbols of various
degrees of legibility. Modern critics as well as contemporary artists are much
more sympathetic to the use of signs and symbols than was the case a generation
or two ago, hence we can be more understanding of symbols and more subtle in
seeing them than was possible in the recent past. Modern man has an enormous
repertory of symbols available: the psychic residues defined by Jung; those more
common ones whose unconscious meanings were revealed by Freud; and Renaissance, Platonic, and Christian ones.[27] In Romanticism there was an implication
that the true fall of man was the development of the intellect. The modern view
is that imagistic thinking is as necessary for the artist as it is irrelevant for the
scientist, for those who think of problems as soluble and of obscurities as un-
desirable. The high valuation placed upon primitive image-making powers has
increased through the work of Kant, Herder, Bergson, Hulme, Cassirer, and
Langer. The ideal state is one in which name and object are the same and one
in which there is no distinction between thought and emotion. Many others have
contributed to our understanding of the importance of sign and symbol: Erich
Auerbach in *Mimesis*, Northrop Frye in *Anatomy of Criticism*, Helen Gardner
in various works, and Jacques Maritain, who discriminated fully between various kinds of signs. There is an effort to recover imaginative patterns and relations
so subtle that in our brutality we have lost them. Their significance depends on

25. Piranesi, *L'Antichità* . . . (4 vols. Rome, 1756), pl. 53.
26. Mario Praz, *Gusto neoclassico* (2nd ed. Naples, 1959), p. 102.
26a. Summerson, *Architecture in Britain*, p. 284.
27. Frank Kermode, "On David Jones," *Encounter, 13* (Nov. 1959), 76–79.

historical deposits. As Yeats said, art must be constantly flooded with the passions and beliefs of ancient times. Hence, in order to comprehend the architecture of Romanticism, we must see how much of its language of form, symbol, and image we can decipher today.

Our best guide to the symbolic language of Romantic architecture comes from the French writers Boullée and Ledoux, who interpret their architectural designs for us. Boullée, for example, comments on the way in which buildings may express the moods of the four seasons. Spring, he says, is light and agreeable and may be expressed in architecture by light, elegant proportions and tender, delicate color. The mood of summer is magnificence, which an architect can echo by using noble masses, a play of light, considerable movement, and the multiplication of elements. Autumn was a laughing season to him, since it was the time for fairs, theatres, visits to baths, and Vauxhalls. Hence the architecture should be picturesque, full of flights of the imagination, piquant contrasts, and the unexpected. This is not a traditional view of autumn but a farfetched one used in order to make melancholy available as an expression of winter. In the Middle Ages it was usual to represent autumn as harvest time in accordance with the agricultural orientation of the time. Boullée's ideas are those of a townsman. So winter is a sad and sombre season and its mood may be caught architecturally by using low masses, absolutely bare walls, burying the building partially in the earth, and creating an architecture of shadows by using materials which absorb light.[28]

An effect which most architects sought to achieve at one time or another had various names—"the sublime," "grandeur," "vastness," "magnificence," "nobility," and "majesty." The "sublime," according to Burke, could arouse in the sensitive beholder feelings of fear, infinity, difficulty or pain, vastness or obscurity. The means to achieve it included the use of monumental scale.[29] Italian *terribilità* as seen in Piranesi's etchings is closely related. Summerson cites an example of this in Bonomi's Church of Great Packington, Warwickshire, of 1790, which seems to derive from Piranesi's dark views of Paestum.[30] Ledoux was the master of this quality in its aspect of grandeur. He achieved this by increasing the solids in relation to the voids, spacing his bays far apart both horizontally and vertically, thus slowing the beat to a processional measure. Ledoux used other devices to the same end: contrasting masses with flat bare planes, repeating vertical elements such as orders as though they were bays, omitting details on large elements where the dominance of the main mass would tend to

28. Helen Rosenau, ed., *Boullée's Treatise on Architecture* (London, 1953), pp. 41–45.
29. Rosenau, "The Engravings of the Grands Prix of the French Academy of Architecture," *Architectural History, 3* (1960), 20.
30. Summerson, *Architecture in Britain*, p. 284.

obliterate them, increasing the imposing effect of the elements by reducing breaks in the surface, and using the colossal order.[31] Boullée also reduced the variety of elements to a minimum but increased their number so as to invoke the vastness of a panorama made up of an incalculable number of objects. In so doing he tried to avoid what appeared to him to be the excessive giganticism of St. Peter's and the overabundant details of Gothic, and kept to the justice of the Greeks.[32] Boullée, in common with many authors, thought that nothing achieved magnificence so effectively as colonnades. This led to the extreme of stylophily usually confined to paper projects but which, when executed, were noble in spite of greatly reduced dimensions. It was nearly a century after Durand's *Précis*[32a] had appeared that his mania was realized at full scale in the great expositions beginning with the Columbian of 1893 in Chicago.[33]

The closely related feeling of nobility was best insured, Boullée said, by due care in the surroundings to enhance or maintain that quality in the building itself. Temples should have a fine portal, colonnades, and a considerable extent of empty space as in antiquity. St. Gervais in Paris, he felt, was marred by the lack of a suitable precinct. Porches like that of the Pantheon also established nobility and should be more widely used. In order to make sure that a Palais de Justice was sufficiently majestic, Boullée urged that it be raised high so that it dominated its environment and "belonged to the heavens." The "Throne of Justice" could be given the utmost grandeur by using a simple mass without subdivisions or breaks.[34] This idea, common at the time, was a legacy from the Renaissance.

The Greek Doric, too, had similar associations. This was sometimes considered to be typical of primitive nature uncontaminated; "Dorismo" or Dorism is a term used by Praz to describe the young German architect Gilly's style with its nude walls, ponderous arches, crepuscular interiors, and nocturnal scenes.[35] These features can be seen in his well-known project for a temple-tomb to honor Frederick the Great. It was never built, just as his short life was unfulfilled in every sense. Dorism was meant to express virility, integrity, strength, and the heroic spirit. The heroes of this period were men, as those of the preceding period had been women like Catherine the Great, Maria Theresa, and Marie Antoinette. Napoleon, Wellington, and the marshals were the soldierly heroes of the new age, and women like George Sand and Mme. de Staël attempted to

31. J. Ch. Moreux, *Claude-Nicolas Ledoux* (Paris, 1945), p. 47.

32. Rosenau, *Boullée*, p. 48.

32a. J.-N.-L. Durand, *Précis des leçons d'architecture* (2 vols. Paris, 1802–05).

33. Carroll L. V. Meeks, "Wright's Eastern-Seaboard Contemporaries: Creative Eclecticism in the United States around 1900," *Studies in Western Art, 2* (New York, 1963), 64 ff.

34. Rosenau, *Boullée*, p. 65.

35. Praz, *Gusto neoclassico*, p. 105.

adapt themselves to this by being as masculine as possible, often finding their greatest admirers among delicate men. The Doric column is an obvious symbol of masculinity, and this aspect of it is clearly shown in the Fountain of Hercules at La Favorita near Palermo, where a single huge Greek Doric column, modeled after one at Agrigentum, rises from a basin of water to support a relatively tiny version of the bull-like Farnese Hercules. Several arched jets of water descend from lion heads on the echinus (Figure 30). Dorism ranged from this sort of archetypal association to the specific heroes of Plutarch who were considered to have exhibited admirable virtues. A more elementary association with sheer strength occurs in the preference shown for using Doric antae in place of rustication or mere pilasters.[36] Some, like Isaac Ware, however, felt that rustication gave a very great sense of stability. "It looks as a rock upon which all the rest is raised."[37]

The emotion of horror was one sometimes deliberately sought. Horror was considered capable of evoking a sort of admiration. Boullée wrote that a Vulcan emitting flames and death was a horribly beautiful image.[38] Something similar was evoked in the design of prisons. As late as 1862 Charles Blanc was strongly moved at the sight of Ledoux's prison for Aix-en-Provence which he called "farouche."[39] Moreux says of it that it is so expressive as almost to be a caricature of the idea of a prison. George Dance the younger, in his Newgate Prison, London, designed in 1769, had earlier achieved the same effects with overtones of sardonic humor. The *Carceri* were in everyone's mind as the Bastille would also be. The formal means employed in such designs include, in addition to military overtones, allusions to medieval fortresses—stern, nearly windowless walls, great scale, and a sense of impenetrable dignity. In 1827 Cacialli published in Florence a book of designs which included such a prison. It rises in three rusticated tiers of which the lowest is battered. There are four squat spool-shaped towers whose small windows are Roman, and Greek Doric columns appear in lunettes high above the ground. All the openings are round-headed, except for a few pointed ones in the towers. The plan is bold and simple and contains a circular courtyard. Thus the prison overtones have been achieved by using features which express withdrawal, medievalism, militarism, masculinity, and fierceness.[40] Today any yearning we have for horror is not intentionally gratified by architecture.

At the opposite pole a number of buildings expressed gaiety and frivolity, such as Porden and Nash's Royal Pavilion at Brighton, Cockerell's Sezincote,

---

36. Summerson, *Architecture in Britain*, p. 304.
37. Isaac Ware, *A Complete Body of Architecture* . . . (London, 1756), p. 323.
38. Rosenau, *Boullée*, p. 48.
39. Moreux, *Ledoux*, p. 42.
40. Giuseppe Cacialli, *Raccolta di progetti* . . . (Florence, 1827), pl. 2.

Vauxhall, or the Hameau at the Petit Trianon. The means used to induce this mood included frail materials and forms insubstantial in themselves, such as tents, screens, or lattices, suggesting transitoriness; brilliance of color; and an air of extemporization. A frivolous function called for these associations.

The Critical Decades: The 1740s and 1750s

The middle third of the century was the decisive one. Wittkower, for example, ends his book on Italian architecture in 1750 with many tantalizing glances beyond, and says that by 1770 "Neoclassicism was conquering Europe."[41] Lavagnino traces the many efforts toward a return to greater simplicity and purity in the first half of the eighteenth century as preliminary to the treatises of the second half.[42]

Kaufmann says, "The momentous symptoms, then, of growing uneasiness about 1750 will not appear as a sudden break with the past, but as the outcome of a century-old process. It may be said in advance that this uneasiness found vent not so much in building as in acid criticism of tradition, in the most daring formulation of an entirely new architectural program, and in delineations in the graphic arts which tell of the breakdown of the old outworn system and the desire for a new architectural order."[43]

Hitchcock places the concerted stylistic revolution as coming shortly after the mid-century, with the new style taking form during the forty years between 1750 and 1790.[44]

The decade of the 1750s is filled with the publication dates of important treatises, such as that by Rousseau in 1750, *Discours sur les arts et sciences;* Pancrazi's *Antichità siciliane spiegate,* one of the earliest to show Greek buildings; J. F. Blondel's *Architecture françoise,* with its radical theories; Count Algarotti's redactions of Lodoli's rigorist ideas; the Abbé Laugier's purist doctrines published in his *Essai sur l'architecture* in Paris in 1753 and in England in 1755; Winckelmann's *Gedanken über die Nachahmung der griechischen Werke,* one of the earliest to pronounce the superiority of the art of Greece, followed in 1758 by J. D. Le Roy's *Les Ruines des plus beaux monuments de la Grèce,* the first publication to give accurate drawings of Greek architecture. In 1757 Edmund Burke had published *Of the Sublime and Beautiful,* the most concrete statement which had appeared up to that time concerning the widened range of aesthetic satisfactions and objectives. Once launched with such bril-

41. Wittkower, *Art and Architecture,* p. 287.
42. Emilio Lavagnino, *L'Arte moderna dai neoclassici ai contemporanei,* Storia dell'arte classica e italiana, 5 (rev. ed. 2 vols. Turin, 1961), *1,* 4 ff.
43. Kaufmann, *Age of Reason,* p. 75.
44. Hitchcock, *Architecture,* p. xxi.

liance the flood of publications kept on through the rest of the century (see Appendix A).

So many landmarks occur in the '50s that one must look back into the '40s for preliminary stirrings. These are to be seen in the doctrines, discussed below, the publications listed in Appendix A, and, according to John Harris, in the projects executed by students in the French Academy in Rome even before the arrival there of Clérisseau.[44a] Thus the contribution of Italy is important.[44b]

The Rôle of Italy

The second half of the century was peaceful in Italy. This encouraged the flow of travelers and tourists. In Venice, in particular, the last years of the Republic were ones in which, as Focillon says, individualism flourished.[45] Venice became the most relaxed and licentious city in Europe. In the years 1787–89, Tarchiani says, there were crowds of travelers studying Greek and even Egyptian monuments.[46] In Rome the papal and lay princes were surrounded by the treasures of the past. Italy's churches, her academies, and her climate exercised their perennial appeal to the men from the North. The cafés and the Corso were full of them (see Appendix B).

This magnetic combination drew students of architecture from all over Europe. Many bearing illustrious names followed in the footsteps of Inigo Jones, who had made two trips a century earlier; Thomas Archer, who had spent four years there at the end of the century; James Gibbs, who had studied for several years (1707–09) with Carlo Fontana; Lord Burlington, who had there met his lifelong friend and collaborator William Kent, who had lived in Italy from 1710 to 1719. These were followed shortly after by Isaac Ware and by Jacques-Germain Soufflot, a student at the French Academy who returned later to visit the temples of Sicily. The Spanish Academy's pensioners included Diego and Juan de Villanueva.

Another wave of Englishmen included Nicholas Revett, who arrived in 1742 and stayed for nine years, joining up with James Stuart, Matthew Brettingham, Jr., and Gavin Hamilton to travel extensively in the south of Italy and eventually to Greece. In the decade of the '50s other important visitors included Sir Joshua Reynolds (1749–52); Sir William Chambers (1750–55), who was elected a member of the Florentine Academy (he had already returned from his voyage

44a. Unpublished letter from John Harris to the author, April 1964.

44b. This opinion was expressed by Louis Hautecoeur, in 1912, in his *Rome et la renaissance de l'antiquité . . .* (Paris, 1912), p. 79, and reaffirmed by him forty years later in *Histoire de l'architecture classique en France* (7 vols. in 9. Paris, 1943–57), *4*, 12.

45. Henri Focillon, *Piranesi* (Paris, 1928), p. 13.

46. Nello Tarchiani, *L'Architettura italiana dell'ottocento*, p. 7.

to China); Marie-Joseph Peyre from Paris (1753–57), who exercised a considerable influence over Robert Mylne; Charles Louis Clérisseau, who went to Nîmes, Venice, and the Dalmatian coast with Robert Adam, and who later assisted Thomas Jefferson with his Nîmes-derived scheme for the Virginia Capitol. Robert Adam was in Italy and Dalmatia from 1754 to 1758, and became a member of the Academy of St. Luke (the art and architecture school of Rome) and a friend of Piranesi, a leader of one of the new movements in Italy. Robert Mylne (1755–59) won a prize while studying at the Academy of St. Luke and became a member of the Academies of Florence and Bologna. J. J. Winckelmann arrived in Rome in 1755 and remained until 1768. Three years later George Dance, Jr., arrived and studied in Rome, Naples, Florence, and Parma, where he won a gold medal from the Academy there. Jacques Gondoin came in 1759 and stayed four years. Nearly all of these men came in their youth and at an age when they were receptive to new ideas and to the stimulation of the vibrant environment. They all left their mark on the architecture of their native countries.

The illustrious procession continues through the '60s and '70s with James Wyatt, Karl Gotthard Langhans (whose Brandenburg Gate of 1789–94 in Berlin was the first German monument of Neoclassicism), Bernard Poyet, Thomas Harrison, Jean-Louis Desprez, Sir John Soane, and others. With singularly few exceptions, the men who created the architecture of Romanticism had spent some time in Italy, a fact which is not usually given sufficient emphasis. Italy, and Rome in particular, was the meeting place of the young architects and the new ideas. Italy was as important to the development of the new architecture as it had been to the birth of the Renaissance. It occupied a position similar to that of Paris in the late nineteenth and early twentieth centuries. In Italy, more than anywhere else, architects from all over Europe had an opportunity to meet, discuss, and argue the radical ideas promulgated by Lodoli and Algarotti, to take sides in the controversies about the Greeks and the Romans waged by Winckelmann and Piranesi. This occurred where the ancient models lay about to be studied and revered.

The great Italians of the period were the teacher Carlo Lodoli of Venice, who died in 1761; Ferdinando Fuga, who was fifty-one years old in 1750; Luigi Vanvitelli, who worked in Naples and Caserta until his death in 1773; Giovanni Antonio Scalfarotto in Venice, who died in 1764; Carlo Marchionni, who erected revolutionary buildings with the advice of Winckelmann and was forty-eight when the '50s began; and Tommaso Temanza, the Venetian architect, historian, and teacher, who lived until 1789. Count Algarotti, who was familiar with the courts of Germany, France, and England and who was an intimate of Frederick the Great, Voltaire, Lord Hervey, and Lady Mary Wortley Montagu, preached a modified version of Lodoli's rigorist ideas. The following important Italian architects were coming to artistic maturity during the decade of the '50s: Antonio Asprucci, Michelangelo Simonetti, Pietro Camporese, Niccolò Gaspare Paoletti, Giuseppe V. Marvuglia, Cosimo Morelli, Giovanni Stern, Giuseppe Piermarini, and Simone Cantoni. At this time Piranesi was in his early thirties and the Grecian Winckelmann about the same. The international galaxy thus met with an equally formidable array of local talent and changed the architecture of Europe.

The painters, too, came and went at Rome, such as Canaletto and Bellotto, or spent the best part of their lives there, like Panini, who died there in 1765, or Hubert Robert, who lived there from 1754 to 1765, or Gavin Hamilton, who lived in Rome from the age of twenty-five until his death at seventy-five in 1798. Raphael Mengs became the Director of the Vatican Art Academy in 1754.

Finally there were the patrons, the tourists, the young milords and princes with their "bear-leaders," as their tutors were called, and the duchesses.

One might expect that the ideas of men like Rousseau would tend toward austerity; however, the lavishness of princes continued unchecked. Neoclassic buildings were no cheaper to build than Baroque or Rococo ones, requiring at least equally good materials and finely executed decoration. The furniture made to their order cost them about as much as it does us today, when it has become rare and is sought after by collectors and museums.

It was under these conditions that the new theories concerning the nature of architecture arose, came into conflict with one another, and revolutionized the design of buildings.

Concurrency of Systems

Before 1750 the new attitudes toward architecture were relatively minor currents—after that date they became rushing torrents. These new attitudes often coexisted, so that it is important at this point to dispel as far as possible the notion that there has been a marked degree of unity in the arts at any one time—the Zeitgeist. The conception of an homogeneous period has few friends today; for instance, witness such ideas as "the many-faceted art and philosophy of Romanticism."[47] There is also a growing awareness of "the need to clarify the sources and nature of the various romanticisms and certainly to discriminate the very different contributions made by England, France, and Germany."[48] And, of course, Italy. These countries interacted upon one another, each developing new architectural systems to meet the needs of the new philosophy.

47. Jacques Barzun, *Classic, Romantic and Modern* (2nd ed. New York, 1961), p. xxii.
48. Basil Taylor, "Art in the Nineteenth Century," *Listener, 64* (Dec. 1, 1960), 997.

This multiplicity was a relatively new thing. "The challenge of diversity . . . is an historical development peculiar to a mercantile society . . . the joint acceleration of horizontal and vertical . . . mobility. . . . The assimilation of works of art of an alien society, or an alien period in the past, is translation and interpretation. None can survive, or be communicated directly."[49] This implies the presence of eclecticism, and also implies that it may be creative rather than imitative. The new movement is distinguished by Jacques Barzun from the Enlightenment which preceded it "as fundamentally social and political . . . the eighteenth century entrusts everything to the intellect and loves Man abstractly as an archetype, whereas Romanticism studies sensation and emotion and embraces man as he is actually found—diverse, mysterious and irregular."[50] Although he places these movements sequentially instead of concurrently, he has indicated one of the important differences in point of view. One may also call it a movement "away from authority and toward liberty."[51] Or one can say that the older way of looking at Man emphasized the qualities shared by all men idealized, whereas the new way admired the qualities which made each man unique. Such an attitude admits of great variety at any one moment. "Art, in the works of the various creative geniuses alive at any one time, is endlessly varied. . . . It may be an annoying fact when we are trying to uncover the Zeitgeist. . . . But it is also salutary . . . though the climate of opinion is a reality, 'the spirit moveth where it listeth.' "[52]

Another indication of the enormously increased variety concurrently possible is the wide range of meaning attached to the word Romanticism. This has been investigated by Jacques Barzun in the work quoted above and by Arthur Lovejoy in his *Essays in the History of Ideas*.[53] Between them we find dozens of assorted meanings and many more uses. These "various Romanticisms" could be concurrent because, although Intellect and Passion may seem to be the polar opposites, psychology indicates that they are faces of the same coin. Men desire security but seek danger, they demand that order be varied by the irregular, and they enjoy tranquility between passionate interludes. It is the same in architecture; differences in intention may occur in rapid succession in one individual or be concurrent in different individuals. The widely used term "Romantic Classicism" summarizes such conflicts as those between extravagance of feeling and simplicity of form, or indulgence in self-expression and the restraint of reason, or between picturesque irregularity and classic symmetry.

49. Owen Holloway, "Thoughts on 'Art and Anarchy,' " *Listener, 65* (Feb. 9, 1961), 255–56.
50. Barzun, *Classic, Romantic and Modern*, pp. xx, xxi.
51. Ibid., p. xxi.
52. Michael Tippett, "Thoughts on 'Art and Anarchy,' " *Listener, 65* (March 2, 1961), 383.
53. Arthur Lovejoy, *Essays in the History of Ideas* (New York, 1948).

It is generally recognized today that there was a plurality of valid styles at this time. As John Summerson says, "It would be impossible, even if it were desirable, to separate the Classical and Gothic movements, except in so far as the latter has origins remote from those of the Neoclassic point of view."[54] In discussing Wyatt, his famous client William Beckford, and their joint efforts which produced the glorious folly of Fonthill, Summerson says that stylistic catholicity was part of Wyatt's point of view but that Fonthill's architect should have been Ledoux, since the building is more significant as the expression of William Beckford's personality than as a work of architecture. Consequently it had such characteristics as are conveyed by terms like "dramatic," "sensational," "fabulous," "chaotic," and "grotesque sensationalism."[55] These characteristics are the common coin of the Romantic architect, as we have seen.[56]

One of the factors contributing to the new era must have been the desire for change—a desire which is felt most strongly when the old ways have fallen out of touch with new concepts even if these are not yet fully comprehended. There is usually more than one route for change to follow. Wittkower has given an example in the case of landscape design. In 1744 the last Doge of Genoa had new gardens laid out for the Villa Gavotti at Albissola in which "Man's work ennobles the landscape without subduing it."[57] This was a possible alternative to the growing popularity of the English garden. That it had no great influence was probably related to the fact that the power of Genoa was waning while that of Britain was rising.

The Older Architectural Systems

During the eighteenth century a number of architectural systems had currency, some on their last legs, others barely able to stand as yet. The oldest continuing one was that of the Renaissance, which had persisted as the core of the Baroque.

Renaissance

The Renaissance system as evolved through Filarete, Colonna, and Alberti stressed the pre-eminence of one part of a building over the others; the unification of all the parts through gradation, similarity, and repetition; numerical systems of proportion; the integration of all the parts into a whole; and simple clarity of conception. In ideal form these principles are to be seen in Leonardo da Vinci's projects for churches, in which the dominant feature is echoed by a

54. Summerson, *Architecture in Britain*, p. 281.
55. Ibid., p. 282.
56. See pp. 3 ff.
57. Wittkower, *Art and Architecture*, p. 258.

cluster of smaller ones surrounding it, and in which the geometrical relationships and patterns predominate over site, orientation, or any other individualizing factors. Such a conception subordinated decoration and material. The realization of these aims was occasionally achieved—in the magnificent clarity of Santa Maria della Consolazione at Todi (begun in 1508), and in Bramante's simpler Tempietto of San Pietro in Montorio, Rome (begun in 1502). Kaufmann uses the terms "gradation" to apply to the relationship of the ruling and subordinate parts, and "concatenation" to mean the concert between the major and minor parts.

Baroque and Late Baroque

The Baroque masters liked to use a greater variety of forms and to oppose open and closed ones, at the same time preserving the idea of gradation.[58] From the beginning of the eighteenth century in Italy one can see a change in the Baroque which gave it more clarity, although it continued to be varied, rich, and full of unorthodox incidents. It was flexible enough to admit Borrominesque decoration and such a late Mannerist element as an undifferentiated framing band. It had a deliberate scenic quality and used broken colors of light tone. It had some of these qualities in common with the Rococo, which in addition was characterized by freer and more imaginative decoration and a richer play with elegant curvilinear shapes and spatial complexities. The Rococo appealed to both the aristocrat and the rich bourgeois, who enjoyed its elegant window frames, which sometimes made lacelike interconnections between the tiers of a façade. It had strong Italian roots and was influenced by French fashions.[59] The severe late Baroque can be seen at Juvarra's Palazzo Madama in Turin (1718–21) and later at Caserta. The Italian theories taken up in France thus returned to Italy.

Theories of proportionalism and rationalism had transformed this mode into a more additive type of composition with each part clearly separated and independent. A style arose in which the divisions were emphatic, unambiguous, and easily readable, so that canonical systems of proportion could be appreciated. All of this can be seen in Carlo Fontana's San Marcello al Corso, Rome (1682–83), which Wittkower nominates as the key building for this phase of the Baroque in Italy.[60] It is easily read: the single bays are framed by orders, each bay has an identical complement of them; the composition is essentially static; the encased columns form isolated motives; wall projections equal the diameters of the columns; the aedicule, instead of being linked, is detachable; the tiers

58. Kaufmann, *Age of Reason,* pp. 10, 11.
59. Wittkower, *Art and Architecture,* pp. 240–43.
60. Ibid., p. 244.

are repetitions of one another; chiaroscuro is used to clarify and not to complicate the orders and entablatures, which are thus disciplined and precise. Other Roman examples which reflect this attitude are: Nicola Salvi's Trevi Fountain (1732–62), with its almost academic palaces flanking a central motive based on the Arch of Constantine; Alessandro Galilei's Corsini Chapel in San Giovanni in Laterano (1732–34) and in his façade for that church (1732–35), which is grand enough to have served as the façade for St. Peter's itself; Ferdinando Fuga's façade for Santa Maria Maggiore (1743) between earlier flanking palace wings, and his Coffee House in the garden of the Quirinal palace (1741–44). The examples continue down to the end of the century with Fuga's Church of the Gerolomini in Naples of 1780, and Valadier took it into the nineteenth century.

Parallel formal changes were taking place simultaneously not only elsewhere in Italy, but all over Europe: in Milan with Giuseppe Piermarini's La Scala (1776–79) with its disciplined understatement (Figure 2). Naples had been the scene of his training under Luigi Vanvitelli, and in several of that master's works we see the new approach: in the austerity of Arco Clementino of 1735 at Ancona; in the fondness for an absolute geometrical pattern at the country palace of Caserta, begun in 1752; and in the slow rhythms, the unchanneled Roman Doric, the clarity, and the oddly original axial arch at the Piazza Dante (1757–65, formerly the Foro Carolino) in Naples (Figure 4a).

The façades at Caserta exhibit a feature which was becoming international —the giant Composite order used in a long sequence of narrow bays. Other examples were the Capitole at Toulouse by Guillaume Cammas (1750–60); the Academy of Art in Leningrad by Vallin de la Mothe and Kokorinov (1765–72); John Wood's Royal Crescent at Bath (1767–75); and Somerset House, London (1776–86).

In Naples, too, there was Mario Gioffredo (1718–85), who published his strongly Neoclassical *Dell'Architettura* in 1768 and applied this concept to the completion of Santo Spirito, finished by 1774, with its colossal nave and "even, sonorous" Corinthian order.[61]

In Piedmont Bernardo Vittone (1704/5–70) showed a basically Renaissance attitude in his books (published in 1760 and 1766), while in his work as at Vallinotto, he was often stark, using plain frames, panels, and unobtrusive pilasters, all in unrelieved white.[62] His objective was to delight rather than to edify. In this he showed his inheritance from Guarini (1624–83), who believed that architecture was intended to delight the senses and not to be merely rational. Intricate and subtle as was most of Vittone's work, it showed respect

61. Ibid., p. 263.
62. Ibid., p. 283.

for Palladian ideals. He was even puristic to the point of expressing disapproval of the *porte-à-faux,* or cantilever. He approved planning by enfilades, the linking of frames and walls together, and placed maximum importance on the principle of hierarchy and the consequent need of an emphatic portal, as Guarini had done at San Filippo Neri in Turin of 1714.[63]

Neo-Palladianism

In another system the principles of the Cinquecento were carried on as Palladianism and Neo-Palladianism, with implications for Neoclassicism. Palladio's principles, as revised by Vincenzo Scamozzi, with their "calculated intellectualism" and their "frigid classicism" left a mark for a long time to come.[64] This is particularly evident in Piermarini's work in Milan. In the Vicentine region Palladianism can be traced as a continuous and direct heritage from the master's death in 1580 through his successor Vincenzo Scamozzi (1552–1616) who completed his unfinished works, to Baldassare Longhena (1598–1682). Of Longhena's Santa Maria della Salute (begun 1631), Wittkower has stated that the following features come from Palladio: the coloring of grey stone and whitewash; the columns placed high on pedestals; the thermae windows with mullions, which Palladio was the first to use in churches; the use of optical devices—scenic integration—to unify separate spaces; the chapels right and left of the main entrance, adaptations of Palladio's façade of the Church of the Zitelle; and the decisive influence of the *scena frons* of the Teatro Olimpico on Longhena's manner of composition.[65] Then came two Venetian façades by Andrea Tirali: San Vitale and San Niccolò dei Tolentini, after 1700 (Figure 5). Tirali was followed by Giorgio Massari (circa 1686–1766), whose Church of the Jesuits (1725–36) is Palladian within and without, though on a very grand scale derived from San Giorgio Maggiore. There was also Matteo Lucchesi's S. Giovanni in Oleo of 1762; Antonio Scalfarotto's San Simeone Piccolo (1718–38, Figure 83). Other Venetian Neo-Palladians include: Antonio Visentini (1688–1782), architect of the façade of the Palazzo Giusti; Ottavio Bertotti-Scamozzi (1719–90), who edited a magnificent edition of Palladio's works in 1776–83 with new plates; Antonio Selva (1753–1819), architect of La Fenice (Figure 27); and Lorenzo Santi (1783–1839), noted for his conspicuously placed Palazzo Patriarcale (1837–50, Figure 61). Santi, born more than 200 years after the death of the founder of this line, continued in the founder's footsteps.

This was not, however, the only important ideology in Venetian architecture. There were other men who were less classical, such as Michele Sanmicheli

---

63. Kaufmann, *Age of Reason,* p. 95.
64. Wittkower, *Art and Architecture,* p. 73.
65. Ibid., pp. 192–95.

(1484–1559) and Jacopo Sansovino (1486–1570), who were leading another procession. The latter was a pupil of Andrea Sansovino and had come to Venice from Florence and Rome. Some of their successors were freer than those of Palladio. It would be a long time before the Venetian architectural scene froze, if in fact it ever did. The later men in both processions increased the amount of ornament, manipulated the scale and indulged in the opulent, the sensuous, and the vulgar. One of these is again Longhena, who was flamboyant in the Palazzo Pesaro (circa 1663–1710) as compared with his much more Palladian mood at Santa Maria della Salute (begun 1631).

Another line of succession in England was led by Inigo Jones (1573–1652), who made the first of his visits to Vicenza not long after the master's death and a later one in 1613–14. His pupil and assistant John Webb (1611–72) carried on the discipline, which was then taken up by the Burlingtonians. These were led by Colin Campbell (1680?–1729), by the Earl of Burlington himself (1694–1753) assisted by William Kent (1685/6–1748) and Giacomo Leoni (1686–1746), who had come to England in 1715. He issued an heretical edition of Palladio in 1715 and one of Alberti in 1726. The Burlingtonians opposed the more baroque tradition of Wren and his school; their part was taken by the following: Isaac Ware (d. 1776), Robert Morris (d. 1744), and Sir William Chambers (1723–96). All of these men published books and nearly all of them had been to Italy. Their devotion to the cause was assisted by the uninterrupted reprinting of the master's works in every language.[66]

A useful key to the continuation of the old systems of composition and the emergence of the new ones is to follow the relative importance of the pilaster, wall, and column. The Palladians made the pilaster paramount. In the Baroque system the pilaster, the framing band, and the wall formed parts of a plastic complex. Although Palladio in the courtyard of the Palazzo Porto-Colleoni in 1552 used a giant order, he also used pilasters as forceful clear-cut entities. Before him architects had handled them with less respect and, particularly at corners, resorted to various expedients such as half and quarter pilasters or thin, ghostly vestiges. A master of the Baroque style such as Borromini took the giant pilaster and bent it around a corner, as in the Oratory of San Filippo Neri (begun 1637), thus showing his concern with the integral character of a coherent dynamic system. A similar comparison can be made between the interiors of Palladio's chapel at the Villa Maser (1560s) and Bernini's at Ariccia (1662–64). In the first, pilasters are used rhythmically, and in the second they are used to define a single unit of space.[67]

66. Carroll L. V. Meeks, "Books and Buildings, 1449–1949, 100 Great Architectural Books . . . ," *Journal of the Society of Architectural Historians (JSAH), 8* (1949), 55 ff.

67. Wittkower, *Art and Architecture,* pp. 118, 147.

Eventually the framing bands and other elements of Baroque plasticity fall out of use. The pilaster regains its independent status and is ultimately replaced by pure, free-standing columns, their cylindrical form, not a complement to nor a part of, but a sharp contrast to the naked plane of the wall. The orders are in the ascendant and the pilaster on the decline. Eventually even the idea of a pilastered respond to the orders will be eliminated. This is the most violent break with a tradition which felt that the parts of a complex, highly articulated system could not be expressed without a liberal use of pilasters, as in Rainaldi's Sant'Agnese in Piazza Navona, Rome (1653–55), where overlapping pilasters were deemed necessary. To omit the pilaster was to stiffen the wall, to unlock the pieces and let each stand forth on its own. The analysis of a few more examples will show this process at work. Piermarini in La Scala at Milan in the 1770s (Figure 2) remains Neo-Palladian, since he uses pilasters in the old way. At the Vatican there is a clear sequence from Michelangelo Simonetti and Giuseppe Camporese's Sala della Biga (after 1786) with still bolder engaged columns to Raffaello Stern's Braccio Nuovo (1817–22) with no pilasters and fully isolated columns standing free at key points (Figure 17). Similarly in Valadier's quite Palladian façade of 1833 for San Rocco in Rome (Figure 64) the two pairs of columns do not have the full Neoclassic independence yet they seem much less integrated into the design than in a normal Palladian composition. They are squeezed together like a pair of huge buttresses, and the pediment they support has no attic behind it and no skyline figures. Hence it comes close to the Neoclassic ideal of a temple front, but only tentatively, a compromise between the old principles of hierarchy, climax, and dominance and the new ones of simplicity and purity. From 1823 on, in his reconstruction of the transepts of San Paolo fuori le mura (Figure 62), Poletti departed completely from the pre-fire plasticity of pilasters and framing bands. Instead he used free-standing columns independent, widely spaced and without pedestals or pilastered responds. Another variant can be seen in Niccolini's façade of the Teatro San Carlo in Naples (1810–44), where there are no pilasters and an almost uncountable, seemingly endless row of free-standing columns which act as a textural variation, contrasting with the rustication of the lower zone (Figure 51). Some of these changes are of course due to another architectural concept of the period—Purism.

The Newer Architectural Systems

Eclecticism; Gothic, Egyptian, Neoclassic

That men with new objectives should make use of old traditional vocabularies has been explained in various ways. The main problem has been to account for their lack of originality, today considered a grievous fault. Elsewhere I have said that architects were so absorbed in solving new functional and technical problems, buildings for wholly novel ends such as railroad stations and office buildings, or wide-span structures, that they used much of their creative energy in those concerns.[68] Kaufmann said the revivals "were, perhaps, necessary for men dazzled by the tremendous possibilities contained in the revolutionary discoveries needed to take breath before continuing on the new and arduous path."[69] Still another and plausible explanation is that these old forms were essential as grammar for the kind of literary and emotional communication they had in mind. Using these familiar forms they then attempted an unprecedentedly wide range of expression. Unhappily this often failed to communicate, and recourse was had to frank labeling, as in Piranesi's inscriptions justifying or clarifying his compositions, Ledoux's carefully tagged designs which often would be unintelligible otherwise, such as in his "House for a Cooper," and in numerous projects such as those in the *Atti della Accademia della Pace* (published in Florence, circa 1825), in which the function would elude us without the title, although perhaps at the time it was only necessary to provide clues for the newer, less sophisticated elements of the audience. An example of this trend is in the marble Canovan tablet in the vestibule of Santissimi Apostoli in Rome that contains an allegorical figure which is inscribed *amicitia*.

Gothic, on the whole, played an unimportant rôle except in England until the nineteenth century was well advanced. It was sometimes used in Italy for pleasure pavilions, as at Racconigi (Figure 105) in the 1830s and at Il Pedrocchino in 1837 (Figure 53), merely to evoke a nostalgic mood. But since there were those who avoided it because it seemed to them to suggest an extreme of restlessness, others could have used it deliberately to evoke that reaction. If the architect sought geometrical purity, he succeeded better with the Romanesque. The English combined purity of form, derived from Norman keeps, with medieval detail in such castles as Ashridge and Eastnor, and at St. John's College, New Court, Cambridge; here Rickman and Hutchinson in 1825–31 were very nearly as pure as Wilkins had been in Greek at Downing College twenty years before and was subsequently to be in Gothic at King's.

The Egyptian vocabulary was often found in association with other antique vocabularies. It was usually meant to convey durability and hence immortality. This is easily seen to be appropriate for a tomb or cemetery gate, but is a little less obvious on a prison as a symbol of hope, not of escape but of redemption.[70]

---

68. Carroll L. V. Meeks, *The Railroad Station, an Architectural History* (New Haven, 1956), p. 44.

69. Kaufmann, *Age of Reason*, p. 205.

70. Richard Carrott, "The Egyptian Revival: Its Sources, Monuments and Meaning, 1808–1858," Ph.D. dissertation, Yale University, 1962.

Neoclassicism is one of the variants of eclecticism which grew up after 1750. It combines many of the elements of the concurrent new styles subsumed under the general head of Romanticism, such as purity, geometry, and the eclectic use of antique forms to convey sentiments of nobility and the like.

The first phase of Neoclassicism has been given various names. Wittkower refers to it as Late Baroque Classicism.[71] Pevsner calls it "Rococo if anything."[72] Herrmann explains that Laugier and his circle admired " 'delicacy, gracefulness, and lightness' as well as 'the high degree of loftiness' and the 'elegance and noble simplicity' " which have nothing to do with the robust primitive early Greek temples, which were imperfectly known at the time. The admired qualities were those to which Robert Adam also gave expression in his style.[73]

Summerson adds the following characteristics: the tendency to smooth over and flatten out forms; the new contexts assigned to old forms (as in Adam's portico at Osterley); and the increased freedom of grammar, as with Dance and Soane, who abbreviated the orders and de-emphasized the center of their compositions. Such devices were noted in 1804 by Thomas Hope, who seems to be echoing the Italians when he says that pilasters were to be avoided, the parts of the entablature to be used functionally. He added that the only orders permissible were those of Greece.[74] Innovations in form and a widening kind of eclecticism had been taking place since early in the eighteenth century, not only in the temple front of San Niccolò dei Tolentini (1706–14) in Venice (Figure 5), but also in England, France, and Germany. In England both Wren and Nicholas Hawksmoor had used Gothic when the setting seemed to call for continuity, but Hawksmoor was much interested in the buildings of antiquity and made sketches based on both Greek and Roman precedent. He had, after all, illustrated Henry Maundrell's *Journey from Aleppo* in 1703. He had based his spire for St. George's, Bloomsbury, 1720–30, on Pliny's account of the Tomb of Mausolus.[75] Wren had built a severe, unfluted Tuscan portico at the Chelsea Hospital in 1682–89, which John Evelyn had said was intended to be the "conception . . . of monastic austerity."[76] This stern portico and its giant order were a step toward the more classical and more complete temple front which James Gibbs employed at St. Martin-in-the-Fields of 1721–26. After that the examples of a stricter classicism become more common, and the new sense of com-

71. Wittkower, *Art and Architecture*, pp. 240 ff.

72. Nikolaus Pevsner, *An Outline of European Architecture* (6th ed. Baltimore, 1960), p. 592.

73. Herrmann, *Laugier*, pp. 24, 179, 200, and n. 28, p. 179. See also my review, *JSAH*, 22 (1963), 234 ff.

74. H. M. Colvin, "Observations on the Plans and Elevations designed by James Wyatt, Architect, for Downing College, Cam.; in a letter to Francis Annesley, Esq., M. P., 1804," *A Biographical Dictionary of English Architects, 1660–1840* (Cambridge, Mass., 1954), p. 298.

75. Summerson, *Architecture in Britain*, p. 180.

76. Ibid., p. 138.

position can be seen in such English country houses by James Wyatt as Heaton (1772), Heveningham (1788), and Dodington (1798–1808).[77] Their counterparts in France were some of Ledoux's Barrières, his Maison de M. de Saiseval, and Pierre Rousseau's Hôtel de Salm in Paris of 1783–87. Jefferson and Clérisseau's project for the Capitol of Virginia of 1785–96 brings the new system to the New World.

Eclecticism began to include Greek forms about the middle of the century. Johann Joachim Winckelmann (1717–68) had published his first book on the superiority of the Greeks before he came to Italy to live in 1755.[78] Once there, he became associated with Cardinal Albani's classical collections as librarian. At the same time, a villa was being erected for the Cardinal by Carlo Marchionni (1702–86), the architect of the Sacristy at St. Peter's, which Milizia attacked so severely. A number of classicizing buildings appeared at the Villa Albani which are presumed to be the consequences of Winckelmann's presence. The two outstanding ones are the "Greek" *tempietti* added to the wings of the villa (Figures 6, 7). They are not very Greek, nor very Neoclassical. They are not archeological but associative in the same way that the Gothic Pavilion at Hagley (1749) and Strawberry Hill (begun the same year) are Gothic. Winckelmann remained in Italy from 1755 until his violent death in Trieste in 1768, commemorated there by Antonio Bosa's Neoclassic monument dedicated in 1833. In contrast to the late Baroque style of the villa, these little temples are strikingly new, heralds of the architectural revolution. They illustrate somewhat tentatively Winckelmann's thesis that the art of Greece was superior to that of Rome:

> Good taste began in Greece which offers us the purest models . . . to take the ancients for our models is the only way to become great . . . Raphael and Poussin did this . . . Roman work is inferior . . . the Greeks provide us with the perfect canon . . . certain ideal beauties of nature which exist only in the intellect . . . only the inner sensation brings forth the essence of truth . . . the intention to achieve something more beautiful and more perfect than nature . . . we do not value them as models because of their age only . . . imitating the Greeks can teach us to become wise more quickly than by trying for ourselves to find greatness directly in nature, ideal beauty

77. Douglas Lewis, "The Image of Greece in 18th Century English Architecture," Master's thesis, Yale University, 1963.

78. Johann Winckelmann, *Gedanken über die Nachahmung der griechischen Werke* (Friedrichstadt, 1755). This was preceded by the Comte de Caylus, *Recueil d'antiquités* (Paris, 1752 ff.), and was followed in 1758 by A. Y. Goguet, *De L'Origine des loix, des arts, et des sciences et de leur progrès chez les anciens peuples* . . . (Paris, 1758), and in the same year J. D. Le Roy, *Les Ruines des plus beaux monuments de la Grèce* (Paris, 1758).

being the objective, a product of: nature, art, and the human mind as in the Apollo Belvedere. The ancient concept of the unity and perfection of nature will clarify our concepts of nature in its diversity.[79]

Winckelmann joined the chorus deploring the excesses and innovations of Michelangelo and declared that Borromini was guilty of bad taste. He decried the discontinuities and extravagances of Baroque architecture which lacked beginning and end. "Antiquity," he said, "provided us with excellent examples of simplicity and solidity."[80]

Insofar as they denigrated the Romans these views were regarded with abhorrence by Giovanni Battista Piranesi (1720–78), a Venetian who settled in Rome. He was a close friend of Robert Adam, whose work and style of presentation owe much to him. But of more far-reaching influence were his widely collected prints. They were also revolutionary, and were not only pictorially striking but also novel in concept. In the *Carceri* series (1744–45) he introduced a mystical, theatrical, psychological, more-than-Baroque space.[81] In his numerous and popular views of Rome he demonstrated his belief that the accomplishments of the past were greater than those of his contemporaries, and that however man struggled, nature would inevitably conquer. In his late works he introduced new vocabularies, Egyptian and Tuscan, and, more important, a new system of composition in which the elements became more and more independent, agglomerated, heaped up and anti-traditional. Finally we have the application of this in three-dimensional form in his startlingly unconventional church of Santa Maria del Priorato on the Aventine (1765–66, Figures 9–12). His essay *Parere sull'architettura* appeared in 1765. By way of his prints his messages were carried to every corner of the Western world. They were an effective force in bringing about the collapse of the old systems and the rise of both Revolutionary architecture and Neoclassicism, to which they contributed romantic and psychological color.

Thus eclecticism becomes an indispensable part of the means of expression for an architecture which has as its deepest function the communication of feeling. If necessary, new and unheard-of forms could be invented since the horizons were considered limitless, but this was not mandatory. The mood was close to Tennyson's "spontaneous overflow of powerful feelings," Rousseau's "great passions" and "naked self," and Wordsworth's, speaking of a mountain peak, "as if with voluntary power instinct."

79. Winckelmann, *Gedanken*, translated in Elizabeth A. Holt, ed., *A Documentary History of Art* (2 vols. New York, 1958), *2*, 336–351.

80. Tarchiani, *Ottocento*, p. 6.

81. Andreina Griseri has demonstrated that Piranesi's compositions and moods owe something to Juvarra's sketches of Rome; "Itinerari Juvarriani" *Paragone*, 8 (1957), 40 ff.

The Picturesque; Gardens

A rising system was that of the Picturesque. This has been dealt with at length in other places.[82] I have called it "Picturesque Eclecticism" and said that its compositional character was given by the following qualities: Variety, Intricacy, Irregularity, and Movement, which can be called by the acronym "Virim." I also asserted that it was the dominant aesthetic system of the nineteenth century. This may be an exaggeration, but it was unquestionably one of the most important systems.

Its origins lie far back in the eighteenth century. It begins with the cult of the natural as advocated by the Earl of Shaftesbury in 1711, Addison in 1712, and Pope in 1713.[83] It was put in practice by Pope, Burlington, Kent, and many others and finally developed into a fully defined creed by 1796. The basic idea was anti-formal and favored the irregular, the varied and the naturalistic. The Picturesque derived authority from Pliny and was intended in a fully romantic way to evoke moods such as grandeur, melancholy, sublimity, or gaiety. The garden was to have literary associations, which were more important than aesthetic appeal. For this purpose the garden was to contain objects of varied character: columns, ruins, grottos, and inscriptions.[84] Thus the Picturesque system made eclectic use of the styles, irregularly composed to evoke moods and feelings.

Purists, Rationalists, Rigorists, Revolutionaries, and Pure Geometry

Another new concept of architecture was that of the Purists, Rationalists, and Rigorists. Parts of their doctrines can be traced back to the beginning of the eighteenth century in France, notably in J. L. de Cordemoy's *Nouveau Traité*.[85] For him, good architecture must have rational clarity in its external aspect and must relate construction and appearance in a suitable manner. These two principles would create beauty. Furthermore, a building must be suitable to its function. He condemned most of the Baroque devices and some Renaissance ones, such as twisting, bulging, channeling, jutting, interrupting pediments and cornices, and the picturesque modeling of masses and volumes. Some of these so-called "abuses" had been attacked before, and most of them would be vilified for the next two centuries; however, he put the case for a clean functional architecture with some force.[86]

---

82. Meeks, *Railroad*, pp. 2 ff., 175.

83. The Earl of Shaftesbury, *The Moralists . . .* (London, 1709). Joseph Addison in *The Spectator* (London, 1712). Alexander Pope, anonymously, "Essay on Gardens," *The Guardian* (London, 1713).

84. James Lees-Milne, *Earls of Creation* (London, 1962), pp. 140 ff.

85. J. L. de Cordemoy, *Nouveau Traité de toute l'architecture . . .* (Paris, 1706 and 1714).

86. Angela della Chiesa, *L'Età neoclassica in Lombardia* (Como, 1959), p. 17.

The most stringent doctrine of all was that advocated in Venice by Abbé Carlo Lodoli (1690–1761). Although he wrote an illustrated treatise, this was never published and the manuscript is lost. His message has come to us via two of his students, the Count Algarotti and Andrea Memmo. The former (1712–64) has been mentioned above. He published two works dealing particularly with architecture, which went through many editions: *Saggio sopra l'architettura* (Pisa, 1753), and *Lettere sopra l'architettura* (about 1764–65). Memmo's publication did not appear until 1786, the *Elementi dell'architettura Lodoliana* (Rome, with later editions in 1833, Milan, and Zara in 1834). Algarotti refers to Lodoli as the "Socrates of architecture" with some justice, since he was as rational and functional as Socrates himself. Lodoli pronounced the three essential qualities of architecture to be Commodity, Firmness, and Durability. Unlike Vitruvius and his imitators he omits "Delight," saying that his triad will of itself produce beauty almost automatically. There is no place in architecture for Taste or Fashion. Beauty arises from fixed principles which in turn grow out of the nature of the material, "indole della materia." He even claimed that architecture, unlike painting or sculpture, was a science and hence must show an intrinsically logical reason for every part. He rejected "useless ornament" and was opposed to plastic art in general. He was thus in a more puristic position than anyone who had preceded him from Vitruvius to Palladio. Such views were not palatable to his contemporaries, and while they acted as a sort of brake they seem never to have been taken very literally. It would be interesting to know what his lost illustrations showed. One imagines unornamented prismatic structures like those of Soane's pupil and illustrator, Joseph Gandy, or the early International Style. Could he have meant to abolish traditional form? What remains to us is a negative doctrine without a positive corresponding aesthetic.[87]

The earliest publication of these ideas was that by Algarotti. He was critical of these concepts, although he admired their general tenor. He considered them excessively austere, since they rejected the whole humanist tradition from antiquity on. Algarotti ingeniously demonstrated, for instance, that ornament was one of the original and natural components of architecture. His position was palatable enough to his contemporaries for him to be called one of the "restorers of true architecture." He feared the consequences when the reforms proposed by Lodoli would be generally accepted. In 1759 he was writing Temanza about these matters, saying that, while he could on the one hand support the rigorists,

87. Edgar Kaufmann, Jr., may have found the outline of Lodoli's book and one illustration for it in the edition of Memmo published in Zara in 1833. See his "Memmo's Lodoli," *Art Bulletin, 46* (June 1964), 159 ff. The illustration shows a heavily rusticated masonry framed doorway, the joints cut to express the forces at work, but producing a highly Mannerist effect. See also Emil Kaufmann, *Age of Reason*, p. 96.

on the other he did not feel disposed to accept so-called authority. Discussions of this kind must have been very common in Italy in those years. Algarotti rejected the idea that architecture was a pure science.[88] He was disinclined to accept the old legend that all architectural forms were descended from the wooden hut of ancient times, pointing out that we cannot know this, since none of the archetypes have survived, whereas man's passions emerge directly from nature and are still susceptible to study by sculptors and poets. Architecture, however, has to be intellectualized and so is as different from all the other arts as metaphysics is from the other sciences. Algarotti was indifferent to the nature of materials. He held that all forms of architecture are derived from wood, this having been the universal material immediately available. He deduced from this the unity of architecture, unity being as necessary to the perfection of the arts as variety, derived from the multiplicity of wooden shapes. However, only stone by its nature could give rise to arches found in nature in grottos, but the exclusive use of arches would produce the grave fault of boredom. Lodoli had urged that walls should be flat or at the very most given some contrast by the use of rusticated ashlar. Algarotti traced the wooden origin of every part of the architectural vocabulary with differing degrees of plausibility and some disagreement with Vitruvius. He demonstrated a wide knowledge of both ancient and modern authorities in his quotations and in his footnotes. His list of abuses or errors is conventional; he was opposed to repeating the full cornice for each story of a building, since it belongs only at the top to shed water, but if used intermediately should logically have less projection. Similarly pediments over windows shed water, so there is no reason to put one indoors, as Michelangelo did, or to break them in the middle or to back the broken halves together, as Buontalenti did. He finds Vitruvius' assertion that the different orders were invented to express the massiveness of man or the slenderness of woman farfetched—the true origin being, he said, the variation in tree trunks. He called architecture the "art that is the daughter of necessity," following the authority of the *Encyclopédie,* or the embellished mask of one of man's basic needs.[89] He concludes, contrary to Lodoli, that the lie is more beautiful than the truth in this case, but that nevertheless we must be grateful to Lodoli for raising the question, and also for pointing out that many abuses can be avoided by not using forms which require chains, cramps, and such artifices, and thus become "held together with shoe laces."[90]

What Algarotti has done is to take the stern Lodolian doctrine and make it acceptable by modification and compromise. His main effort was to justify the

88. Kaufmann, *Age of Reason,* pp. 96 ff.
89. Algarotti, *Saggio sopra l'architettura* (Milan, 1831), p. 38, quotes "Discours préliminaire . . . ," *Encyclopédie, 1* (Paris, 1751).
90. Ibid., p. 39.

use of ornament and decoration on rational grounds, saying that they have been part of architecture from the earliest times and evolved logically and organically from the basic wooden structures of primitive man, finding a feasible archetype for each part of the order. Nevertheless he is opposed to what Palladio also called "useless decoration," meaning elements which either no longer served their original function, such as shedding water, or those which were added purely for form's sake. "Useless" in this context is not susceptible to close definition. It is, like Goodness, Beauty, and Nature, a term which can be given many meanings and needs clarification each time it is employed. Winckelmann likewise was not very explicit. He merely said that "ornament must be appropriate." From the point of view of the designer or architect, ornament is used to serve some aesthetic purpose relevant to the character of the building. The critic may disagree, but is he justified in calling it useless? Furthermore, what may have appeared necessary to one generation may appear gratuitous and extravagant to another. It is hard to know how far these men meant to go. Algarotti admires "the strong foundation which rivals those of ancient buildings" in the Tempio Malatestiano at Rimini, and speaks of stripping the walls ("nudar gli edifici"), citing both Perrault and Frézier in his support.[91] On the whole his views were enlightened and somewhat eclectic. He could admit of the desirability of "drinking from the most pure fountains of Greece,"[92] could recognize, with reservations, that the French had superior standards of convenience, and conclude that he preferred Italian formalism.

It has been suggested by Wittkower that Venice would have been particularly receptive to Lodoli's ideas, because there was almost no Rococo movement there, apart from furniture and interior decoration.[93] This would also allow classicizing ideas, such as those of Tirali and Massari, to exist in the 1690s. There were a good many treatises of a conservative nature coming out in Venice in the eighteenth century, such as Antonio Visentini's *Osservazioni* (1771), which argues that reason supported the traditional conservative Palladian forms, and Passeri's *Discorso della ragione dell'architettura* (1772), in which the reasonableness of nature was invoked.

The Rigorist attitude was reiterated toward the end of the century in Italy by Francesco Milizia (1725–98). His essays, which appeared from 1768 on, were reprinted in French, Spanish, Portuguese, and English, some of them as late as the 1820s.[94] Milizia's importance has been variously appraised. Profes-

91. Tarchiani, *Ottocento,* p. 6.
92. Kaufmann, *Age of Reason,* p. 98.
93. Wittkower, *Art and Architecture,* p. 243.
94. Francesco Milizia, *Del Teatro* . . . (Rome, 1771; Rome, 1772; Venice, 1773; Venice, 1789); *Trattato completo, formale e materiale del teatro* . . . (Venice, 1771; Madrid, 1789); *Dell'Arte di vedere nelle belle arti del disegno* . . . (Venice, 1781, 1792, 1798, 1823; Halle, 1785; Paris, 1798; Barcelona, 1823; Madrid, 1827); *Dizionario delle belle arti del disegno* . . . (Bassano, 1797); *Prin-*

sor Hitchcock ignores him. Tarchiani, Kaufmann, and Lavagnino discuss his message and its influence, and the most recent opinion, that of della Chiesa, is that he was highly influential. His earliest publications, in the 1760s, would have exerted an influence on the generation born about 1750, and would have been shown in their work about 1780. This notable generation in Italy included Antonio Selva (1753–1819), whose first modern work was the Teatro La Fenice (Figure 27), dedicated in 1792, Leopold Pollack (1751–1806), whose first major work was the Villa Reale-Belgioioso in Milan (1790–93, Figures 24–26), and Giovanni Antonio Antolini (1756–1841), famous for his grandiose project for Milan, the Foro Bonaparte (1801–06, Figure 32).

The generation of the 1760s was more markedly Neoclassical: Mario Asprucci, Luigi Cagnola, Ferdinando Bonsignore, and Carlo Barabino.

Milizia's doctrine was closer to Algarotti's than to Lodoli's extremist one. He accepted the dichotomy that architecture was both an art and science. He was somewhat eclectic and changeable, hence his nickname, "the Don Quixote of Ideal Beauty." At times he seemed to think of the Baroque as a "Black Beast." He held that Neoclassicism was inferior to Greece in its golden age and hence would advocate Greek over Roman. Thus he could approve the use of the pure baseless Greek Doric order. It first appeared in Italy at the chapel in the Borghese gardens by Mario Asprucci (circa 1787, Figure 23) about thirty years after James Stuart had used it in the temple at Hagley (1758–59). On other occasions he would announce that the Greeks had gone astray by disregarding nature, so that they were not to be followed in principle or detail. He was not an antiquarian in the usual sense, since he did not worship the cadavers of the past.[95] He could also admire the impressiveness of Gothic vaults and dislike the restlessness occasioned by the multiplicity of buttresses and pinnacles. He favored grandeur of mass and form, and disliked the pettiness of the typically alveolate theatres of his day, as well as the complexity of the typical church with its infinitude of bays and chapels. Even St. Peter's was guilty in this respect. Milizia advocated a high degree of correspondence between the interior and exterior of buildings seeking for a total unity, and complained that the façade of Sant'Andrea della Valle was not closely related to its interior, which is true, and that the Pantheon portico was not closely enough related to the cylindrical mass behind, which is doubtful. He enjoyed shock treatment—saying he pre-

---

cipi di architettura civile . . . (Finale, 1781; Leipzig, 1784–86; Bassano, 1785); *Roma, delle belle arti del disegno: parte prima: dell' architettura civile* (Bassano, 1787; Paris, 1789); *Le Vite de' più celebri architetti d'ogni nazione e d'ogni tempo, precedute da un saggio sopra l'architettura* (Rome, 1768 [later, *Memorie degli architetti antichi e moderni, terza edizione, accresciuta e corretta dallo stesso autore Francesco Milizia* (Parma, 1781; Bassano, 1785)]; Paris, 1771; trans. Mrs. Edward Cresy, London, 1826).

95. Kaufmann, *Age of Reason,* pp. 102–04.

ferred the Cloaca Maxima to Marchionni's Sacristy at St. Peter's or to Michel-angelo's Porta Pia, thus stressing the high value he placed on simple, geomet-rical, and rigid forms. On the subject of decoration he was particularly forceful: if used it must be an integral part of the building and have a clear reason for its presence. Rich and profuse decoration not derived from utility or necessity only makes a bad building uglier, as a homely woman only makes herself more frightful by overmuch jewelry. He also said that if a building corresponds ex-actly to its purpose, even though it has no decoration and is intended for some ordinary purpose, it will be beautiful. He felt that the beauty of architecture lies in the perfection of its construction, and derives from necessity and utility. These opinions were considered so shocking that in some places, in spite of the papal imprimatur, his books were censored and destroyed. This happened to the first volume of his *Roma, delle belle arti del disegno* (1787).

Rigorists tend to draw false analogies between architecture and vehicles. In Lodoli's case it was with the gondola, just as later on it would be the clipper ship with Horatio Greenough and the automobile and airplane with Le Cor-busier. Milizia was not guilty of that error in logic. His comparisons were al-ways with civil engineering, an error of another sort.

Kaufmann criticized Milizia for being changeable and eclectic. It is true that these qualities have less impact than a stricter fanatical dogma, yet they are more representative of and normal to the average man's way of thinking, and this in the long run may be more effective. His position was therefore more "modern" than the more controversial views taken up by Winckelmann and Piranesi, which added fuel to the fires destroying the old systems.

During these years of the eighteenth century, related doctrines were being advocated in France as well as Italy and England. One of the most significant is the well-known essay by the Abbé Marc-Antoine Laugier (1713–69), *Essai sur l'architecture,* first published in 1753, with a second edition in 1755 and anonymous pirated English ones in 1755 and 1756.[96]

Laugier's ideas were derived, as Herrmann has shown, from a considerable body of French theory going back to the late seventeenth century. To this he added a number of personal items such as an aversion to pilasters and an antip-athy to niches.[97] He objected to the harsh contours of pillars. He found the Doric order to be "crude." His dislike of the wall was as strong as Alberti's, from whom he probably derived the antipathy.

Did Laugier draw upon Lodoli? To this question Herrmann devotes consid-erable space. His effort to establish the independence of Laugier, though valiant,

96. Laugier's dates are usually given as 1713–69, but Hitchcock gives 1770, and Herrmann, April 5, 1769.

97. Herrmann, *Laugier.* This has been drawn upon extensively in the following discussion. See also my review in *JSAH, 22* (1963), 234 ff.

is not conclusive. Contemporary evidence and the opinions of many less partial historians cannot be thus dismissed, nor is the begging summary that both men drew upon a common fund of ideas a sufficient answer. Lodoli's dramatic *pronunciamentos* were well known in Venice, and he was the older man by twenty-three years. There is Laugier's deep interest in Venice, his authorship of a history of the Venetian Republic, his one certain visit there, and the possibility of an earlier one.[98] It is not necessary for Laugier to agree with or even discuss Lodoli's ideas to prove a connection. Lodoli's freedom from conventional thought may have been enough to start Laugier off on his own course. He could have heard about Lodoli's teachings in a dozen ways, since he was a prominent member of a well-known intellectual group and had a special interest in things Venetian. There is not at present any way of proving this connection, but it is far more likely that Laugier knew of Lodoli's ideas than that he did not. Algarotti, for instance, knew both men at the right time to have been the intermediary. Probably there were many other intermediaries.

Laugier, too, was a rationalist. He deduced from the primitive hut that only a few elements of architecture were necessary and truthful: those which had a structural and functional reason for being. This was to be seen in perfection in the Maison Carrée at Nîmes. Professor Hitchcock calls Laugier both a Neo-classicist and a Functionalist, partly because he was among those Frenchmen who praised Greek architecture from enthusiasm rather than knowledge, and partly because of his emphasis on the plain primitivistic forms which appealed strongly to Sir John Soane.[99] Like Lodoli, Laugier emphasized logic and reason. The Maison Carrée was a paradigm: the portico columns are detached from the wall, free-standing and cylindrical, and standing directly on the pavement; above them is a simple trabeation without arches; everything is smooth and rigorously rectilinear, without angles and recesses; there are no false gables on the long sides, no untruthful details, no bits and pieces, no concave or convex window frames, no string courses, no archivolts, no useless cupolas, no superfluous decorative balustrades, no niches with or without statues (niches came to be widely used by Neoclassicists).[100] Laugier says:

> Do not let us lose sight of our little rustic cabin. I can see nothing therein but columns, a floor or entablature; a pointed roof whose two extremities each of them forms what we call a pediment. As yet there is no arch, still less of an arcade, no pedestal, no attique [sic], no door, even nor window. I conclude then with saying, in all the order of architecture, there is only

98. Marc-Antoine Laugier, *Histoire de la république de la Venise* (2 vols. Paris, 1759–68).
99. Hitchcock, *Architecture*, pp. xxii, xxiii, 59.
100. Della Chiesa, *L'Età neoclassica*, p. 18.

the column, the entablature, and the pediment that can essentially enter into this composition. If each of these three parts are found placed in the situation and with the form which is necessary for it, there will be nothing to add; for the work is perfectly done. There is remaining with us in France a very fine monument of the ancients, it is what they call at Nismes the square house, connoisseurs or not connoisseurs, everybody admires this beautiful building: What is the reason? because all therein is agreeable to the true principles of architecture. A long square, wherein thirty columns support an entablature, and a roof terminated at the two extremities by a pediment, this is all it contained; this collection hath such a simplicity and grandeur that strikes every eye. Let us enter then into a detail of the essential parts of an order of architecture.[101]

These declarations left an architecture of form, volume, ratio, and proportion, and could be summed up: "a well-constructed building with good proportions will always look well, whereas one prodigal of ornament but without good proportions will not."[102] There are two difficulties with this: "good" is a matter of taste and constantly changing, and the absence of ornament does not make a building any less dateable and less free from the vagaries of fashion. In essence it merely meant that to him a simple, plain, boxy building is more likeable than a richly ornate, plastic one. Further light on his ideas is shed by his criticism of specific buildings.

The portal of St. Gervais in Paris, he felt, would be more nearly perfect if the Doric columns were disengaged like the upper orders. The Jesuit church in the Rue St. Antoine is condemned because of its use of overlapping columns. The pedestals under the columns of the screen of the Hôtel de Soubise are faults. Domes should not be allowed to hang over the space below on pendentives. St. Sulpice is full of errors: it has gross pilasters and thick masses of wall, and the lobby hides the entrance, of which the columns should have been doubled in depth to free it and to disengage the towers. Notre Dame is striking. Anticipating Goethe, who read his work, Laugier admires Strasbourg Cathedral extravagantly, using ecstatic terms such as "ravishing masterpiece," "fineness of labor," "more art and genius," etc.[103] He liked Le Camus de Mézières' Halle aux Blé in Paris (1763–67) because this round building, entirely isolated, had adequate solidity and simplicity.[104] He approved of it functionally as well as aes-

101. Marc-Antoine Laugier, *Essai sur l'architecture* (2nd ed. Paris, 1755), pp. 10, 11; Eng. trans., anon., *An Essay on the Study and Practice of Architecture* . . . (London, 1756), pp. 13, 14.

102. Quoted by della Chiesa, *L'Età neoclassica*, p. 18.

103. Laugier, *Essai*, p. 201.

104. Kaufmann, *Age of Reason*, pp. 149 ff.

thetically. He advocated that someone attempt a triangular building, which his disciple Sir John Soane obligingly designed, although it was never executed.[105] He was highly critical of Versailles, saying that the chapel had good columns but there was no necessity for having piers in addition, that the pilasters of the main front pinched the wall, that the entrance was obscure, that the rooms did not function well and lacked privacy.[106] These points were, of course, partly due to the number of changes and additions, and to the standards of the earlier periods. Significantly he finds the formality and grandeur of the garden unpleasingly austere, uninviting, and lacking in variety. It was, in short, old-fashioned by the new English landscape standards. Laugier summed up his position as follows:

> An artist ought to give a reason for every thing he does . . . so that he may tell if a thing be good or bad, not purely by instinct, but by reasoning. . . . Architecture . . . has hitherto been abandoned to the caprice of Architects, which have given us precepts of it without discernment. They have determined its rules at hazard upon the bare inspection of ancient buildings. . . . Vile imitators, all that has been authorized by examples has been declared legitimate . . . their lessons have only been a fountain of errors.[107]

Like Milizia, he combined a desire for simple straightforward logic and a passionate admiration for the spectacular qualities of Gothic.

In France, Laugier's message was echoed in a quieter form by the younger Blondel, Jacques-François (1705–74), whose six-volume *Cours d'architecture* appeared from 1771 to 1777, although the ideas date back to 1750. He was more revolutionary, but praises such qualities as simplicity, nourishment by the ancients, proud masculine beauty, and vigor. He said that genius was not enough, since simplicity, regularity, and beauty of proportion were to be preferred to the enjoyment of being singular, or being trifling. He used "picturesque" as a pejorative term. He admired the ancients, and refers frequently and respectfully to the beauties of the Greeks and Romans. He favors the quality of being "august," which is presumably an equivalent of Burke's "sublime."[108]

Other Frenchmen followed with new and even startling ideas. Claude-Nicolas Ledoux (1736–1806) published his great treatise two years before his death. It was the fruit of years of enforced inactivity during the revolution and followed his productive years like a peroration. It was called *L'Architecture considerée sous le rapport de l'art, des moeurs et de la législation.* The elaboration of the title shows a social consciousness which was timely in the work of a for-

105. Laugier, *Essai,* p. 207. Kaufmann, p. 57, discusses the influence of Laugier on Soane.
106. Laugier, *Essai,* pp. 147, 159 ff., 181 ff. and elsewhere.
107. Ibid., pp. xxxiv–xxxvi; Eng. trans., anon., *Essay,* pp. iv–vii.
108. J.-F. Blondel, *Cours d'architecture,* quoted in Holt, *Documentary History, 2,* 334.

mer royal architect. Mario Praz called him an "architect of hallucination," whose prose was full of rhetoric, who coined "classical" names for some of his projects, and who "dreamed of an age of heroes."[109] He designed buildings for every conceivable function and aimed to express their character and purpose in their form. These forms ranged very widely indeed, from pure abstraction through various dramatic and original interpretations of Palladio and the Italian Cinquecento to the phallic. His manner of composition was, as Kaufmann has pointed out, revolutionary, in that he did not accept the old principle of gradation but often reversed it, stressing the isolation of the parts rather than their unity or subservience. His buildings are often "literary" to the degree also affected by Boullée.

The popularizer of revolutionary and Neoclassical ideas in France was the teacher Jean-Nicolas-Louis Durand (1760–1834). From 1802–05 he published his *Précis des leçons d'architecture données à l'Ecole Polytechnique* in two volumes with numerous plates. They were free from what Hitchcock calls Ledoux's "recondite symbolism."[110] The designs fall into two general categories: either those astylar ones derived from the Italian villa, with masses, towers, pergolas, and arcades thus providing picturesqueness within a symmetrical outline, or a more Neoclassical group which stresses an impossible proliferation of columns often in multiple rows, a case of extreme stylophily. Every part and element, however pompous, has its counterpart at least once, often four times, as symmetry is extended in two directions around a network or grid of intersecting major and minor axes. The doctrine is clear and straightforward, stressing character, regularity, simplicity, and materials. Durand's handbook of design provided a variety of schemes which could be easily adopted for real buildings by eager students, though in execution there was always a marked reduction in the number of elements and dimensions. The Durandesque idea can be seen clearly in such examples as the Paris Bourse (1808–15, enlarged 1902–03) by Alexandre-Théodore Brongniart (1739–1813); the Rue des Colonnes, Paris, by Bernard Poyet (1797 ff.); the Altes Museum, Berlin, by Karl Friedrich von Schinkel (1824–28); the British Museum, London, by Sir Robert Smirke (south front, 1824–47); the Piazzetta San Carlo in Milan by Carlo Amati (Figure 88); and many others in the first half of the century. Most of the Beaux-Arts projects of the following decades, whether executed in Paris itself or in any of the other schools of Europe, exhibit the same characteristics. The remarkable thing is that in this phase of Neoclassicism the temple form was rarely used, pediments were scarce, and, when they do appear, are likely to be Neo-Palladian, since trabeated colonnades were generally preferred.

Among Germans, Winckelmann was the first to preach the new concepts. He

109. Praz, *Gusto neoclassico,* pp. 102–03.
110. Hitchcock, *Architecture,* p. 20.

quoted Algarotti on at least one occasion and was in favor of "noble simplicity and quiet grandeur" which he considered to be characteristic of Greek master-pieces.[111] The qualities are not such as to permit a very wide range of expression but are clearly Neoclassical and opposed to the violent and transitory work of his contemporaries. In the next decade Lessing drew some boundaries for the conveying of expression in art; he felt that the emotions, such as pain and joy, should be carried only so far as was compatible with beauty and dignity.[112] The conflict inherent in the ideals of Neoclassicism and Romanticism is apparent and unresolved. Goethe, whose essay on Strasbourg Cathedral, "Von deutscher Baukunst," was published in 1773, was a complete Romantic. He had read Laugier and did not agree with him.[113] In this famous essay Goethe goes into ecstasies of feeling induced by the contemplation of Strasbourg Cathedral. In it he sees genius, desire, suffering, enjoyment, the expression of a gigantic spirit, exaltation, and the spirit of the nation. To him, even its ruggedness was more significant than the meaningless smoothness of other buildings. Feeling is implicit in the work and in the viewers' appreciation of it. Goethe has evoked the typical Romantic idols: power, nation, nature, hero. Goethe repeated the notion that art is image-forming long before it is beautiful. This is a completely anti-classical attitude.

The Revolutionary System

One of the consequences of these new ideas about the nature of art and architecture was the invention of a new system of composition, called "The Architecture of Revolution" by Emil Kaufmann. It has the following features: the reduction in the number and variety of components by the elimination of minor parts, and a reduction in the quantity of ornament. If a building was intended to be very large, the necessary dimensions could be obtained by repetition of a few forms; simplicity, clarity, and purity were the avowed objectives. These could be secured without any change in vocabulary or the implication that antique forms should be revived. It was a matter of thinking freshly and rationally. In looking at antiquity, these architects were more struck by the piles and masses of the buildings which had been stripped of their surface ornament such as the Tomb of Caecilia Metella, the Pyramid of Cestus, the aqueducts, and the bare brick and concrete cores of the baths. These could be used as arguments for simplicity and truth, and at the same time could inculcate a taste for the picturesque and romantic. In practice no one seemed quite ready to be as

111. J. J. Winckelmann, *Gedanken,* quoted in Holt, *Documentary History, 2,* 349.

112. Gotthold Lessing, *Laocoön,* quoted in Holt, *Documentary History, 2,* 358.

113. Johann Wolfgang von Goethe, *Of German Architecture,* quoted in Holt, *Documentary History, 2,* 361 ff.

"nude" as the doctrine demanded. Ornament was reduced but not eliminated. It was frankly tacked on. A frieze would be hung on a wall as one might hang a picture. Niches and panels were placed arbitrarily where the designer felt that the walls would otherwise be too stark. Interiors were always decorated with care. There was often as much ornament in such an interior as in a Rococo one, though the effect was usually quieter. At times it seems as though this was more a style of interior decoration than an architectural style, as was inaccurately held, until recently, to be the case with the Art Nouveau.

There were many Italian projects and designs which exhibited the revolutionary trend. Some of the key buildings will be discussed in following chapters. One must heed Kaufmann's warning not to let a classicizing vocabulary blind us to underlying achievement.[114] He concluded that the new idea motivating the Architecture of Revolution was individualism, the goal of which was the freedom to devise new configurations which had in common the quality of being different from any previous ones. By this he implied that the architect had the right to make his buildings express feelings.

Strongly contrasting basic geometrical forms are commonly used, such as those of the Pantheon; although the basic idea of contrast was anti-Renaissance. It was derived from the Baroque, but it was executed with less intricacy and obfuscation. Contrast was a means indulged in by Piranesi and his follower Valadier, along with the independence of the parts, their variety, and the free coexistence of diverse elements, thus minimizing the old virtues of balance and coherence. These principles were used by Piranesi in his *Carceri, Cammini,* and the plates of the Via Appia.[115] Valadier made the wings of his compositions as heavy as his central mass in order to reduce its importance. This can be seen more readily in his numerous sketches than in executed work. In other instances he makes the central mass so overwhelmingly important in relation to the minor ones that the parts are "incongruous." An example of this is a *rotonda* surmounted by a pyramid with very small wings—an idea which was still current when Carlo Barabino made his first project for the Cemetery Chapel at Staglieno. There are echoes of Mannerism in some of these ideas as well, such as making the superstructure abnormally heavy for the supports, or making the two equal in height. The combination of incongruous features seems to have been deliberate, for one sketch is marked "in a mixed style" (*in stile misto*). Giuseppe Valadier often showed the commonly accepted preference for simple, pure geometric forms, a fondness which he shared with Ledoux, Gilly, Boullée, and many others. The forbidding character of unrelieved geometry tends to further separate the parts, as does the use of such self-contained and withdraw-

114. Kaufmann, *Age of Reason,* p. 118.
115. Ibid., p. 112.

ing forms as pyramids, cones, and cylinders.[116] Similar in intent is the use of stepped forms or particularly platforms, which isolate the building or buildings from any accidents of environment and thus stress the purity of form. This is exhibited in the works of Boullée and Ledoux, the books of Durand, Valadier's San Pantaleo, Rome, and his projects for the Teatro Valle, Rome, 1819.[117]

The seekers after a new revolutionary style seemed to hesitate for some time between such objectives as the wholly rational and the sensual, and between the hierarchical order and the opposed isolation of the components.

Many of these general ideas had been known in antiquity and were never quite lost from sight. What marks the difference is not the novelty of form but the handling of it. The effects obtained by manipulations of space, movement, and vocabulary must be carefully discerned. The presence of a pure baseless Greek Doric column does not in itself indicate that we are in the presence of the new style. Leopold Pollack's Villa Reale in Milan (1790–93) has some Neoclassical elements, but the basic composition is predominantly traditional with a considerable debt to Palladio (Figures 24–26). The historian must be alert to detect minute changes in vocabulary, composition, and emotional content. This is not unlike what Henri Foçillon directed to our attention as the analysis of effects.

Here it will be useful to trace some common denominator, or what Giedion called a "constituent factor," through a series of examples, such as we did above with the pilaster and column.[118] The rise and fall of the silhouette of the dome is such a talisman. The domes of the early Renaissance are sometimes entirely internal or they rise a little above the main roof, as at the Pazzi Chapel or at Santa Maria delle Carceri at Prato, or become semicircular and external, as at Todi and Montepulciano. The dome of St. Peter's, though raised on a high drum, was not very steeply pointed in Michelangelo's model but became more so in della Porta's execution. The Baroque masters tended to make more of the drum than of the dome, as Borromini did in Sant'Ivo, or to make the dome and its drum dominate everything below it, as was done at Sant'Agnese on the Piazza Navona, Rome, at Santa Maria della Salute, Venice, and at the Superga, Turin. Presently the reverse process sets in. This can be observed in Venice, where G. A. Scalfarotto's San Simeone Piccolo of 1718–30 (Figure 83) has an absurdly high dome which is "corrected" in 1748 by Temanza in his use of a low saucer dome on Santa Maria Maddalena (Figure 84). This trend is paralleled by minimizing the external expression of the dome as was done by Vittone at Santa Maria di Piazza, Turin (1751–68), and Marchionni at the sacristy of

116. Ibid., p. 113.
117. Ibid., p. 114.
118. See p. 22.

St. Peter's in Rome (1776–84). Thereafter, the low Roman Pantheon dome becomes dominant and is to be found in nearly all projects using domes from 1780 onwards, rarely with a drum, as at San Carlo in Milan (1836–47) by Carlo Amati (Figure 88). The effect of the lower dome is to place more emphasis on the temple front so frequently used in conjunction with it. This was coming to be regarded as more "classical" than the dome. Later on, as the mania for towers spread and the picturesque silhouette required lofty vertical accents, the dome and drum rise again to almost spire-like heights in such domed towers as in the Town Hall at Leeds, the Capitol in Washington, the Capitol at Hartford, the Palais de Justice in Brussels, and the Mole in Turin.

Symbolism, Allegory, and Iconology

Other less recondite symbols were often used to provoke the desired reaction, so that buildings and their ornament could clearly communicate with the beholder.

The pure cube is often used symbolically. Not only is the equality of its six faces an expression of perfection, but Ledoux considered it a symbol of immutability upon which one should seat the Gods and Heroes. Mario Asprucci, in the gates of the Villa Borghese at Rome, may have had a similar idea when he raised the Borghese dragon on cubical gatehouses.

The pyramid had several meanings. To Ledoux it was a crowning feature as necessary to a building as a head to a man. It also had mystic overtones. It was associated with cabalistic symbols, the secrets of the pyramids, eternity, and the like. To him it was also the image of a flame shaped by the pressure of the atmosphere.[119]

The sphere or the hemisphere represented heaven or the firmament. Ledoux referred to "the celestial harmonies."[120] For Vaudoyer it was the ideal form for a "House of a Cosmopolite," a project he designed in Rome in 1785.[121] For Houel it was the "perfect symbol of equality.[122] Kaufmann calls it the most perfect of withdrawing forms and therefore an expression of self-contained individualism. Much of this was an inheritance from Alberti and Palladio, to whom the geometrical perfection of circular and equilateral plans partook of the divine.

The shell, particularly the scallop shell, has had a number of symbolic meanings: an adjunct of the goddess Venus, and of the crusader who had returned successfully from his dangerous journey; by extension it could be read as a

---

119. Moreux, *Ledoux,* pp. 45–46.
120. Ibid., p. 54.
121. Kaufmann, *Age of Reason,* p. 185.
122. Ibid.

symbol of a voyage, a journey, or the quest. Its use to adorn the upper surface of a niche thus might mean something particular beyond a happy harmony of form and decoration. Michelangelo Simonetti, who used the shell to head the niches of his Sala Rotonda in the Vatican in 1773 (Figure 15), was not only being traditional but might possibly have been alluding to the journeys the antique statues within them had made through time, and also perhaps to the quest his own age was making for the values of antiquity.

As we have seen above, the eighteenth century believed with Descartes that certain formalized gestures which expressed the actor's mood were natural.[123] This sort of naïveté makes some of Ledoux's symbolism more tolerable though, as we have said, some of them are in the same class with the cute names given cottages, such as his calling the house of a ballerina a "Temple of Terpsichore," or a roof garden "The Garden of Zephyr and Flora."[124]

Among the more easily understood accessory devices were laurels for glory, wheat for plenty, the sphinxes as the guardians of the mysteries of royal and everlasting life. The sophisticated architect Borra, for example, placed sphinxes at the Castle of Racconigi in 1756. They were also used at the approaches to a suspension bridge in southern Italy, perhaps to persuade the timid traveler to accept the novelty (Figure 43).

The allegorical tradition continued in force, drawing strength from Palladio's statement that the four loggias of his Villa Mocenigo were "arms which tend to the circumference to receive those which come close to the house," and Bernini's idea that his colonnades at St. Peter's are the embracing arms of Christ, whose head is symbolized by the dome.

Jean-Charles Delafosse, in his *Nouvelle Iconologie historique* (1768), made decorative compositions of symbols which are like the themes set nowadays for flower arrangements. One, called "L'Amérique" combines a table, a mask, flaming torches, arrows, and a primitive figure holding a wheel, with an alligator at his feet. Some of this is easily readable, but for other parts a key would help us understand it better. In some cases he had recourse to medallions and ordinary illustration instead of symbols. When this approach is used in architecture much of the content is lost without a key. The decorative friezes and sculptured figures must have given clues to the initiated which are difficult to recover today without the learning of a Panofsky. Abstract architectural language alone is not always clear.

There is a collection of projects by distinguished Italian architects, the *Atti dell'Accademia della Pace,* which makes extensive use of symbols and associative forms. Ferdinando Bonsignore in a "Monument to Michelangelo" uses a

123. See p. 6 and also Sypher, *Four Stages,* pp. 274 ff.
124. Praz, *Gusto neoclassico,* p. 103, referring to Ledoux.

tabernacle formed by partially fluted Doric columns supporting a sarcophagus to enclose a cube. The attendant figures and decoration are partly Egyptian.[125] This combination of symbols is easily read, but its application to Michelangelo in particular is obscure. Mario Asprucci designed a "Country House for a Literary Gentleman."[126] The country location is suggested by the use of rustication; the main building is a cube resting on a high base penetrated by fountains "of learning." At the summit is an observatory in the form of a circular domed temple, the well-known symbol of the skies.

Scenography

Romanticism fostered scenography, although purists opposed it. It had developed under the many geniuses of the Bibiena family, continued its sway in the works of Piranesi, and persisted with hardly diminished vigor into the nineteenth century, not only on the stage itself but also in the engravings of men like Antonio Basoli, or in projects by men like Giovanni Antonio Antolini, and in the work of designers, topographical painters, and imaginative architects. Scenography was consistent with the ideas of the picturesque, the heroic, and the sublime. The opposition to it was the product of an unnaturally severe rigorism far removed from the emotional wellsprings of the common man, who was being taught to cultivate his sensitivity.

Scenography can exist, as in Panini's decorations, without a stage, but in Italy and elsewhere the theatre and opera flourished at the end of the eighteenth century. The attendant scenographic effects were a part of everyone's experience. In the Neoclassic style of opera, very elaborate stage effects were the rule, as in the productions of *The Magic Flute*. These were highly profitable to their producers. There was also a series of "rescue operas" which drew huge crowds.[127] They filled an emotional need. In them the hero or heroine went through scene after scene of tribulation, each requiring an elaborate change of scenery, until the final rescue took place, the whole plot being contrived primarily to give the stage technicians opportunities for displaying their skill.

Character

The application of such symbols to give buildings character became the preoccupation of architects. In the mid-eighteenth century J.-F. Blondel had said,

125. *Atti dell'Accademia della Pace* (Florence, c. 1825), 1 plate, unnumbered.
126. *Atti,* 3 plates, unnumbered.
127. The following explanation of this term is given by David Ewen, *Encyclopedia of the Opera* (New York, 1963), p. 420: "A genre of French opera enjoying a brief span of popularity during the French Revolution. The typical libretto shows the hero or heroine being saved after many vicissitudes. Cherubini's *Les Deux Journées* is such an opera." Such operas continued to be popular for some time in Italy. In the early days of the cinema, "The Perils of Pauline" formed a sort of parallel.

"Character is more important than visual Beauty."[128] Boullée helps us understand this language, too, by his explanations of his own designs. His Palais de Justice contains a prison in its substructure and culminates in an august palace which thus rises above the gloomy pits of crime, an allegory of the Vices crushed beneath the weight of Justice. His design for a Municipal Palace is in three tiers, the lowest open to all, since it is the people's house, but not wholly open, as it is controlled by four guardhouses symbolizing force. The intermediate floor contains offices, and the uppermost the main public rooms. The character achieved is dignified, proud, republican, and imposing—but not magnificent, which would be inappropriate. He has, he says, accomplished this by using widely separated openings and avoiding the use of breaks and recesses which would be too grand. In a project for a National Palace, more grandeur is required, and utter simplicity of form. However, in this case the meaning is not conveyed by the architectural forms so much as by figures bearing the books of decrees and some low reliefs. His comments on domestic architecture reveal the limitations of the system. To him houses were hopelessly sterile as vehicles for expression; one could only make them more or less rich. The true vehicles for poetry are palaces, theatres, cenotaphs, and temples. Thus he limited the rôle of expression to monumental buildings. Others were bolder and made symbolic houses, like the project of Vaudoyer mentioned above.

Ledoux, by using pyramids, masculine forms, and generally nude walls in his Cannon Foundry, conveyed reasonably well its utilitarian function if not its specific one.

It was partly a legacy from tradition that determined the character considered suitable for certain types of buildings. Juvarra orchestrated large forms in an impressive manner for a royal town palace, the Palazzo Madama in Turin (1718–21); in a merely aristocratic residence there was less parade, and at Stupinigi, a country villa (1729–33), an even cooler, simpler handling was deemed appropriate. The dome was usually reserved for churches.[129] A great man's monument must be made to look like a temple to a hero, a bourse must recall a basilica, a castle should be Gothic. Some thought that Gothic might be suitable for a church, as it could be interpreted as symbolic of pure pre-Jesuit religion.

Stockmarkets were a relatively new type of building and a favorite subject for competitions; Durand offered several designs in his *Précis.* Many others appeared in the *Grand Prix,* and some of these influenced actual designs. One by Giuseppe V. Marvuglia, included in the *Atti dell'Accademia della Pace,*[130] recalls the basilica, considered the correct association, and does so without

128. Kaufmann, *Age of Reason,* p. vii.
129. Wittkower, *Art and Architecture,* p. 276.
130. *Atti,* 3 plates, unnumbered.

recourse to the Corinthian order. The front consists of a double colonnade of fourteen Greek Doric columns under a simplified entablature; within the great hall the Ionic pavilions have saucer domes. Its geometry is intricate; its detail simplified; its character is businesslike and civic without being excessively grand. Another example is furnished by Giuseppe Cacialli in his volume of projects published in 1827.[131] Cacialli's Bourse is more like that by Thomas de Thomon, built in Leningrad from 1804–16, which in turn uses features from several *Grand Prix* "Exchanges," such as P. Bernard's of 1782 and Tardieu's of 1786; the descent from the former was observed by Helen Rosenau.[132] As in the Paris Bourse of 1808, colonnades and not temple fronts were deemed appropriate. Even when there is a sloping roof and gables they are not handled as pediments. Instead, the Roman window at large scale supplies the axial accent. There must also have been an association between the shape of this window and that of the Cloaca Maxima so much admired by the purists for its functional directness. This shape is popular among the Neoclassicists for openings, be they windows, portals, or merely niches, with or without fountains.

To another project in the *Atti,* Barabino imparted a suitable character: forbidding, grand, military, and virile.[133] The problem was the enlargement of the famous Mole at Genoa. The main mass is huge, battered, dense, and overwhelming. The plan is a system of crepuscular geometric burrows, more solid than void. The few openings are relatively tiny and set into deep embrasures. The only order used is Greek Doric.

The influence of Gilly's tomb for Frederick the Great is shown in another project by Cacialli which is simply called a "Monument."[134] The components include a domed interior chamber, a pyramid, "Cloaca Maxima" portals, and the Greek Doric order. In addition he uses rustication in two scales. His order is a primitive, stubby type of Doric. Some of the columns stand on cubical blocks, which may have been meant to convey Egyptian overtones. His pyramid is as steeply sloped as that of Cestus. The tomb is undeniably sepulchral in mood—grim, rigid, and withdrawn.

Conclusion: The Longevity of These Systems

The architectural history of the eighteenth century is thus revealed as containing a wide spectrum of stylistic coloring. To the parts of this spectrum many names have been applied, and for them many sources have been proposed. The common denominator of the new or revived stylistic vocabularies is above everything else the desire of the architect to communicate to the observer by means of

131. Cacialli, *Raccolta,* pls. 31–32.
132. Helen Rosenau, "Engravings of the Grand Prix," *Architectural History, 3* (1960), 17 ff.
133. *Atti,* 3 plates, unnumbered.
134. Cacialli, *Raccolta,* pls. 10–12.

associative values. From this desire arise such phenomena as the Picturesque, Purism, and the many forms of Eclecticism including Neoclassicism. The sources of these ideas and vocabularies are many, and they include, to a greater extent than has been generally observed, Italy, and particularly Rome. It is to confirm these observations that Appendices A and B have been supplied. From them it is deducible, first, that many countries offered revolutionary concepts and that their authors compiled volumes of exotic or inactive vocabularies, and second, that the Italians were active in this program and that Rome more than any other place was a meeting ground for the interested parties—the young zealots and the powerful prophets. There the old and new systems of design were brought into contact.

At the end of the nineteenth century and the beginning of the twentieth, some of these systems could still be identified. The Eclectics flourished using all three of their vocabularies and received most of the commissions. The Purists and the Architects of Revolution were a minority but emerged as the Functionalists, De Stijl, and finally the International Style. The extreme Romantics would enjoy short reigns in the Art Nouveau, *Stile Floreale,* Expressionism, and Futurism. By the middle of the twentieth century some of these attitudes have become minor, such as that of the Eclectics, and others have merged, the most striking merger being that between the Architects of Revolution in their modern guise as Functionalists and their opposites, the Expressionists, which we are today calling the Brutalists and the Neoromantics. The evidence would indicate that these attitudes correspond to some of the basic drives of man and continue to find expression in architecture.

The most recent stage in this movement toward expression in art took place in the twentieth century, when the artist became free to record his experience, however personal and however imperfectly communicated. There was a wide audience prepared to accept a work of art shorn of the familiar means of communication: vocabulary, images, and associations. We may today be on the verge of another revolution in feeling which will be based on a new concept of "natural man" derived from Freud and Fromm, one in which authority and tradition will play a respected role. It has been suggested that the beatniks in their disrespect for any kind of authority—moral, legal, societal—are the last protest of the old kind of romanticism. In their clannishness there may be a token of a new kind of authority—that of "togetherness." This may be a reaction to the frightening doctrine of self-expression, which implies that man is alone.[135]

Today expression of mood and symbol are again, after years of disuse, coming

135. Michael Polanyi, "The Two Cultures," *Encounter, 13* (Sept. 1959), 61–64.

into vogue both in the language of critics and the designs of architects. An unusually subtle analysis occurs in a work by Edmund Crispin, *Buried for Pleasure*. "Sanford Hall . . . was discreet rather than arrogant, demure rather than impressive—and this in spite of its rather considerable dimensions . . . it lay along the crown of a hill like an elegant toy, its carefully spaced sash windows tactful and unobtrusive."[136] Architects again attribute symbolic meanings to their forms. As James Stirling wrote, the courtyard of his modern college was carefully enclosed to symbolize the restricted size of the group, and the whole was placed on a raised podium like the turfed platform of an earthworks to suggest security.[137] Eero Saarinen, describing his highly original designs for Morse and Stiles Colleges at Yale, said that he could not use conventional forms or materials to get the appropriate meaning and take cognizance of the peculiarities of the site.[138] He wanted effects of diversity, variety, individuality, roughness, and a play of light and shade; therefore he used polygonal shapes varied in their siting, a sequence of spatial experiences, a large scale bending back and forth, strength, simplicity, romantic texture, and an image of "citadels of earthy monolithic masonry." He used not only the terms of the Picturesque but also those of the Romantics.

136. Edmund Crispin [pseud.], *Buried for Pleasure* (London, 1948), pp. 98–99.
137. James Stirling, "The Functional Tradition and Expression," *Perspecta, 6* (1960), 96.
138. *Yale News Supplement* (Nov. 12, 1959), p. 3.

2

The Neoclassical Architecture of Italy

Introduction

The Transitional Period 1765–1795: Continuations of the Renaissance, Neo-Palladian, and Other Systems

The Rise of Neoclassicism

The Triumph of Neoclassicism 1795–1840
Introduction
Urbanism, Gates, Gardens, Triumphal Arches, and Cafés
Palaces, Public and Private
Churches
Villas
Temple Fronts
The Pantheon as a Paradigm

Survivals of Neoclassicism After 1840
Sarti and Marchese
Antonelli

2

The Neoclassical Architecture of Italy

Introduction

This chapter will trace the rise of the new systems of architecture in Italy as they can be seen in actual buildings, concentrating on those with some sort of classical vocabulary, which were overwhelmingly dominant for four decades. There are a few examples of the Revolutionary Style, a number of lingering Renaissance- and Palladian-oriented buildings, and a much greater number of designs derived at varying removes from the antique, chiefly from Rome but with some from Greece. This is Neoclassicism. First we will see the gradual introduction of new details, then of new compositions and their application to buildings for diverse purposes. Finally the architect will evolve variations on antique themes with powerful associational values, such as triumphal arches, the Pantheon, and temple fronts. Some of these will be motivated by projects of urbanistic embellishment—such as city gates, public buildings, and the adornment of piazzas—others by the desire to enhance and modernize older or incomplete buildings, and still others by the wish to garb in classical dress new buildings of utilitarian function, such as meat markets, stock exchanges, and factories. Neoclassicism will be seen to be the dominant mode after Napoleon's conquest and to have survived almost to the moment of unification in 1870.

From time to time an occasional note of a broader eclecticism will be found, motivated either by a desire for continuity or, more often, by a wish to enlarge the range of associations. This will result in the appearance of a Gothic, Egyptian, or Chinese motive.

Although there was much that was "classic" in late Baroque, it was a deflection of the spirit. The proportion of traditional elements was larger. The cerebral was not to be dimmed by the sensual. There are some instances of this in Guarini, Vittone, and Juvarra. Stupinigi is particularly intricate and full of sub-articulations. The next generation tends toward simplification; thus, Giuseppe Piermarini (1734–1808) comes nearer to being a "classicist."[1] While far more

---

1. Wittkower, *Art and Architecture,* p. 256.

"modern" than Vanvitelli or than his contemporary Cantoni, he makes only tentative advances toward a pure, bare style. He is content to take his master's ideas and "refine" or "correct" them in the direction of Neo-Palladianism.

The Palladian, Neo-Palladian, and Neoclassical systems all used an antique vocabulary. The Palladian system mixed Roman and Renaissance forms. The Neoclassic system tended to eschew the latter and included Greek elements. The range of elaboration and texture in the Palladian and Neo-Palladian systems was restricted, but Neoclassical buildings could be light, papery, and ornate as in the Adam and Federal styles or heavy, massive, and stark as in some of the work of Ledoux and Cagnola.

Everywhere the march of giant pilasters across the wall slows down to a decorous gait: at the Royal Crescent, Bath; at the palace, Caserta; at Somerset House, London; at the Hôtel des Monnaies, Paris, begun 1768, and so on. Hence it is not surprising that when Piermarini is entrusted with his first major commission, the new façade (1769–78) for the Royal Palace in Milan (Figure 4), he is as quiet and restrained as was his master Vanvitelli ten years earlier in the Piazza Dante (1755–67) in Naples (Figure 4a). He reduces the florid and irregular old palace (Figure 3) to seemliness. There is no recall in detail, but the funereal pace of the pilasters and the extreme restraint are common to both.

The use of orders in the new buildings is also a measure of the increase in simplicity and severity which was shared by many of the new systems. The unfluted Tuscan Doric had never been entirely dropped. The Baroque masters liked it as a starting point for their intricacies. They used it to frame portals—as had Vignola at the Cancelleria in Rome, Carlo Fontana in Genoa's Palazzo Reale (1705), and Alessandro Specchi in Rome's Palazzo de Carolis (1727). It became increasingly favored in the later eighteenth century, and may have acquired a variety of meanings by then. There was the Palladian idea that it was suitably employed on wings and in forecourts; Bernini had used it this way in his colonnades at St. Peter's. It was also agreed that, if several orders were to be employed in tiers, the lowest order should be the simplest. Pietro da Cortona may have had both principles in his mind when he designed the curved porch for Santa Maria della Pace, since that is also part of a piazza. Marchionni had used it in the 1750s in the wings of the Villa Albani to support both lintels and arches inserted between pilasters and paneled frames, with a considerable indebtedness to the Capitoline and the Palazzo Odescalchi. Cosimo Morelli, in his Palazzo Braschi (1790–92) for the family of Pope Pius VI, now the Museo di Roma, flanked his arched entrance portal with a Tuscan order. The confirmation of this as symptomatic of the growing fashion for antiquity is that he crowned the building with a stark Doric frieze and cornice.

To Neoclassicists the column and the wall were entirely different elements, not just one more means of articulation. The column was not something to be recessed into a wall, nor to be applied to it, nor to be half buried in it, but was instead a complete form with an individuality which must in no way be impaired by any kind of symbiotic relationship. The column became for them, as it had been for antiquity itself, a primary element of architecture. Stendhal says, "These Baths have no columns—which, in my opinion, deprives them of all *expression*."[2] Their expressive function may have been capable of a far wider and more subtle range than we are tuned to register. Several generations had been made to believe that the achievements of the ancients made their own efforts seem puny. They would, therefore, invest the features of classical architecture with additive attributes. As in antiquity, columns came to be regarded as more admirable the larger they were and the more precious their material; and they were most particularly prized if they were monolithic. These qualities appealed to primitive associations with wealth and power.

In this period in Italy, certain effects of lowness and elongation became more and more frequent, as had become common in France. The overall mass flattened down and gained length at the expense of height. This had been accomplished partly by lowering interior ceiling heights, partly by the compression or elimination of the traditional high basements, particularly evident in new villas like that at Monza (Figure 13) or the Villa Olmo, which start directly at the ground level, or very near it. Balustrades above cornices and their accompanying skyline figures tend to disappear. This had the effect, as it had in Paris in the Hôtel de Salm, of reducing the formality and increasing the feeling of intimacy. Low massing was given to monumental buildings as well, such as triumphal arches, gates, and even temple fronts, which now seem to touch the ground without the intermediary of a stylobate, though they do not appear to be rising out of the ground. One can therefore say that at this time the less a building is separated from the ground the more it takes on an early Neoclassical appearance; sometimes buildings were set directly on platforms to obtain similar effects, particularly in France.

A related tendency can be observed in the work of painters of this time. Andrea Appiani and certain landscape painters bring the figures very close to the edge of the frame, reduce the space below them in relation to that above, and often cut off the figures at the knees. All of these devices tend to bring the viewer closer to the subject.

It is revealing to compare two three-storied Italian buildings of this time, Simone Cantoni's Palazzo Ducale in Genoa (1777, Figure 1) and Piermarini's La Scala in Milan (1776–78, Figure 2). Both use paired orders one to a story in a pre-Palladian manner. The latter building has garlands in the frieze and sculpture in the pediment, both features already Neoclassical. Otherwise the

2. Stendhal, *A Roman Journal*, Haakon Chevalier, ed. and trans. (New York, 1957), p. 17.

Figure 1. Simone Cantoni: Genoa, Palazzo Ducale, 1777

Figure 2. Giuseppe Piermarini: Milan, La Scala, 1776–78

detail is sparse, the relief low, the articulation clear in a Renaissance hierarchical building-up from the lateral wings to the central attic. The skyline figures have been replaced by urns. Both buildings face upon a square, have rusticated basements, are seven bays wide, and bring the three central bays forward as a block. Piermarini brings his forward for a porte cochere on the ground floor, and sets his lateral wings back in two stages, thus achieving more plasticity of mass. There is a faint echo of Palladio's Palazzo Iseppo da Porti, Vicenza, about this design. Cantoni's decoration is more robust. His two lower floors are heavy with pairs of engaged columns—Roman Doric below Ionic—both unfluted. The pilaster strips in the attic are in high relief, have statues squeezed between them, have brackets attached to them, and each pair of brackets supports an active trophy. This palace is heavy, ornate, cluttered, and yet lacks plasticity of mass. The façade of La Scala is smoother, lighter, and more graceful. The huge, inflated theatre façades of a later period would lean more on Cantoni's style than on Piermarini's, although the latter's building was more elegant and otherwise more progressive. Its composition was late Baroque, but its simplicity was forward-looking, and was allied to his Palazzo Reale, Milan (1769–78, Figure 4), which is even more monotonous, with only one powerful accent—the three-bay unit at the main entrance. This is heavily rusticated, with engaged Ionic columns topped by a high attic, a motive from Caserta.

The Transitional Period 1765–1795: Continuations of the Renaissance, Neo-Palladian, and Other Systems

In the 1760s there are a number of tentative approaches to a new system. These occur primarily in Rome where so many visitors and architects had been exchanging ideas. Previously there had been some slight Neoclassical activity in Venice. Tirali, for instance, had added a startlingly classical temple front to San Niccolò dei Tolentini (1706–14, Figure 5), destined to be the forerunner of a long line of such additions although it is clearly more Palladian than Roman. There, too, had risen early in the century two small churches which can be considered to be remotely derived from the Pantheon. These will be discussed below. These, and the Roman examples which we are about to discuss in detail, exhibit characteristics of three significant systems, Neo-Palladianism, the Revolutionary mode of composition, and traces of the Neoclassical vocabulary. They all tend to be ground-hugging. Some of them are richly ornamented in a Rococo spirit but others are pure and stark.

About 1760 Cardinal Albani's architect, Carlo Marchionni (1702–86), and Johann Joachim Winckelmann added several novel edifices to the Cardinal's villa and gardens. The work at the villa had begun in 1746. Both it and the gardens were well along under Marchionni's direction when Winckelmann appeared in Rome. The late Baroque style of the main buildings turned in a new direction in the three new *tempietti*. This may be due to Winckelmann's presence, his emphasis on things Greek, and his enthusiasm over the Cardinal's collections (Figures 6, 7, 8).[3]

The three edifices at the Villa Albani correspond in function to the pavilions so important in other eighteenth-century gardens, in which so many stylistic experiments and mood-inducers were occurring at this time: Cirencester Park, Hagley, Kew, Strawberry Hill, Sans Souci, et al. But they were not fully Neoclassical. They were a sort of "Rococo-Neoclassic." The porticos and cellae were small, the scale dainty, the ornament abundant, neither pure nor simple. The vocabulary was eclectic. The Ionic order with garlands suspended between the volutes had been popular ever since the Capitoline and had already been used on the main villa. It can be traced through the Certosa at Pavia to antiquity.[4] Much of the ornament is Hellenistic rather than fifth-century Greek. The extraordinarily large figures serving as acroteria are among the numerous Palladian features, as are the pilaster responds, the wide central intercolumniations, and the low steps. Two of these tempietti, tacked onto the older structure, are without much reference to it in scale (Figures 6, 7). They are amusing exercises. The columns of the third one, Tempietto Diruto (Figure 8), with spiral channeling in reversed cutting, may owe something to Palladio, who depicted similar ones. The rare pier-order, rectangular in section and very thin, is to be found at Hadrian's villa, from which it may have been brought; others have recently been found at the new excavations at Pompeii. This artificial ruin is largely composed of authentic ancient fragments. A similar little temple, not a ruin, is to be seen in the background of Poussin's "Gathering of the Ashes of Phocion," and may also owe its form to Palladio.

One of Marchionni's Greek tempietti (Figure 7) here uses tall channeled shafts, Attic bases, and floreate Corinthianesque capitals which may be Hellenistic. The frieze of confronting sphinxes suggests Egyptian influence, and the pediment figure is an Ephesian Diana. Winckelmann's influence or no, there is little archaeological exactitude.

Piranesi (1720–78), with his overwhelming inspirations and his total disagreement with Winckelmann's Greek tastes, introduced intense novelty in his most important architectural realization, the well-known Santa Maria del Priorato (Figures 9–12) which he remodeled in 1764–65, and to which he added a new forecourt. It is a prime example of Kaufmann's "Architecture of Revolu-

3. Carl Justi, *Winckelmann und seine Zeitgenossen* (3 vols. Leipzig, 1923), *2,* 351 ff.
4. While not unknown in antiquity, the Ionic capital with garlands swung from the volutes was rare. It was revived and became popular from the sixteenth century onwards.

Figure 3. Milan, Palazzo Reale, before the reconstruction of 1769–78

Figure 4. Giuseppe Piermarini: Milan, Palazzo Reale, 1769–78

Figure 4a. Luigi Vanvitelli: Naples, Piazza Dante, 1755–67

Figure 5. Andrea Tirali: Venice, San Niccolò dei Tolentini, 1706–14

Figure 6. Carlo Marchionni: Rome, Villa Albani, Tempietto Greco, c.1760

Figure 7. Carlo Marchionni: Rome, Villa Albani, Tempietto Greco, c.1760

Figure 8. Carlo Marchionni: Rome, Villa Albani, Tempietto Diruto, c.1760

tion," although he calls it "incoherent."[5] The complex shows an eclectic mingling of styles: sixteenth-century Mannerism from Scamozzi, and seventeenth-
century Baroque in the handling of the Borrominesque interior. The altar owes
much to Bernini, and Neoclassicism is shown in the rigidity and rectilinearity.[6]

Piranesi's use of a mélange of traditional and novel attitudes changed their
meanings and made them, as Praz says, "romantic, morbid, and hallucinated."[7]
We are in the presence of something profoundly disturbing. The eclecticism is
far-ranging, the novelties and juxtapositions highly literate and complex, and
the use of symbols and devices carried out further than commonly attempted.
It is Neoclassic, Rococo, and full of feeling—an intensely personal style in
which not only the old system of composition has been negated, as Kaufmann
says, but a new one applied. "Frozen baroque" is not sufficiently descriptive.
This style communicates on several levels, literally through its symbols and
formally through its ingenuities, which are only apparent to those familiar with
the normal, conventional way of doing things. Similarly, the allusions to the
architecture of the Venetian Mannerists, and of Borromini and Bernini, were
directed to an informed audience.

There is a kind of delight in watching the master's tricks and games, an intellectual formal entertainment. Something like this can also be found in some
of the works of Valadier (Rome, Casino Valadier, 1809–14, Figure 69), Japelli
(Padua, Caffè Pedrocchi, 1816–42, Figures 52–54), and Antonelli (Novara,
Duomo, 1854–69, Figure 102).

Lavagnino says that Piranesi's church was rebuilt in 1765 on a structure in
sixteenth-century taste, and that the new paneling and stucco, although unquestionably after antique models, was handled with an eighteenth-century
fantasy and picturesqueness. The church does not quite become Neoclassical
because, in his view, that term should be reserved for works in which antique
motives are taken up with strictness and used in an archaeological spirit.[8]

As we see it today without its lateral wings, the chapel façade is a simple
temple front of four pilasters with a pediment over the central door and an
oculus above. The pilasters share a common base which extends toward but is
interrupted by the door-frame. The capitals, conventional in form, are surprising
in detail, being composed of castles, animals, and other emblems related to the
arms and history of Knights of Malta. A similar insistent use of symbols characterizes the whole complex and conveys numerous overtones, sometimes of

5. Kaufmann, *Age of Reason*, p. 111.

6. Rudolf Wittkower, "Piranesi as Architect," in: Smith College Museum of Art, *Piranesi*
(Northampton, 1961), pp. 99 ff.

7. Praz, *Gusto neoclassico,* p. 98.

8. Lavagnino, *L'Arte moderna, 1,* 28.

Figure 9. Giovanni Battista Piranesi: Rome, Santa Maria del Priorato, façade of church, 1765

fantasy, sometimes of surprise when such forms are substituted for conventional architectural elements.

The door and its window form an independent composition, a frontispiece with its own unit of relief: a frieze, part of a cornice, and a frame which comes to an abrupt stop on the corner of the pediment. None of these architectural elements have architectonic qualities. The pilasters are frames for decorated crosses, the window and door hang like a tapestry. The spaces between are filled with ormolu-like decoration. It could have been executed in wood as well as in stucco.

The use of appliqués in Santa Maria del Priorato and the treatment of the doors was carried on by Canova and Valadier.[9] This breaking-up and recombination had also been used by Cosimo Fanzago in the façade of San Lorenzo in Lucina, Rome, a century and a half earlier and not very far away.

The clean white interior is rich with eclectic and original ideas, one of the most notable of which is the way in which moldings, pilasters, and window frames are manipulated to form crosses. The gorgeous decorations of the ceiling are placed ingeniously in frames of various patterns. The lighting of the altar group from behind is theatrical in the Baroque tradition. The relief ornament is abundant and yet self-contained, appliquéd as on the exterior. What had been exuberantly framed panels in Rococo stucco work had stiffened into geometrical compartments infused with a new spirit, not merely an exhibition of learning. Among the aspects of this spirit was a Baroque-Picturesqueness, as Wittkower calls it, which was more dynamic than the "dry-precision" of the later topographical views.[10] The oblique perspectives, which added a new dimension of drama and spatial expansion, derived from Bibiena's *scena per angolo* and wedded two contradictory traditions, that of the Baroque stage and that of the architectural landscape.[11]

The garden wall sometimes can be read as a five-bay composition, sometimes as a three-bay one, because the wide, nearly square lateral bays have incomplete minor axes indicated by the beam-ends of the entablature, the blank window frames, and the base moldings. But these axes are interrupted by the horizontal panels, the main feature of which occurs above the interval between the windows and thus ignores them.

Other curiosities are the omission of the frieze, the discontinuity of the base line, and the rhythm of the skyline ornaments, which places minor accents above the pilasters and major ones above the incomplete subordinate axes and the apex of the pediment. The central door, usually closed, contains the key-

9. Praz, *Gusto neoclassico*, p. 98.
10. Wittkower, *Art and Architecture*, p. 236.
11. Ibid., p. 237.

Figure 10. Giovanni Battista Piranesi: Rome, Santa Maria del Priorato, interior of church, 1765

Figure 11. Giovanni Battista Piranesi: Rome, Santa Maria del Priorato, garden wall, 1765

Figure 12. Giovanni Battista Piranesi: Rome, Santa Maria del Priorato, piazza, 1765

hole through which thousands of visitors enjoy a peepshow view of St. Peter's. The low relief ornament in the lateral bays spreads outward and upward like inverted pyramids. Kaufmann might consider this disturbed and individualized.[12] But it is not incoherent; there is a clear system.

The wall of the piazza is equally original. Its plain base is interrupted by slabs supported by curved brackets and serving as benches. The mass of the wall breaks in and out, sometimes down to the ground, sometimes only in the cornice, a disquieting unevenness of movement. There is also a gradual increase in activity upward from the taut base to the animated skyline. Praz compares the piling up of elements with Piranesi's plate, "Urne, cippi, e vasi canerarej, . . . nella Villa Corsini."[13] The largest composition on the wall is a round-headed stele with trophies applied to its channeled surface. Its base is grossly oversized and hence tends to crush the cornice which barely supports it. At this point the cornice is made to dive down to surround a deeply shadowed panel. As if for reassurance, there are curved brackets like those under the benches, here turned at right angles. There is a large keystone but no arch. The channeling of the stele surface may be a deliberate transposition from a column to ennoble it, or may be used for textural contrast, or may be just an engraver's trick transferred to another medium. There are two other frontispieces of squat panels, round-headed, pedimented, bearing trophies, and sunk low in the wall instead of precariously tottering on the cornice. They are flanked by paneled obelisks rising from sarcophagi clamped over the top of the wall. The upper edge of the wall rises, falls, splits, and even disappears in a disturbing manner. The silhouette is further animated by a repeated motive—a concave coping supporting a pair of cannon balls. These are recognized in the cornice. They flank the lateral "frontispieces" and are variants on the theme of the looser pairs which crown the courtyard pilasters. Elsewhere they are combined with the sarcophagus-and-urn motive. The urns recur on the peaks of the pediments. Fertility of idea and unconventionality thus are exhibited to perfection in these dazzling inventions which elude definitive classification.

Works like these remained rare. Other architects broke less violently with traditional ways. The royal villa at Monza (1777–80) by Piermarini is largely Neo-Palladian (Figure 13). Since it was a country house, he made it low and small in scale. The main axial motive is five bays wide, reached by two staircases. A balustrade replaces most of the attic. The composition is long and broken up. The orders are only one story high. It is more restrained than Palladio's work, although there is variety in the articulation, both horizontally and vertically. Its window areas, being in a villa, are relatively larger than those of a town house.

12. Kaufmann, *Age of Reason,* p. 109.
13. Praz, *Gusto neoclassico,* fig. 29.

Figure 13. Giuseppe Piermarini: Monza, Villa Reale, 1777–80

In an earlier country house, the Villa d'Adda (later Borromeo) at Cassano (begun in 1765), the mixture of traditions is also apparent, the most prominent constituent of which is the Palladian villa, with its giant order of pilasters on the high basement of the main block flanked by curved screens and many subordinate parts, open and yet stiff in character.[14]

Piermarini's Palazzo Belgioioso, Milan (1777), differs from an earlier project, which was more traditional than the executed version.[14a] Both Bernini's and Fuga's influences can be felt. As in the former's Palazzo Montecitorio, a high attic links the eleven central bays. The idea of treating the wings like five-bay palaces could have come from Fuga's Palazzo della Consulta, though Fuga's bays have more vertical emphasis. The final version is less Baroque and more Palladian in such features as the academic formula complete with pediment, the complexity of organization, and the richness of texture. It is only Neoclassical by comparison with the work of the first part of the century. Old prints show it complete with the typically Palladian skyline figures perched on the parapet. Many details, such as the special Composite order, come from Caserta. Others are used in modified form, such as the panels sunk between the windows and here flattened into delicate low reliefs kept clearly apart from the adjoining motives. The lintels of the *piano nobile* windows come from the basement ones there. Pediment, balustrades, and attics all have the same source. Certain omissions, such as frieze windows and modillions in the cornice, occur because of the lesser size of this building; the basement is lower, and the attic proportionally heavier. A great axial niche would have been out of place here. The Milan palace is much less Late Baroque and more Neoclassic than Caserta. Its unity is less complete and less taut. The detail is simpler, the parts are clearer, the character is less royal and more feminine.

The architect in Rome who corresponds most closely to Piermarini in Lombardy was Michelangelo Simonetti (1724–81), whose most important work was done in the Museo Pio Clementino in the Vatican, where he built several rooms and a court (Figures 14–16). The earliest part is the reworking of the Cortile Ottagono from 1771 to 1773 for Pope Clement XIV.[15] The new work consisted of the portico and the four cabinets at the angles in which sixteen antique oriental granite columns were used. The theme, an arch between short lintels, can be traced back to Bramante, the courtyard of the Villa Giulia, and Palladio. Antique low reliefs were incorporated in the attics. The alternations,

14. This was in part a remodeling which was not completed until 1859. Luca Beltrami and others, *Ville e Castelli d'Italia* (2nd ed. Milan, 1907), pp. 458–59.

14a. Lavagnino, *L'Arte moderna, 1,* fig. 27.

15. The original court had been designed and probably built by Bramante before 1514. J. Ackerman, *The Cortile del Belvedere* (Rome, 1954), pp. 117 ff.

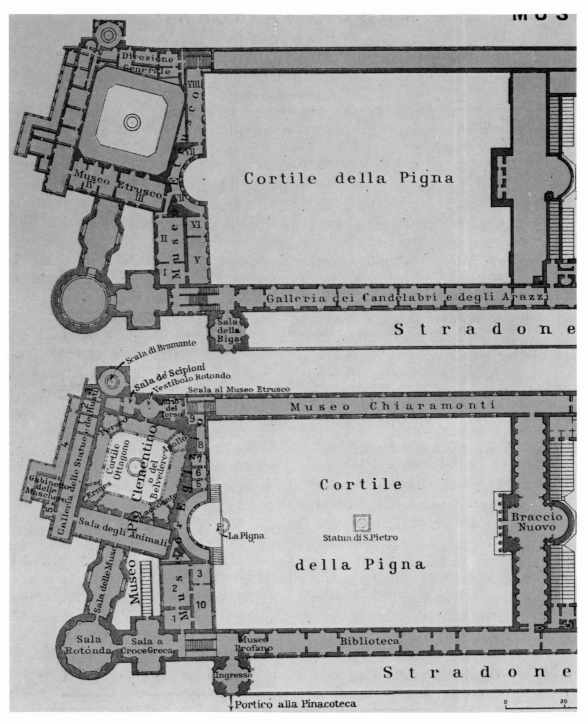

Figure 14. Rome, Vatican, Museo Pio Clementino and Braccio Nuovo, plans

basically High Renaissance, are the following: straight and arched lintels; segmental and pointed pediments; wide and narrow bays closed, partially open, and fully opened; and the play with panels and framing strips. These are, however, treated Neoclassically—the columns are unchanneled, the Ionic capitals are severe, and the molded entablature is not decorated and lacks a frieze.

The Sala Rotonda (Figure 15) has been mentioned above with reference to the symbolism of its shell-headed niches.[16] As its name implies, it is a cylindrical room topped by a drum pierced with lunettes and crowned by a coffered dome. The main order is a channeled Composite one. The capitals incorporate elements from the Braschi arms of Pope Pius VI, eagles and seraphim. It is difficult to know how much of the original design is preserved for us, since the room was completed by the Camporese, and Pope Pius IX added "splendor" to it in 1861. The present color scheme and painted decoration have a nineteenth-century flavor. The room is a handsome interpretation of a Renaissance circular hall, with niches containing pagan sculpture instead of Christian altars. The echo of the Pantheon is very faint.[17] There is no trace of the Baroque.

The adjoining room, the Sala a Croce Greca (Figure 16), is of the same period and also recalls Renaissance schemes. As its name indicates, its plan is a Greek cross inscribed in a square and roofed by intersecting barrel vaults. The corner spaces are accessible through low openings. An order of unfluted Tuscan pilasters articulates the lower zone. The room contains two sphinxes, one from the Villa of Julius II and the other found near St. Peter's, and two great Constantinian porphyry sarcophagi from Santa Costanza, an instance of eighteenth-century eclecticism. The mutules of the frieze bear an eagle, a star, and a fleur-de-lis. Those in the faceted angles show a zephyr quickening a garland. This is trickily but deftly handled.

One of the most admirable creations of the later, full Neoclassicism at the Vatican is the Braccio Nuovo (Figure 17) built from 1817 to 1822 by Raffaello Stern (1774–1820) and Pasquale Belli (1752–1833). This is one of the series of great Neoclassical museums being built at this time.[18] Like the iron and glass gallery added to Attingham Park by John Nash in 1810, the lighting is entirely from above. Two lofty wings meet a domed central space. The great length is interrupted by diaphragm arches, which spring from colorful columns of cipollino, alabaster, Egyptian granite, and yellow marble, emphasizing the perspec-

16. See pp. 41 ff.

17. Gertrud Sutton, "Architecture in Eighteenth Century Rome," *Gazette des Beaux-Arts, 59* (1962), 27.

18. Other museums of this period include: London, Dulwich Gallery, Sir John Soane, 1812; British Museum, Robert and Sydney Smirke, 1823–57; Berlin, Altes Museum, Schinkel, 1824–28; Munich, Glyptotek, von Klenze, 1816–30; Possagno, Canova Museum, Selva, 1819–20; Copenhagen, Thorwaldsen Museum, Bindesböll, 1839–48.

Figure 15. Michelangelo Simonetti: Rome, Vatican, Museo Pio Clementino, Sala Rotonda, 1776 ff.

Figure 16. Michelangelo Simonetti: Rome, Vatican, Museo Pio Clementino, Sala a Croce Greca, 1776 ff.

Figure 17. Raffaello Stern: Rome, Vatican Museum, Braccio Nuovo, 1817–22

tive of the three spaces and forcefully recalling such inventions of Boullée as his "Métropole," "Madeleine," and "Library."[19] The way the barrel vaults penetrate the domed area is unusual in classic architecture. The lozenge-shaped coffers may have been suggested by Maxentius' restoration of the Temple of Venus and Rome and are also to be seen at Sant'Andrea at Mantua. The installation of busts on corbels recalls the streets of Palmyra. The treatment of the lateral walls is one common at the time; the long friezes "float" above the deep, darkly painted niches. The use of niches as a setting for sculpture was a common device going well back before the nearby "rotunda" of Simonetti, though here they are treated more broadly and simply, as Sir John Soane had treated them. The great length, the barrel vaults, and the top lighting suggest, too, the room streets of the train sheds that were to follow, such as that of the Gare de l'Est of 1849 in Paris.

Similar tendencies can be seen in the great rooms decorated by the Albertolli family in Tuscany and Lombardy in the 1770s. The seven members of this family taught, practiced, and wrote for half a century about the new taste. Their first work is the *gran salone* at the Villa Poggio Imperiale, Florence, decorated for the Grand Duke Leopold II of Tuscany from 1772 to 1775 by Giocondo Albertolli (1742–1839), a magnificent room decorated entirely in white and looking as though it might have come from the Petit Trianon. A Corinthian order of pilasters, occasionally standing in pairs and with capitals close to those of Mars Ultor, lines the walls. The scale is very large for an interior, as can be seen by comparing the main order with the doors (Figure 18). The applied decorations of garlands, trophies, and low reliefs are confined for the most to their tidy frames. There is none of the enchantment of Piranesi nor of the lavishness and freedom of Stupinigi. The same man much later did a more sumptuous room, the Sala del Buffet, or Pranzo, in the Royal Palace in Milan (Figure 19). It is in sharp contrast to his earlier work there, the over-elaborate Hall of the Caryatids, with its mirrors and caryatid-supported balcony, dating from 1776. In the later room Composite pilasters, in imitation marble with gilded capitals, stand on a high wainscot. The painted frieze runs below the architrave and flanks the capitals. There is a coved ceiling and an octagonal skylight. Plaques in low relief fill in the overdoors. The detail is as classical as at Florence but richer and less restrained. Alinari labels it "Stile Impero." A brother, Grato Albertolli, was responsible for much of the decoration (1775–80) in the Pitti Palace. The later work in the Villa Reale in Milan was more grand and more classical.[20]

There are two transitional buildings in Lombardy by Simone Cantoni, who

19. Rosenau, *Boullée*, figs. 2, 7–9, 31.
20. Due, perhaps, to Napoleonic influences.

Figure 18. Giocondo and Grato Albertolli: Florence, Villa Poggio Imperiale, interior of Grand Salon, 1772–75

Figure 19. Giocondo Albertolli: Milan, Palazzo Reale, Sala del Buffet, after 1776

has been mentioned above in connection with his Genoese Palace.[21] At Como there is the splendidly situated Villa Olmo, formerly Odescalchi, now the property of the city of Como and used today for concerts and exhibitions. This was begun in 1780. It is more Neo-Palladian than Neoclassic. It is composed of many subordinate parts, each with its counterpart on the other side of the main axis. The importance of the individual parts is minimized, since they eschew axes of their own. To gain emphasis, the main block uses an engaged colonnade of six Ionic columns above a rusticated first floor. The use of semispherical recesses containing busts is Neoclassical. Numerous Late Baroque devices are employed to unify the various elements. In character it is aristocratic and dignified but not ostentatious. Its numerous entrances at the terrace level make it friendly and welcoming. Some of the interiors remodeled in the mid-nineteenth century are more ornate.

From 1780 to 1794 Cantoni built a palace for the Serbelloni family in Milan, which is far more in the new manner (Figure 20). It is fifteen bays long and three stories high. Its central feature is stressed. It has a recessed loggia surmounted by a pediment. The order is an unchanneled Ionic widely spaced in the Palladian manner. All the wall surfaces are smooth and without rustication, and the windows are quiet rectangles. This further concentrates attention on the central feature, which has the only two arched openings on the whole façade: the portal and a lunette-loggia in the tympanum. The façade is stopped quietly by paired pilasters at the ends. The one rich decoration is a transposed frieze in low relief which, held up by lion-heads, hangs above the windows of the main floor and slides back of the two free-standing columns of the axial pavilion. It is as though everything else were subordinated to this daring innovation. This frieze, by Francesco and Donato Carabelli, represents episodes from Lombard legends. The simple Renaissance balusters which run along the two loggias are low and seem dwarfed. This may be a deliberate touch of megalomania. On the whole, the design is characterized by marked simplicity and restraint. It does not go so far in this direction as Lodoli or Milizia would have liked. Cantoni, apparently siding with Algarotti, continues to use ornament such as moldings; it would have been very early for an Italian to omit them altogether. In his criticism of this building, Gino Chierici notes the compactness of the mass, the nudity of the walls, the reduction of the number of moldings, the imprint of classical antique forms in combination with more modern forms, the severe sobriety, the solemnity of expression, the temple-front motif, and the insistent rigidity of line.[22] In spite of the novelty of some of the features, the main lines are predominantly Palladian, so that in this case the new spirit shows

21. See pp. 53 ff.
22. Gino Chierici, *Il Palazzo italiano* (3 vols. Milan, 1952), *3,* 458–59.

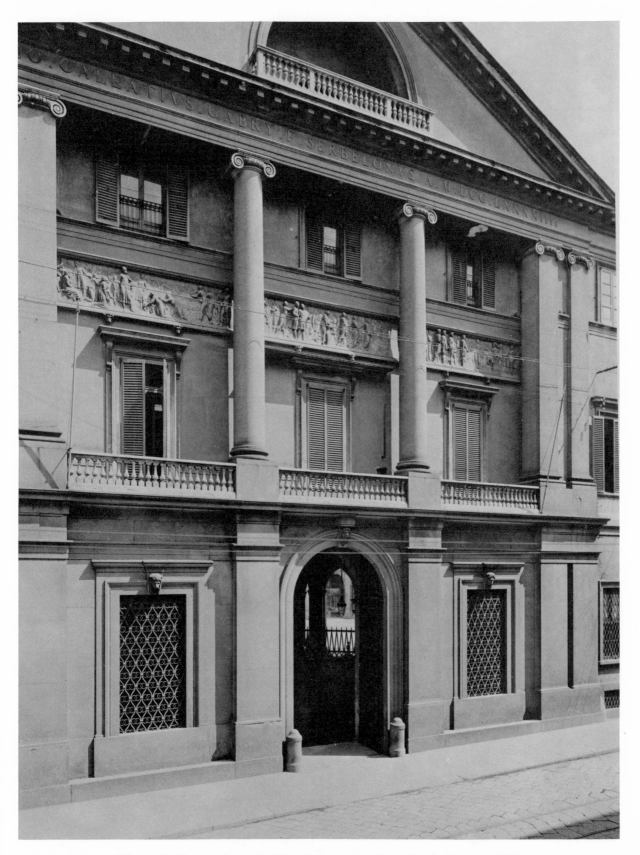

Figure 20. Simone Cantoni: Milan, Palazzo Serbelloni, detail of façade, 1794

Figure 21. Giacomo Quarenghi: Subiaco, Monastery of Santa Scolastica, interior of chapel, 1777

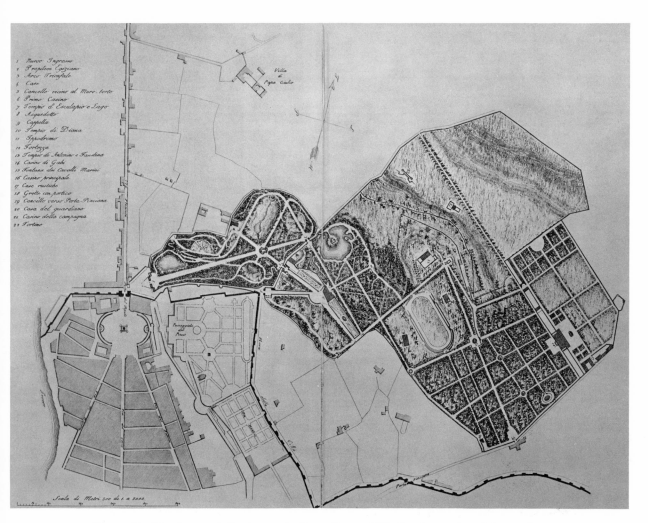

1 Nuovo Ingresso
2 Propileo Egiziano
3 Arco Trionfale
4 Case
5 Cancello vicino al Muro-torto
6 Primo Casino
7 Tempio d'Esculapio e Lago
8 Acquedotto
9 Cappella
10 Tempio di Diana
11 Ippodromo
12 Fortezza
13 Tempio di Antonino e Faustina
14 Casino di Gabi
15 Fontana dei Cavalli Marini
16 Casino principale
17 Case rustiche
18 Grotto con portico
19 Cancello verso Porta Pinciana
20 Casa del guardiano
21 Casino della campagna
22 Fortino

Villa di Papa Giulio

Scala di Metri 500 di 1 a 5000

Figure 22. The Asprucci, Canina, and others: Rome, Villa Borghese, plan of the gardens

itself in the handling rather than in the vocabulary. Napoleon, as King of Italy, chose to live in this palace, perhaps because it was so new and hence conveniently arranged but possibly because its style and decoration were so close to his own taste. With the advent of Napoleon, Neoclassicism, as will be shown later, came to maturity in Italy.

The Rise of Neoclassicism

The first of the early Neoclassical churches and one that subsequently provided a model for others, although it was only an interior, was that reconstructed at the Monastery of Santa Scolastica at Subiaco from 1774 to 1777 by Giacomo Quarenghi (1744–1817). The nave is barrel-vaulted and flanked by chapels in the form of exedra (Figure 21). The transepts are shallow and marked by columns. The apse is a larger exedra with a coffered half-dome rising above the main cornice line and following the curve of the main vault. The unchanneled Ionic is close to that of the fourth-century Temple of Saturn at Rome. Again there are strong traditional features and some Baroque plasticity in the apse, but the overwhelming effect is that of simple, first-phase Neoclassicism: light tones and sparse ornament taken from antiquity. The apses and detail recall the elegance of Robert Adam. Quarenghi also had been influenced by Piranesi, Winckelmann, and Mengs before being sent to Russia by Baron Grimm in 1779, where he carried out important buildings for Catherine II and her successors.[23]

More indications of the application of Neoclassical principles can be seen in the work of the numerous members of the Asprucci family. They were active in Rome, chiefly at the Villa Borghese, which they redecorated sumptuously, also enlivening the park with pools, temples, arches, pavilions, and ruins (Figure 22). Antonio, the father, lived from 1723 to 1808. His son Mario (1764–1804) was responsible for most of the work in the gardens of the Villa, the plan of which was by the Scottish landscape painter Jacob More (1740?–93).[24] Antonio built the remarkable Chiesetta di Piazza di Siena about 1787 (Figure 23). The porch of this chapel is long and low and is opened up by a colonnade of four unchanneled baseless Doric columns resting directly on a low step and supporting a stark entablature without responds. He was the first Italian to revive the pure classical Doric. The rest of the building is more conventional though severely simple. The order, however, is not quite Greek. It conforms to Palladio's ideas but shows no awareness of the proportions or detail of Magna Graecia. Palladio had noted that the Doric had no base peculiar to it, as could

23. Maria Catelli Isola, *Restauro di disegni di Giacomo Quarenghi* (Rome, 1963).
24. Jacob More came to Rome about 1773.

Figure 23. Mario Asprucci: Rome, Villa Borghese, Chiesetta di Piazza di Siena, c.1787

Figure 24. Leopold Pollack: Milan, Villa Reale-Belgioioso, entrance façade, 1790–93

Figure 25. Leopold Pollack: Milan, Villa Reale-Belgioioso, garden façade, 1790–93

be seen in the Theatre of Marcellus, but had then gone on to say that the Attic base is often used with it and that this "greatly increases its beauty"; this is the way it was commonly used.[25] There is an example by Giorgio Massari (c.1686–1766) in the courtyard of the Palazzo Grassi-Stucky (1749–66) in Venice. None of the other edifices in the park comes so close as this one to Lodolian austerity.

A still more advanced taste was shown in 1790 in the villa built by Leopold Pollack (1751–1806). Originally the Villa Belgioioso, it later became a royal villa and is currently the Galleria d'Arte Moderna in Milan (Figures 24–26). Pollack, although educated in Vienna, is said to have introduced a French approach. However, he had also been on Piermarini's staff at the Palazzo Reale in Milan. There are several novelties which can perhaps be laid at the door of French taste. The most striking is the composition of the entrance front with its screen wall, a court flanked by *corps de logis* and terminated by the main block. This ancient French arrangement was still in use in Paris, as at the Hôtel de Salm (1782–86). On the garden side there is a Gabriel-like use of a colonnade of ponderous orders terminating in pedimented end pavilions.[26] Palladian features also occur: a rusticated arcaded ground floor under a giant order, a balustrade and skyline figures, and both plain and rusticated wall surfaces. The entrance front builds up hierarchically from the flat-decked entrance screen to the two-storied gabled wings and up to the three-story main block with its hipped roof behind a balustrade. The variation in roof forms tends to emphasize the individuality of the components. The great order marches across the garden façade, sometimes engaged, sometimes as pilasters, but the central axis is played down in respect to the end pavilions, which express the side wings of the other façade and bring the composition to a firm stop by their bold projection and emphatic pediments. This is new for Italy. The entrance façade is built up around an elaborate system of triplets: the three portals; the two sets of blank windows which flank them; the three bays of the end pavilions; the three triplets facing the court along each wing, of which the centre ones with their segmental, not alternating, pediments repeat those on the gable ends; and the triplets with alternating pediments which flank the engaged order of the entrance motif. The garden façade is two bays wider, seventeen instead of fifteen, and the grouping is partially in triplets, two pairs of them on either side of the central five-bay pavilion. The orders throughout are channeled, and the Ionic of the garden façade, with its horns and rose, is like that of the Temple of Saturn in Rome, but the frieze has another source. Neoclassicism makes a

---

25. Palladio, *I Quattro Libri dell'architettura . . . 1*, 22. The matter is discussed by Ware, *A Complete Body of Architecture*, p. 155.

26. Gabriel's palaces on the Place de la Concorde, Paris, 1753 ff.

Figure 26. Leopold Pollack: Milan, Villa Reale-Belgioioso, Sala da Ballo, 1790–93

Figure 27. Antonio Selva: Venice, Teatro La Fenice, detail of principal façade, 1790–92

tentative appearance in some details: most conspicuously in the extensive use of low reliefs above the windows of the *piano nobile* on the entrance side, and over some of the arcades of the basement on the garden side; in the stiff garlands of the frieze on both sides; in the tympani sculpture; and in the Greek look of the fluted baseless Doric at the entrance. There is a notable vertical emphasis to the garden façade, in which the numerous motifs fill the narrow bays between the orders. The shift of emphasis to the highly articulated end bays is, of course, not Palladian, and is anti-hierarchical. The villa is mixed in derivation and in effect. The entrance front is discreet and dignified while the garden front is ostentatious and, one would think, unsuitable for a private villa. The French version of Neo-Palladianism has been combined with Neoclassicism.

Compared with earlier great salons (Figures 18, 19), the Sala da Ballo here (Figure 26) is more robust. This is particularly noticeable in the engaged columns and coffered ceiling.

There was very little being built in Venice at this time. Its last doge was about to surrender to Napoleon. An exception is the Opera House, La Fenice (1790–92), on which Antonio Selva placed an elegant "modern" frontispiece between more conventionally handled wings (Figure 27). This composition seems very pure, with its handsome tetrastyle porch of Corinthian columns standing on a graciously spreading flight of low steps. The much taller upper part, which runs through two stories, is a simplified triumphal arch. Its central window, flanking niches, and inset panels and ornament, although punched into and pulled out of the neutral plane of smooth masonry, have the right degree of relief to harmonize with the orders below. The piazza is very small; anything on a larger scale would have been overpowering, anything more delicate would have seemed too frivolous, even for Venice. The character is just right; a semi-public building to be used by a select and sophisticated audience, yet neither residential nor governmental.

This decade also saw the rise of the new style in Sicily. Again the spark seems to be French influence—a Francophile court and the presence of the young architect Léon Dufourny (1754–1818), pupil of the archaeologist Le Roy and of Peyre, who from 1789 to 1792 built the extraordinary Ginnasio in the Botanical Garden of Palermo (Figure 28). This building, which originally served as both a school and museum, is eclectic. Léon Dufourny came to Italy in 1782. He built this Ginnasio seven years later. When he left Paris at the age of twenty-eight, he would have been able to see, among others, such Neoclassical buildings as Charles de Wailly's Odéon going up (1779–82). The cubical mass of the Ginnasio, with fluted pilasters contrasting with rusticated wall, and the coarse scale, was very modern. The battering of the pilasters emphasizes the massiveness. The cornice is huge and archaic and seems to be part of the wall, not its termination. The melon-shaped dome has overscaled antefixae at its base.

Figure 28. Leon Dufourny: Palermo, Orto Botanico, Il Ginnasio, 1789–92

Figure 29. Giuseppe Patricola: Palermo, Villa della Favorita, Palazzina Cinese, 1799–1802.

The stylobate runs all the way around the building instead of the conventional basement, and yet this is not a temple; it has no colonnade, no pediment. The entrance steps rise between sphinxes and lead to a pair of archaeologically correct, fluted Greek Doric columns *in antis* and a loggia behind. The undercutting of the stylobate, and practically every other detail including the rustication, can be found in Greek ruins on Sicily. These were being studied at this time by French architects such as Houel. This building is, nevertheless, not an attempt to imitate a specific ancient building. Neither is it Vitruvian nor Palladian. It is an example of creative eclecticism applied to a building which was too lowly to be treated as a temple and too important to be handled as a palace or villa. Dufourny had said that architecture would be reborn through geometry.[27]

Since the principal local architect, the aged Giuseppe Venanzio Marvuglia (1729–1814), changed his style immediately after the completion of this building, it is evident that either Dufourny or his patrons were rapidly bringing Palermo into the vanguard of the new taste. This is shown at the Villa della Favorita in the Palazzina Cinese and the Fountain of Hercules. The Palazzina (Figure 29) is a fantasy of the same family as the Brighton Pavilion and Sezincote, or the Japanese tea house at Sans Souci. Built between 1799 and 1802, it is sometimes credited to Marvuglia but is probably the work of Giuseppe Patricola, the Royal Surveyor.[27a] Basically a cubical mass on a raised platform, it is girdled by a balcony and cut into by loggias. A semicircular columnar portico projects from one side. The ornament is exotic Muslim as well as Chinese in origin. There was a Pompeian room within. It lacks the finished and consistent effects of the more successful buildings mentioned above.

The Fountain (Figure 30), by Marvuglia, is another example of a carefully archaeological Greek Doric order. It is a paradigm of the associational values attributed to the Doric order at this time: its masculine strength is reiterated in the association with Hercules; the fountain and pool allude to his paternity.[28] The single column isolated from its fellows in colonnade or portico carries the whole weight of the traditional aesthetic and historic role of the Doric order.

The fourth important building of this Palermo group is the Villa Belmonte (1801 ff.), also by Marvuglia, then aged seventy-two (Figure 31). The Palladian model is most evident, with the academic formula applied with exactitude, the rusticated basement—part of it arcuated for emphasis—and a colossal order under a pediment as the main feature. It is, however, larger than the usual Vicentine ones, with its portico of five bays and its flanking wings of three bays

27. Kaufmann, *Age of Reason,* p. 196.

27a. Edward Croft Murray, "The Palazzina Cinese at Palermo," *Country Life, 102* (Oct. 10, 1947), 724–25.

28. See p. 12.

Figure 30. Giuseppe Venanzio Marvuglia: Palermo, Villa della Favorita, Fountain of Hercules, c.1814

Figure 31. Giuseppe Venanzio Marvuglia: Palermo, Villa Belmonte, 1801 ff.

each. It is severely plain. The portico is an Ionic temple-front without piers or wings. The rear elevation is said to have a Greek Doric order and a number of caryatids.[29]

Influences other than that of Dufourny may have also been at work. Marvuglia had been a pupil of Vanvitelli's, and there had been a nationalistic interest in the Grecian antiquities of Sicily for a generation. The novelties include the balustrade used as a continuous pedestal for the order, the string course with a wave fret, and the frieze occupying the position of the mezzanine windows in the loggia. The decoration of the main frieze is not of garlands, but is more like that of the Villa Farnesina, Rome. The windows are sensibly small in this hot, exposed site. Very monumental in effect, it is a firm, positive statement which holds its own in that forbidding location of exposed rock faces. The mood is one of self-confident optimism.

The Triumph of Neoclassicism 1795–1840

Introduction

Wherever Napoleon or his victorious generals went, Neoclassical buildings were likely to spring up. What began as a fashion continued after Napoleon's fall as a habit, for when the old legitimate rulers returned, the buildings they built to celebrate this event of doubtful benefit were also Neoclassical. It has been asserted that in periods of upheaval, such as those following a war, people seek a return to classical forms. "When things go haywire you go back to the Grecian urn."[30] In other words the Grecian urn is not a product of peace but a reaction to the absence of it.

In Milan, as is so often the case with the buildings of the period, the Palladian influences continued almost to equal the Neoclassical ones. Palladio had also used colonnades on his façades, notably on the Palazzo Chiericati, the Villa Valmarana, and the unfinished Palazzo Porto poi Breganze.

Curved and curvilinear elements are eschewed unless they are niche heads and semicircular windows. They rarely are used in plans except as semicircular apses or under Pantheon-like domes. But no other types of curve appear. No undulations, for example, were tolerable.

In this period the work of dilettanti and amateurs has great merit. We can see this in England in the work of Lord Burlington, Lord Pembroke, and Horace Walpole.[31] In Italy at Possagno we have a program devised by a sculptor and carried out by almost unknown men. Such literary and associative programs

29. Lavagnino, *L'Arte moderna, 1,* 128.
30. Jean Devoluy, *New York–Paris Herald* (Oct. 10, 1959), p. 8.
31. Lees-Milne, *Earls of Creation,* passim.

reflect the ideals of the period more uninhibitedly than those buildings in which the intervention of trained architects tended to obscure the immediacy of the intention. This is understandable in a period so influenced by Rousseau's doctrine of the natural man. When the expression of feeling is the architectural objective, amateurs may achieve the goal more directly.

The use of pure, strong, prismatic, classical motives such as cylinders, saucer domes, and temple fronts may be partly accounted for by the oscillation of taste. Since the preceding period, the Baroque, had favored the intricate, subtle, low-relief type of façade, then the following period might well react by preferring simplicity and sharp definition. It would follow the geometry of Euclid rather than that of Descartes. Similarly mass would be emphasized rather than space, and immobility rather than movement.

In Italy there was another factor. It was commonly believed with Piranesi that modern art was inferior to that of the ancients, but that it was proper to try to emulate their accomplishments and to seek to create cities and buildings which would have some of the grandeur of those ancient ones, whose remains confronted them on every hand. Copying or imitating was not the program of the Neoclassical architect. Hence the exact prototypes for eighteenth-century Neoclassicism are very seldom identifiable. His goal was to create new buildings true to his time, deriving general ideas and even details from the treasuries of the past as all architects have done, but in doing so to make a new work of art expressive of his feelings. To accomplish this he strove to achieve simplicity, orderliness, solidity, majesty, and clarity. As there was no desire to copy, so there was no desire to push the program of the Purists and Rigorists to its logical extremity. None of these architects, however much they favored clarity and the independence of the parts that they juxtaposed so boldly, sought wholly to eliminate ornament and decoration. It was still their intention to establish the character of the building in an unequivocal manner and to defer to the hieratical distinction between the ordinary and the monumental, more often than not by using forms with traditional associations. The goal of Neoclassicism was not archaeology but evocation.

In the direction of simplicity we can observe a consistent effort to reduce the number of geometrical elements. When the image of the Pantheon is evoked, for example, only the portico and cylinder are used. The attic is omitted. This is less imitative and heightens the effect of contrast almost to the point of making the parts appear to collide.

Urbanism, Gates, Gardens, Triumphal Arches, and Cafés

Italy, in the nineteenth century, gave its attention more to beautification than to slum clearance. Early in the century arches and gates were commonly erected

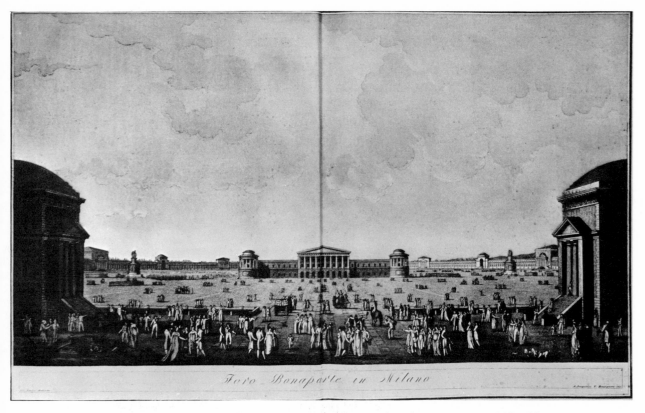

Figure 32. Giovanni Antonio Antolini: Milan, Project for Foro Bonaparte, 1801–06

Figure 33. Luigi Cagnola: Milan, Porta Ticinese, 1801–14

both by the government in the cities and by private individuals in their gardens, along with temples and bridges.

While Lombardy was within the charge of Eugène de Beauharnais, Napoleon's stepson who served as viceroy, great works were undertaken in Milan. The most grandiose was the Foro Bonaparte by Giovanni Antonio Antolini (1756–1841), which was to include a modernization of the Castello Sforza (Figure 32). The remains of this project include the curved street surrounding the Castello, and still called the Foro Bonaparte. Antolini had been educated at the Clementina di Bologna and at Rome, but his design was megalomaniac, like those of the French academicians. It was to have been 600 meters in diameter. Long, low blocks would have been interrupted infrequently by temple-like blocks of slightly greater height. The Greek Doric order would have been used exclusively. Geometry, purity, and antiquity were combined in the manner of Ledoux. While Antolini's project was far too grand to be executed in the short time available before the military reverses began, other projects were carried further.

Among these was a plan for modernizing the street system, a part of which was carried out. The committee working on this plan was comprised of Luigi Cagnola, Luigi Canonica, Paolo Landriani, Giocondo Albertolli, and Giuseppe Zanoia. The committee worked between 1801 and 1807.[32]

More apparent today are the new gates, functionally related to the Barrières in Paris, which rose at intervals along the walls. These include Luigi Cagnola's Porta Ticinese (1801–14, Figure 33). Cagnola (1762–1833) was the most important architect of his day in Lombardy. This gate, in contrast to its attendant custom houses, was light and open. Each front consisted of a pair of tall unchanneled Ionic columns *in antis*. The end walls were perforated in the Palladian manner by arched openings. The order is ten diameters high, which is more Corinthian than Ionic and suggests Vicentine more than Roman proportions. The pediment above is light and the tympanum empty. The character is rural, not military. Many other gates survive. Two of them are works of the late 1820s: the Porta Venezia (Figure 35) by Rodolfo Vantini (1791–1856) and the former Porta Comasina (Figure 36), renamed Porta Garibaldi in 1859, by Giacomo Moraglia (1791–1860). The latter was erected servilely to commemorate the visit of Francis I of Austria, although he was hated. Both gates lack the simplicity of Cagnola's and turn to the Ledulcian manner, combining columns, pilasters, textured walls, niches, and ornament into massive blocks. There is some indebtedness to Michele Sanmicheli (1484–1559), too. Strictly Neoclassic elements are minor: fluted and unfluted Doric columns without bases, string courses decorated with a wave motive, and plaques of stiffly clas-

---

32. Lavagnino, *L'Arte moderna, 1,* 89.

Figure 34. Giuseppe Zanoia: Milan, Porta Nuova, 1810–13

Figure 35. Rodolfo Vantini: Milan, Porta Venezia, 1827–33

Figure 36. Giacomo Moraglia: Milan, Porta Comasina, now Porta Garibaldi, 1826

Figure 37. Luigi Canonica: Milan, Arena, Triumphal Gate, 1806–13

sical ornament. These and other gates continue to give the circumferential *viale* of Milan dignity and monumentality.

Milan has other buildings with clear classical backgrounds begun during the Napoleonic regime. The arena near the Castello was built by Luigi Canonica (1762–1844) from 1806 to 1813 (Figure 37). This oval enclosure, for somewhat less savage sports than those of the Romans, is enclosed by a Piranesian wall, battered, made of large stones, and punctured from time to time with the Cloaca Maxima motive. Its most elegant feature is the main portal, a simplified triumphal arch consisting of a relatively thin slab pierced by an arched portal, set between pairs of free-standing fluted Roman Doric columns supporting an entablature and pediment, of which the tympanum is richly but delicately carved, set against an attic. The columns, each pair of which share a common podium, are widely separated. The architrave is reduced. The temple-front motive is merely appliquéd to the wall, but in a Neoclassical way, with Palladian overtones.

The Milanese Duomo begun at the end of the fourteenth century remained unfinished when the nineteenth century began. Napoleon, to gratify his Italian subjects, ordered the façade to be completed. There was ample precedent elsewhere for continuing incomplete Gothic buildings in a Gothic style: the towers of Westminster Abbey, built between 1735 and 1740 by Nicholas Hawksmoor, and the eighteenth-century work at the Cathedral of Orléans by Jacques Gabriel and Louis-François Trouard. There was by this time both an archaeological knowledge of Gothic and a Romantic interest in it. The design was the joint work of the elderly professor Giuseppe Zanoia (1752–1817) and his pupil and assistant Carlo Amati (1776–1852). This was their only exercise in Gothic (Figure 38). While it did well enough at the time, the building was a hurried job, being completed in the seven years following 1806, and soon ceased to satisfy, so a series of new competitions was held to launch a better façade. These will be described below because of their great interest as barometers of taste, although nothing came of them and the present façade is still that of Zanoia and Amati.[33] All they did was frugally to overlay the existing but incomplete buttresses and the gables with a thin veil of motives taken from the flanks. The portals and most of the windows had been designed by Pellegrino Pellegrini in 1567. These in turn were part of one of the late Renaissance designs which proposed to range great orders across the front. The existing façade is thus an example of synthetic eclecticism by happenstance rather than design.

The Piazza San Marco in Venice, "the finest drawing-room in Europe" as Napoleon called it, was completed by him (Figure 38a). In 1810 he began the new wing of the Palazzo Reale called the "Ala Napoleone." It was by Giu-

33. See pp. 230 ff. and figs. 116–18.

Figure 38. Carlo Amati and Giuseppe Zanoia: Milan, Cathedral, façade, 1806–13

Figure 38a. Giuseppe Soli: Venice, Piazza San Marco, Ala Napoleone, 1810 ff.

seppe Soli (1745–1822), possibly following a design by Giovanni Antonio Antolini. The design of the exterior follows in a general way that of the adjoining Procuratie Nuove, and this in turn follows Sansovino's design for the Libreria Vecchia. However, the idea of achieving complete and boring unity by a slavish copying of the older design was happily avoided. Instead, the upper story was made heavier and was treated as a blank attic. The skyline figures on the Piazza side are Roman emperors who would not have been dismayed by the temporary absence of the famous Byzantine horses, and those on the other side are Roman Gods. Tactfully, there was no allusion to the former glory of Venice. Within, there is a magnificent stairway, partly genuine and partly imitation marble. This leads to an interestingly articulated ballroom, of 1822, by Lorenzo Santi (1783–1839), with a balcony supported on columns and a lofty coved ceiling. The whole was over-richly decorated by Giuseppe Borsato (1771–1849). Some adjoining rooms, now part of the Museo Correr, were pleasantly decorated in an Empire manner.

In Rome shortly after the turn of the century, Giuseppe Valadier (1762–1839), who may have been trained in France, became the most prominent member of the second generation of "new" architects.[34] His work at the Milvian Bridge shows how *au courant* he was (Figure 39). In 1805 Pius VII commissioned him to rebuild the old gate through which so many celebrities had passed. Valadier found a ruinous work of Nicholas V's day, which in turn may have been a reworking of the original, already reworked in the second century A.D. It consisted of a massive block perforated by a rusticated arch and surmounted by a second block. Valadier emphasized its military character. He omitted such frivolities as orders, battered the wall of the lower section, restored or added a heavy unmolded cornice, and permitted only narrow windows in the upper zone. Less creative than the Ledulcian Barrières, it is nevertheless executed in a Lodolian spirit: nothing unnecessary, strictly masculine and severe. The geometry recalls Sir John Vanbrugh's military toys at Castle Howard.

The *loggiata* which Valadier built on the side of the Pincian hill between 1816 and 1820 is a curiosity (Figure 40). It combines a loggia formed by three arched openings with a colonnade which stands in front of it on its own pedestals and supports an entablature. Both of these elements rest on a high, rusticated basement indented by three niches. An equestrian statue is framed by the middle arch of the loggia. The allusions here seem to be to a triumphal arch taken apart and rearranged, or perhaps to a Roman fountain such as the Fontana Paola or that of the Acqua Felice.

Although the triumphal arch often appeared in Renaissance paintings, Renaissance architects seldom took it as a model for actual and permanent building.

34. Elfriede Schulze-Battman, *Giuseppe Valadier* (Dresden, 1939), and Paolo Marconi, *Giuseppe Valadier* (Rome, 1964).

Figure 39. Giuseppe Valadier: Rome, Ponte Milvio, reconstruction, 1805

Figure 40. Giuseppe Valadier: Rome, Giardino del Pincio, Loggiato, 1806–14

Alberti was an exception, since he took it as a paradigm for the façades of all three of his churches. He handled it with relaxed freedom. The next few generations may have felt that the form was too pagan for Christian churches. Palladio did not assign a single plate to the subject and only suggests the motive in his "Ponte di Pietra" on the flanks of the terminal pavilions and as the enclosing motive of the Forum of Nerva and the Temple of Antoninus and Faustina.[35] None of these are any more pertinent than the Mannerism of his title page.

Examples of the casual Renaissance attitude are the many free variants of the theme at the Villa Giulia, Rome (1551–53), probably by Bartolomeo Ammannati on the villa façade, the court, and the garden buildings, including rusticated ones, some curved in plan, some lopped off as well as some superimposed. It is not until nearly the middle of the next century, in Venice, at Longhena's Santa Maria della Salute (1631–87), that we find the motive being used conspicuously on a church. There it is not archaeological. It is just one of the numerous scenographic features. Again in Venice, in the entrance to the Accademia, an approximation of the themes is achieved, though without the arched portal. It may have been begun by Giorgio Massari in 1765 and finished by Francesco Lazzari in 1820, or, as other authorities state, it may have been the work of Antonio Selva (d. 1819).[36] In Rome Simonetti introduced it (1776 ff.), in a functionally logical situation, although indoors, at the entrance to his Sala a Croce Greca, where it can also be read as a classicizing version of the Palladian motive. A little earlier, in 1741, Fuga had devised a motive for the entrance to the atrium of Santa Cecilia in Rome, which combines the idea of a Baroque palace doorway with that of the Roman triumphal arch with its triple portals and flanking orders. In 1757 Vanvitelli had played freely with the theme in the central feature of his Piazza Dante (formerly Foro Carolino) where he framed a large arched opening between pairs of columns. The arched opening in turn frames a niche which encloses a portal (Figure 4a).

The first permanent modern triumphal arch in Italy was that by Jean-Nicolas Jadot (1710–60) in the Piazza Cavour (now Piazza della Libertà) in Florence, which was built between 1739 and 1745 in honor of Francis III of Lorraine (Figure 41). Derived from the arch of Septimius Severus, it is only half as large, but more ornate, and more plastic—a Baroque handling of a Classical theme.

Napoleon and the Austrians gave Italian architects further opportunities to

35. Palladio, *Quattro Libri, 3*, pls. 26, 27; *4,* pls. 24, 27, 34.

36. On the arch of the Accademia, Venice: according to Thieme-Becker, the façade was the work of Giorgio Massari in 1765. However it was remodelled in 1829 by Francesco Lazzari. Antonio Selva worked on transforming the old buildings into an academy from 1800 until his death in 1819. See Giulio Lorenzetti, *Venezia* (Venice, 1926), p. 633, and Elena Bassi, *Architettura del sei e settecento a Venezia* (Naples, 1962), p. 330, who states that Massari's design was executed by Bernardino Maccarozzi and that it is difficult to attribute the existing parts with assurance.

erect triumphal arches after the Roman pattern. There was by that time the French tradition of arched city gates as in the Porte St. Denis and the Porte St. Martin of Paris. Two were also built at Stowe in the 1760s, and there was the Gloriette at Schönbrun (1775) by J. F. von Hohenberg. There had been the portals of the Royal Palace in Berlin by Eosander von Goethe (circa 1707–09) and more recently the Brandenburger Tor in Berlin (1789–94) by K. G. Langhans. Antolini had proposed some for his Foro Bonaparte.[37] The new series of city gates in Milan carried on the idea.[38]

In 1806 the Arc de Triomphe de la Place du Carrousel in Paris was begun by Percier and Fontaine, to honor Napoleon's successful campaign of 1805, and Chalgrin began the enormous Arc de Triomphe de l'Etoile in the same year, while Cagnola was designing the most impressive Italian Neoclassical arch, in Milan, to honor the marriage of Eugène de Beauharnais to the Princess Augusta-Amelia of Bavaria (Figure 42). First built in wood, it attracted such admiration that it was decided to rebuild it in stone. Begun in 1807, it was stopped in 1808. Work was resumed in 1826 by the Emperor of Austria, to whom it was rededicated, and it was renamed the Arch of Peace.[39] It was completed under Ferdinand I in 1838. In 1859, following another political change, it was named the Arco del Sempione, in honor of the peace between France and Italy achieved by Victor Emanuel II and Napoleon III, Sempione being the name of the avenue which runs north from the Castello Sforza under this arch and on to the Simplon pass. A good many architects and sculptors contributed to its completion. Cagnola's successors, after his death in 1833, were Carlo Landonio, Francesco Peverelli, and Domenico Moglia (1780–1862). As were the other Milanese gates, this one was flanked by a pair of guard and custom houses, still extant.

Cagnola's design was not so complex nor so polychromatic as Percier and Fontaine's in Paris, which seems to have been influenced by the Baroque Florentine design mentioned above (Figure 41). The Milan arch is larger than the Arc du Carrousel, but not so large as Chalgrin's Arc de Triomphe. It is less original and less "sublime." It is, however, more modern than the Arc du Carrousel, perhaps because of the presence of Pollack with his advanced tastes. It is based on the Arch of Septimius Severus in Rome but is freely handled. The order is Corinthian instead of Composite, the masses are regrouped, and the effect is less weighty. The frieze seems too light and the effect is vivacious rather than solemn. The new mode of composition of Cagnola's own time was used to change and simplify the model.

Giuseppe Zanoia turned to the Arch of Titus when he designed the Arch of the Porta Nuova, Milan, in 1810–13 (Figure 34). This stands between low

37. See p. 101.
38. See pp. 101 ff.
39. T.C.I., *Lombardia* (Milan, 1939), p. 142.

Figure 41. Jean-Nicolas Jadot: Florence, Triumphal Arch, 1739–45

Figure 42. Luigi Cagnola: Milan, Arco del Sempione, 1806–38

arched screens which terminate in custom houses. Although the resemblance to the Arch of Titus is marked, it is related to the Arch in its simpler, pre-Valadier restoration state. The combination of arch, screen, and wings is scenographic. Its sturdy Greek Doric order *in antis* and the severe detailing of the screens serve to heighten the greater richness and size of the main arch. The effect is that of a lingering Late Baroque type of Classicism. The Porta Nuova at Bergamo is identified by a pair of partially colonnaded small temples, using a Greek Doric order but with wide intercolumniations and other characteristics of the Palladian system.

Near Lucca, in 1839, Lorenzo Nottolini (1787–1851) used triumphal arches functionally as supports for the chains of his suspension bridge over the river Lima. Lavagnino says that the prototype for this was the similar bridge over the Thames at Hammersmith (built 1824–27) by W. T. Clark, which Nottolini had seen.[40] The association of triumphal arch and suspension bridge by this time was well-established in Britain at Clifton, Menai, and other places. Here, massive arches with a relatively small passage through them are handled without orders and a minimum of decoration. They are splendidly robust.

At Minturno near Gaeta, the suspension bridge over the Garigliano River built in 1832 followed a relatively rare precedent in adopting the Egyptian style for its compression and anchoring members (Figure 43). The suspension members are wrought iron "I" bars. The association of durable Egyptian forms with works of engineering is comprehensible and recurrent. The connotation is that of simple, primitive strength. The use of Egyptian forms in Italy began with the Roman importation of obelisks and sphinxes. These were reused in the Renaissance and revived at this time, as in Canina's pylon-obelisk-sphinx complex in the gardens of Villa Borghese (Figure 44).[41]

Triumphal arches provided a popular motive for garden features, as can be seen as early as the Aspruccis' embellishments at the Villa Borghese. Antonio worked there, as did his son Mario. It is assumed that both Antonio and Mario worked on these gardens in the 1780s and 90s. The ornamental features used by them had by that time become familiar in the gardens of northern Europe. The range includes: a small circular temple to Diana with a curious, rare type of Doric capital; a temple to Esculapius, with rusticated walls, arched portal, and Ionic order beneath a pediment, standing on an island in an artificial lake (Figure 45), and recalling features from Lord Burlington's garden at Chiswick;

40. Lavagnino, *L'Arte moderna, 1*, 320. See also A. A. Jakkala, "History of Suspension Bridges," *Bulletin of the Agricultural and Mechanical College of Texas, 12* (1941), 65 ff., and Charles S. Drewry, *A Memoir on Suspension Bridges* (London, 1832), pl. 6. Arches were commonly used to support the chains or cables of suspension bridges as in the Neoclassical examples at Norfolk and Marlowe (Drewry, p. 82).

41. See p. 118.

Figure 43. Anonymous: Minturno, Bridge over the Garigliano, 1832

Figure 44. Luigi Canina: Rome, Villa Borghese, Egyptian Propylea, 1820s

Figure 45. The Asprucci and Christoph Unterberger: Rome, Villa Borghese, Temple of Esculapius, 1785–92

a Corinthian temple front; two columns *in antis* dedicated to Antoninus and Faustina; the small church with a Doric colonnade mentioned above (Figure 23); a Corinthian temple to Herod Agrippa; and sundry other architectural inventions such as the Piazza di Siena, recalling a Roman circus, and the nearby Casina dell'Orologio, with its battered walls, oversized voussoirs, and temple-crowned tower. This and several other of the more rustic structures, with their picturesque irregularities and allusive names ("Casina di Raffaello," "la Fortezza," etc.), show how comprehensive the range of eclecticism had become. At Saonara and in other gardens, Giuseppe Japelli also used many styles. The English fashion, perhaps through French intermediaries, was spreading. Luigi Canina (1795–1856) demonstrated a notably archaeological bias in his gates at the gardens of the Villa Borghese.[42] The screen at the principal entrance from the Piazza Flaminia is adorned by two lodges with Ionic columns *in antis* owing not a little to Cagnola's gates in Milan (Figure 46). The treatment here is even more archaeological. The placing of small, closed temples beside and behind each of the main open ones, prefaced by heraldic columns, makes the composition scenographic, all of it designed to frame the vista up the long straight avenue.

Canina built an Egyptian propylea in the 1820s beside a bridge over a public lane which connected newly acquired lands with the older part of the villa grounds. This example of the Romantic use of Egyptian pylons appears to be the earliest in Italy (Figure 44).

His Fountain of Esculapius in the same garden is a not very serious exercise in providing a setting for an ancient statue (Figure 47). Nature and man seem to be the themes, since a miniature and very simple triumphal arch stands on a naturalistic formation of rocks, among which flow the waters of an elegant fountain, in allusion to the healing properties of water. The Borghese may well have been hypochondriacs, since they already had a temple to the same divinity in the older garden, on an island in the lake (Figure 45).

Canina's third use of the "arch" motive, also at the Villa Borghese, stands near a second bridge linking the old and new parts of the garden. This is larger than that to Esculapius but more simplified, being astylar and almost without ornament, recalling Chalgrin's arch more closely than any of the Roman ones, and thus demonstrating in their homeland the influence of the theories of Lodoli and Milizia (Figure 48).

A much smaller but equally fashionable garden, now a public park, was designed by Japelli in Padua for the Villa dei Baroni Treves de'Bonfili. Here the artificially "natural" topography has been accented with a circular Temple of Love and a triumphal arch of drawing-room size. Bosquets, serpentine paths, and bridges were contrived on a scale comparable to Alexander Pope's garden at Twickenham.

42. Luigi Canina, *Le Nuove Fabbriche della Villa Borghese dominata pinciana* (Rome, 1828).

Figure 46. Luigi Canina: Rome, Villa Borghese, Gates from the Piazzale Flaminio, 1825–28

Figure 47. Luigi Canina: Rome, Villa Borghese, Fountain of Esculapius, 1818–28

Figure 48. Luigi Canina: Rome, Villa Borghese, Triumphal Arch, 1818–28

The principal urban improvement in Rome was the replanning of the complex of the Piazza del Popolo and the Pincian by Valadier, which has been discussed in detail by Siegfried Giedion.[43] Valadier was also entrusted with work on the Arch of Titus (Figure 49). This arch, so conspicuously placed on the edge of the Palatine, challenged attention. Erected in 81 A.D., it is one of the earliest examples of the Composite order. Old prints show that it was partly engulfed in other buildings and was in ruinous condition. Raffaello Stern (1774–1820) began the restoration about 1817. He was followed by Valadier in 1821, who published an illustrated account of his work there in 1822.[44] Two of the original capitals above engaged channeled columns and part of the richly worked entablature remain. All the other capitals, with uncut leaves, are restorations, as is most of the attic. This arch was greatly admired after its restoration, and it influenced numerous designs, notably Virgilio Vespignani's addition to the Porta Pia in 1852–68 (Figure 50). This is the last of the Neoclassical arches.

The older façade of this gate, begun by Michelangelo in 1561 to 1565 toward the then new Via Pia, now the Via XX Settembre, one of his most original works, was far too unconventional to be used in the midcentury as a prototype for the new façade.[45] Instead another but more "correct" model, the Arch of Titus, was selected. It had been much featured in the decades just prior to this work as it had gradually been cleared of impingements. The paradigm is, however, so much altered that to copy it was evidently not the architect's intention. The Composite order is used, but it is unfluted and freestanding rather than engaged. The keystone of the original is copied. The spandrel ornament is omitted. Niches replace the smaller portals in the lateral bays, the ornament of the frieze is not duplicated, and the inner pair of columns support a pediment which is an added feature.

In Naples, two areas near the palace were improved at this time: the piazza in front of the church of San Francesco di Paolo to the north, and the façade of the Teatro San Carlo to the east.[46]

Antonio Niccolini's (1772–1850) remarkable theatre façade was designed between 1810 and 1812 (Figure 51).[47] An analogous building is the extraordinary Women's Prison (1809–10) at Würzburg by Peter Speeth. In both

43. Sigfried Giedion, *Space, Time and Architecture* (Cambridge, Mass., 1949), pp. 84–89.

44. Giuseppe Valadier, *Narrazione artistica dell'operato finora nel restauro dell'arco di Tito* (Rome, 1822).

45. See p. 251.

46. See p. 23.

47. T.C.I., *Naples* (Milan, 1938), p. 108, states that this theatre was built originally by Angelo Carasale in 1737 after designs by Giovanni Antonio Medrano. Niccolini added the ponderous atrium and the elegant loggia which were destroyed by fire in 1816 which he then rebuilt. He also was in charge of the reconstruction of 1841.

Figure 49. Giuseppe Valadier: Rome, Arch of Titus, reconstruction, 1821

Figure 50. Virgilio Vespignani: Rome, Porta Pia, new façade, 1852

there is a piling-up of nearly independent layers and surprising changes of motives. At the San Carlo the part below the long balcony is all rusticated, but it has been divided into two sublayers, the lower one more heavily scaled than the upper. The lower one sits perversely on an oversized course of smooth ashlar in front of which stand overscaled, rusticated bollards the height of a man. Below the string course which divides these two lower layers runs a series of unexpected relief panels of garlands or heads tightly compressed in low boxes. The heavy rustication of the five portals is carried into the upper rusticated layer, and, just where the voussoirs flatten out, a new motive four courses high is introduced—a discontinuous frieze and four panels of intertwined, rigidly geometrical wreaths. Above this comes the far-projecting balcony. Its balusters are stubby, conical, archaic columns. Access to this is gained between the fourteen unchanneled Ionic columns without pilasters or responds referred to above as "endless."[48] The frieze above them is delicately adorned with slight garlands and wreaths. The broad, smooth end bays are carried up through the cornice and serve to terminate an incomplete pedimental attic of unusually low slope, echoing the similar device at the Villa Poggio Imperiale.[49] The lower half of the façade seems to be aggressively masculine and the upper distinctly feminine, a contrast which could not have escaped the designer in that age of acute sensitivity. Theatrical effects extend into the architecture here.[50] Nikolaus Pevsner has declared of this theatre, "surely the arcaded and rusticated ground floor comes straight from the Odéon, and equally surely, the splendid colonnade on the upper floor . . . from such designs as Ledoux's Maisons Hosten of 1792."[51] However, the ground floor of the Odéon, with its more numerous and smaller-scaled arches, lacks the intricate irregularities and inventions of Niccolini. Similarly, the colonnade at the Maisons Hosten and its pediment are far more regular and stark than Niccolini's. This is not to deny Pevsner's main point, that French influence upon Italian Neoclassic buildings is a "most interesting and important problem," but to suggest that, as usual at this time, architects played freely with the paradigms in a creative way and that the French influence was only one among many.[52]

At Padua stands the most unusual of all the Neoclassical buildings of Italy—the Caffè Pedrocchi, begun in 1816 by Giuseppe Japelli (1783–1852).[53] Japelli was the most eclectic Italian architect of his day. He had studied in the Acca-

---

48. See p. 23.

49. See p. 142.

50. See Chapter 1.

51. Nikolaus Pevsner, "Review of *Architettura neo-classica a Napoli*," *Architectural Review, 131* (1962), 307.

52. Ibid.

53. There is an excellent biographical study of Japelli by Roberto C. Mantiglia, "Giuseppe Jappelli (sic) architetto," *L'Architettura, 1* (Nov.–Dec. 1955), 538–52.

Figure 51. Antonio Niccolini: Naples, Teatro San Carlo, principal façade, 1810–44

demia Clementina, Bologna, and Selva had been his master. He traveled extensively in Germany, Belgium, England, and France and was fully aware of the latest works of the greatest European masters. He was closely associated with Antonio Gradenigo (1806–84) who is said to have collaborated with him in Padua (Figures 52–54). Japelli's most famous work, the Caffè, was but one of his many buildings in and around Padua, including villas, gardens, the Market, and an opera house.[54] The Caffè took a long time to complete, as new parts were added, the most surprising of which is an English Gothic wing of 1837, "Il Pedrocchino" (Figure 54). The Caffè was a family enterprise and was bequeathed some time ago to the Commune which now operates it. It seems to have been run as a gentlemen's club, something after the manner of Whites and Brooks, i.e. privately owned by an individual proprietor whose source of livelihood it was. The rooms on the upper floors include private dining rooms, a ballroom, reading rooms, and billiard rooms; undoubtedly a good deal of cash changed hands in some of them. These rooms exhibit the greatest variety of styles: the ballroom is Empire, there is a Gothic suite, and, in one of the corner pavilions facing the piazza (on the left in the figure), a lofty and dark Egyptian lodge room. None of these are in good repair but all deserve careful restoration. The main building dates from 1816 to 1831, "Il Pedrocchino" from 1837, and the Casino from 1842. Its general scheme is academic, an H-shaped plan with symmetrical elevations where the site permitted. There is a giant order over rusticated basements, on the street side in pilasters, on the piazza side in a loggia of free-standing columns with half-column responds. The pavilions, with their single windows, flat lintels, and recesses for floating friezes, perhaps originally in fresco, are all normal parts of the Venetian-Palladian tradition. The projecting porches, two toward the piazza and one on the narrower opposite façade, are strikingly different in character. They are composed of baseless, channeled Greek Doric columns *in antis,* with echini of eggs and darts, supporting a massive entablature enriched with overscaled ormolu-like decorations. These may have been additions to the original Palladian core, and may have been executed subsequent to the building of the city gates in Milan.[55] In front of each porch lies a handsome pair of recumbent sphinxes, of which there were also many pairs displayed in Rome. The handling is, therefore, by no means archaeological, but freely eclectic and imaginative. The character seems a little less than festive for a building in which so many kinds of pleasure could be sought.[56] But so were many of the other cafés and pleasure resorts of the time,

54. See p. 158.
55. See p. 101.
56. Hitchcock, *Architecture,* p. 56, calls this Caffè: "a charming ornament, delicate in scale, interestingly varied . . . most urbane . . . the handsomest nineteenth-century café in the world and about the finest Romantic Classical edifice in Italy."

Figure 52. Giuseppe Japelli: Padua, Caffè Pedrocchi, 1816–42

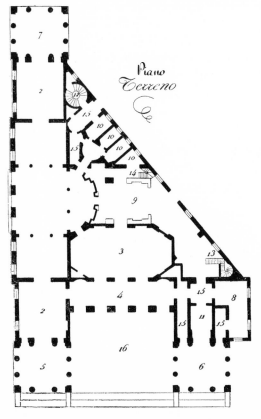

Figure 53. Giuseppe Japelli: Padua, Caffè Pedrocchi, 1816–42, plan before 1837

Figure 54. Giuseppe Japelli: Padua, Caffè Pedrocchi, "Il Pedrocchino," 1837

such as the minor buildings at the Villa Albani, the Piranesi decorations for the destroyed Caffè Inglese (1760) in Rome, and the present Caffè Greco on the Via Condotti. Fuga's coffee house of 1741 in the garden of Quirinal Palace is somewhat more intimate, but not much more, while the least solemn of all is Lorenzo Santi's Caffè in Venice of 1838.[57] After a trip to England Japelli brought to Padua the newest fashion, Gothic. Italy had thus far seen very little in the way of Neo-Gothic.[58] The exceedingly picturesque "Il Pedrocchino" was added to the Caffè at the restricted southwest corner in 1837. This is complete, with all the devices of English Neo-Gothic that characterized it in its playful Strawberry Hill phase.[59] With Japelli we are in the presence, for the first time in Italy, of an architect capable of using any eclectic style.[60]

The most delightful of the Venetian Neoclassic buildings is the very late one on the Riva, the coffee house, now the clubhouse of the Società Canottieri Bucintoro (1838) by Lorenzo Santi (Figure 55). Here an open site permits a centralized and plastic form which seems inviting because it is executed in small scale, something like the Palladian bridges at Bath and Wilton or a temple in the garden of the Trianon. Lavagnino considers it to be Santi's masterpiece.[61]

Down in the heart of Rome facing the Piazza Colonna an old building of Innocent X's day, now the Palazzo Wedekind, was improved by the addition of a stoa-like colonnade at the piazza level (Figure 56).[62] This remarkable bit of antiquarianism and urbanization was accomplished by Pietro Camporese the younger in 1838, as the inscription relates. The columns are part of those from a building of the Augustan age at Veio. The handling of the columns is not so much classical as Renaissance, with strong terminations of paired pilasters and an emphatically projecting central feature. The new disposition occurred at just about the time Antonelli was demonstrating his excessive stylophily at Novara.[63] The contemporary rage for temple fronts is a parallel phenomenon.

Leghorn received a number of Neoclassical additions at this time, the most famous of which is Il Cisternone by Pasquale Poccianti (1774–1858) of 1829–42. The frontispiece of this reservoir puts a Roman Doric portico of eight columns before a huge coffered niche (Figure 57). The cross-section shows the elaborate system of columns and vaults of which it was composed (Figure 58). There was also an aqueduct at Lucca by Lorenzo Nottolini (1787–1851),

57. See fig. 55.
58. See pp. 210 ff.
59. Nikolaus Pevsner, "Il Pedrocchino and Some Allied Problems," *Architectural Review, 122* (1957), 112–15.
60. Lavagnino, *L'Arte moderna, 1,* 394.
61. Ibid., pp. 324–26.
62. Luigi Càllari, *I Palazzi di Roma* (Rome, 1944), p. 477.
63. See p. 198.

Figure 55. Lorenzo Santi: Venice, Caffè, now Società Canottieri Bucintoro, 1838

Figure 56. Pietro Camporese, the younger: Rome, Palazzo Wedekind, Portico di Veio, 1838

Figure 57. Pasquale Poccianti: Leghorn, Il Cisternone, principal façade, 1829–42

Figure 58. Pasquale Poccianti: Leghorn, Il Cisternone, longitudinal section, 1829–42

opened in 1832, which terminated in a fountain in the form of a circular temple with a baseless Doric order and a domed superstructure.

Urbanistic activities of this time were usually as episodic as this.

Palaces, Public and Private

The mature Neoclassic style was widely used for palaces of several types—those for private individuals or kings and those for governmental functions ranging from city halls to meat markets.

The Palazzo Rocca Saporiti, now Archinto, Milan, dating from 1812 (Figure 59), takes up the use of orders from Pollack's nearby Villa Reale and Piermarini's Palazzo Belgioioso and makes a robust colonnade. It has a channeled Ionic order somewhat widely spaced so that the columns read almost as independent units and clearly reveal their supporting role. Palladio tended to bunch his columns more than this, but he did favor the wide central intercolumniation as used here, which was fortunate, since the keystone of the entrance comes so close to the loggia floor. Tarchiani's observations on this palace are followed closely by Lavagnino.[64] The design was supplied by Giovanni Perego, a scene designer, in 1812, and executed by the engineer Francesco Gloria and the architect Innocenzo Giusti for Gaetano Belloni.

This colonnade is confined by strong opaque blocks which act aggressively to hold the loggia in place. Gabriel's end pavilions facing the Place de la Concorde in Paris are looser, because they stand free instead of being set between party walls. The long frieze above the *piano nobile* windows is typically Neoclassical. Palladio showed some friezes in his "Salle Egittie," where the capitals are linked by a band of low relief under the entablature and on some exteriors.[65] This is doubtless the authority for Inigo Jones' use of this device on the Whitehall Banqueting House. Palladio thickened up the horizontals by adding balustrades, bands, and pedestals above the entablature. It is no great step to turn such features into a frieze or to weave them behind the order, as he did in the Palazzo Porto poi Breganze, Vicenza.

Curved elements in Perego's design are restricted to semicircular shapes—three portals and two lunettes. The balustrade between the pedestals of the columns is too small. This is Palladian, as are the roofline balustrade, the skyline figures, the Roman windows, and the rusticated basement. Such references in Lavagnino's view make it an example of Purism.[66] There is Rationalism in the carrying of the balustrade and frieze of the loggia right across the façade by moldings which tie the loggia to the end pavilions. The moldings which continue the frieze appear to run under the Ionic responds to the colonnade. The level of

64. Tarchiani, *Ottocento*, pp. 22 ff.; Lavagnino, *L'Arte moderna*, *1*, 315.
65. Palladio, *Quattro Libri*, *2*, 14, 15, 40, 42.
66. Lavagnino, *L'Arte moderna*, *1*, 4–12, 315.

Figure 59. Giovanni Perego: Milan, Palazzo Rocca Saporiti, 1812

the cornice is maintained in the later adjoining buildings. Everything seems to fit well and to reflect the ideals of clarity and rationality without straining. The coloration, a dark layer between two lighter ones, emphasizes the length. Though this may be due to age, it looks deliberate.

The dry Palazzo Besana (circa 1815) on the Piazza Belgioioso, by G. B. Piuri, was for a time the Unione Fascista dei Commercianti (Figure 60). Its bare, smooth walls are broken by eight engaged Ionic columns. It is an example of the way in which the Palladian formula could be adapted to the larger buildings needed by the nineteenth century, and shows how the juice was extracted from it under the pressure of Neoclassicism.

The Palazzo Borghese in Florence (1835) by Gaetano Baccani (1792–1867) is composed pyramidally; the lowest floor receives the most elaborate detail and most complex rhythmical handling, the next floor is more centralized, and the uppermost is the least emphatic.[67] The rhythm quiets down and the number of parts decreases as one's eye moves upwards. The effect of bareness is augmented by the absence of fluting and responds, but the round-arched motive was used as follows: seven times on the ground floor, four times on the second floor, and once on the third. The dry flatness also recalls the illustrative technique of the period. The total length seems much greater and the whole much calmer than would be the case in more conventionally handled compositions of the same dimensions.

Lorenzo Santi was responsible for the new Palazzo Patriarcale on the Piazzetta dei Leoncini adjoining San Marco in Venice (Figure 61). This work of 1837 to 1850 is both florid and conservative. Although not without originality, it derives to a great extent from Palladio. The giant order rests on a tall basement of smooth ashlar, with windows and panels so treated that at a quick glance it seems to be two-storied and to belong to the Venetian palazzo tradition with mezzanines in the basement story. The tall order of six channeled Corinthian pilasters frames a most unconventional device—the unequal stories are reversed, with the taller windows above the short ones separated, furthermore, by the balconies. The general scheme recalls that of Palladio's Palazzo Porto poi Breganze, which has tall windows close to the capitals between a giant order. But Santi's pilasters are flat and farther apart and have none of the tension of Palladio's. This is true of all the changes from the presumed model: the garlands between the capitals are comparatively slack and shriveled; the balconies are not compressed but relaxed; and the window heads are flat and uniform with none of the positive rhythm set up by Palladio's alternating ones. As Palladio had done, the frieze is widened to admit windows, with the interstices filled with trophied panels instead of the more plastic beam-ends. The air of immobility reveals an aspect of the nineteenth century's ideal of classicism.

67. Ibid., fig. 267.

Figure 60. Giovanni Battista Piuri: Milan, Palazzo Besana in Piazza Belgioioso, c.1815

Figure 61. Lorenzo Santi: Venice, Palazzo Patriarcale, 1837–50

Figure 62. Luigi Poletti and others: Rome, San Paolo fuori le mura, north transept, rebuilt 1823 ff. and new campanile

Figure 63. Luigi Poletti and others: Rome, San Paolo fuori le mura, nave, rebuilt 1823 ff.

Churches

Apart from the numerous churches which received temple fronts at this time, which will be discussed below,[68] there are two important Neoclassic ones in Rome, for in spite of her political difficulties, her architects seem never to have lacked work.

The Quirinal Palace, the Vatican, and many other buildings of less importance were enlarged or altered, but the most famous rebuilding was that of San Paolo f. l. m. This venerable and imposing shrine suffered terribly from fire in 1823. There was no question but that it would have to rise again, though there was considerable disagreement about the form it should take. Some were for an archaeological restoration, others for a wholly new work. The first party would have been in some difficulty, since the old fabric had been repaired, rebuilt, and renovated many times in its long history. The question would have been (as it was so frequently in the nineteenth century) which of its many styles should be favored? In England and France this usually meant going back to the oldest surviving fragment and eliminating everything subsequent to it. For San Paolo, this would have meant eliminating some fine Baroque additions. In the end, the second party, led by Luigi Poletti (1792–1869), won out with an ingenious argument for a wholly new work, the success of which he insured, it is said, by ordering the rapid destruction of all sound surviving parts.[69] This shows not only the prevailing relaxed attitude toward archaeological accuracy but also the boundless self-confidence which so many nineteenth-century architects exhibited. The work dragged on for many years. The expenses were very great and a number of architects took part. The resulting structure is therefore a work of the mid-nineteenth century, the character of which shows most clearly in the apse and north transept (Figures 62, 63). The loose individualism of the composition is one such trait, as shown by the placing of the single, nearly detached, campanile behind the half-dome of the apse. Other traits are the airy openness of the porte cochere, the eclectic use of Classical and Renaissance elements, such as the framing bands, string courses, and rustication, together with the more medieval style of the wheel window. The domed circular temple on the final stage of the campanile is a little like Cagnola's at Ghisalba (Figure 87), although the proportions are less elegant and the lower stages are like Sangallo's at Montepulciano, but it was held to be based upon the ancient Pharos of Alexandria. The wholly new nave, with its forest of shiny columns reflecting on the polished floor, is impressive and even sublime.

In 1833 Valadier added a façade to the church of San Rocco, which had been rebuilt in a Baroque manner in the mid-seventeenth century (Figure 64). This

68. See pp. 152 ff.
69. See pp. 23, 165–66.

Figure 64. Giuseppe Valadier: Rome, San Rocco, 1833

is usually brushed off as a dull work, but it has a certain interest as a reworking of the Palladian church façade formula at a time when a much more Neoclassic solution would be expected.[70] The formula is the one which involves the interweaving of a wide and low temple front with a tall and thin one, thus adapting classical forms to the medieval shape resulting from a high nave and low aisles. In this case the lower order is an unchanneled Ionic pilaster on a low base and in a shallow relief. The tall order is a giant Corinthian one in full relief, with channeling, decorated frieze, and pediment. The paired orders standing on pedestals as high as the lateral doors, but widely separated, are in strong contrast with the modesty of the lesser order. Valadier's way of handling the formula seems arresting and abrupt.

Villas

In Florence a great villa-palace at Poggio Imperiale was rising slowly (Figure 65). An important part of it was commissioned by Queen Maria Luisa of Etruria, that ephemeral, revived kingdom which lasted from 1801 to 1807. The long line of architects and artists concerned included the original architect, Giulio Parigi (d. 1635), those of the mid-eighteenth century, Niccolò Gaspare Paoletti (1727–1813) from 1770 to 1781, the decorator Grato Albertolli, Giuseppe Cacialli (1770–1828), Pasquale Poccianti (1774–1858), and Luigi Pampaloni (1791–1847), who also supplied elegant decorations in the famous bathroom of the Palazzo Pitti (Figure 67). Between 1770 and 1781 Paoletti added the garden façade, two courtyards, and the great ballroom.[71] Poccianti began the entrance façade and executed the rustic portico between 1804 and 1806. Cacialli carried on and finished it and the rest of the main floor from 1807 to 1828. Paoletti's garden façade shows less of the new spirit than had Piermarini's work. It is quiet and academic, with regular spacing and the parts defined by pilasters, one order to a story and often paired. The orders are Roman. On the main floor they stand on pedestals. The crowding both of features and of panels strikes an eighteenth-century note.

The nineteenth-century entrance façade is Neoclassic. Like Monza, this country villa extended a considerable distance, thus making for a long, low building set directly on the ground without even a half-basement. Today it stretches to the limits of the property, but this may not always have been the case. The effect of length is heightened by the coloration—a dark layer below a light one—and by the absence of balustrades or skyline figures above the cornice. The most notable feature of the excessively stark entrance front is the enormously long, low pediment which, like the ones at Würzburg and Naples, are not temple fronts but pure geometrical shapes. The four unfluted columns, widely sepa-

70. See p. 23.
71. T.C.I., *Firenze* (Milan, 1950), p. 260.

Figure 65. Giuseppe Cacialli and Pasquale Poccianti: Florence, Villa Poggio Imperiale, entrance façade, 1812 ff.

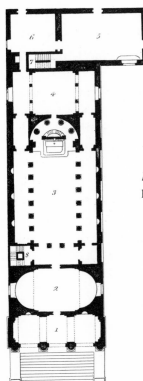

Figure 66. Giuseppe Cacialli and Pasquale Poccianti: Florence, Villa Poggio Imperiale, plan of chapel, c.1812

rated, do not support the pediment. They lack responds, piers, pilasters, or anything which might unify them into a colonnade. The weight of the pediment is
carried by the end bays, which then push through it and emerge above it like
the interlocking bits of a Chinese puzzle. All of this is set off against a high,
massive, and utterly bare attic, like those shown by Durand.

The rusticated ground floor of the entrance is on a massive scale approaching
that of the Palazzo Pitti more than that of the Rucellai. Arched elements are
few. Semicircular ones are allowed only in the entrance pavilion, while all the
other openings are quiet rectangles without pediments.

The long uphill approach ends in a pair of guard houses which frame a view
of the entrance. They are as severe as Asprucci's at the Villa Borghese, but in
place of the Borghese eagles these are topped by figures of Jove and Atlas by
Jacopo de Settignano. Poccianti and Cacialli must have worked with considerable harmony, because Cacialli's engravings show a consistent Neoclassicism:
low Pantheon domes, Roman windows, Greek Doric columns, geometrical
blocks, and masses.[72] All his designs for this villa and for the new work at the
Pitti are consistently "Impero" and imbued with a real desire for plasticity.

The chapel which occupies the east wing is entered through a one-story porch
of engaged, unfluted, Roman Doric columns (Figure 66). The interior is a full-
dress Vitruvian basilica, with colonnades, niches, coffered half-domes, and
friezes, all done at a bijou scale which, to some observers, makes it appear overly
busy.[73] The other interiors are for the most part richly frescoed; some echo
Tiepolo, some Mengs; others are clearly "Victorian."

While the execution of the architectural detail is sometimes rather thin for
the grandeur of the design, on the whole the villa is Neoclassical in its bareness,
simplicity, and majesty.

The qualities aimed for can also be seen in the famous bathroom in the Palazzo Pitti (Figure 67). Here, in a compressed area, after the model of those
achieved in France for the Napoleonic court, a handkerchief dome supported
on four full Corinthian columns is flanked by two narrow barrel-vaulted recesses. In one of these the bathtub stands, flanked by figures in niches. A marble floor, and fine low-relief decoration by Pampaloni completes this sumptuous
incident in the long series of rooms decorated here at this time. Many of these
follow Cacialli's death and therefore must be the work of Poccianti, who added
the severe conservatories at the Villa del Poggio a Caiano.

These stand to the east of the old villa, and lower down (Figure 68). They
have an imposing front toward the south. The roof slopes down and back, and

72. Giuseppe Cacialli, *Collezione dei disegni di nuove fabbriche e ornati . . . regia villa del
Poggio Imperiale . . .* (Florence, 1823); *Raccolta di progetti architettonici ideati dall'architetto
Giuseppe Cacialli . . .* (Florence, 1827).
73. Lavagnino, *L'Arte moderna, 1,* 99 ff.

Figure 67. Guiseppe Cacialli: Florence, Palazzo Pitti, bathroom, 1812 ff.

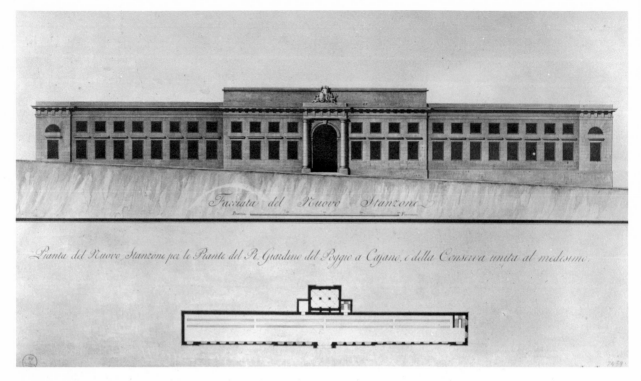

Figure 68. Pasquale Poccianti: Poggio à Caiano, Villa Medicea, Orangery, original design, elevation, and plan, c. 1825

all the openings on the front, which appears to be two stories high, open into the single shed-like space. The composition is severe, having very little ornament, and it is not so intricate as the Orangery at Kew. The imposing attic which rises over the axis is a false front. The central pavilion is nine bays long, and its central bay is marked by a high arch which encloses a barn door and is framed by a smooth Tuscan aedicula. The wings are nine bays long and end in narrow pavilions with a lunette in the mezzanine level and a bit of architrave. This is as pure as Lodoli could wish. The projects in the *Atti dell'Accademia della Pace* are rarely as severe as this, but then they do not attempt such utilitarian tasks. This could be a factory. It also has the dry, linear look of a plate from Durand. The large, bare, bold elements contrast with the delicately lined window edges, which just miss being merely punched out of the wall mass. The thin planes of the window cornices are also linear. The Roman Doric frontispiece is standard Vignola. Alternate, richer schemes are shown in Poccianti's drawings in the Uffizi.

The beautifully located Casino Valadier, built between 1809 and 1814 on top of the Pincian Hill, was originally intended as a residence, some say for L'Aiglon (Figure 69). It is one of the freshest inventions of Valadier's nimble fancy. Three different elevation schemes are employed, one for the entrance, one for the terrace, and one for the two sides. This is Rationalist, since the different functions are thus expressed. The main block rests on a wide terrace perforated by loggias, employing the Greek Doric order. The capitals on some of the Doric columns appear to have slipped; this could be a deliberately romantic device to suggest age. The roof piles up with great emphasis on the separateness and individuality of the blocky elements. The terrace is ringed round by "idle" columns of polished granite set on travertine bases, whose only duty is to uphold terra-cotta urns. Though the building is of brick and stucco, the texture is varied throughout. The motives vary widely and so does the plasticity of the wall planes. It would be difficult to give so small a building more intricacy and variety. The interior is a collection of vaults, domes, and half-domes. The Casino reflects many trends, since it is eclectic, picturesque, and Neoclassical, as well as being an example of Revolutionary architecture.

A fine example of Japelli's versatility is shown in the main building and gardens of the Villa dei Conti Cittadella Vigodarsere near Saonara, in the vicinity of Padua. Work was begun here in 1817. The chapel at the gate is placed in the customary way, so that it can be used both by the family and the villagers (Figure 70). Its ultimate reference to the Pantheon is clear enough: cylinder, low dome, and temple front. Its diminutive size puts it in the category of garden pavilions, such as Lord Burlington's at Chiswick in 1717. Its geometrical emphasis is augmented by the pair of rectangular prisms inserted between the cylinder and the wall, which make it intensely Neoclassical. While the stark bareness of the surfaces and the lack of channeling on the order suggest Rigorist

Figure 69. Giuseppe Valadier: Rome, Casino Valadier, 1813–17

purity, the handling of portico, order, door, and windows does not escape allusions to Palladio.

The villa itself is of an almost unequaled Rigorism. As Lavagnino says, it is an extreme example of Purism in its revolutionary sense.[74] The central motive of seven bays and the end wings of four bays each are all subsumed under one weighty, unbroken, hipped roof. All openings are rectangular. There is almost no ornament and a minimum of plasticity. This is barer and starker than anything else we have encountered, including the conservatories at the Villa Medicea at Poggio a Caiano (Figure 68).[75] Japelli's villa stands in a fashionably Romantic park, of which the once orderly avenues were transformed into a rolling English meadow dotted with clumps of trees and containing an irregular artificial lake. Within the park there are a number of minor structures, some recently ruined: grottos, temples, a Gothic cellar, and the like. The effect today is distinctly melancholic.

A much more decidedly archaeological step had been taken by Luigi Cagnola in 1813, in the design of his villa at Inverigo (Figures 71, 71a), now called the Villa d'Adda, after the family who had it completed after Cagnola's death in 1833 by the architect Ambrogio Nava (1791–1862). In it Cagnola apparently aimed to exhibit in one building—his own country residence—the breadth of his archaeological knowledge. On the side facing Como and the mountains, a colossal flight of steps rises between two temple fronts to a larger one through which one enters a domed *rotonda*. The stairs are supported in the Roman manner on a segmental vault. The dome is the low Pantheon type. Both orders on this façade are unfluted Ionic engaged along the flanks. The temple fronts are shallow, not the deep porches of Rome but more Palladian. On the other façade there are rusticated walls, arcades, and round-headed windows suggestive of the Renaissance. There are said to be some Egyptian details, a Roman Corinthian entrance gate, and a caryatid portico composing a veritable compendium of styles.[76] Many tendencies of the time are fused in this example of synthetic eclecticism—an eclecticism made up of a gamut of styles with widely differing associations, and composed in a scenographic Piranesian manner to which one can justly apply such adjectives as romantic, stupendous, unique, didactic, incongruous, impressive, and heroic.

Quite different in character is the Villa Torlonia on the Via Nomentana in Rome, where Sarti, working there from 1841, was but one of the numerous architects engaged over a long period of time on the villa and its grounds (Figures 71b, 71c).[77] The exact history is obscure. Much of the older building

74. Ibid., p. 396.
75. See pp. 144–45.
76. Tarchiani, *Ottocento*, pp. 26 ff.
77. Ferdinando Castagnoli and others, *Topografia e urbanistica di Roma* (Bologna, 1958), p. 485.

Figure 70. Giuseppe Japelli: Saonara, Villa dei Conti Cittadella Vigodarsere, chapel, c. 1817

Figure 71. Luigi Cagnola: Inverigo, Villa Cagnola d'Adda, north façade, 1813–33

Figure 71a. Luigi Cagnola: Inverigo, Villa Cagnola d'Adda, detail, 1813–33

Figure 71b. Antonio Sarti: Rome, Villa Torlonia, entrance façade, c.1840

Figure 71c. Antonio Sarti: Rome, Villa Torlonia, Orangery, c.1840

remained and was modernized by such devices as the great Ionic portico over a rusticated basement and the bulky Greek Doric loggias extended out from the ends at the terrace level. The pilastered wings of the main building have a full entablature which is more Neoclassical than Palladian. The garden, like that of the Villa Borghese, was full of pavilions in a variety of exotic styles, Moorish and Chinese among them. The Orangery curves back of a commemorative Corinthian column. It is Neoclassical in detail and Baroque in composition.

Temple Fronts

It is generally held against the Italians that they left so many of their churches with unfinished façades for so long, and that they were never much concerned to have the façades bear a direct relation to the naves, i.e. a classical temple front could be applied to a building of any period.

The best known examples of these peculiarities were the vast medieval cathedrals of Florence, Bologna, and Milan. The later examples to be mentioned here will indicate that there were many churches of more recent periods for which new façades were supplied in the nineteenth century. Of the 363 Italian cathedral sites listed in Franklin's *The Cathedrals of Italy* more than one-third have been subjected to major rebuilding, reconstruction, remodeling, or such significant additions as new façades since the seventeenth century.[78]

The conditions which fostered the embellishment of old churches with new façades were, as far as I know, peculiar to Italy. In the United States the problem was usually to build new and cheap buildings fast enough to meet the demand. There were few old ones to embellish. In England and on much of the continent, the economy was advancing at great speed, and again it was a question of meeting the needs of a growing but more prosperous population, whereas in Italy, the last country to share in the benefits of the Industrial Revolution, the reserve of old buildings to rehabilitate was enormous and the economy weak.

In Neoclassic times the preferred façade treatment was indubitably the "temple front," thus making such Neo-Gothic façades as that of 1806 at Milan (Figure 38) and the remarkable "Strawberry Hill" Gothic of the porch and decoration of 1825 by B. C. Marandono of the Duomo at Biella (Figure 106) conspicuous exceptions rarely to be imitated in Italy until the generation of Selvatico.[79]

The addition of a temple front to a Christian church sometimes produced incongruous results, sometimes pleasant harmonies. Alternately wholly new buildings, often churches, were built after some pagan model, also with temple fronts. Such conceits were not new in the Neoclassical period, having been

78. J. W. Franklin, *The Cathedrals of Italy* (New York, 1958).
79. See pp. 211 ff.

Figure 72. Antonio Mollari: Trieste, Bourse, 1802–06

tentatively essayed by some of the Renaissance masters, such as Alberti in his three religious edifices. Even the notion of adding an impressive portico to an older building found most respectable authority in the prevailing notion of the history of the Pantheon.

Michelangelo's desire to revive the boldly projecting temple front was unfulfilled. He had hoped to build one at St. Peter's. Since this yearning was widely known, it was shared by his admirers. Carlo Rainaldi's church fronts on the Piazza del Popolo, as executed by Carlo Fontana by 1675, are classical in spirit. They stand forth boldly and completely as tetrastyle prostyle pedimented temple fronts standing above low flights of stairs. These approximations of antique building elements are proto-Neoclassic rather than Palladian.

Lavish as Palladio had been in recording the temple fronts of antiquity in Book Four, he himself had built only one on a church, that at Maser in the 1560s. They were commonplaces on his villas, where the full Roman majesty was rarely invoked, since the order was more likely to be Ionic rather than Corinthian, and still more likely to be without fluting. The hexastyle prostyle Corinthian portico at Maser has more the air of a garden decoration than of a serious exercise in ecclesiastical design (Figure 82).

Following Carlo Fontana's pair, the family of tetrastyle prostyle temple fronts includes Juvarra's at the Superga near Turin, handled as a porte cochere, an ancestor via Dublin of that at the White House; Galilei's dynamic Composite one at St. John Lateran, a version of Maderna's calmer central motive at St. Peter's; and Vanvitelli's on the garden façade at Caserta, with both fluting and reeding but with a simpler capital which may be derived from Galilei's.

The great Roman gardens of the eighteenth century, like those of the rest of Europe, were sometimes three-dimensional echoes of the painted landscapes of Claude and Poussin, both of whom often introduced temple fronts. At the Villa Albani, Carlo Marchionni and Johann Joachim Winckelmann had constructed several of these small temple fronts (Figures 6–8).[80] Shortly afterward, at the Villa Borghese, members of the Asprucci family together with Christoph Unterberger (1732–98) built a tetrastyle prostyle temple to Esculapius (Figure 45).[81] There is another tetrastyle composition there: a pair of Corinthian columns *in antis,* with a fragment of a pediment but no cella. It is known as the Tempio di Antonino e Faustina, and may in part be made up of antique fragments.

From time to time wholly new tetrastyle prostyle porticos appeared on such buildings as the Bourse at Trieste (1802–06, Figure 72), or as the frontispiece to a school at Lecce, or, in the old Palladian way, to a villa such as Nottolini's at Marlia near Lucca. Hexastyle Ionic ones were usually favored for villas, as at the Villa Torlonia in Rome (Figure 71b), or, without a pediment,

80. See pp. 56 ff.
81. See p. 115.

as at the parish church at Montecatini. But architectural ambitions were often much greater, and a remarkable series of grandiose porticos resulted.

The series begins in Baroque Venice with the great hexastyle prostyle Corinthian temple front added to the Church of San Niccolò dei Tolentini by Andrea Tirali (circa 1660–1737, Figure 5) at the beginning of the eighteenth century.[82] The bricks of the nave rise high above this Neoclassic-Palladian addition. The setting is romantic, partly obscured by neighboring buildings. Set back on a small piazza, fronting a canal and backed against the near-ruin of the west front, it might well have sparked Piranesi's youthful imagination. Corinthian temple fronts often have such an attic behind the pediment, as in the Pantheon. Tirali's design indicates an intention to make the forms clear and sharp. He has omitted the frivolous garlands suspended between the capitals at Maser and also its solid flank walls. Returned columns are used, as in antiquity. The feature which best suggests the early eighteenth-century date is the oval oculus, and its ornament, in the tympanum.

The next major temple front to be planned was that at S. Filippo in Turin, which has a long and complicated history (Figure 73). The gist of this seems to be that although the front had been designed by Filippo Juvarra, who died in 1736, its execution was delayed until 1835 and was not finally completed until the 1890s. The eighteenth-century design was not executed for a century, and presumably was then somewhat revised, thereby including traces of the taste of both centuries. Again the order is Corinthian, and again it is fluted and reeded. But the six main elements are four columns and two piers standing on paneled pedestals with stairs sliding between them. These support a pediment with a strongly projecting and modillioned cornice. The tympanum in two planes bears a tablet and forceful classical garlands. The temple-front motive is not permitted to stand forth clearly in its own right, but is attached to slightly recessed wings, the pilasters of which continue the main order. The wings are then perforated by unglazed windows which permit a restricted oblique view of the inner depths of the porch through perforated wing walls. Through these and numerous other devices, the basic idea of a temple front has been altered to achieve a Baroque spatial complication, an hieratic unity, and is made to play a more integrated role in the total composition.

In the early nineteenth century, a number of wholly new churches were built with prominent temple fronts, such as Luigi Cagnola's (1762–1833) at Ghisalba (Figure 87), the new cathedral of Alessandria, Ferdinando Bonsignore's church at Turin (Figure 90), Pietro Bianchi's at Naples (Figure 94), the Tempio Canova at Possagno (Figure 97), and Carlo Amati's at Milan (Figure 88).[83]

82. See p. 56.
83. These are described in detail elsewhere as follows: Ghisalba, p. 174; Turin, p. 177; Naples, p. 181; Possagno, p. 188; Milan, pp. 174 ff.

Figure 73. Filippo Juvarra and others: Turin, San Filippo, 1730s–1890s

Figure 74. Antonio Diedo: Schio, Cathedral, 1805–20

One of the first of the series of old churches to receive a temple-front façade in the nineteenth century was the cathedral of Schio. The façade was begun by Antonio Diedo in 1805 (Figure 74), and its construction lasted until 1820. The building had been rebuilt in 1740, and as late as 1879 narrow side aisles were added. Diedo's majestic pronaos stands above a lofty complex of stairs and terraces, giving it an almost acropolis setting. This circumstance did not lead to the introduction of any other Greek characteristics. The flank walls, with their arcades, are Palladian, as are the "ass's ears" standing on the attic behind the pediment, and the four stout columns *in antis*. More Neoclassical is the long frieze running across the rear wall of the porch. The whole is a graceful scenographic combination—imposing, varied, and harmonious.

At almost the same time and a few miles to the south, another prominent Venetian architect, Antonio Selva (1753–1819), began the rebuilding of the old Duomo at Cologna Veneta, giving it an octastyle Corinthian pronaos standing at the summit of a long flight of steps.[84] The treatment is less Palladian and more Neoclassic, anticipating in some features Bernard Poyet's (1742–1824) portico added to the Chamber of Deputies in Paris between 1806 and 1808. Both porticos are backed against a wide rusticated wall and stand at the summit of a flight of steps, and neither have pilaster responds, though there is one column returned on each flank. Selva came very close to achieving Roman grandeur.

At nearby Padua, Giuseppe Japelli (1783–1852) built the new Meat Market in 1821 with a squat Greek Doric portico, octastyle prostyle with shallow channels supporting an austere pediment (Figure 75). Behind the portico, a half dome on a shorter Doric order and lit by an oculus created a monumental setting for slaughtering. Today the building serves more appropriately as an art school. The portico springs abruptly from the road, a characteristic often found in Neoclassical buildings, in part, perhaps, because the bases of so many antique temples were still concealed by accumulated debris. A far more rational treatment was given to the one- and two-story flanking wings in brick with minimal ornamentation, looking as though they had been designed by J.-N.-L. Durand. This meat market, curiously, was far more imposing than the contemporary Capodimonte observatory, which also had a Doric temple front.

In 1826 another important example of the use of the Greek Doric was Carlo Barabino's (1768–1835) hexastyle colonnade on the flank of his Teatro Carlo Felice on Genoa's Piazza de Ferrari (Figure 76). The columns are remarkably thin and deeply channeled. The returns are piers, and pilastered responds occur on the rear wall. The entablature supports a massive attic crowned by a pyramidal roof and a large statue. This colonnade was not required for the functioning of the theatre, of which the main entrance is around the corner, but exists

84. Lavagnino, *L'Arte moderna, 1,* fig. 89.

Figure 75. Giuseppe Japelli: Padua, Meat Market, 1821

primarily for the embellishment of the piazza and perhaps secondarily as a substitute for a triumphal arch in honor of Carlo Felice. Barabino was, by this time, becoming an expert on temple fronts. He had been one of the judges in 1806 of the temple-studded designs for the Foro Bonaparte in Milan. In 1824 he had placed a small tetrastyle prostyle temple front against the cylinder of his new Pantheon-like Church of the Rosary in Genoa. In 1820–21 he had skillfully applied a pilastered temple front to the existing church of San Siro, and in 1835 he was to design another for the cemetery of Staglieno (Figure 98).[85] But in 1830 he tackled the much more difficult problem of adding a temple front to the sumptuous old Church of the Annunciation (Figure 77). His design was harshly criticized, and, after his death in 1835, other schemes were proposed. Finally in 1843, for lack of a better solution, Barabino's design was partly carried out by other hands. He had intended that a high, flat, pedimented wall be used to cover the old Cinquecento brick façade against which his new pronaos would have looked somewhat less out of place. The side towers were standing, and the Baroque quality of most of the building would imply a Baroque design such as that proposed for it in the late sixteenth century by Giacomo della Porta (1539–1602). Although the mid-nineteenth century ranged widely in its use of old styles, it did not yet tolerate Neo-Baroque. This point of view is implicit in Stendhal's comment on the Michelangelesque palaces on the Capitoline which he found to be "without character," saying, "In such a place, two façades of antique temples were called for. Nothing could be too majestic or too severe."[86] "Majestic" is the word which Stendhal uses over and over in association with ancient columns, and he consistently prefers classical porticoes to Baroque façades.

The usual exception to such rules is provided at Turin, where, at the south end of the magnificent Piazza San Carlo, there was a pair of churches flanking the Via Roma, not unlike the pair flanking the Corso at the Piazza del Popolo in Rome. At Turin, however, the left-hand one had a fine façade added by Juvarra in 1718, but the one on the right, San Carlo, did not, so between 1834 and 1836 a matching baroque façade was applied by Ferdinando Caronesi (1794–1842). This was clearly an exception, because to another Turinese baroque church, the Santuario della Consolata, on which Guarini had worked, a tetrastyle prostyle Corinthian temple front was added as late as 1860. A still later one in Turin will be mentioned subsequently. The inference is that persons of taste were convinced that Neoclassicism was *the* style of their day, and were hardly aware that it was but one of several concurrent eclecticisms.

When built as we now see it, the new front of the Church of the Annunciation caused evident discord. Agitation to destroy it was constant, one citizen leaving

85. See pp. 188 ff.
86. Stendhal, *Roman Journal*, p. 89.

Figure 76. Carlo Barabino: Genoa, Teatro Carlo Felice, 1826–28

Figure 77. Carlo Barabino: Genoa, Chiesa della Santissima Annunziata, façade, designed 1830, constructed 1843

the city a large sum conditional on its demolition. From the point of view of a later century, a less dogmatic one, which tolerates contrast and has affection for pleasing decay, this complex is a vivid record of the fate of inflexible self-confidence and a witness to the mutability of taste. Barabino's elegant Ionic hexastyle prostyle pedimented temple front, with its fluted columns and carefully balanced pilaster responds, its delicate cornice and glissade of steps, furnishes its piazza with admirable picturesqueness from most of the sharp angles from which it is customarily viewed.

In the meantime, in 1842 another Neoclassical façade was added to another old Genoese church, Santa Maria delle Vigne. The architect was Ippolito Cremona (died 1844). This front was a ribbon of columns and pilasters wrapped across the lower part of the façade, with lunettes and pediments above, a mixture of Palladio and Valadier.

In the 1820s it was thought necessary to bring the old cathedral at San Marino up to date, and a little-known architect, Antonio Serra (1783–1847), rebuilt it, beginning in 1826, although political events delayed the consecration until 1855 (Figure 78). Here, too, a grandiose Corinthian pronaos was achieved. It is somewhat wider than the nave and without a pediment.

In the 1830s the Municipal architect of Verona, Giuseppe Barbieri (1777–1838), who a few years before had begun the Neoclassical cemetery there,[87] was given the magnificent opportunity of building a wholly new Municipal Palace close by the ancient Roman arena (Figure 79). What pleasure this must have given this Neoclassical architect! How could he do otherwise than use a colossal Corinthian octastyle pronaos supporting a pediment? Barbieri must have felt that he and Verona were recreating a civic center worthy of the city's ancient Roman one.

Alessandro Antonelli (1798–1888), the most widely known of all nineteenth-century Italian architects, was fanatically addicted to the Corinthian temple front, employing it in novel and intricate ways in such new buildings as the Sanctuary at Boca (1830 ff., Figure 101), the parish church at Oleggio (1853–58), and the Cathedral at Novara (1854 ff., Figure 103), as well as in the Mole Antonelliana at Turin (Figure 104).

The rage was widespread. The town of Treviso swung into line in 1836 by adding a temple front to Ricatti's (1709–70) eighteenth-century cathedral there. Another piazza was being furnished with a dominating classical portico, this one hexastyle prostyle, supporting a bare pediment. The order is Ionic, the portico is shallow and there are no flanking columns, merely pilastered responds, austere and powerful, dominating the multi-storied adjoining palace and the numerous small domes behind.

It will be sufficient to mention in passing the numerous porticoes added by

87. See p. 186 and fig. 96a.

Figure 78. Antonio Serra: San Marino, Cathedral, 1826–36

Figure 79. Giuseppe Barbieri: Verona, Palazzo Municipale, 1830s

various hands to San Paolo f. l. m. in the long rebuilding which followed the fire of 1823. The porticoes are the whims of the architects concerned. They are not reconstructions of the porches standing prior to the fire, but emendations undertaken in a creative and non-imitative spirit.[88] Poletti himself also added a Corinthian temple front to the Cathedral of Chiavari in 1841.

The final and belated example of this series is the Corinthian portico added in 1870 by Carlo Ceppi (1829–1921) to the not very old Turinese Church of the Sacramentine (Figure 93). Twenty years before, a low saucer dome had been raised on an octagonal drum over a Greek cross plan. It was a neat sequence of geometrical volumes, unhappily left with the structural brick exposed and no significant façade. Since the church was situated in a fashionable section of a prospering city, this had to be remedied. The architect added a hexastyle prostyle Corinthian portico supporting a bare pediment. The portico is a little wide for the attic behind it, but the problems of adding on to the existing core were doubtless considerable.

This account of the Neoclassical use of the temple front in Italy for buildings of so many functions does not review the total. Like the triumphal arch and the Pantheon the temple front was a theme, given authority by the ancients, capable of many variations and expressions of feeling: jewel-like at Saonara, picturesque at Schio and Genoa, scenographic at San Carlo at Milan, and sublime at Cologna Veneta.

The Pantheon as a Paradigm

"The Pantheon, built by the son-in-law of Augustus, was the first great monument of non-useful architecture."[89]

For many Neoclassicists, especially in Italy, the Roman Pantheon was the most admirable building of antiquity, yet they never sought to copy it (Figures 80, 81). "Pantheons" sprang up in many places and for many purposes, but none of them can really be mistaken for the original. It is merely a careless habit of architectural historians to toss off phrases like "innumerable copies of the Pantheon were erected all over Europe and America in this period," and "many Pantheon imitations about 1800." The use of "copy" and "imitation" in such comments is perhaps owing to hasty observation and only partial comprehension of the aims and spirit of the architects of Neoclassicism. Wittkower implies this concerning the relationships between Bernini's church at Ariccia and the Pantheon, stating that modern critics "fail to understand the subjective and particular quality with which seemingly objective and timeless classical forms have been endowed,"[90] echoing Stendhal's remark, a phrase without novelty may

88. See p. 140.
89. Stendhal, *Roman Journal*, pp. 103–04.
90. Wittkower, *Art and Architecture*, p. 119.

Figure 80. Rome, Pantheon, exterior, A.D. 120–125

Figure 81. Rome, Pantheon, interior, A.D. 120–125

express or give birth to a sentiment. Wittkower notes that both Palladio and Bernini had interpreted the original Pantheon as the union of two basic forms, the vaulted cylinder and portico, and that, in Bernini's case, these were given an "entirely non-classical meaning."[91] This is emphasized by the fact that, in addition to the two basic elements which Bernini had employed, there were in his day two more which he omitted at Ariccia. These were the great attic against which the portico butts, and the pair of towers. The towers had been there in the sixteenth century. They were medieval and quite small. In the 1660s, Bernini himself regularized them into a pair of larger domed belfries, which became known as the "ass's ears." They were removed in 1883 or 1893. The rebuilding of these towers had probably been based on the century-old earlier ones which Palladio had introduced in his free version of the Pantheon at Maser (Figure 82).[92]

How Palladio arrived at this composition is an unresolved problem. The theme of dome and towers was at least as old as Bramante. Sometimes the towers were planned to be detached and free-standing. Palladio probably had seen the various minute structures then standing on the roof of the Pantheon portico, but he did not show them in the plates of his Fourth Book. It is possible that he was alluding to the medieval practice of paired church towers on west fronts. It is more probable that he had a brilliant idea, which was in the direction of the Baroque effort, to increase the polyphonic richness of the portico and dome elements by incorporating additional sharply contrasting forms and integrating them with the main masses. The architects of Neoclassicism often emulated the architects of Renaissance, who also had found the Pantheon a great stimulus to their imaginations, and whose versions of the paradigm were equally innocent of the idea of literal imitation. Architects of both periods liked to change the proportions or to add new elements. The Renaissance masters, on the whole, were inclined to see the Pantheon in terms of lines, planes, and decoration, whereas the Neoclassicists emphasized the mass, bulk, and weight. In both cases the aims were distinct from those of academicism—it was not a matter of rules but of invention. Just as Palladio was not an academician himself though his followers generally were, the Neoclassicists were relatively independent and their followers less so. In this sense, Palladio was a Neoclassicist.

Palladio's attitude toward antiquity was immensely influential. Neoclassicism was born in his part of Italy. By 1775 every sophisticated person in Europe must have been aware of the Neoclassic program. Italy contributed many of the major monuments; hence the importance of Palladio's attitude toward antiquity and particularly toward the Pantheon.

91. Ibid.
92. Ibid., p. 118.

Figure 82. Andrea Palladio: Maser, Chapel, 1560s

At Maser he linked the columns of his portico with garlands swinging across the compressed intercolumniations and adopted a bichromatic color scheme, which gave the design a light-hearted air of frivolity, intensified by its small size. There is no sycophantic solemnity about the Palladian version of the great paradigm. This is typical, I believe, of the relaxed attitude of most of his successor architects toward the ponderous original. None of the Neoclassical versions seems to be hamstrung by considerations of archaeological accuracy.

Palladio had done much to emphasize the importance of the original, but had said nothing about copying it. In his Fourth Book he singles out the Pantheon for very particular attention. He devotes plates 75 through 84 to it, nearly twice as many as he allocates to any other building, and two pages of text in which he uses terms like "most celebrated," "most notable," and "most beautiful," and alludes to its symbolism.

Neoclassical designs were often meant to have the qualities of coolness, rigidity, and severity. These we recognize more easily in the paintings and sculpture of Mengs, Canova, and Thorwaldsen, and accept in the white-and-gold Empire interiors. The sculptors', and particularly Canova's, interpretation of the *beau ideal* was to make objects to be looked at calmly and rather dispassionately, as Mario Praz has said of Canova's nudes.[93] The buildings, too, are deliberately reserved and aloof. They are intended to be admired, not as picturesque ruins stained and fragmented with an "air of pleasing decay," but as calm statements of ideal grace and purity. The spectator was to be impressed, but not aroused nor transported.

The factor of materials should not be ignored. In America, Pantheon variants were only occasionally executed in the traditional masonry of Europe. A wooden or stuccoed building, painted white, would, to this extent, be further removed from the original, and the temptation to cry "copy" would accordingly be lessened.

The elevation of the Pantheon to supremacy as the architectural paradigm—Stendhal called it "the finest remnant of antiquity . . . sublime . . . daring"—before the Parthenon achieved that status, is easily explained.[94] It was the most completely preserved building of antiquity, the only one with an impressive interior. It was of awe-inspiring dimensions and solidity, such as few of its admirers could hope to emulate, and it stood prominently in the heart of contemporary Rome, whereas the Colosseum was then on the outskirts. Furthermore, on less accidental grounds it could be admired aesthetically for a variety of effects.

Those ascribed to Bernini have been mentioned. The Lodoli-Milizia school

93. Praz, *Gusto neoclassico*, pp. 156 ff.
94. Stendhal, *Roman Journal*, pp. 123 ff.

could carry these further—the stark severity and almost total lack of ornamental additions, such as the portico columns innocent of fluting. Those who
sought an *architecture parlante* could find a prototype in these rugged, majestic,
and masculine forms. There are many other grounds for admiration, such as
the concept that this building represented the supreme achievement of ancient
architecture, combining in one forceful unit the Corinthian temple front derived from Greece, and the enormous vault of Roman invention. Some Neoclassicists felt that ideally such a temple front should be Greek Doric. This
objective was apparently first achieved in Italy by Vantini at Brescia in 1815
and subsequently by others at Possagno and Genoa (Figures 96, 97, 98).[95]

The notion that an exact copy of the Pantheon was desirable seems to have
been alien to Neoclassic architects, partly no doubt because no one would pay
for it, but more importantly because they still believed in the creative powers
of the architect. The doctrine of progress based on reason had not yet suc-
cumbed to pessimism. Henry Bacon, in his infrequently admired Lincoln Memorial in Washington, was truly Neoclassical, with an equal emphasis on both
parts of the term. To demonstrate how much invention went into the major
monuments of Neoclassicism, I will discuss a few Italian examples.

There are two proto-Neoclassic Pantheons in Venice, San Simeone Piccolo by
Giovanni Antonio Scalfarotto (circa 1700–64), probably completed by 1730
(Figure 83), and Santa Maria Maddalena (Figure 84) by Scalfarotti's nephew
and follower Tommaso Temanza (1705–89) about twenty years later. Wittkower calls the latter "a corrected version" of the former.[96]

It is unlikely that either architect thought he was copying the paradigm or
even that one thought he was correcting the other. Each was creating a personal
variation on the theme. The first does not adhere to the prototype in proportions, in scale, or in any other important respect. The portico is six units wide,
not eight, and all the corner elements are piers. It stands at the top of a high
flight of steps which confines access to the front. There is a projecting element,
the sanctuary, at the rear of the cylinder. The dome rises to a spectacular, almost rocket-like height, and indeed the whole structure, within as well as without, has a vertical soaring feeling in sharp contrast to the static massiveness of
the paradigm. A further difference, the separateness of the parts and not their
unification, is stressed. It is full of the lightness of the eighteenth-century Italian
Rococo. It is true that the novelties of this building are largely eliminated in
Temanza's, but again the departures from the paradigm are far more significant
than the reminiscences of it. The cylinder is topped this time by a saucer dome,
but the portico is flattened out against the cylinder, and consists of two widely

95. Brescia, p. 186; Possagno, p. 188; Genoa, pp. 188 ff.
96. Wittkower, *Art and Architecture*, p. 253.

Figure 83. Giovanni Antonio Scalfarotto: Venice, San Simeone Piccolo, c.1718–30

Figure 84. Tommaso Temanza: Venice, Santa Maria Maddalena, 1748

separated pairs of Ionic columns on low pedestals. The Ionic order is also used on the interior and in both places without fluting. The inner wall of the cylinder moves with a regular rhythm of column, arched recess, niche, column, and so on, in no way recalling the model, but strongly reminiscent of Palladio, even down to the bichromatic color scheme. If anything is being improved upon here, it might be said to be the master's own version at Maser. Temanza was regarded by Milizia as the greatest architect of his generation. One cannot agree with Milizia, but one can see why he might have come to this judgment about the younger man's work, which in this instance is so orderly, unified, and disciplined. Yet Temanza has not carried Milizia's program to its rational end, since he has not quite eliminated all ornament. It was still part of the architect's duties to establish an unequivocal character by a discreet use of associative elements.

Further east, at Trieste, Pietro Nobile's (1774–1854) Sant'Antonio (Figures 85, 86), completed in the 1840s, takes the elements of the low dome and the temple front and arranges them over and before a long-naved church with a rectangular exterior. Sited most strikingly as the terminal feature of a long canal, it reminds one of a garden temple at Chiswick, Wrest, or Stra, rather than of the urban model.

The two most important examples of the theme in the Lombardy region are Luigi Cagnola's (1762–1833) at Ghisalba, of about 1834 (Figure 87), and Carlo Amati's (1776–1852) San Carlo al Corso in Milan (Figures 88, 89). Cagnola uses the two basic elements of the paradigm with considerable fidelity: the deep Corinthian portico, hexastyle rather than octastyle, and the cylindrical body supporting the saucer dome. But the static quality of the original is disrupted by his third element, a detached campanile placed to the left of the portico and in advance of the curving flank of the cylinder. This and the elimination of the attic create a loose "revolutionary" composition of three strikingly disparate elements varying in form, density, and surface. From the classic paradigm, Cagnola has created an asymmetrical, picturesque composition, enhanced by the elevated site.

Carlo Amati adapted the Pantheon image in his masterpiece, the impressive Milanese church of San Carlo al Corso (Figures 88, 89), built between 1836 and 1847. He used the Corinthian order consistently, and established an integrated forecourt for his temple front by lining the court with additional rows of columns, presumably echoing the temple settings of ancient Rome, though not that of the Pantheon itself. This colonnaded setting establishes a majestic as well as a scenic atmosphere, dominated by the dome raised on its lofty drum. The drum, with its alternating niches and columns, is an interloper in the Pantheon family and Renaissance in inspiration. The original is recalled by the stepped flanks of the saucer dome. The contrived setting also hints at the fifteenth-century fondness for architectural perspectives. The interior at Milan,

Figure 85. Pietro Nobile: Trieste, Sant'Antonio, exterior, 1826–49

Figure 86. Pietro Nobile: Trieste, Sant' Antonio, interior, 1826–49

Figure 87. Luigi Cagnola: Ghisalba, "La Rotonda," 1834

with its coffered dome lighted from the drum as well as the oculus, has a serene unity of scale, a pleasant gradation of accents and of richness culminating at the apse. Its pavement is closely derived from the original at the Pantheon (Figure 89). The oculus is for practical reasons covered by a small cupola, as Palladio had done at Maser, but made more interesting by the use of angels as caryatids, perhaps derived from Soane's similar use of figures in the Old Dividend Office of the Bank of England (1818–23), or from Borromini's Campanile at Sant'Andrea delle Fratte in Rome. A recapitulation of the un-Pantheon-like elements will indicate how far Amati was from being a copyist: the fora-like colonnades in front, the linking of the portico scenographically with the colonnade, the exaggerated width of the central intercolumniation, the smoothness of the surfaces, the introduction of a quiet Renaissance drum with windows, niches, and another Corinthian order, the use of an ornamented cupola, the changed rhythms of the interior, and the altered proportions (the height being greater than the diameter). Amati, therefore, has built an eclectic domed church, incorporating a variety of traditional elements and giving the combination a distinctly original meaning, the realization of a scenographist's dream dear to men like Poussin, Claude, and Antonio Basoli.

In another northern area, Turin, we find three nineteenth-century variations on the theme, not to mention the eighteenth-century Superga on its nearby hill. The earliest is the Church of the Great Mother of God (Figure 90), by Ferdinando Bonsignore (1767–1843), which is reached by crossing Turin's earliest permanent bridge. The bridge was erected by Napoleon's order, but the church itself was designed to celebrate one of the consequences of Napoleon's fall, the return to the throne of Victor Emmanuel I. The construction took from 1818 to 1831. Bonsignore was of late middle age when he designed this, his masterwork. He had spent some years in Rome, was a distinguished teacher, and of an archaeological bent. These circumstances may account for certain eighteenth-century qualities of lightness and elegance in his work, such as the unusually slender and widely spaced columns. They do not account for certain other novel features which may be attributed to the requirements of the site. Since the church was to be approached across a long square and the bridge, and was to be seen against an irregular hilly background, it was set upon a high cylindrical base. The portal was reached by a long flight of thirty-two steps rising between massive podia supporting sculptural groups—a scenographic composition. The distracting "ass's ears" have been omitted, so that the main forms read clearly from a distance. The single cylinder of the original has been modified by a set-back at the level of the portico cornice, thus tying the upper cylinder and the attic masses together and adding more interest to the silhouette, which is formed by three superimposed cylinders and a dome. The character of the interior reflects

Figure 88. Carlo Amati: Milan, San Carlo al Corso, exterior, 1836–47

Figure 89. Carlo Amati: Milan, San Carlo al Corso, interior, 1836–47

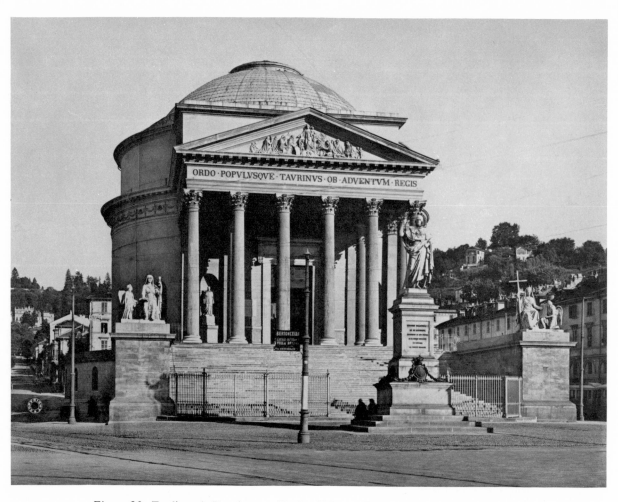

Figure 90. Ferdinando Bonsignore: Turin, Chiesa della Gran Madre di Dio, 1818–31

the elegance and lightness of the exterior decoration of the cornice and pediment.[97]

The two later Turinese examples, begun less than a generation after Bonsignore's was completed, depart still more widely from the paradigm. San Massimo (Figures 91, 92), built in 1845–53 by Carlo Sada (1809–73), looks more "Georgian" than Roman, with a belfry over the apse, a dome on a high drum, a long nave, and a four-column pronaos. The youngest of this trio, Alfonso Dupuy's Chiesa delle Sacramentine (1846–50, Figure 93), returns somewhat more closely to the paradigm. Its saucer dome dominates the exterior, even though it rests on a polygonal drum which stands over a Greek cross. Its portico, added in 1870 by Carlo Ceppi (1829–1921) is a shallow hexastyle Corinthian one, somewhat awkwardly attached.

One of the most original variations on the theme is Pietro Bianchi's (1787–1849) well-known San Francesco di Paola in Naples (Figures 94, 95). This church also has Napoleonic connections. Joachim Murat endeavored to beautify many of the cities of his kingdom. He proposed to erect here a great semi-elliptical colonnade to regularize the area opposite the Royal Palace. This was begun by Leopoldo Laperuta in 1808 and was part way along when the Bourbons returned to their throne, an event which, as in Turin, was commemorated in a church of thanksgiving. Ferdinand I gave the commission to Bianchi, who began the construction of the church at the axis of the colonnade about 1817, and the work dragged on until nearly the middle of the century. Laperuta's colonnade obviously owes something to Bernini's Roman one in the use of the Doric order and its semi-elliptical shape. A rather more recent example stood at hand in Vanvitelli's regularization of the Piazza Dante in 1755–67 (Figure 4a). Laperuta, in a typically Neoclassic spirit, substituted decorum for panache. Nikolaus Pevsner states that in Naples "the turn to Neoclassicism came with Joseph Bonaparte and Joachim Murat" and that the Foro Murat (now the Piazza del Plebiscito) is derived from the "Pantheon and the piazza of St. Peter's, or indirectly via Peyre and the style of the Parisian *Grands Prix*."[98] By this time, 1806, the number of Neoclassical buildings in existence and in projects was considerable. They all shared the classical sources, and it was not necessary for an Italian to get his ideas via Paris or the French. However the rôles of the French conqueror must often have been decisive.

Bianchi had studied with Cagnola and, like his master, was not inhibitingly archaeological. Once more, the differences from the paradigm are telling. The portico is Ionic hexastyle *in antis* with pierced end walls. There is no attic, but

97. Although the resemblance to the Pantheon is obvious, there were two other Roman buildings which are still closer. Both were recorded by Palladio as well as others; the Temple of Fortune at Palestrina and the "Tomb of Romulus" on the Via Appia.

98. Pevsner, *Architectural Review, 131* (1962), 307.

Figure 91. Carlo Sada: Turin, San Massimo, rear view, 1845–53

Figure 92. Carlo Sada: Turin, San Massimo, detail of principal portico, 1845–53

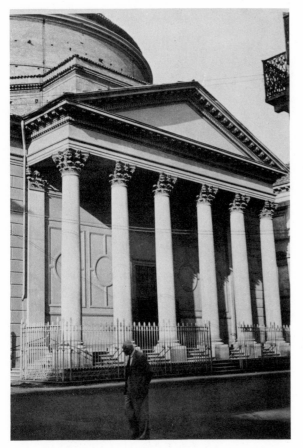

Figure 93. Alfonso Dupuy: Turin, Chiesa della Sacramentine, 1846–50, portico added by Carlo Ceppi, 1870

Figure 94. Pietro Bianchi: Naples, San Francesco di Paola, exterior, 1817–46, colonnades by Leopoldo Laperuta, begun 1808

Figure 95. Pietro Bianchi: Naples, San Francesco di Paola, interior, 1817–46

instead a pair of domed cylindrical chapels link the main dome with the portico and colonnade. The Corinthian order is reserved for the interior and is used in relatively taller tiers. There is a marked change in proportions, with the diameter-to-height ratio of three to five instead of one to one. The rhythmical system is simpler, with an uninterrupted colonnade of thirty-four columns, more Classical than the alleged models. Bianchi has blended elements from the Roman, Palladian, Baroque, and scenographic systems, in which the independence of some parts is contrasted with the unification of others to make an imposing and self-confident contribution to the cityscape.

Four other variations on the theme remain for special comment. This quartet have in common the idea, typical of synthetic eclecticism, of creating a new building type by combining elements from two of the most famous buildings of antiquity, the Parthenon and Pantheon.[99] Something new is thereby created, something partaking of the universally acknowledged excellences of these archetypes. It is too much to say that the combinations surpass either of the models, but it cannot be denied that the resulting contrasts of form are productive of novel and provocative effects. Similar juxtapositions of well-known and strongly associative forms were of course commonplace in the projects of imaginative architects at this time; Robert Mills had proposed a combination of a Doric colonnade and an obelisk for the Washington Monument.

The earliest of the four Italian combinations is Rodolfo Vantini's (1791–1856) monumental cemetery at Brescia (Figure 96), begun in 1815, which is also the first of a series of monumental Italian cemeteries. Another cemetery in which the theme was used is that by Giuseppe Barbieri at Verona, begun in 1828. The overall plan is Durandesque (Figure 96a). The third major example is at Possagno, the Tempio Canova begun in 1819 (Figure 97). It is not clear whether Vantini or Canova (1757–1822), or his good friend the architect Giovanni Antonio Selva (1753–1819), was responsible for the idea. It might well have been Selva who inspired all these projects. As young men, he and Canova had traveled throughout Italy looking at antiquities. Selva had also visited Austria, Holland, France, and England. He was an admirer of Robert Adam's work and had translated Sir William Chambers' *Civil Architecture*.[100] He was a friend of the widely traveled and open-minded Casanova, had been a pupil of Temanza, and was himself the master of the most original North Italian architect of the next generation, the urbane and eclectic Giuseppi Japelli, whom he, in turn, urged to travel widely.

Vantini's chapel was a step in the direction of Possagno, since he combined

99. The combination of the Pantheon and temple had occurred to others elsewhere, for example, to Giacomo Quarenghi, sometime between 1796 and 1817, and to Latrobe in 1798.

100. Architectural Publication Society, *Dictionary of Architecture* (8 vols. in 5. London, 1853–92), *6–7, 50.*

Figure 96. Rodolfo Vantini: Brescia, Cemetery, 1815–49

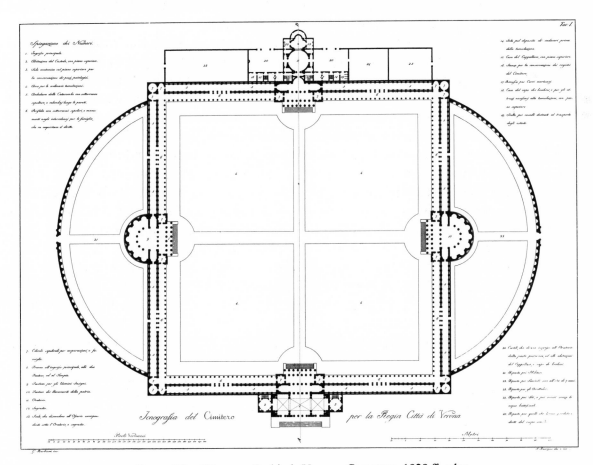

Figure 96a. Giuseppe Barbieri: Verona, Cemetery, 1828 ff., plan

the cylinder and saucer dome of the Pantheon, much reduced in size, with tetra-style Greek Doric porticoes, and applied the same order at smaller scale to extensive flanking colonnades. Vantini's work at Brescia was spread over many years. The chapel described above came first, then colonnades and subsidiary chapels (some pedimented, some domed), and in 1849 the Pharos in the form of a Greek Doric column sixty meters high. One quality which lifts this complex above the commonplace is the scale. The giant imbrications on the roof of the chapel and the relatively puny order create a relaxed rather than pompous effect.

The temple at Possagno (Figure 97) dominating Canova's native village was undoubtedly intended to have a didactic effect on the villagers. The cornerstone was laid several months after one of its alleged architects, Selva, had died in 1819. Canova himself died in 1822, and the construction of the temple seems to have been conducted by relatively unknown local people. One of Canova's disciples and close friends, Melchiorre Missirini (1773–1849), published in 1833 an illustrated work describing the building and relating its history.[101] Lavagnino discussed the problem of authorship at some length, since he regarded the building as the best example of Neoclassicism in North Italy.[102] Set above a curious mixture of decorated polyhedral surfaces and stairs, its double octastyle pronaos, Doric frieze, and bare tympanum clash violently with the unruffled cylinder. The brutality of the contrast, the severity of the detail, the empty tympanum and the absence of color are instances of the Neoclassic tendency to be more Classical than antiquity. The element of economy is not always critical, since some of the buildings were only a little less costly than copies would have been. The architects took pride in their unswerving adherence to the Doric order of the Parthenon, but did not attempt to reproduce it at full size. The height is only three-quarters that of the Pantheon, but the equality of height and diameter is retained. The interior abandons the polychrome veneer and double-story treatment, and merely resorts to a system of niches and panels without columns, producing an *Empire* rather than a Roman effect. The lighting is from the central oculus. The Christian requirement of a large chancel is met by a projecting apse also lighted by an oculus. An iron armature and relieving arches were used in the portico. Some of the metopes are conventionally decorated, but the central eight depict scenes from the Old and New Testament.

It is obvious that a building which incorporates elements of two disparate prototypes will not be a copy of either one. In spite of a didactic intent, absolute fidelity was not the architect's dominant concern, for his originality is apparent in many of the elements, as well as in the total conception.

The fourth major example of this fusion is that of the cemetery of the Stag-

101. Melchiorre Missirini, *Del Tempio eretto in Possagno da Antonio Canova* (Venice, 1833).
102. Lavagnino, *L'Arte moderna, 1,* 114 ff.

Figure 97. Attributed to Giovanni Antonio Selva, with others: Possagno, Tempio Canova, 1819–33

lieno, near Genoa, which in the end was less synthetic than had been at first proposed (Figure 98). Sometime before his heroic death in the plague of 1835, Carlo Barabino (b. 1768), urbanist and architect, proposed to build the chapel at this cemetery with a Greek pronaos, a Roman cylindrical body, and an Egyptian pyramidal superstructure. The execution of the project was delayed for some years, until 1844–61, and was then carried out by Barabino's pupil and assistant, Giovanni Antonio Resasco (1799–1872), who rather timidly abandoned the typically eighteenth-century idea of the pyramid, and, following Vantini and the builders of Possagno, reverted to the saucer dome. The magnificent conception of the use of the hillside, however, seems to have been Barabino's. He may have had the example of Palestrina in mind. He had spent his life coping with city-planning problems in the difficult Genoese terrain. The chapel placed high on a hill is the central feature, and is approached across an enclosed forecourt with a puristic gateway. The axis is marked by an imposing statue of Faith, and back of this rises a noble but knee-wrecking flight of stairs flanked by ramps. At the chapel level, long arcades reach out laterally to short returned wings. The dark hillside at the rear, against which this brilliant orderly complex is silhouetted, quickly abandons formality in favor of picturesque irregularity.

Once more many liberties have been taken with the paradigm. The pronaos is hexastyle Greek Doric, there is no second row of columns, the metopes depict seraphim, the entablature changes from Greek to Roman when it encircles the cylinder. The massive wings butt directly against the cylinder without transition and obscure its basic form. The upper entablature has an ornamental cresting of Greek origin. Within, there is a circular aisle separated from the nave by a row of polished black columns, a notable departure from the single static space in Rome. This is an area set apart for memorials to the architects of Genoa, an honor infrequently assigned to members of that profession. Again we have a liberal mingling of antique elements which coalesce to form something characteristic of the time in which it was built.

Survivals of Neoclassicism After 1840

Sarti and Marchese

Antonio Sarti (1797–1880), an architect to whom all architectural historians are indebted for founding the Biblioteca Comunale Sarti in the Accademia di San Luca, worked in a Neoclassical vein in Rome. The Villa Torlonia has been mentioned above.[103] His most conspicuous building is the Manifattura dei Tabacchi on the Piazza Mastai in Rome, which was completed in 1863, according to the inscription on the frieze (Figure 99). The manufacture of tobacco was

103. See pp. 149 ff.

Figure 98. Carlo Barabino: Genoa, Staglieno Cemetery, projected before 1825, executed by Giovanni Antonio Resasco, 1844–61

Figure 99. Antonio Sarti: Rome, Manifattura dei Tabacchi, 1859–63

a Vatican monopoly at this time. The factory is an example of the way in which old formulae were blown up to accommodate new functions. In this case the formula is Palladian and everything has been both enlarged and ruthlessly simplified. The central block is eleven bays wide, the end wings three bays each except the attics, which have five bays. The rusticated basement has a mezzanine. The applied temple front is engaged and octastyle. In order to accommodate it, some of the windows of the upper floor have been cut down, whereas beyond the temple front the entablature has been reduced to a cornice. The detail is severely plain, which is appropriate to its industrial function. Sarti is thus seen to have conservatively handled Palladian and Neoclassic ideas.

In the 1840s one of the greatest of the Neoclassical halls of Italy was begun at Pavia, the Aula Magna of the University (Figure 100). The architect was Giuseppe Marchese. The façade is a temple front of six Corinthian columns *in antis* under a pediment standing on three low steps, with a low tower above. The interior is a version of the Vitruvian-Palladian basilica, of which a much earlier version was built at the York Assembly Rooms by Lord Burlington between 1731 and 1732. In the Pavian interior, majesty and weight are stressed far more than in the York example. The effect is handsome, masculine, and stately, more like Robert Adam's hall at Kedleston House and not without echoes of the grandiose projects of Boullée.[104] The top light of the apse is such a feature. An unusual detail is the way in which the bases of the order are allowed to project over the sill on which they stand. This room is roughly contemporary with St. George's Hall in Liverpool (1839), which was considerably larger and also freer, but closely linked in form and concept.

Antonelli

The last of the great classical masters of nineteenth-century Italy was Alessandro Antonelli (1798–1888) who is justly famed for creating the highest building in Europe south of the Alps in the Mole Antonelliana, formerly a synagogue, which he began in Turin in 1863 and which is beyond question the most lofty columnar masonry building ever built (Figure 104).

Antonelli was a native of Piedmont and most of his work, finished and unfinished, is there. He was a man of genius, original, dogged, opinionated, and one who walked with grandiose visions. His Neoclassicism shows itself in an unusual fixation on the orders, which to him were more basic than the wall. However gigantic his project, it was always built within the rules of conventional masonry procedures, though these were sometimes pushed beyond hitherto accepted limits. In this he is like Gottfried Semper (1803–79) and Antoni Gaudí (1852–1926) and unlike E.-E. Viollet-le-Duc (1814–79) or Gustave Eiffel (1832–1923), who explored the possibilities of metallic construction.

104. See p. 11.

Figure 100. Giuseppe Marchese: Pavia, University, Great Hall, c.1845–50

An early work which has progressed very slowly since it was begun in 1830 and is still unfinished, due in part to calamitous earthquakes, is the Santuario del Crocifisso di Boca (Figure 101) in an excessively isolated position. Piedmont has many such sanctuaries on its hills, such as Juvarra's Superga (1717–31) outside Turin and the Santuario di Vico with its mammoth oval dome.[105] The former is grouped by Wittkower with the Madonna di San Luca (1723–57) by Carlo Francesco Dotti outside Bologna as an expression of eighteenth-century taste for such shrines in elevated places.[106] Antonelli at Boca was attempting to achieve a fantastically tall nave. The apse end, with its gates, courtyard, and minor buildings, uses a Piranesian trick of making a great structure look more immense by surrounding it with minor structures. The unfinished capitals of the façade recall the similar ones at San Giovanni Battista at Carignano of the middle of the eighteenth century by Conte Benedetto Alfieri, with its unique U-shaped interior. The entrance porch is composed of six columns set between terminal piers standing on a raised platform reached by both stairs and ramps. The ends of this porch are extended to the sides, an idea found earlier at the Panthéon in Paris, but terminate in piers, not columns. The member which supports the re-entrant angle is a column and not, as one would expect, a pier. The intercolumniations of the extensions are very wide. Typical of Antonelli is the lavish use of orders of varying sizes within and without. The round-headed opening is used here for windows and arcades.

At Novara both San Gaudenzio (Figure 102) and the Duomo (Figure 103) bear the imprint of Antonelli's imagination. The former, a large early Baroque church begun in 1577 by Pellegrino, was radically altered in 1841 by the addition of a dome and spire over the crossing of 1679. This remarkable structure reaches a height of 121 meters and is said to have been built without recourse to metal. It totally dwarfs the nearby campanile and contrasts its cylinders with the former's prisms. The method of composition is typical of Antonelli—the multiplication of stories, the only way in which one can achieve great height within the traditional confines of orders and entablatures. The pointed dome is supported on two zones, the upper one narrower than the lower, both consisting of circular Corinthian colonnades over pilastered basements, and is crowned by a pilastered attic. The ribbed dome is steeply pointed, and from its apex emerges a slender, rocket-like spire with more columned layers. The effect of lightness and upward movement contradicts the traditional technique and forms. It is overpoweringly dramatic when seen from the closely built narrow streets surrounding it, an effect common in Italian cities.

One thinks of the iron domes built at this time: in St. Isaac's Cathedral by

105. One of the ingenious constructions of the century.
106. Wittkower, *Art and Architecture,* pp. 255, 279.

Figure 101. Alessandro Antonelli: Boca, Santuario, 1830 ff.

Figure 102. Alessandro Antonelli: Novara, San Gaudenzio, dome and spire, 1841–88

August Montferrand between 1817 and 1857 in St. Petersburg, over the reading room of the British Museum in the 1850s by Sydney Smirke, and on the Capitol in Washington, D.C., after the scheme established in 1855. It would appear that Antonelli was aware of this trend toward lofty domes but could emulate them only in masonry, since Italian industry was not yet able to fabricate large metal structures. Too, he may have felt that he was more "correct" in using metal only for ornament. It was during these decades that there was a world-wide striving for tall buildings—in the buildings named above, in church spires, and in the verticality of Victorian Gothic towers in England.

The Duomo of Novara, which Antonelli also completed, does not aim to compete with San Gaudenzio in height but rather to outdo it in the number and variety of its columns. Tarchiani calls this Early Christian.[107] The extensive use of columns within and without may have been influenced by the celebrated rebuilding of San Paolo f. l. m., which was still in progress in Rome. In spite of his addiction to columns, one can feel that Antonelli was not a pure Neoclassicist; he used so many Renaissance devices—pilasters, framing bands, arcuated and molded windows, and blind tabernacles—and he never eschewed ornament. There may have been something vaguely Early Christian, namely the columnar galleries running along the clerestory and up the gable, but since the latter is not arcaded and stands precariously above a large Roman window, the context is different. Furthermore, as one's eye travels downward, it encounters batteries of the Corinthian order at three different, larger sizes: those applied to the exterior wall of the nave, wholly gratuitous structurally since they are part of a second external perforated wall system; the next larger size, which stands in marshaled rows at street level, extending along the side walls of the church and enclosing a grandiose *quadriportico* like that of San Paolo f. l. m. in Rome; and the third and largest order which forms an aggressive temple front projecting out into the narthex as the climax of this hierarchy of orders. Through it one can see the returned ends of the narthex colonnades pointing up the gigantic size of the main order, which is the only one to have channeling. The high altar is also a great Antonellian confection full of bravura and scenic effects.

The fourth of his major buildings is Turin's Mole Antonelliana, already mentioned (Figure 104).[108] So great was the interest taken in this ambitious project that it ultimately became a civic museum. Its final height was 167.50 meters, about half that of the Eiffel Tower and within two meters of the Washington Monument (completed in 1884). But unlike the other two giants, the one in Turin contained a large room projected for use as a synagogue. Like the Washington one it was built entirely without structural metal. The repetitive simple module of the lower stories suggests utilitarian or low-ranking civil buildings

107. Tarchiani, *Ottocento,* p. 47.
108. See p. 193.

Figure 103. Alessandro Antonelli: Novara, Cathedral, remodelled, 1854–69

rather than a religious edifice. As usual with this architect, the grandiose pile is built up like a coral reef of small units, layers, and sublayers. This is particularly noticeable in the zone below the arcuated clerestory, where four colonnades of twenty columns each frame a square space. Above this, the pointed square dome rises very high to support a motive which inescapably suggests a dovecote in the form of a villa: a four-sided, four-pedimented, two-storied structure with airy colonnades on both stories. A short conical section follows and supports a pagoda-like spire of eight additional stories or layers, recalling the well-known pagodas at Kew and Chanteloup, particularly the latter, which is likewise a pagoda in form and classical in its details. The square dome is not a common Italian feature though it may be found on other synagogues. Regrettably the spire has proved vulnerable to wind. Thirty-seven meters of it were destroyed in 1953. It is being restored. It is a truly remarkable edifice, and one characteristic of many aspects of the nineteenth century: the competition for extreme height, the hesitation to use wholly new forms or new means of construction, the megalomaniac ambitions of the architect supported by an enthusiastic and equally coarse-fibered public, all of which combine to produce a work with an eclectic vocabulary and a creative form.

Antonelli's other work cannot be reviewed in detail, save to mention another oddity, a small apartment house on the Corso San Maurizio in Turin, which is one narrow bay wide on the avenue front. The width of the building made it a fertile source of such legends as: that it was built to prove that so narrow a building could be made to stand up; that it was the only lot Antonelli could afford (indeed, he lived in it for many years, perhaps to quiet skeptics); and that it was an experiment in reinforced concrete, etc.

Antonelli, as has been said above, was the last Italian Neoclassicist of the nineteenth century. For his time he was a wild man and a romantic architect. Given to self-expression, defying gravity and convention, he became a hero. It does seem, however, that he is a restricted one, since his contribution to modern architecture as a whole is very limited and even to that of Italy not very noteworthy, although some enthusiastic claims have recently been made for him.[109]

Neoclassicism in the broadest sense never died out completely anywhere, and it is even less threatened with extinction in Mediterranean countries. One can say that all those cinquecento palazzi of Gaetano Koch, such as those on the Piazza dell'Esedra and the American Embassy in Rome, belong to it. They express the same love for bygone, if not ancient, forms. They are revived with the same freedom and dilution that masters like Cagnola and Barabino used upon themes of greater antiquity—a blending of veneration and innovation. These themes were revived again, and for didactic purposes, by Mussolini.

It is remarkable that Neoclassicism in Italy accomplished so much in view of

109. See p. 407.

Figure 104. Alessandro Antonelli: Turin, Mole Antonelliana, 1863–88

the incessant political difficulties. Perhaps the strength of her magnificent architectural traditions carried her through. Her architects were no more nor less successful than those elsewhere in re-employing antique forms for new buildings, thus giving their cities many new monuments expressive of Italy's age-old feeling for monumentality, the sublime, the noble, and the elegant, as well as the picturesque. This last quality was more readily achieved by the use of more picturesque vocabularies, as we shall see in the following period and chapter.

3

The Picturesque System and Medieval Vocabularies

3

The Picturesque System and
Medieval Vocabularies

Introduction

Picturesque Eclecticism, with its preference for variety of form and color, intricacy of composition, roughness of textures, irregularity of outline, and movement of masses (Virim), was becoming a common denominator in western architecture. The full picturesque system, however, was rarely applied in Italy to urban buildings. Asymmetry was reserved for rural projects like castles and villas. This was different from the practices of the Anglo-Saxons and Northern Europeans. The recourse to national medieval vocabularies was shared by all countries. But Neo-Medievalism came late to Italy. At first, as we have seen above, it emulated the national styles of other countries and particularly of England. Later, an interest in Italy's own medieval styles arose, intensified by the Austrian repression and the straining toward independence and unification. Byron, Leopardi, Manzoni, Cavour, Garibaldi, and many other patriots fanned the slow fires which finally, in 1870, melted down the old bars and chains. Hence the feelings conveyed by Neo-Medievalism included nationalism, idealism, and veneration of the Middle Ages. What had begun as a folly ended up as a serious attempt to express sublimity.

The most outspoken and influential architectural high priests of the mid-nineteenth century were Medievalists: Viollet-le-Duc in France; Pugin, Ruskin, and the Camdensians in Britain; Richard Upjohn, A. J. Downing, Peter B. Wight, and Russell Sturgis in America; and in Italy Pietro Selvatico (1803–80) and Camillo Boito (1836–1914). Many of these men were contemporaries. They all came to their prime at the close of the long reign of classical ideals to which they reacted by championing the minor but persistent current of medievalism. The distinctive note in the Italian version of it was that of heroism associated with the Risorgimento.[1] To many of these men medieval architecture

---

1. Liliana Grassi, *Camillo Boito* (Milan, 1959), p. 13.

was not only their own, rather than something belonging to the Ancients, but it was held to be more "truthful." This was an idea which, consciously or not, was partly due to the visual structural system so noticeable in the novel and daring work of the successful engineers of their own time, though the Italian variants of this international movement were not usually so structurally expressive as those of northern countries. In this relative indifference to expressive structure, they were true to their own traditions, in which the technically able vaults of wide span achieved in Florence, Bologna, and Milan were subordinated to the decorative effects. Some exceptions will be described in the next chapter.

Pietro Estense Selvatico published a volume of essays, which included some on architecture.[2] One of these was a lecture given to the students at the Academy in Venice in 1856. In this he explains that, in his view, the study of architectural history has hitherto failed to stress the influence of materials on design, since an architectural idea may be very much impaired by the limitations of the material available. The architect, he said, should be taught construction first and design second. His study of history should make him aware of the influence of granite on Egyptian edifices and of fine marble on those of Greece. Similarly the Romans exploited their clay, the French their sandstone, and the Swiss their wood. This was being said just as improved transportation was about to make any of these materials available to all these people, and just as the new materials, iron and glass, were beginning to be exploited all over Europe. He continued by saying that the academic concentration on the Italian styles of the Cinquecento was a mistake, since they were systematized, cold, inopportune, and lasted only a short while before being superseded by "a rival as licentious and corrupt as the other was severe of taste and form." In imitating the models of antiquity, architecture ceased to be an art and became a craft, "a matter of construction not of aesthetics."[3] Durand, Percier, and Fontaine had, he thought, sterilized a ready-made architecture. Clearly, Selvatico writes, the architecture of the past twenty years in France, Germany, Russia, and England, although tainted with eclecticism, is better suited to our present manner of living since it is attuned to our feelings and ideas, which are derived from the Middle Ages.

This leads him to his main point, that the Italians were complacently following Vignola and Palladio and almost ignoring their own Lombardic and arcuated styles, except for his predecessor, Japelli, who had initiated the study of them. He warns students against seeking after novelty for its own sake, saying that novelty should lie in the concept, not in the elements used to carry it out, for tradition is the cornerstone of civilization and architecture is its interpreter. From this he concludes that students should apply themselves to the study of their own medieval styles, all of them beautiful and reflecting the ideas and

2. Pietro Estense Selvatico, *Scritti d'arte* (Florence, 1859).
3. Ibid., pp. 293 ff.

customs of the Italian people. Vitruvius must be abandoned. The day would soon come when the public would approve buildings executed in this spirit, noble in inspiration, varied, original, and growing out of customs and needs.[4]

He emphasized on another occasion the fact that Venice, the London of the Middle Ages, was rich with a great variety of noble buildings of the arcuated and Arabic styles, from which could be derived an architecture superior to that of Rome, Florence, or Segesta because of its picturesque variety of line and delicacy of ornament. As with Ruskin and G. E. Street it was the forms and colors of Italian, and particularly Venetian, architecture of the Middle Ages which evoked the greatest response. The allusion to London is perhaps a key; the architecture of both cities represents a high level of material display reflecting their power and wealth. This is also indicated by his references to the Exposition of 1851, and to the Panoptico in Leicester Square of 1853, both approved for their machine-made art. Note, too, the names of the English architects and manufacturers which he gives individually: Scott, Carpentier (sic), Cundy, Ferry, Pugin, Minton, Barton, Hardemann, and Boisserees.[4a]

Selvatico, owing to his receptive mind, wide reading, and extensive travels, was simply bringing the new message to a lagging Italy. He lacked Ruskin's eloquence. His style is much less "Italian" than that of the English author of the *Stones of Venice,* nor is there the moral fervor of Pugin, though he mentions the Christianity of the styles of the Middle Ages. An awareness of the structural potential of new materials is absent. It had not yet been made a doctrine anywhere; Viollet-le-Duc and Horatio Greenough were yet to issue their proclamations. The nearest approach to this idea in Selvatico is, on one hand, his response to the machine in all its revolutionary character, and, on the other hand, his appeal for truth of structure and materials, though this is less stressed than in later writers.[5]

The torch for Medieval-Nationalism was taken up by Camillo Boito, who followed von Schmidt at the Brera.[6] Friedrich von Schmidt (1825–91), who later worked for fifteen years on the continuation of the cathedral of Cologne, taught architecture at the Brera from 1857 to 1859 but resigned when Milan was lost by the Austrians. He was highly esteemed in Milan, and though urged to remain at his post, he declined. While he was in Milan, he was engaged on the restoration of Sant'Ambrogio and taught Carlo Maciachini and Gaetano Landriani. His teaching strongly influenced his youthful successor at the Brera, Boito, who filled the gap left by Schmidt's sudden resignation.[7]

Boito was born in Rome in 1836 and died in Milan in 1914. His family moved

4. Ibid., pp. 305 ff.
4a. Ibid., pp. 371–72.
5. Ibid., p. 295.
6. Grassi, *Boito,* p. 37.
7. Lavagnino, *L'Arte moderna, 1,* 542–43.

to Venice, and Boito studied there under the Neoclassicist-Purist Francesco Lazzari (1791–1856). He also studied in Padua and traveled abroad in Germany and to his mother's native Poland. As a student he had first been taught to purify the designs of the Venetian palaces with the object of correcting "errors."[8] Boito began to oppose this limited curriculum and to follow Selvatico's as yet unpopular principles. He succeeded Selvatico at the age of nineteen, but in 1859, in danger of arrest by the Austrians, he fled to Milan where he shortly thereafter took up von Schmidt's abandoned chair. He kept this position for forty-eight years. Among his famous pupils were Brentano, Beltrami, Moretti, and Sommaruga.[9] He believed in a stripped medieval style which was so personal that it came to be known as the "Stile Boito." It had marked affinities with High Victorian Gothic.

He wrote, in *Architettura del medio evo in Italia,* that the house should be the characteristic architecture of the modern day, whereas, regrettably, the character of modern building was being established according to economic and banking values, ostentatious on the one side, parsimonious on the other. He cited the Ministero delle Finanze in Rome, the Cassa di Risparmio in Milan, and the Banca Nazionale in Florence. He noted that railroad stations and markets should provide architecture with new opportunities.[10] He was vividly aware of the wide range of the eclecticism of his day. He felt that an architecture suitable to modern Italy was bound to come to united Italy, and that it would be an architecture like that of the Trecento: varied, suited to the needs, climates, and characters of the provinces, worthy of a cultivated society and of the progress of science. In spite of the adverse influences of classical rhetoric and Catholic nostalgia, both of which were fortunately declining, the impulse to be more practical would increase, he thought, and the organic part of architecture would become the main line of development. The program for architecture should limit itself to serving the special function of each building completely. One danger which arose from the traditional divisions of construction, distribution, and beauty was that beauty was sometimes considered to be independent from the other two. If all three were thought of as interconnected, the discovery of a new symbolic language would follow. There was, however, the essential factor of a national tradition or language. America, which was vast, powerful, and very rich, he observed, found no national style perhaps because it lacked the aid of past centuries. Boito disregarded the fact that the Americans had brought their cultural roots with them from Western Europe. He continued by

8. Ibid., *1,* 548.

9. For Brentano, see p. 232; Beltrami, p. 328; Moretti, p. 407; and Sommaruga, p. 429.

10. Grassi, *Boito,* p. 29, quotes from Boito's preface to his *Architettura del medio evo in Italia* (Milan, 1880).

saying that art, unlike science which can start freshly from new discoveries, is based, like literature, upon a language. He frequently uses the term "organic" as the key adjective for good architecture, and in one place says that architecture originates in utility and has for its object the embellishment of utility.[11]

Boito's doctrine was sensible and, for the most part, clearly thought out. He did not carry the idea of functionalism to the exaggerated claims of pure utility made for it in the twenties of this century. He always kept the useful and the beautiful in balance. In his own work, he made little or no use of modern materials but felt free to adapt and simplify traditional forms. His early style, as seen in work of the 1860s and 1870s, has much in common with some aspects of High Victorian Gothic, though it tended to get richer with time. The common features include the emphasis on flat planes, the positive articulation of changes in stress by changes in materials, and consequently a delight in structural coloration. The acrid effects and brutal realism of Frank J. Furness in Philadelphia were present but toned down. He was not as inventive as Viollet-le-Duc. His influence spread from what he taught and what he wrote more than from what he built.

An important part of Medievalism was the restoration of medieval monuments. The architect continued, however, to be creative rather than archaeological in this rôle. Viollet-le-Duc's comments are typical of the restorers of his day: "To restore a building is not to preserve it, to repair it, or to rebuild it; it is to reinstate it in a condition of completeness which could never have existed at any given time."[12] In other words, it is a highly subjective creative act in which imagination plays a larger part than archaeology. Similar ideals, though widespread in the eighteenth and nineteenth centuries, shock us today as much by their self-confident arrogance as by their indifference to historic truth. In another passage Viollet-le-Duc implies that the link between the restorer and the architect is creative ability:

> Italy, imbued though it is with local traditions of undeniable power, does not abstain from efforts to free itself from them, as far as they hinder the development of novel conditions imposed on the architect. It is restoring ancient buildings with a highly developed critical intelligence; and this is a step towards the application of the same spirit of criticism to novel conceptions . . . the Italians have the good sense not to separate their architects into two classes,—the restorers of ancient buildings and the constructors of those adapted to novel requirements.[13]

11. Ibid., p. 13.

12. Viollet-le-Duc, *Dictionnaire raisonné de l'architecture française du XIe au XVIe siècle* (10 vols. Paris, 1854–68), *8*, 14.

13. Viollet-le-Duc, *Discourses on Architecture,* trans. Benjamin Bucknall (2 vols. Boston, 1889), *2*, 387–88.

The first class in his view is at least as well fitted as the second to construct. This is partially special pleading, since its writer had fewer opportunities to build *de nuovo* than he would have liked and had received his own training in architecture largely by studying and restoring medieval monuments. Archaeological exactitude is not mentioned. The point of view of the Camdensians in England was, however, nearly as permissive if one observes their practice. The totally archaeological approach to restoration is a twentieth-century concept, and is still honored as often in the breach as otherwise.[14] Another hallmark of nineteenth-century Medievalism is the insensitivity to scale. It is impossible in a photograph like that of Santa Croce (Figure 110), without people or vehicles, to grasp that it is an enormous building. The height of about one hundred and twenty-five feet is not appreciable; even the flight of steps does not give the clue.

The air of economy seen at Santa Croce and elsewhere also strikes us as regrettably unmedieval. The severe, linear geometrical decoration like that on the Baptistry is hard and machinelike, which may have been the case at the latter when it was new. But there the variations from bay to bay are sufficiently noticeable to give it vitality. Most nineteenth-century restorers ran into this problem: how to reproduce the spontaneous quality which is associated with medieval architecture. Perhaps they felt that this quality was due more to time and neglect than to intention. Therefore they sought what they assumed the original master builders had sought in exactness of finish but failed to achieve for lack of power-driven machines. Or this may be an example of accepting the taste of one's own time as the logical conclusion of an evolutionary process. Or if the "hand-made" quality was appreciated, it may have been too costly to reproduce.

The consequence of all of these factors, such as creativity, scale, dryness, and economy, is that the expert can easily distinguish a Neo-Medieval building from a genuine one.

Early Examples

In the first quarter of the century Medieval forms were used principally in stage sets. Among these there is a notable series by Antonio Basoli of Bologna recorded in engravings. An occasional funerary monument, such as in that in Milan for Francesco I in 1835, also preceded the serious revival.[15]

An early example of the decorative use of Gothic forms occurred in Piedmont in the garden pavilion, La Margheria (Figure 105), at Racconigi (1834–39) and attributed to Pelagio Palagi (1775–1860), the decorator-architect. Racco-

14. Recent examples of this are the new Spanish chapel at the Cloisters in New York, and the Arnold House at Lincoln, Rhode Island.

15. Paolo Mezzanotte and Giacomo Bascapè, *Milano nell'arte e nella storia* (Milan, 1948), pp. 118 ff.

Figure 105. Pelagio Palagi: Racconigi, Palazzo Reale, La Margheria, 1834–39

Figure 106. B. C. Marandono: Biella, Cathedral, façade detail, c.1825

nigi was at that time one of the seats of the Savoys, whose relatively liberal kingdom also saw the first steps toward freedom.

At about the same time, the cathedral at Biella received a porch, façade, and interior decoration in Gothic (Figure 106). The various works undertaken here have not been clearly recorded. There was activity in 1772, 1795, 1825, and 1840.[16] The porch could have been derived from an orangery. It is an elegant pastiche, with lofty arcades of pointed arches supported by clusters of columns, the capitals of which have distinctly Egyptian detail: the spandrels are as Moorish as they are Gothic, as is the cresting along the parapet. Egypt returns in the obelisks clustered on pedestals. The roof of the porch is ribbed. The iron grills between the piers are Gothic. The interior walls of the apse are richly painted with imitation arcades, tracery, and diaper work in light stone colors, and have small rose windows. It is a scene painter's fantasy and could serve as the setting for an opera. There is a playful air to it which is not equaled by anything surviving in Italy from this period except the "Pedrocchino" in Padua (Figure 54).

There were also some Medieval elements in the architectural projects of the period. In Rome, bits of some richly treated rooms in the destroyed Palazzo Torlonia are preserved in the Museo di Roma. In Rome, too, the Villa Mills once stood.

The Villa Mills was an improbable Gothic mansion, an example of uninhibited Romanticism. It stood on the Palatine, of all places, from 1818 until 1926. Some of it was reconstructed from the Domus Augustana and some from the Renaissance Villa Mattei or Spada. The Gothicizing was done by Charles Andrew Mills (1760–1846) and his friend Sir William ("Topographical") Gell (1777–1836). Its spires and pointed arches were painted a lively red. Everywhere the symbols of England, Scotland, and Ireland were to be seen—the rose, the thistle, and the shamrock. Mills had served the British Government in the West Indies before retiring to Rome, and Sir William Gell was a member of the Society of Dilettanti, the Society of Antiquarians, and the like. He published books on Troy, Ithaca, Pompeii, and Rome.[17]

Both "truthfulness" and nationalism are expressed in the Medieval church façades built or completed in nineteenth-century Italy. As has been emphasized in Chapter Two, the adding of new fronts to older, unfinished churches was a major architectural activity in Italy. Those which had not received some form

16. T.C.I., *Piemonte* (Milan, 1940), p. 597.

17. H. V. Morton, *A Traveller in Rome* (London, 1957), pp. 417 ff. Margaret R. Scherer, *Marvels of Ancient Rome* (New York, 1955), pp. 55–56 and pl. 86. A. Bartoli, "La Villa Mills sul Palatino," *Rassegna contemporanea, 1* (1908), fasc. 1, pp. 89–102. Visitors included Queen Caroline, "Madame Mère," Lady Granville, Lord Byron, Sir William Drummond, Lady Blessington, Sir Walter Scott, Edward Dodwell, and Henry Fox. The successive owners included Colonel Robert Smith and the Order of the Visitation.

Figure 107. Pietro Selvatico: Trento, San Pietro, façade, 1848–50

of temple front now received a Medieval one. One of the earliest, after that of Milan, was added to San Pietro at Trento (Venezia Tridentina) from 1848–50 by Pietro Selvatico (Figure 107). His clients usually, but not always, allowed Selvatico to practice what he preached. At San Pietro, begun when he was forty-five, there is, however, no emphasis on structure. The façade looks like an enlargement of a triptych. A century earlier, Walpole and his friends had taken similar liberties with the scale and associations of the motives they revived for Strawberry Hill. To the purist such freedom was deplorable, but to those who merely sought evocation by means of association the purists seemed pedantic. Sir George Gilbert Scott's famous sneer that archaeologists would criticize moldings if they were "half an hour too late" was attacking an anti-creative attitude which no Victorian Gothic architect could tolerate.

At Trento the vigorous early tower with its broached spire contrasts with the atectonic handling of the façade elements. The fitting of a new façade to an old church seems always to have presented great difficulties to the designer. The numerous competitions for the façades of San Petronio at Bologna, San Lorenzo and the Duomo at Florence, and the Duomo at Milan, both in Renaissance and modern times, demonstrate this. The façade schemes of Alberti and Palladio, which served their successors so well, were no help to the Neo-Medievalists who could not solve their problems by interweaving or otherwise adapting classical temple fronts. Selvatico's solution, with its floating main portal, its cornice now flat and now raked, and its pairing of buttresses, belongs to no architectural family. It can be read as two symmetrical compositions built up around the aisle windows and loosely connected with each other by an ogee arch drawn lightly across the surface of the nave. Only the ornament suggests a real knowledge of Gothic.

At about the same time an equally factitious structure went up in Florence on the old Via del Prato, the Palazzo-Studio "der Villa" (Figure 108). The façade of this flat-fronted building with six stories of varying heights was an ingenious but unconvincing display of ornate Gothic motives—suggesting architecture used like a billboard to attract attention, or like a *stuccatore* showing off his stock of molds. The scale is that of jewelry at one point, of a *duomo* at another, and of a carved picture frame at a third.

In the suburbs a much more serious work was underway. John Temple Leader was restoring the eleventh-century castle of Vincigliata near Florence, which he had found in ruins and where later he was visited by Queen Victoria. It is hard to determine how much he had to go on and how much he invented. Rebuilding became a kind of hobby with him, an absorbing activity which has some Beckfordian aspects. He discovered a talented youth, Giuseppe Fancelli, and trained him as his personal architect. In its present aspect, his castle (Figure 109) is

Figure 108. Anonymous: Florence, Palazzo "der Villa," c.1850

remarkably clean and free from clutter, and, what is rare, the masonry is free of the usual stucco coating.[18]

The fact that Leader was British is probably significant. Florence was the center of an Anglo-American colony of which the English components would have approved an active program of restoration such as was flourishing in England. So we find three important new Medieval works being undertaken there: at Santa Croce (Figure 110) a new campanile by Gaetano Baccani (1792–1867) and a new façade by Nicola Matas (1798–1872). These works had been begun before Florence became the temporary capital of a nearly united Italy. The third was the completion of the façade of the Duomo.[19]

The façade of Santa Croce was executed in a Tuscan idiom. There had been a competition held for the design, and Matas' project was selected over that of Luigi Veneziani who had built several chapels there in the 1830s.[20] Matas' project, outlined in 1842, was not begun until 1857 and only completed in 1863. The model can be seen in the Museo dell'Opera. It is said to be based on an old seventeenth-century project which in itself owed something to the flanks of the Duomo. As can be seen in the Zocchi etching of 1744 and the pre-façade, post-campanile photograph, there was almost nothing there to go on (Figure 111).[21] In addition to the Duomo, Matas seems to have drawn upon the Porta della Mandorla for his portals, and the *tricuspidale* (three-gabled façade scheme) with pinnacles could have been suggested by Orvieto and Siena. The elaborate polychromatic incrustation had ample precedent right at hand in the Duomo, Baptistry, Campanile, San Miniato, and Santa Maria Novella. As will be seen later, in discussing the complex history of the new Duomo façade the question of tricuspidale or single pedimental front was a matter of intense disagreement among the experts at this time. At Santa Croce, with its relatively low aisles and vast barnlike nave, the former is an appropriately expressive solution, even though there was no sign in the old masonry of the new lateral gables, which are copied from those on the flanks. All the other principal elements had good traditional sources. The bareness of some parts and the richness of others, such as the pinnacles, make sharp contrasts. The blunted central gable is awkwardly handled and the height of the base courses is exaggerated in relation to the portals. The whole effect, perhaps inevitably considering the date, is more industrial than religious. We have become so accustomed to the hygienic look of

---

18. An interesting account of two visits to this castle appeared in the Roman periodical, *L'Italia artistica* (1883), *1*, pp. 66 ff. G. Cesare Carraresi had written about it in a romantic vein before Temple Leader bought it in 1855. Twenty-seven years later, he revisited it and admired the restoration. He noted that the architect had died and that the loggia was a memorial to him.

19. See pp. 220 ff.

20. W. Paatz and E. Paatz, *Die Kirchen von Florenz* (6 vols. Frankfurt-Am-Main, 1940–54), *1*, 504, 519.

21. G. Zocchi, *Scelta di XXIV vedute . . . di Firenze* (Florence, 1744), pl. 24.

Figure 109. Giuseppe Fancelli: Vincigliata, Castello dei Visdomini, restoration, c.1855

Figure 110. Nicola Matas: Florence, Santa Croce, façade, 1857–63. Gaetano Baccani: campanile, 1847 ff.

Figure 111. Florence, Santa Croce, unfinished façade, prior to 1857

white tile with narrow bands of contrasting black, seen so effectively in Austrian and German work of the Secession, that we have a prejudice against the use of such decoration for ceremonial buildings.

The campanile, which was finished (1847 ff.) before the new façade was barely started, is more successful (Figure 111). Its bare, unstuccoed walls and strong silhouette fit unobtrusively into the cityscape and pass for most viewers as genuine medieval work. The architect Baccani had had some experience in restoring medieval buildings, such as the façade of the Compagnia della Misericordia and interiors in the Duomo in 1842.[22]

History of the Façades of the Cathedrals of Florence and Milan

Among the scores of such projects two stand out: the competitions for the completion of the façade of the Duomo of Florence and that for redoing again the façade at Milan.

The completion of the façade of the Cathedral of Florence was of interest not only to the Florentines and all of Italy but also to much of Europe. The discussions about it began in 1822 and the work was finally brought to completion in 1887, four years after the death of its architect, Emilio de Fabris (1808–83).

The old Medieval façade, which had never risen more than one-third of the way, was partly Romanesque by Arnolfo di Cambio and partly Gothic by Francesco Talenti, who worked on it from 1355–65, doing the first door and adjoining wall on the right flank (Figure 112). This was entirely out of fashion by 1586 when Bernardo Buontalenti recommended that it be taken down.[23] Then followed a flurry of competitions: 1587, 1596, 1634, 1635, and 1636. Wooden models for many of these have been preserved and can be seen today in the Museo dell'Opera del Duomo.[24] They range from the extreme Mannerism of the project designed by Buontalenti himself to more restrained academic-classic ones. That by Gherardo Silvani (1579–1675) is said to have been the one preferred by the Grand Duke, Ferdinand II. Somewhat astoundingly, it included some Gothic features, such as Gothic towers at the ends, and much marble inlay.[25]

In 1688, a very simple, academically conceived façade was painted on a

22. He could also design Neoclassically. See p. 135.

23. Jacopo Sansovino had designed and built a temporary façade in wood in 1515. It was apparently based on a design by Giuliano Sangallo, and displayed twelve Corinthian columns. Vasari, *Le Vite . . .* , ed. by G. Milanesi (9 vols. Florence, 1906), *7,* 494 ff.

24. Vera Daddi Giovannozzi, "I modelli dei secoli XVI e XVII per la facciata di Santa Maria del Fiore," *L' Arte, 17* (1936), 33 ff. See also Adolfo Venturi, *Storia dell'arte italiana* (24 vols. Milan, 1901–39), *11,* part 2, pp. 494 ff.

25. See summary of my paper "Mannerist Churches in Florence," in *College Art Journal, 1* (1942), 73. There were numerous projects for the façade of San Petronio at Bologna, including Medieval, Renaissance, and Palladian projects.

Figure 112. Arnolfo di Cambio: Florence, Cathedral, unfinished façade, as it appeared c.1500

Figure 113. Florence, Cathedral, façade prior to 1868

brick-and-stucco base according to designs by Ercole Graziani (Figure 113).[26] This façade stood until 1868, when a new design had been settled on, but it would have been of much aid to the judges and competitors concerned with a new façade if it had been removed to permit some archaeological study of the surviving old work, which might have guided them toward the original intention if they were so inclined. This sensible step was not taken at the logical moment.

Throughout the first half of the nineteenth century, the incongruous factitious Renaissance façade, which clashed with the Medieval environment, bothered citizens and critics. In 1822 Giovanni Silvestri (1796–1873) had proposed a Gothic one.[27] Nicola Matas, who erected the new Medieval façade at Santa Croce, proposed one, and in 1852 yet another was published by a Swiss, Johann Georg Mueller.[28] In 1859 an official competition was announced under the patronage of the Grand Duke, who had been urged on by his favorite architect, Emilio de Fabris. Ten years later de Fabris ended up with the commission in his own hands.

De Fabris was of humble origin and had to struggle to achieve his education. After studying with Baccani, he won a fellowship to Rome at the age of thirty and later came to the attention of the Grand Duke, who took him with him on long trips to paint views of antiquity. In 1858, when the completion of the Florentine façade again became a live issue, he was called in to advise on the merits of the existing collection of projects. Since these were largely of the sixteenth and seventeenth centuries, they were no longer acceptable. The proceedings for the next decades are a comedy of errors, if not a scandalously high-handed, politically controlled series of unethical practices, entirely characteristic, however, of the universal attitude toward architectural competitions in the nineteenth century and not wholly unknown a century later.

In August 1859, the proposal of the *Associazione Fiorentina* to erect a new façade was approved. De Fabris had advised that a new competition be held since he found nothing suitable and he felt that modern architects should be given an opportunity. In April 1859, the Commission announced a competition open to artists of all nations and offered prizes ranging from £ 12,000 to £ 2,000. Ten days later, due to political disturbances, the competition was canceled. After an interval of a year the Commission was reappointed by Prince Eugène of Savoy, the capital of expanding Italy having meanwhile been transferred to Florence from Turin. Although no design had yet been adopted, King Victor Emanuel II laid the cornerstone. The competition was revived and a new announcement made in November 1861, with a deadline of September 1862. No conditions were laid down until general ones were established in Jan-

26. Paatz, *Kirchen, 3,* 336.
27. Ashton R. Willard, *History of Modern Italian Art* (New York, 1900), p. 530.
28. Ibid.

uary 1863, after the designs had been received: the design must be in profound and complete harmony with the rest of the building.[29] The jury was a distinguished group consisting of the heads of the principal academies of Italy, as follows: Alessandro Antonelli from Turin, Baccani from Florence, Fortunato Lodi from Bologna, Enrico Alvino from Naples, Boito from Milan, Pietro Camporese from Rome, and Scala from Venice. Nearly everyone on the Commission took to print at one time or another as the controversies raged.

The basic and fundamental problem, still open to argument, was the nature of the crowning feature. Should it have three gables, "tricuspidale," following the precedent of the Spanish Chapel at Santa Maria Novella and the façades of Orvieto and Siena, or should it be "basilican," that is, end in a great single pediment or gable? The pro-basilica group felt that the surviving masonry indicated that this was the intention of the medieval builders. If one is to attempt an opinion today—realizing that the nave, dome, and other features had not been built in conformity to the designs of the thirteenth and fourteenth centuries, and that the antique design for the façade showed sloping terminations to the aisles leading up to a single gable over the nave as in the seventeenth-century work— one is still unsure of what the correct decision should have been. The antique sketch shows some irresolution in other matters, such as the disposition of the oculi, of the corner treatment, of the deep slot on the left which has no counterpart on the right, and numerous other differences in fenestration and detail from one side to the other. Careful study of the masonry at the very beginning of the sixties might have indicated the dates at which these features appeared, and thus, as Beltrami argued, might have guided the committee in formulating a detailed program.[30] This, however, was not the spirit of the nineteenth century, which was more inclined to the belief that what was wanted was a sympathetic original work which would be an idealized version of what might have been built in the Middle Ages. This attitude prevailed, and the existing façade shows very little regard for the previous work. For example, the two ancient, deep, vertical, round-headed recesses were ignored.

Forty-two submissions were received, and were judged after the Secretary of the Commission had elaborated one or two additional general requirements. The Committee gave close scrutiny to sixteen of the superior solutions, but found none of them worthy of the larger premiums, and so gave three lesser awards to Count Carlo Ceppi of Turin, Professor Mariano Falcini of Florence, and Vilhelm Petersen of Denmark, with less valuable awards to six others. Twenty-two of the designs submitted had been tricuspidale, but the Committee

29. The details of this confused and controversial history can be found in Willard, p. 530, and in a magnificently illustrated folio: Luigi Del Moro, *La Facciata di Santa Maria del Fiore* (Florence, 1888), as well as in Paatz, *1,* 504 ff.

30. *Edilizia moderna, 8* (1899), 45 ff.

now favored a basilical effect. In May the Committee decided to try again, and invited new submissions from the three principal winners named above and seven other architects. Count Ceppi declined. Falcini and Petersen accepted. The other members of the select group included six of the men who had served on the first jury. One suspects, although they were as well qualified as any Italian architects of the period, that self-interest had played some rôle in this development. The other members of the new group were Antonio Cipolla and the Grand Duke's protégé, de Fabris. He had worked on a design for the first competition which he had not completed in time. He may have been waiting to see how the wind would blow. When he accepted an invitation to enter the second competition, he said that it was his patriotic duty to do so. Again the announced deadline was revised and the problem of new jurors arose, since so many of the old ones were now competitors. Selvatico, aged sixty-one, was selected to organize the jury, and he chose the Marchese d'Azeglio and Messrs. Edward Van der Nüll, Emil von Förster, Malvezzi, Giovanni Duprè, and Monti. Viollet-le-Duc was considered. The jury was not chosen until January 1865, although the submitted designs had been on view since July 1864. In view of the opinions expressed by the previous jury, only one tricuspidale design was submitted and this was by de Fabris (Figure 114). A pamphlet by de Fabris was published posthumously, defending his nonconformity.[31] Many of the contestants submitted more than one design, and the jury had a total of forty-three to review. They eliminated twenty-eight quickly, then grouped the balance according to their treatment of the crown. Selvatico himself could not take part in the judgment because his eyes were failing. One judge voted for Petersen's project, one abstained, and the remaining four voted for de Fabris, the one design which disregarded the recommendations of the previous jury. They did, however, advise him to redesign it in some minor particulars. The selection of de Fabris' design was highly unpopular as well as, shall we say, quixotic, and the Commission decided to call another jury. They had to defer to popular opinion, since the costs were being raised by public subscription and much more money was needed.[32]

The most generous donors to the building fund are commemorated, just as the merchants and guilds who gave windows to medieval cathedrals had been immortalized, in the tiers of square panels, bearing their coats-of-arms, above the base. These included Pope Pius IX, the King, and the Grand Duke.

Among the rejected designs were two by Guglielmo Calderini, which were greatly praised by Gottfried Semper.[33]

This time the three leading designs from the first competition, together with

31. Emilio de Fabris, *Del Sistema tricuspidale per il coronamento della facciata di Santa Maria del Fiore e delle sue linee organiche* (Florence, 1886).

32. Del Moro, *La Facciata*, p. 39.

33. Thieme-Becker, "Guglielmo Calderini."

Figure 114. Emilio de Fabris: Florence, Cathedral, façade competition project

the principal ones from the second, were submitted to a jury of outsiders: Viollet-le-Duc, Selvatico, and Professor Giuseppe Bertini, Director of the Brera. In May 1865 Selvatico declared himself in favor of de Fabris' scheme in particular and the tricuspidale parti in general. Viollet-le-Duc also approved de Fabris' scheme, with the reservation that it should be more plastic to accord with the Frenchman's interpretation of Arnolfo di Cambio's intention. Bertini, on the other hand, objected to the tricuspidale idea in general and to de Fabris' project in several other respects as well. The Commission, after reviewing these experts' critiques, was not much further ahead, and in desperation decided to hold a third competition due in July 1866 (later postponed to December so that more Venetians could enter designs). A jury of nine was appointed, on which Viollet-le-Duc declined to serve.

In the final competition, the dogged contestants were de Fabris, Antonio Cipolla, Alvino, Giuseppe Partini, Vilhelm Petersen, and Marco Treves.

The jury's deliberations were prolonged. There was still no agreement on general principles, but finally in March 1867 de Fabris' design was approved five to three, with one judge abstaining. In June the Commission accepted the jury's decision and authorized de Fabris to develop his design. His larger scale drawings were presented and accepted in May 1870. By June 1871 a color presentation of the design was completed at one-tenth full scale and exhibited publicly to encourage contributions. But the troubles were not yet at an end, because the tricuspidale scheme was still unpopular. Preliminary work on the upper parts was held up until an agreement could be reached. In order to arrive at a decision, de Fabris prepared an alternate scheme. It was assumed that this would show the merits of the tricuspidale one to be clearly superior. This was published in 1875. De Fabris had meanwhile been building the new façade, although the legal position was dubious. In August 1875 La Relazione Galeotti was published to quiet public unrest and increase the flow of contributions. A nine-man executive committee was appointed in January 1876. Work on the foundations of the four major buttresses had begun. The marble incrustation began to be applied in 1877. De Fabris fell ill in 1878 and asked that Luigi Del Moro be made his successor. All this time, de Fabris was secretly at work on an alternate scheme, the one that eventually was built, although it was his personal conviction that the tricuspidale solution was the only aesthetically satisfactory one. De Fabris was a practical man. He had his second design in readiness in case he failed to achieve his favorite one. He was insuring, as well as he could, that the final design, whichever it was, would be his. In 1883, the year he died, the work as far as the horizontal galleries was unveiled and well received. Temporary triangular gables were erected in situ over the aisles for public comment and vote. In 1884 it was finally determined to omit lateral gables and complete the façade according to de Fabris' alternate design. This was finished in 1886, and unveiled in May 1887, nearly thirty years after the project had been reborn (Figure 115). That the final design has been moderately well received is remarkable, considering the vicissitudes to which it had been subjected.

Tarchiani said that it was most freely conceived, heavy with ill-digested decoration but executed with great skill.[34] Lavagnino says that it has even less merit than that of Santa Croce, solid and heavy, crowded with every kind of decoration, a banal, dry-as-dust compendium executed with the most extraordinary skill by local craftsmen in whose blood runs an incomparable technique for this craft.[35] Heavy and solid it undoubtedly is, and the great gable is topheavy. The scale is very large. Even though it is derived from the lateral façades, it seems to have been intensified. Selvatico's lighter treatment at Trento emphasizes the clumsiness of this outline.[36]

Recently, critics have been intolerant of richness and bombast and, however unconsciously, have felt that a veneer is not quite honest. It is, I think, necessary to accept the premises of this problem: to complete a façade in harmony with the elaborate polychromed side walls of the building and its celebrated neighbors; to find a composition which would accommodate itself to the existing core and to what little could be determined about its intended effect; and to reconcile this with the honest conviction of every nineteenth-century architect that it was his primary duty to be creative. De Fabris did create a composition without precedent, one which, in a rough way, expressed the existing interior spaces, used materials and a decorative system indigenous to the region, and also conformed to the late nineteenth-century reverence for sumptuousness, the spirit which was so exceedingly gratified by Charles Garnier's Paris Opéra. The façade is heavy and rigid, but it took courage even then to introduce on a medieval building such "classical" conceptions as the horizontal cornices, which minimize

34. Tarchiani, *Ottocento*, p. 56.

35. Lavagnino, *L'Arte moderna, 1*, p. 402.

36. Willard, *Modern Italian Art*, p. 537, writes that the façade as built seems to be propelled in a certain direction and then arrested before it reached the point at which it would naturally have come to a standstill. Logically, he said, the removal of the projected gables demanded the elimination of the frieze of statues and the window tracery, but this would have lessened the "absolute beauty" which results from the façade being tied in with the flanks.

The author of the article on de Fabris in *Thieme-Becker* comments that opinion is still divided on its aesthetic merit; the bold veneer of colored marbles laid in bands relates it to the older portions, but the baldacchino is not very successful, and the statues and doors are both without character and damaging to the general impression. The *Enciclopedia Treccani* says that the decoration is over-crowded with detail but the overall effect is one of harmony and grace appropriate to the mass, space, noble simplicity, and structural discipline of the rest of the building. Vincenzo Costantini, *Storia dell'arte italiana* (4 vols. Milan, 1949), *4*, 385, dismisses de Fabris as a meticulous imitator, lacking spirit. Hitchcock, *Architecture*, p. 200, says that although it is better than the façade of Santa Croce, it is carefully archeological and does not come alive in the way that English High Victorian Gothic does.

Figure 115. Emilio de Fabris: Florence, Cathedral, façade, 1867–87

the important diagonals of the old core wall, and to introduce the four massive buttresses instead of developing the original pair of tall, deep recesses. The immense weight of the upper parts in proportion to the lower is purely nineteenth century in spirit and, although clothed in a less aggressive and original idiom than Frank Furness', might otherwise be said to conform to his preference for the overpowering, overhanging quality of the superstructure. There is an almost brutal severity about the silhouette which lacks any of the conventional softening elements, such as pinnacles and turrets or visible pyramidal roofs. Certainly no student of nineteenth-century architecture can fail to recognize the "Virim" of it any more than an expert Medievalist could mistake it for a work of the Middle Ages. It is de Fabris, not di Cambio.

The fantastic chronicle of the façade of the Duomo of Milan is hardly less dramatic. In this respect it conforms with the wrangling that had gone on over the other aspects of its design.

The turmoil of its Medieval beginnings, one of the most interesting chapters in the history of late Medieval architecture, has been splendidly recounted by James Ackerman.[37] The façade had been left unfinished for centuries while the main fabric was slowly progressing. The older temporary or incomplete façades had left few traces. Some early ideas for the façade can be deduced from fragments of sketches, paintings, and engravings, such as those in the Cesariano edition of Vitruvius of 1521. The earliest work on the present façade was begun in the sixteenth century, part of a project in a late Medieval style by Antonio Seregno about 1537. Pellegrini Tibaldi (1527–1600) began work on a much more up-to-date design later in the century, the influence of which remains to this day. His colleague Martino Bassi, who died in 1591, had suggested a screen of colossal Corinthian columns culminating in a pediment considerably wider than the nave. His idea was clearly derived from Michelangelo's proposed façade for St. Peter's in Rome. Bassi's opportunity to substitute his design arose because Tibaldi had been called to Spain to work on the Escorial. It was a proto-Neoclassic design with very little of the Renaissance in it. Tibaldi proposed, alternatively, to flank the enormous façade by a pair of detached campaniles.

In the early seventeenth century, further discussion continued and additional projects were offered. Ultimately, a proposal was made to continue the lower part according to Tibaldi's project but to give the upper parts a more modern "German" air. No major work could be accomplished, however, until permission had been received from Madrid for altering a corner of the Ducal Palace

---

37. James Ackerman, "Ars sine scientia nihil est; Gothic Theory of Architecture at the Cathedral of Milan," *Art Bulletin, 31* (1949), 84–111. The subsequent history is in Carlo Romussi, *Intorno alla facciata del Duomo di Milano* (Milan, 1903), and two works by Luca Beltrami, *Per la Facciata del Duomo di Milano* (Milan, 1887), and *Il Coronamento nella fronte del Duomo di Milano* (Milan, 1900).

to make room for the corner of the new façade. An attempt was made to use monolithic columns, but the first one broke and this discouraged the committee. Little was done until Carlo Buzzi (died 1658) arrived on the scene in 1638. He proposed to incorporate in medieval designs the Pelligrini-Richini door and window frames, most of which he had executed, and the bases for the great columns. A revised design without campanile was approved in 1653.

The work proceeded slowly, and new designs were made from time to time. These included a curious Gothic-Rococo one by Francesco Castelli in 1657. Bernini commented that, while there was no piazza from which the façade could properly be seen, the addition of a campanile would give the sightseer a hint of the magnificence to be found at its foot. Baldassare Longhena also admired the beauty of Castelli's Gothic project. A surprising number of critics did approve of the use of Gothic in this situation, and some were entirely tolerant of the mixture of styles that would result from the proposed Gothic additions. English and French critics were not yet so liberal. Throughout the following century, the Buzzi project was considered to be the definitive one and artists chose to show it as though completed even though the wood engraving by Marc'Antonio Dal Re of 1741 reveals that the fabric at that time was still lacking any of the proposed Gothic elements. Juvarra presently submitted two designs, one in a pure *romano* (Baroque) style and one in a mixed or Gothic style. He was asked to prepare a second version of the mixed one, but left for Spain, where he died in 1735.

Numerous projects suggested the addition of a porch in the Gothic style in order to conceal the Renaissance portals and windows. Among these was one by Vanvitelli of 1745, with columns adorned with spiral fluting like an enlarged Cosmatesque cloister. Bernardo Vittone also proposed a porch of this sort flanked by tall, thin stepped towers which has been called "half Chinese."[38] Luigi Cagnola submitted several designs before 1800, three of which assumed the demolition of all the Renaissance work. Only in his fourth project did he yield to the obvious economic advantages of retaining it. As late as 1790, the Chapter was still ordering work to proceed according to the Buzzi design of 1653, under the direction of Felice Soave (1740–1803). What little had been done on the Neoclassic pilasters was pulled down at this time. In 1797 Napoleon ordered the work to go ahead faster. In 1805, when he returned to Milan to be crowned King of Italy, he summoned the Committee, demanded how much money they required to get the job done, and authorized the sum named. This, however, was a hasty estimate and not adequate. A new design had to be prepared which would involve the least possible expense. The Academy at the Brera was assigned to the task. Giuseppe Zanoia and his assistant Carlo Amati prepared the new design by 1807, and it was practically complete by 1813 as we

---

38. Romussi, *Duomo di Milano*, p. 41.

see it today (Figure 38). Haste and economy had their aesthetic drawbacks. Ever since, the discord between the Renaissance and Neo-Gothic elements has been constantly condemned.

So uncomfortable were the proud Milanese made by their seeming lack of taste in this matter that in 1881 the Accademia delle Belle Arti raised the question of a new competition for the façade. In 1884, a citizen named Aristide de Togni died, leaving a large sum to be used for the remodeling of the façade. The money was to go to the hospital if not used for this purpose within twenty years. There were some legal problems raised by the term *riforma* (remodeling) versus the widely held desire to reconstruct the façade entirely. This idea was to some extent the result of the views of Viollet-le-Duc.

It was decided in 1886 to hold an international competition in two stages for a wholly new façade. No restrictions as to cost were laid down, lest they might inhibit the imagination of the contestants. This proved very popular and drew submissions from all Europe. One hundred and twenty architects submitted four hundred designs. The identities of the competitors were supposedly concealed from the Jury, since the drawings were signed with mottoes. With remarkable prescience, one was signed "Noli me tangere." The international jury, which included Camillo Boito, selected fifteen competitors for the second stage, as follows: eight Italians—Gaetano Moretti, Giuseppe Brentano, Luca Beltrami, Tito Azzolini, Enrico Nordio, Carlo Ferrario, Paolo Cesa Bianchi, and Giuseppe Locati; two Germans—Ludwig Becker and the firm of Harterl and Neckelmann; two Austrians—Anton Weber and Rudolph Dick; one Frenchman—Edouard Deperthes; one Englishman—Daniel Brade; and one Russian—Theodore Ciaghin. The second jury, chaired by Camillo Boito, awarded the prize to his brilliant pupil, Giuseppe Brentano (1862–89), then only twenty-six (Figure 116). The jury approved his project, although it had but three portals and would involve the total elimination of the old work, except for some of the buttresses. The jury also added that a single free-standing campanile, as proposed by Beltrami, should be given consideration. He had submitted a relatively conservative scheme in the first competition (Figure 117).

Emilio Marcucci's project was one of many solutions which proposed to mask the old façade by building a new porch in front of it and raising tall spired towers (Figure 118). This idea had also been proposed in the eighteenth century. The costs would have been formidable in either period. Marcucci also proposed to regularize the piazza by building an arcaded block across the small piazza in front of the Royal Palace, thus reducing the number of styles visible from the main piazza.

In 1889 Brentano died, and the large wooden model of his scheme revealed a number of unsolved problems, which had been less noticeable in his small drawings. Brentano's project seemed to harmonize smoothly with the flanks,

Figure 116. Giuseppe Brentano: Milan, Cathedral, final project for façade, 1888

Figure 117. Luca Beltrami: Milan, Cathedral, project for façade, first competition, 1886

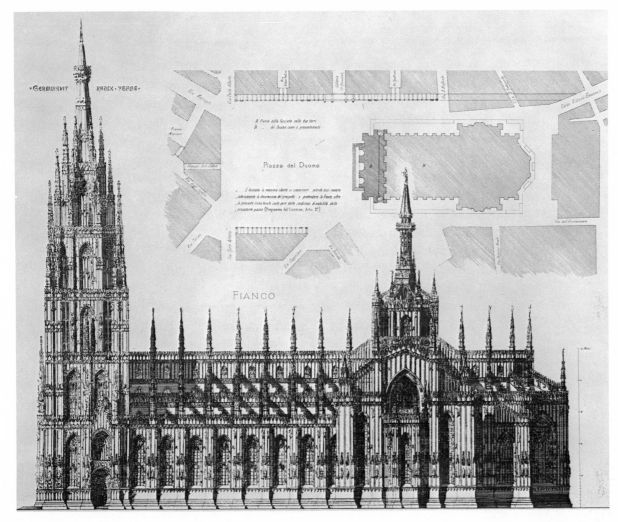

Figure 118. Emilio Marcucci: Milan, Cathedral, project for façade with new porch and towers, plan and side elevation, 1887

but, as Beltrami pointed out, this effect was achieved by altering the existing masonry and corner piers and would have involved some serious questions of stability. The buttresses of the Napoleonic façade were arranged aa, b, cc, cc, b, aa, which was the rhythm set up by Tibaldi for his columns and pilasters, and made use of the foundations as carried on by Buzzi (Figure 38). But Brentano would have changed this to aa, bbbb, aa. He would also have eliminated all the Renaissance work, closed the portals to the outer aisles, and linked the superimposed windows into single tall ones. The oblique angle of the termination would have been altered, but the general overall lushness of texture, characteristic of the flanks and apse but followed by the Zanoia-Amati scheme in an impoverished manner, would have been continued as, indeed, it would have been by all the late nineteenth-century designs. The orchestration of the pinnacles, so prominent on the transepts and flanks, would have been altered to conform with the new buttress system and a crowning system added to the gable. The three portals would have been relatively low and crowned with steeply pointed gables. The designs of the competitors usually showed their national characteristics, some of the English ones being High Victorian Gothic. Moretti's proposal took something from de Fabris' recently completed façade at Florence, and used heavy galleries with varying pitches to terminate all five aisles, unlike the smoothly continuous and more horizontal proposal of Brentano. The French project by Deperthes terminated the outer aisles in a pair of towers whose finials would have risen as high as the *tiburio* over the crossing. Beltrami, who undoubtedly knew the fabric more intimately than anyone else and who published nearly two dozen pamphlets on its problems, offered the most conservative solution, one which would have involved the least destruction, rebuilding, or alteration of the lines and proportions, but this cautious rationalism did not have enough *brio* to appeal to the jury. Italian architects, however, were generally in agreement with his good sense. These included architects who practiced the much freer inventive *Floreale* style, such as Giuseppe Pirovano, Luigi Broggi, and Giacomo Santamaria.

The Commission decided, in view of the costs involved, to proceed only with the upper part of the façade, and went ahead with the erection of some scaffolding and the ordering of marble. The public intervened as they had in Florence. It had become fond of the old façade as it existed, did not care for the new design, and protested loudly. Beltrami urged the conservation of the lower parts, but suggested numerous alterations in the proposed terminations with scholarly and structural logic, but to no effect.

At this time someone proposed to preserve the existing façade by moving it to stand between the two wings of the nearby palace.

In 1902 a new Committee was appointed, which came to the sensible conclusion that repairs to the existing façade be undertaken, but nothing more. This

Committee consisted of five men, two of whom, Luigi Conconi and Giuseppe Sommaruga, were architects. Thus Buzzi's synthetic eclecticism has survived for three centuries. That so many man-hours of labor went into the four hundred designs, the models, and the deliberations preceding and following these two competitions for a single part of this building shows how exceedingly wasteful the nineteenth-century system of competitions was. That this practice continued so long and has not entirely died out is deplorable.

Secular Buildings and Churches

As has been mentioned, the generation of architects born in the first quarter of the nineteenth century were often Medievalists. In addition to those Italians already noted, there were, among others, Count Edoardo Arborio Mella (1808–84) in Piedmont and Giacomo Franco (1818–95) in Venezia. They, and their followers, preached and practiced the Medieval-traditional-national philosophy of design.

Of them all, Camillo Boito (1836–1914) was one of the most original.[39] He was the brother of Verdi's librettist, Arrigo Boito. Two of the architect's early buildings are to be found at Gallarate, north of Milan toward Stresa: a cemetery built in 1865, when he was twenty-nine (Figure 119), and a hospital six years later (Figure 120). The cemetery has properly been admired as a work of genius, original and simple.[40] He had a more rational approach than most Italians of his time. In the center of the cemetery stands a massive white chapel. The gates to the enclosure are flanked by a series of attached small chapels in red brick, gabled, with white stone springers and voussoirs, i.e. stone used logically at the points where greater strength is needed. Nothing is extraneous. It is Gothic, of the rational Viollet-le-Duc kind. The young Boito might well have been aware of Viollet-le-Duc's ideas, since the *Discourses* were published by this date and the two men might even have met, both being active in the affair of the façade for the Florentine Duomo. Boito, in spite of his youth, was one of the judges in the first competition in 1860.

The hospital by Boito has a harshness and acridity which is also characteristic of some British buildings of about the same date, such as those of William Butterfield, combined with an integrity that recalls Philip Webb's. The two Italian buildings lack the high-powered drama and splurge of British examples, but instead have an air of quiet, self-confident mastery. This quality became less evident in Boito's later work, though perhaps more pronounced in his writings. In the early 1870s Boito was at work in Padua on the Palazzo delle Debite, so called because it was built on the site of an old debtors' prison (Figure 121).

39. See pp. 206 ff.
40. Grassi, *Boito*, pp. 19 ff. Tarchiani, *Ottocento*, p. 69.

Figure 119. Camillo Boito: Gallarate, Cemetery, detail, 1865

Figure 120. Camillo Boito: Gallarate, Hospital, 1871 ff.

It was begun in 1872 and completed in 1874. It is on a large scale: a man's head comes to the top of the column base of the great arcade. Two lofty stories rest on it, and there is an elaborate cornice. The detailing is medieval Venetian, handled in a typically stiff nineteenth-century way. Here and there are details which, like those of Viollet-le-Duc, seem to express "truth revealed," such as the colonettes on brackets supporting the balconies of the second story. Though regional in origin, they may well have been chosen for this quality. There is a careful interweaving of motives—the arches of the ground story arcade are repeated in the second story in a slightly different form, where they enclose *bifore* which are used on the third floor without the enclosing arch. Colonettes support balconies from the ground floor, form the balusters of those balconies and of those on the third story, and serve as visual supports for the arches of the cornice. The balconies alternating from story to story give a skipping rhythm to the façade—a device which was widely used in the *Stile Floreale*. With this building's increased richness of detail and eclectic elements, such as the almost classical use of Medieval forms in the capitals and cornices, we are on the verge of what was to be known as the *Stile Boito,* an Italian equivalent of High Victorian Gothic, a style rich in polychromy, variety, and movement.

At the end of the decade of the seventies, Boito built the Municipal Museum at Padua, adjoining the piazza in front of the Basilica of Sant' Antonio and the sturdy Gattamelata. The interior, particularly, is typical of his later style (Figure 122). The upper hall is divided into three aisles by rows of columns. The main staircase starts under the central aisle, winds up through the left-hand aisle, and finishes in the central one. There are no stairs in or under the third or right-hand aisle. This sort of spatial manipulation is frequently to be noticed in English and American buildings of the same period, such as the Manchester Town Hall or the State Capitol at Hartford, Connecticut. The decorative scheme also recalls the latter building, with its glaring white marble, each harsh element of which is identical with its neighbor. The abundant painted decoration is in a tonality and pigmentation which strongly recalls the plates of French folios of the previous decade, such as César Daly's *L'Architecture privée au XIXe siecle* (Paris, 1864), or the second volume of V. Calliat's *Parallèle des nouvelles maisons de Paris* (1864). The full "Victorian" battery has been unleashed—colored tile, frescoes, inlay work on capitals, stilt blocks, profuse moldings, and chamferings. The work of the architect quite eclipses in splendor and scale the objects displayed. The culmination of Boito's style will be seen in the "Casa Verdi" of 1899.[41]

Throughout the post-Neoclassical period, Neo-Medievalism was persistently though not exclusively invoked for religious buildings. The interior of San Do-

41. See Chapter 5.

Figure 121. Camillo Boito: Padua, Palazzo delle Debite, 1872

Figure 122. Camillo Boito: Padua, Municipal Museum, staircase, 1879

menico Maggiore (Figure 123) at Naples has preserved a fine Neoclassical ceiling supported by Federico Travaglini's (1814–91) incongruous medievalizing interior.[42] His restoration was accomplished between 1850 and 1853. The columns, ribs, and ornament, though executed in paint and plaster, nevertheless have an unusually tectonic expression.

Considerably later, the Neapolitan Cathedral received a new façade (Figure 124) first sketched by Enrico Alvino (1809–72). Alvino was prominent in the architectural activities of Campagna during his lifetime, and yet did nothing of remarkable quality.[43] His sketches for the Duomo façade were insufficient, so that after his death the actual façade was designed and built by Nicola Breglia and Giuseppe Pisanti of Potenza (1826–1913) from 1876 to 1907.[44] Neither architect paid much heed to the existing portal of 1407 by Antonio Baboccio, choosing instead a Tuscan idiom made fashionable by the controversies then raging over the façade of the Duomo of Florence. Alvino had been haunted by Florence—his new Cathedral at Cerignola, built between 1868 and 1936, has justly been called a parody of that edifice.[45] He had been a judge of the first competition for the Florentine Duomo façade and a competitor in the second. He was also one of the architects, with L. della Corte and G. Raimondi, involved with the new façade for the Duomo at Amalfi, a bizarre and unarchaeological flight of the imagination.[46] His claim to immortality lies in the design and construction of the important Corso Vittorio Emanuele in Naples, begun in 1852.[47]

The peculiarities of the Neapolitan Cathedral façade include the narrow aisle fronts, with their steep isosceles gables, and the recession of the three main bays behind rectangular wings. The wings are the bases of towers, an unusual feature in Italy. The richly carved figural friezes in the lighter stone flanking the gables of the principal windows have touches of Neoclassicism, and also of High Victorian Gothic reminiscent of the Albert Memorial (completed in 1872). The overall effect is severe, stiff, and dry. It lacks the warmth and variety associated with southern Italian architecture. The verticality and large scale are typically Neapolitan, as at Santa Chiara.

Old photographs show that there were, once upon a time, a number of amusing, light-spirited Gothic buildings in Naples and Genoa, now destroyed. At least one was a hotel. Perhaps its Gothic dress was designed to appeal to the ubiquitous English tourist.

42. Travaglini, a professor of architecture, restored a number of buildings in the Neapolitan area and published his autobiography in 1891.

43. Lavagnino, *L'Arte moderna, 1,* 584.

44. *Edilizia moderna, 16* (1907), p. 59. In 1907 the towers were still unfinished.

45. Lavagnino, *L'Arte moderna, 1,* 585.

46. Ibid., *1,* 405.

47. Ibid., *2,* 644.

Figure 123. Federico Travaglini: Naples, San Domenico Maggiore, interior restoration, 1850–53

Figure 124. Enrico Alvino, Nicola Breglia, and Giuseppe Pisanti: Naples, Cathedral, façade, 1877–1905

Milan, in the second half of the nineteenth century, was already assuming her present stature as the most industrialized and the most prosperous city in the peninsula. Consequently, she was in a position to lavish funds on such gestures as her unrivaled Galleria. She was also actively restoring and completing her churches, as well as covering many square miles with new buildings for business and residence. Several of the best Medieval designs were by Carlo Maciachini (1818–99). His most prominent work is the chapel of the Cimitero Monumentale (Figures 125, 126). Maciachini had been a pupil of von Schmidt at the Brera, and thus belonged to the rising school of Medievalists, to which he remained faithful.

The cemetery, of which he built the principal buildings, was not a wholly new one. The site had been selected in 1838 outside what is now the Porta Garibaldi. A competition was held and work begun according to Neoclassical designs by Giulio Aluisetti (died 1868), architect of the Neoclassical church at Rho. However, by 1859 this seemed quite old-fashioned, and a new competition was held in 1865. Maciachini, the winner, was authorized to begin work in 1866.[48] It was required that the design be in a Lombard-Romanesque style, since it was both local and Christian. The work dragged on, part of it being completed in 1867, part in 1897. Meanwhile, another change of taste had occurred, and a crematory in the form of a Greek temple was built in 1876 by Clericetti.[49]

The main buildings designed by Maciachini form the frontispiece of the complex, and are more delicate and sensitive than most of the Medieval buildings we have been discussing so far. (The intricate, dynamic flow of the stairs is not particularly Romanesque.) The constructive coloration is Ruskinian, as are the alterating voussoirs and the craftsmanlike ornament. G. E. Street approved the combination of brick and marble, about which he had written and which he was to use later in two churches in Rome.[50] Romanesque was being revived elsewhere, too. There had been James William Wild's Christ Church Streatham in London (1840–42), and the Countess of Pembroke's splendid Church of St. Mary at Wilton by T. H. Wyatt and David Brandon (1838–51). Richard Upjohn had suggested a similar style for his projected Harvard Chapel in 1846, and there were related buildings in New York City, such as All Souls Church by Jacob Wrey Mould in the mid-fifties.[51] At Milan, the variety of geometrical forms achieved by superimposing blocks of differing shapes is more intricate than the works of the Maestri Comacini. Now a century old, the atmosphere of

48. *Edilizia moderna, 8* (1899), 52.

49. Paolo Mezzanotte and Giacomo Bascapè, *Milano nell'arte e nella storia* (Milan, 1948), p. 130; see pp. 799–800 for a bibliography.

50. See pp. 275 ff.

51. Carroll L. V. Meeks, "Romanesque before Richardson," *Art Bulletin, 35* (1953), 17–33.

Figure 125. Carlo Maciachini: Milan, Cimitero Monumentale, chapel, 1863–66

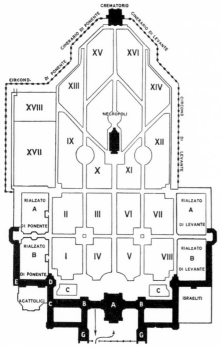

Figure 126. Milan, Cimitero Monumentale, plan

Figure 127. Enrico Holzner and Giovanni Britto: Padua, Cimitero Monumentale, 1880–1900

fresh delicacy at Milan is one not usually found in cemeteries. It is gracious and charming.

The influence of this cemetery was widespread. Two decades later (1880–1900) it was followed at Padua by Enrico Holzner and Giovanni Britto (Figure 127). The similarities include the general scheme, a principal chapel on a raised platform connecting long returned wings which terminate in smaller, simpler versions of the main pavilion. In both, the main chapel is cruciform surmounted by an octagonal lantern with hipped roof, entered through a Lombard porch with a rose window above. The gables in both are arcaded, and voussoirs of alternating colors are used. There are important differences as well. The striped walls and plain buttresses of Milan are reversed at Padua. The lantern at Milan has long and short sides alternately, while those at Padua are equal, and all are perforated by *bifore*. The lanterns of the subordinate pavilions at Padua have *quadrifore* on all eight sides, which at Milan appeared on only the four principal faces. The differences include the squatter proportions, airier arcades, and coarser detailing, which make the Paduan design look more like a functional utilitarian structure and thus closer to the Boitian ideal. Its simplicity is both provincial and progressive, since it anticipates twentieth-century works of equal ruggedness by Cram and Goodhue.

In the seventies Carlo Maciachini completed a new façade for the old church of Santa Maria del Carmine in Milan (Figure 128). Old prints show what he had to start with.[52] His new façade is a variation on the theme of Selvatico's façade at Trento: narrow aisle façades are connected by a pointed arch flung across the wide façade of the nave. But the advance in understanding is great. The later one is unmistakably architectural and unambiguous. Brick and terra cotta are used consistently. The raking cornice of the nave is anticipated by that of the aisles. The buttress-pilasters work logically with all three bays, although the tabernacle finials of the lateral buttresses too obviously eclipse those of the nave gable.

Maciachini's restoration in 1871 of San Marco at Milan is almost as successful. At this time, a good deal of work was being done on the restoration and repair of such ancient churches as Sant' Ambrogio.

Another architect who took part in these Milanese programs was Giovanni Brocca (1803–76), who had been a pupil of Domenico Moglia (1780–1862).[53] One of his principal works was the supplying of a new façade (Figure 129) to

52. Ferdinando Reggiore, *Milano 1800–1943* (Milan, 1947), p. 248.
53. Moglia, who was from Cremona, published a volume of architectural ornament, entitled *Collezione di soggetti ornamentali . . .* (Milan, 1837), and completed much of the decoration on the Arco del Sempione in 1838 in collaboration with Peverelli, according to Lavagnino, *L'Arte moderna, 1,* 87, and Mezzanotte, *Milano nell'arte,* p. 113.

Figure 128. Carlo Maciachini: Milan, Santa Maria del Carmine, façade, 1879

Figure 129. Giovanni Brocca: Milan, Sant'Eustorgio, façade, 1863–65

Sant'Eustorgio (1863–65), celebrated for the early Renaissance Portinari chapel by Michelozzo. The church had elements from the eighth and tenth centuries, a delicate campanile and low, ribbed domical vaults, like smaller versions of those at Sant'Ambrogio, supported on clustered columns with Romanesque capitals arranged logically at varying heights, according to the function of the ribs above. The painted decoration of the vaults was completed in 1882 by Agostino Caironi (1820–1907). Brocca united the façades of the aisles and nave under one wide, low, Medieval gable, the cornice of which is arcaded with the corbels perpendicular to the cornice line rather than to the ground. He has arranged the summit of his windows to echo the gable, and has kept his infrequent buttresses unusually low. The main door is emphasized by a traditional Lombard portal. What is remarkable is the barnlike simplicity of the wide, low, plain brick surface.

In Rome, the Basilica of San Giovanni in Laterano acquired a new apse, altar, and ciborium in the mid-nineteenth century (Figure 130). The strength of the association of Medieval architecture with Christianity at this time could hardly find greater proof. The Baroque nave "modernized" by Borromini in 1650 and Giacomo delle Porta's transepts stood between Galilei's magnificent Late Baroque façade (1733–35) and the Romanesque cloisters. The apse, however, had allegedly fallen into ruin, and a larger Neo-Medieval one by Virgilio Vespignani (1818–99) was begun under Pius IX and completed in 1886.

The Basilica of San Lorenzo in Rome underwent one of its periodic restorations at this time. It has again been restored since World War II in a form which experts consider to be more authentic than the nineteenth-century version by Vespignani. The memorial chapel in San Lorenzo to Pope Pius IX probably decorated by Raffaele Cattaneo is a richly ornamented crypt lacking originality of form or detail (Figure 131). Francesco Vespignani (1842–99) was co-architect, with Father Hildebrand de Hemptine, of the picturesquely situated and handsomely massed Benedictine convent of Sant' Anselmo on the Aventine, built from 1890 on (Figure 132). The inspiration is Lombard Romanesque, shorn of many of its decorative features but adhering to the simple forms with a disciplined straightforwardness which is still appealing.

New buildings in a medieval style were built from time to time. In Turin Count Edoardo Arborio Mella (1808–84) constructed a church in this style —Sacro Cuore di Gesù. Its nave dominates the relatively small aisles. The freedom in handling the familiar motives gives them freshness. He was an eclectic who worked in Renaissance modes as well, but is chiefly noteworthy for his restorations of Piedmontese castles and churches. In this field, his principal rival was the Portuguese-born painter-restorer Alfredo D'Andrade (1843–1915), best known for his part in the Borgo Medioevale in the Parco Valentino

Figure 130. Virgilio Vespignani: Rome, San Giovanni Laterano, apse, 1874–86

Figure 131. Raffaele Cattaneo(?) : Rome, San Lorenzo fuori le mura, crypt, 1878 ff.

Figure 132. Hildebrand de Hemptine and Francesco Vespignani: Rome, Sant'Anselmo, church and seminary, 1890–96

Figure 133. Iorio da Erba: Parma, Santa Croce, façade, 1515

of 1884, an engaging combination of Romantic elements typical of Piedmont and thoroughly picturesque and synthetic, and for his castle at Fenis.[54]

The spirit which lay behind many of the restorations can be judged by comparing the state in which the men of the nineteenth century found the buildings and what they proposed doing to them, as for example the Romanesque church of Santa Croce in Parma as seen with its façade of 1515 (Figure 133) by Iorio da Erba (before 1500–circa 1538), and the grandiose and elaborate proposals of Enrico Bartoli (1837–99) in 1887 (Figure 134). At Lonigo, Giacomo Franco (1818–95) won the competition for and built the Cathedral (1887–95), in a Romanesque revival style (Figure 135).[55] Boito called it "the most beautiful church which has been erected in Italy in many years."[56] It was derived from San' Zeno at Verona. Lombard arcading, porches, octagonal domes, and banding are used freely and with some consistency, but its merits lie largely in an avoidance of the excesses of other contemporary handlings of the same motives.

In 1892 a church in an experimental eclectic variant of Gothic was begun in Genoa by Luigi Rovelli which the late Mario Labò told me he considered the best example of nineteenth-century architecture in Genoa (Figure 136). Well situated on one of those numerous peaks with which Genoa abounds, the Chiesa del Sacro Cuore is still unfinished, but enough has been done by which to judge it. The general effect, with its marked loftiness, is Medieval, though many of the elements, such as the columns and the rustication, suggest the Renaissance. The columns supporting the nave arcade are placed in pairs, with their joint axis perpendicular to the nave. Even without the intended pair of spires, the verticality and simplicity are impressive. They parallel the ecclesiastical experiments of Sir Giles Scott at Liverpool Cathedral (begun 1903) and those of Cram and Goodhue. Proportions, detailing, and decoration all tend toward creative originality without stretching that faculty as far as Gaudí did at Barcelona.

Edoardo Collamarini (1864–1928) is responsible for two interesting Medieval religious buildings: a chapel (Figure 137), at the Villa Doria Pamphili in Rome (1896–1902) and the church of Sacro Cuore at Bologna (begun 1912). The chapel, designed when Collamarini was thirty-two, follows in the tradition of Maciachini's cemetery at Milan.[57] But this version is richer, more in the parvenu taste of Pirovano.[58] The porch is developed as a baldachino, the arcades

54. D'Andrade was highly regarded, and there is a large bibliography including an article by Luca Beltrami in the *Corriere della sera* (August 8, 1906) and an obituary in *Il Marzocco*, 20 (Dec. 5, 1915).

55. Lavagnino, *L'Arte moderna, 1,* 546, and Camillo Boito in *Edilizia moderna,* 4 (1895), 49–51; and A. C. Negrin, *Il Tempio di Lonigo . . .* (Vicenza, 1895).

56. Lavagnino, *L'Arte moderna, 1,* 564. Tarchiani, *Ottocento,* p. 54.

57. See p. 245.

58. See p. 259.

Figure 134. Enrico Bartoli: Parma, Santa Croce, proposed restoration, 1887

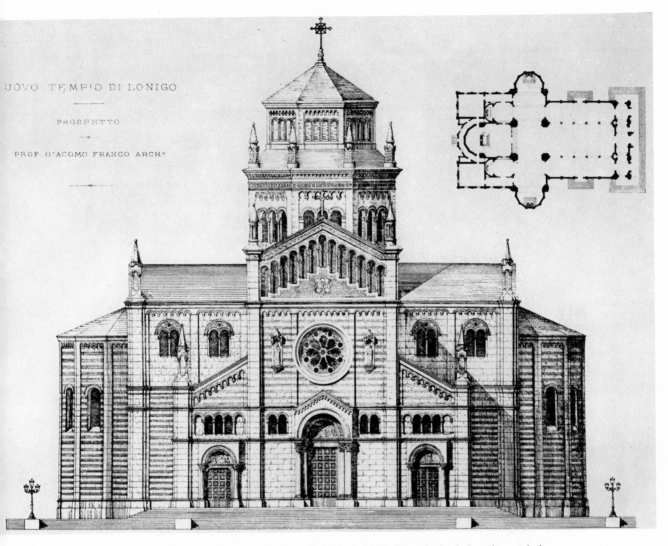

Figure 135. Giacomo Franco: Lonigo, Cathedral, 1877–95, principal elevation and plan

Figure 136. Luigi Rovelli: Genoa, Sacro Cuore, 1892 ff.

Figure 137. Edoardo Collamarini: Rome, Villa Doria Pamphili, chapel, 1896–1902

rest heavily on pairs of colonnettes, and the window frames project far out from the wall plane on more colonnettes. Not only is there more ornament and more variety of motives, but it is all made more plastic. The *Stile Boito,* as handled by the master himself in the "Casa Verdi," was flatter and less sculptural, though equally colorful.[59]

Collamarini's major work is the Bolognese church (Figure 138). Lavagnino does not admire this. He says that it is a grand farrago, a strange melancholic mixture of forms taken from the Orient, Byzantium, and the fourteenth and fifteenth centuries.[60] This, however, is what all the creative eclectic masters of the period were doing, with varying degrees of success. Here the result is harmonious within and without. Within, there are simple spaces formed by clearly articulated domes and vaults. The interior form is revealed externally, and the entrances on three sides are given emphasis by their portals, formed by a bold series of concentric arches. The surface is modeled more deeply than usual in Italy, so that the piers, ribs, and gables seem to be logical and organic. The rugged texture of the walls and the scale is maintained consistently. This is one of the most successful Italian buildings of its time. It was damaged during World War II, being near the railroad, but is now being carefully restored.[61]

The prosperity and security of the latter third of the century was exhibited in the building of innumerable new villas. Many of these were Medieval in style, and most of them seem to have been designed to show off the architect's uninhibited imagination as well as his client's new wealth. Two of these will serve to exemplify the type, which recall the activities of the Rothschilds and the Vanderbilts. The Villa Crespi at Capriate d'Adda (Figure 139) by Ernesto Pirovano (born 1866) is but one of many built for that family. It was begun about 1890 and was published in 1895. Its general form is that of a rectangular block surrounding a galleried courtyard. There is one high, elaborate tower and one stubbier, plain one. The rusticated lower floor supports two other floors with quoining and brickwork, *trifore, bifore,* arcades, merlons, oculi, alternating voussoirs, and jutting bay windows and balconies, which make a rich if undigested mixture of motives. The decoration of the galleried court is almost but not quite as sumptuous as the Alhambra. The main tower is an amazing "wedding cake" ending, after many contortions, in a faceted spire something like that of the Bargello or the smaller spires on the Certosa at Pavia.

At Genoa, Gino Coppedè (1866–1927), more of whose work is discussed in Chapter Five, exhibited an even richer imagination in the Castello Mackenzie high on the Capo di Santa Chiara (Figure 140). This was built for a family of Scottish origin which settled at Genoa. It presents an incomparably picturesque

59. See pp. 409 ff. and figs. 234, 235.
60. Lavagnino, *L'Arte moderna, 1,* 547.
61. It would not have looked out of place in London or New York.

Figure 138. Edoardo Collamarini: Bologna, Sacro Cuore, detail, 1912 ff.

Figure 139. Ernesto Pirovano: Capriate d'Adda, Villa Crespi, c.1890

Figure 140. Gino Coppedè: Genoa, Castello Mackenzie, 1890s

outline when seen from anywhere in the vicinity. It is a minor Neuschwanstein. From close at hand and within, there is abundant, inventive ornament in a wide variety of materials—an example of the almost total lack of restraint or originality which led into the *Stile Floreale* and Futurism.

In Milan, the most significant medievalizing building is the "Casa Verdi" of 1899 by Camillo Boito, which had an important influence on the *Stile Floreale,* to be described in Chapter Five (Figures 234, 235). But there were many other less important buildings which adhered to the Medieval tradition, such as Giovanni Ceruti's (1842–1907) Museo Civico di Storia Naturale, begun in 1892 (Figure 141). It is one of a long series of Medieval style museums for natural history: James Renwick's Smithsonian Institution in Washington (1846–49); Ruskin and Darwin's at Oxford (1855–59); Waterhouse's at South Kensington (1873–80); J. C. Cady's American Museum of Natural History in New York (begun 1869, partly completed 1877). As Lavagnino says, the Milanese example was a strange marriage of Romanesque, Gothic, and Moorish modes, but this combination, not unknown elsewhere in Italy and Europe, was unusually effective and contained some elements of novelty.[62] Ceruti's masterpiece, though damaged in World War II, is now being faithfully restored on its colorful exterior and modernized on its interior. The influence of Boito is marked on the exterior, notably the crowning motive of the central section (short columns on brackets), which Boito had used on his Palazzo delle Debite in Padua.[63] The polychromy of brown-tan with red and black is largely in colored stucco. It is both gay and inviting, and looks very much at home in the park. The striped walls and the alternating colors of the voussoirs are cheerful additions to the rational and uncomplicated scheme, contributing slight accents and minor variations in rhythm. The decision to preserve and maintain this exterior while making the interior consistent with contemporary ideas of installation can be heartily approved, particularly if the installations are up to the standards of other recent work of the kind, such as that by Belgioioso, Rogers, and Peressutti in the Castello Sforza at Milan.

The latter building began in the same year (1893) to undergo a remarkable transformation under the direction of Luca Beltrami (1854–1933), one of the most prominent architects of his day. He had been a pupil of Boito's and had also studied in Paris. In Milan he had a chair of architecture at the Academy and became director of the Monuments Office of Lombardy. While occupying this latter post, he waged a successful campaign to preserve rather than demolish the old castle of the Sforzas, which was in ruinous condition, and in so doing spent vast sums rebuilding it rather as he liked, in an inventive spirit. A critic addressed a letter to him years later as "Senatore Luca Beltrami, Inventore (sic)

62. Lavagnino, *L'Arte moderna, 1,* 555.
63. See pp. 237 ff.

Figure 141. Giovanni Ceruti: Milan, Museo Civico di Storia Naturale, 1892 ff.

del Castello Sforzesco."[64] In 1886 his plans were approved, although the work did not begin for another seven years. He was assisted by Gaetano Moretti (1860–1938). In 1905 the building was opened to the public. Beltrami published a monograph on it, *Resoconto dei lavori eseguiti al Castello di Milano* (Milan, 1898). The central tower is his design. His attitude toward restoration could have been acquired while he was a student at the École des Beaux-Arts in Paris from 1876 to 1880, where he worked on the buildings of the Exhibition of 1878 and the restoration of the Hôtel de Ville.[65] As has been mentioned, further changes within are now under way, but the walls, floors, roofs, cornices, and towers are far more Beltrami than Sforza, so that one may consider it, as we now see it, as a creation of the Medieval revival of the late nineteenth century. It is also another component of that legacy of vast building complexes which lay at hand ready for modern Italy to appropriate for its own purposes—as museums, libraries, or schools.

Other than these few outstanding buildings, the imprint of the Middle Ages on new work was less common in Milan than elsewhere in Italy, with one exception—the almost unphotographable Cassa di Risparmio of 1872 by Giuseppe Balzaretto (1801–74) in a style suggesting that of Michelozzo.[66]

The Palace of the Government of the Republic of San Marino, originally of the fourteenth century, was restored in the 1890s (Figure 143) by Francesco Azzurri (1827–1901) in what Lavagnino calls a mélange and counterfeit of various late Gothic models.[67] However, it is plausible and restrained in both form and ornament. It is not as highly picturesque as might have been expected. This may be due to the fact that Azzurri's work was always restrained, as in his restoration of the early Renaissance Palazzo Cancelleria and the handsome Mannerist stone-and-iron fence he built alongside the Palazzo Barberini in Rome.

Synagogues

The literary use of eclectic forms is beautifully revealed by the associative styles chosen for the wave of new synagogues which flowed across Italy beginning with the unification in the 1860s. The most ambitious of the early ones, apart from Antonelli's in Turin, was that in Florence (begun 1874, completed 1882, Figure 144). Three architects were involved: Vincenzo Michele (1830–95), Marco Treves (1814–97), and Mariano Falcini (1804–85). Oriental forms had by this time become the internationally accepted expression of a

64. Luca Beltrami, *Nuova Lezione* . . . (Milan, 1927), p. 3.
65. Willard, *Modern Italian Art*, p. 559.
66. Lavagnino, *L'Arte moderna, 1,* 554. Hitchcock, *Architecture,* p. 56, says that its nickname the "Ca' de Sass" means house of stone, an allusion to its heavy Tuscan rustication.
67. Lavagnino, *L'Arte moderna, 1,* 600.

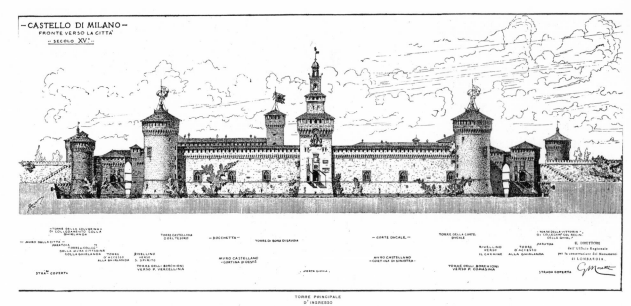

Figure 142. Luca Beltrami: Milan, Castello Sforza, projected restoration, 1893 ff.

Figure 143. Francesco Azzuri: San Marino, Palace of Government, restoration, 1890s

synagogue.[68] The Jews evidently felt that the forms associated with classical antiquity and Christianity would not express their sense of alienation and their pride in their own history, a parallel to the numerous other expressions of nationalism and sectarianism in that century. This led to the introduction into Italian cityscapes of some startlingly incongruous forms, such as minarets, onion domes, and horseshoe arches.

The Florentine synagogue was published in a monograph in 1883 paid for by Engineer Eduardo Votta, though not published in a periodical such as *Edilizia moderna* until 1906.[69] The funds for the building were provided by M. Levi. The plan is of Byzantine derivation, and the exterior uses Arabian and Moorish motives. The aggressive striping of the walls, now much subdued by time, has indigenous affiliations. Arcades and cresting are equally familiar in Italy, though not in exactly these forms. This cresting recalls Persepolis and the Mosque of Kait-Bey in Cairo. Likewise, the swinging semicircular gable was not unknown to Venice. As a whole it is a dignified though exotic statement, pleasing in its restraint and unity.

Enrico Petiti (1832–98) won a competition and built the Turinese counterpart between 1880 and 1884 (Figure 145). (Antonelli's far more ambitious one, his Mole, had been beyond the congregation's means to complete.) Numerous Moorish elements from the Florentine example reappear here: the horseshoe arches, cresting, onion domes, striped walls, and the semicircular gable (the triangular pediment was evidently regarded as an alien symbol). Petiti too used a wide range of textures (all executed in stucco), a number of spirally channeled columns, and a Mameluke Egyptian parapet. The building is placed on a corner lot, and each of the corners is marked by a tower; there is no central dome. The building is less graceful and less unified than the Florentine synagogue.[70] The taste of the time is reflected in the comment that "the four domed towers effectively break the monotonous horizontal line which dominates this part of the new town."[71]

Ruggiero Berlam (1854–1920), son of Giovanni Berlam (1827–92), who had been a pupil of both Franco and Boito, built the most original synagogue of the period in Trieste in 1910 (Figure 146).[72] Lavagnino calls it gross, with heavy masses and mediocre decoration derived from oriental and Romanesque

68. Rachel Wischnitzer, *Synagogue Architecture in the United States* (Philadelphia, 1955), pp. 6, 7, 68, 70.

69. *Edilizia moderna, 15* (1906), 5 ff.

70. *L'Italia artistica, 2* (1884), 124 ff.

71. Ibid., 126.

72. Ruggiero Berlam was assisted in this project by another member of the family—Arduino. The building is often admired. T.C.I., *Venezia Giulia* (Milan, 1934), p. 278, says it is "one of the most original synagogues in existence, of a magnificent austerity of form inspired by fourth-century Syrian art."

Figure 144. Mariano Falcini, Marco Treves, Vincenzo Michele: Florence, Synagogue, 1874–82

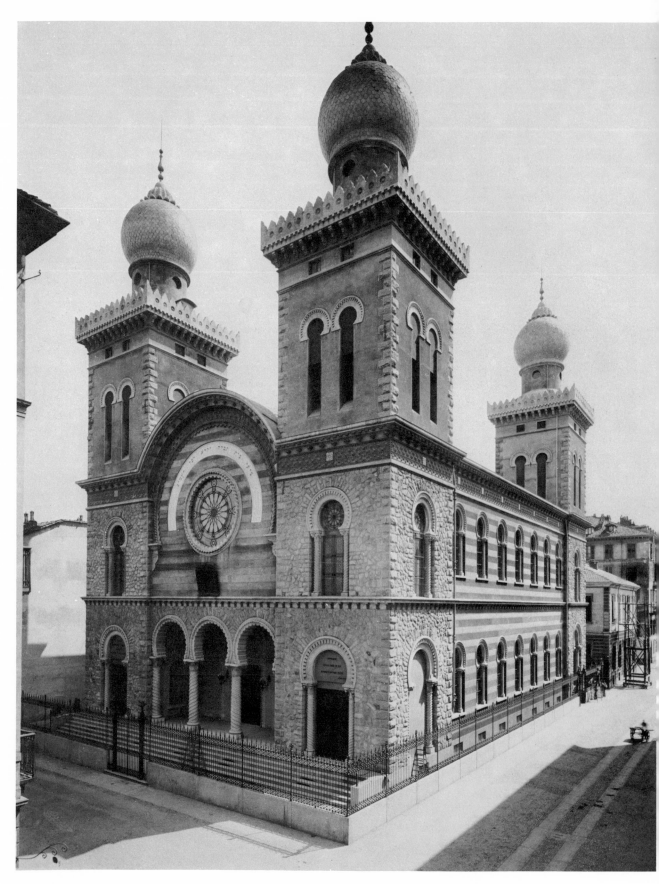

Figure 145. Enrico Petiti: Turin, Synagogue, 1880–85

Figure 146. Ruggiero Berlam: Trieste, Synagogue, 1910

forms, as advocated by Boito but handled with an independence verging on the illogical and arbitrary.[73] It can, however, be seen as a courageous and not wholly unsuccessful attempt at modernization. Like many innovations of the period, the chosen route toward a new architecture was that of simplification and elimination applied to traditional elements. Such was the direction of Berlage in his Bourse at Amsterdam, for which the successive designs became simpler, flatter, and more bare. Richardson's revisions of Trinity Church, Boston, followed a similar course. Berlam's building echoes another current of the early twentieth century—the dawning notion of Expressionism. Berlage, however, seems to have been the strongest influence, even in such things as the diagonals expressing the staircases.

Luca Beltrami's (1854–1933) Tempio Israelitico of the early 1890s in Milan was practically destroyed in World War II. It was published in the 1890s both in *Academy Architecture* and in *Edilizia moderna*.[74] The restored façade glitters with vivid blue and gold mosaics. The original interior, with its central plan, beamed ceiling, and simple detailing, was more classical than Romanesque. It was never a major work and its location on a narrow street opposite a small public garden did not call for a great monument.

The Tempio Israelitico in Rome came late. It occupies a superb site on a bend in the Tiber chosen because it was once the ghetto. A competition was held in 1889 and the results published in *Ricordi* (Figures 147, 148).[75] The existing building was not, however, completed until 1904. The competition was won by Luigi Costa and Osvaldo Armanni (1855–1929). The usual associations were invoked by the architectural styles selected. In this case they were called "Assyro-Babylonian."[76] This is an exaggeration but the obvious fact is that there was little effort to design a building which would fit harmoniously with either its Roman or Renaissance neighbors, a deliberate Zionist gesture of pride and independence. The huge square dome covered with aluminum, rising above its lantern and three large stories of substructure, commands attention. The composition does not depart far from the usual Beaux-Arts practice at the time, and the details, though exotic, are at a distance easily taken to be conventional ones. It is a building which lacks distinction.

Protestant Churches

There were a number of Neo-Medieval churches built in Italy in the last century, made not by or for Italians but by their own architects for Protestant con-

73. Lavagnino, *L'Arte moderna, 1*, 568.

74. *Academy Architecture* (1894), p. 133. L. Tenenti, "Il Nuovo Tempio israelitico in Milano," *Edilizia moderna, 1* (1892), fasc. 7, pp. 1–4, and fasc. 8, p. 4.

75. *Ricordi*, 2nd series, *2* (1891), pls. 25, 26.

76. Guide Bleu, *Rome* (Paris, 1950), p. 147. T.C.I., *Roma* (Milan, 1950), p. 194. Francesco Sapori, *Architettura in Roma 1901–1950* (Rome, 1953), p. 34.

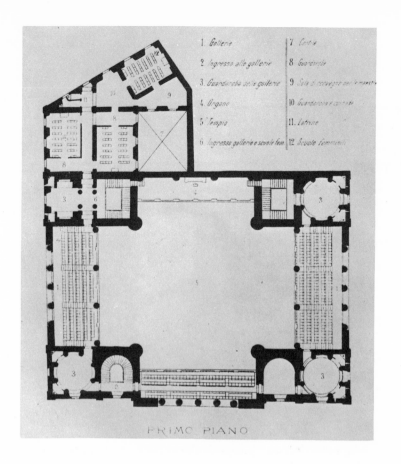

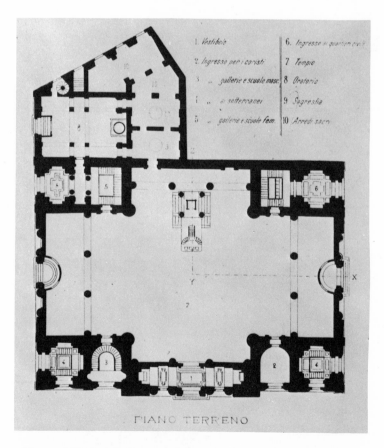

Figure 147. Luigi Costa and Osvaldo Armanni: Rome, Synagogue, plans, project of 1889

SEZIONE SULLA LINEA XYZ

nella propor di 0,015 p. M.

gregations resident in Italy: English, German, and American.[77] Two of the most splendid are those built in Rome for the English and American parishes by the English architect G. E. Street and his son. Since I have published a fuller account elsewhere I will comment briefly on them here.[78] Street had also built the Crimean Memorial Church in Constantinople, which was the only English church on the continent to rival his two Roman ones, although the Diocese of Gibraltar, of which Rome was a part, comprised innumerable English churches and chapels in Italy. As a group, these churches have much of the quality so often ascribed by the unsympathetic to English tourists, a resolute self-confidence which makes it unnecessary for them in any way to moderate their usual way of life or to take into account a foreign environment. This was both the strength and the weakness of Britain's nineteenth-century imperialism, and one finds it manifested in these churches.[79]

The more imposing of the two Roman churches was the earlier, the American church of St. Paul's, or, as it was also called, "St. Paul's within the walls" (Figures 149, 150). This was begun in 1872 and was ready for use in 1876.[80]

George Edmund Street (1824–81), the celebrated architect of the Victorian Gothic Law Courts in London, visited Rome three times in connection with this church. When he visited the site on the Via Nazionale, he said that the campanile, although 139 feet high, must be at the front to be visible, since the buildings already erected nearby were so lofty (Figure 151). However, the city required that it be set back 18 inches from the first intention, thus, unfortunately for its effectiveness, making it flush with the rest of the façade, and ruining its vertical effect.

There was difficulty in having the work built as truly as required by Ruskinian ethic, since Rome was in an era of hurried speculative building, in which the workmen were more skilled at faking than constructing solidly of worthy materials.[81] Street's great love, San' Zeno Maggiore at Verona, was one of the sources of his design. This provided Italian precedent for Gothic forms, as re-

77. Some of the English churches in Italy include: Holy Trinity in Florence; All Saints in Milan; St. Peter's in Siena; Christ Church in Naples; All Saints in Capri; The Church of the Holy Ghost in Genoa; St. George's in Rapallo; Holy Cross in Palermo; and St. George's in Taormina.

78. "Churches by Street . . . ," *The Art Quarterly, 16* (1953), 215–27.

79. See Osbert Lancaster, *Classical Landscape with Figures* (Boston, 1949), pp. 59–60, for a wry criticism of English churches abroad.

80. Sources for the history of St. Paul's include: Dr. R. J. Nevin (the first rector), *St. Paul's within the Walls* (New York, 1878); the Rev. Walter Lowrie (the second rector), *Fifty Years of St. Paul's American Church, Rome* (Rome, 1926); and conversations with a later rector, Dr. H. L. Duggins in 1951–52.

81. The clerk of the works for St. Paul's was Heinrich Kleffler (1840–91), a Swiss architect who also worked in Naples and Florence. His best-known Roman work is the Villa Savoia, outside the Porta Pia. The foundations were placed under the direction of the archaeologist, Rodolfo Lanciani. In some places, the footings had to go down fifty feet to find undisturbed soil.

Figure 149. George Edmund Street: Rome, St. Paul's, exterior, 1872–76

Figure 150. George Edmund Street: Rome, St. Paul's, interior, 1872–76

quired by the theory of the period, which demanded that a church must be Gothic, and in Italy, Italian Gothic.

The first rector, Dr. R. J. Nevin, was responsible for the whole project; he made six trips to America to raise money, and gave liberally to it himself. He may have chosen Street because of his position as one of the prominent architects of the time, or because no American could yet imagine that an American architect could be equal to a British one. Street selected Burne-Jones to design the mosaics. He worked on these for several years, going over them on weekends with William Morris, while Sir Lawrence Alma-Tadema carried instructions to the workmen at Murano. Burne-Jones designed all the apse mosaics, one of the church's claims to artistic fame, though some of them were executed after his death. The architect and his British collaborators gave the building a consistently British look; the windows and most of the fittings were supplied by Clayton and Bell. The tiles of the floor and side walls were directly after William Morris, if not by him. The interior walls are laid up in unequal courses of lake-colored Siena brick and cream-colored Fonteville stone from Arles. The central shafts of the nave, of polished red granite, are surrounded by four smaller ones of dove-colored Carrara marble. Their bases are red marble from Perugia or dark-blue Bardiglio marble. The roof is of fir and chestnut. Heating is by hypocausts under the entire floor. Travertine from Tivoli is used on the exterior.

The campanile was finished shortly after 1876, largely by means of a special gift from Miss Catherine Wolf, who advised that it be built at once and completely, or else it might drag on for years. Her wisdom is proved by the fate of the tower of Street's English church in Rome, which was not completed until fifty-six years after his death and then according to a modified design.

The rectory was begun in 1880. Between 1892 and 1895, twenty rooms were added. It was essentially completed in 1914; an elevator was added in 1933. Four fireplaces, one by Thorwaldsen, and a doorway were incorporated from the demolished Palazzo Torlonia, formerly on the Piazza Venezia.

A second campaign, from 1907 to 1913, added to the series of mosaics. Those on the façade were designed by George Breck, then director of the American Academy in Rome. He also executed those on the west wall of the nave, for which the first sketches had been made by the aged Elihu Vedder. American artists, after 1900, were beginning to be recognized.

The first of Street's two Roman churches surpassed his second in rapidity of erection and magnificence of decor. But there were contributing factors of a non-artistic character: the seasonal presence in Rome of many rich Americans, who had not yet discovered Florida, and the typically aggressive American rector, Dr. Nevin, who was possessed of titanic energy. He used it to get the church built and to secure large gifts from such families as Wolf, Morgan, Fish,

Figure 151. Rome, Via Nazionale, 1880s

Figure 152. George Edmund Street: Rome, All
Saints, showing spire as built, 1880–1937

Astor, Schermerhorn, and Delano. The English parish started its church too late, lacked a rector with Dr. Nevin's energy, and suffered from many other handicaps. Construction began a decade later, and in the end only half as much money was raised as had been lavished on St. Paul's.

The English Church, All Saints (Figures 152–55), on the Via del Babuino was blessed, or cursed, with a plethora of architectural advice before Street was definitely charged, in 1880, with designing the existing building.[82] At an unspecified date in the early 1870s, R. P. Pullan, assisted by "Mr. Philpott," made plans for the old site at the Porta del Popolo.[83] In 1876, Gilbert Scott (1811–78) had made plans for the "ecclesiastical embellishment" of the old building. From 1874 on, a third Victorian personality appears on the scene, John Henry Parker.[84] G. E. Street was in Rome in 1872, 1874, 1878, and 1880 in connection with the plans of this parish. The earlier trips were also in connection with the building of the American church.

The history of the building of the English church is one of frustration. Following the tradition of Empire, the ownership of the property and final authority was lodged not in Rome but in London with the Society for the Propagation of the Gospel, who behaved in an authoritarian manner, and with the inconveniently remote Bishop of Gibraltar. But this was not all. There were constant wrangles with the civic authorities, the clerks-of-the-works (two of whom were fired after a year's service each), several lawsuits with the contractors, and delays due to the absence of many of the committee members during the months between April and November. Some of the difficulties must, however, be laid at the door of the rector, Canon Wasse, who was inclined to ride roughshod over everyone, although he and later his widow gave freely to the costs.

Street provided a nave and two aisles with a deep chancel and choir, a small organ space, made into a Lady Chapel in 1913, and an entrance through the tower. His long experience in picturesque medieval design made it possible for him to fit these elements, including a turret, most ingeniously into the canted site. The tower, too, is placed to get the maximum effect from its location on the narrow Via del Babuino. However, in working out his scheme, he did not pro-

82. The principal sources for its history are: Canon Watson Wasse, *An Account of the . . . Church for the Anglican Communion . . . in Rome* (Aylesbury, 1885); and Muriel Talbot Wilson, *The History of the English Church in Rome from 1816–1916* (Rome, 1916). The latter is not entirely accurate. I was kindly permitted to consult the parish records and the records of the building committee, and I received assistance from the Society for the Propagation of the Gospel.

83. Richard Popplewell Pullan (1825–88) was an architect and archaeologist. He had worked in Asia Minor for the Society of Dilettanti. He designed the English churches at Pontresina, in 1879, and Baveno, in 1873. William Burges was his brother-in-law.

84. John Henry Parker (1806–84) was a printer, historian, and archaeologist. His *The Archeology of Rome* (London, 1874–77) was severely criticized for its superficiality. He was a member of the building committee for the English church and pointed out the inappropriateness of English Gothic architecture in Rome.

vide adequate room for the old organ, intended to be moved into the new building, thus necessitating the expense of remodeling the instrument. Similarly, the new apse was too small for the old reredos designed by William Slater, "the architect," in 1865, at a cost of £400.

The nave is flanked by alternating piers and columns of marble. The columns are monoliths of green Genoese marble, and the piers of layer blocks of Nero di Verona, Rosso di Perugia and Giallo di Siena. The six columns caused addiditional headaches. The detailed drawings for them did not come promptly, and had to be urgently requested from London in October 1883. The columns were then ordered from Greece, but the contractor went out of business. The order was then placed in Genoa. Of the first shipment, in 1885, three were unsafe and another was broken. These disasters led Canon Wasse to wonder how the Romans could have achieved so many large monoliths. Blocks of marble alternate with Roman brick within and without. The roof is constructed of the "best American pitch pine." The length is 130 feet and the width 60 feet. The height of the roof above the floor is about 60 feet; five hundred sittings were provided compared with the eight hundred in the American church. As in St. Paul's, the foundation proved costly. At All Saints, major changes in the design of the nave became necessary. A. E. Street, who succeeded after his father's death in 1880, wrote the Committee on January 11, 1886: "I am afraid that I cannot undertake any responsibility in the matter of the brick arches, I suppose we must substitute wood." This had to be done over the aisles as well, since, because of an error on the part of the clerk-of-the-works, the aisles were twenty centimeters too wide. It was also decided not to increase the weight of the roof by adding the intended wooden panels.

Due to so many modifications coming after the original architect's death, it is impossible to judge the completed building as one of Street's principal works. It does, however, bear an unmistakably English stamp. Like many churches of the time built in England, it was distantly inspired by Italian models filtered and changed to meet a British form-feeling. This was also the case with the first English-designed nineteenth-century church in Rome. George J. Wrigley, a Redemptorist monk, designed the chapel of the order on the Via Merulana, in 1855, in a characteristic blend of Italian and English motives.[85]

Street's picturesque Roman churches seem curiously alien in their surroundings, being more appropriate for somewhat less urban settings. The five- and six-storied cubes amidst which they are set make for startling contrasts. Street, like Ruskin, admired the architecture of North Italy, which, compared to Roman architecture, might be on a different continent. But, for Street, brick and marble architecture was apparently right for the whole peninsula.

85. Wrigley's design was exhibited in London in 1855. Views of it were published by the Roman Congregation of the Redemptorist Order, *Villa Caserta* (Rome, 1905).

Figure 153. George Edmund Street: Rome, All Saints, interior, 1880–1937

Figure 154. George Edmund Street: Rome, All Saints, original design and plan, 1880

It was not until 1937, when all of the personalities mentioned above were no longer on the scene, that the tower of All Saints was completed, the spire built, and the building brought to a conclusion. The design of the upper third of the tower follows G. E. Street's original design, as shown in the lithograph of 1880 (Figure 154). It can be surmised that since Canon Wasse had seen the lower third of the tower executed according to the original design, his widow, in financing the second third, inclined toward the original also, although we know that more drawings were sent out from England at this time. However, twenty years more elapsed before the existing spire was built (Figure 152). The motive of the turrets and the balustrade follow the design of 1880, but the spire of travertine is taller than that proposed by A. E. Street in 1892, and shorter and simpler than that intended in 1880. Moreover, the choice of material seems inharmonious. Street intended the pinnacled parapet to contrast with the richness and polychromy of the slated spire. The present monochrome effect is that of a summer hat worn out of season.

The elder Street can be acquitted of Canon Wasse's charge that he would be very likely to imitate himself. He did not duplicate his effects in general nor in detail. His treatments of the sites were controlled by the special conditions. The American Church was conceived from the beginning on a grander scale and in more sumptuous materials. In both cases, the intended façades have been modified: in the Via Nazionale by the omission of the buttress at the left of the campanile and in the Via del Babuino by the modifications of the spire. The brickwork of the latter, much of it cut and molded, is as pleasing in its way, more pleasing to contemporary taste, than the ornate stratification of the former. The interiors are not as Street planned them. In the American Church, his apse windows have been removed to make way for additional mosaic, a modification toward local tradition but not in keeping with his nave; and his ceiling has been painted. In the English Church, Street's nave ribs of brick and his paneled ceiling were omitted. Nevertheless, we can say that the two Streets left in Rome not two Roman churches but two distinguished examples of Victorian church architecture worthy of comparison with similar buildings in the home island—notable symbols of Britain's far-flung influence, however alien to the main currents of Italian architecture.

In so classically oriented a country as Italy, architects could not for long avoid being classical, as the next few decades would demonstrate.

4

Stile Umberto 1865-1900
Cinquecentismo

Introduction

Innovations: Functional and Structural

Urbanism

Ministries and Monuments; Public and Commercial Palaces

Private Palaces and Villas

Churches

Theatres

4

Stile Umberto 1865-1900
Cinquecentismo

Introduction

Victor Emanuel II was King of united Italy from 1861 until his death in 1878
He was succeeded by his son Umberto, who reigned until his assassination in
1900. During this period the dominant style of Italy was derived primarily from
the developed styles of the High Renaissance, which had been perfected in Rome
by Sangallo, Michelangelo, and Vignola. This was no sudden return to the past.
In a sense the Cinquecento had never entirely died in Italy, much as the Gothic
never died completely in England, where the last ebb of survival coincided with
the first rise of revival. A minor, more florid current was derived from Paris of
the Second Empire, and from time to time even more exuberant Manneristic
designs appeared; but under them all lay a Renaissance core.

United Italy was very conscious of its past, and used architecture, as all governments have done, to state its position. Modern Italy considered itself to be
primarily a continuation of the Italy of the Humanists rather than the Italy of
Imperial Rome. The latter position had been held by the Neoclassicists early in
the century, but its political connotations of foreign domination were unpopular.

The new Italy and the new Rome faced enormous tasks: there was ignorance,
poverty, sectionalism, corruption, and little inclination to submerge local or
personal interests for the good of the whole. There was no complete network
of railroads, no modern industrial system, few technicians, few administrators,
few teachers, and very little capital. In short, Italy faced a bewildering array of
staggering problems and made amazing progress toward solving them, although,
one hundred years and two wars later, many of them are still far from being
ideally solved. The arts, and especially architecture, received a disproportion-
ately large share of the available Italian resources.

Innovations: Functional and Structural

We reviewed in the previous chapter some of the ways in which architects sought to cope with the architectural problems of their day—eclecticism. An alternate way was to make more use of new materials and to think more like engineers. The Italians did not lead in this technological approach, partly because they were not inclined in this direction, but chiefly because their political difficulties were so prolonged. Once these were resolved by the unification of the peninsula in 1870, steps toward catching up with the industrial age followed rapidly and were reflected in its buildings, but even before the great events of the sixties some advances had occurred. The first short bits of railroad were built in the 1840s from Naples to Posillipo and from Milan to Monza, but a complete network was not achieved until the seventies, and the direct route north had to await the completion of the Simplon tunnel in 1906.

A few pioneering works were to be seen even earlier, such as the Galleria de Cristoforis in Milan of 1835,[1] of the same family as the Burlington Arcade (1818–19) in London and the Galerie d'Orléans (1829–31) in Paris, or Japelli's Moorish Greenhouse at the Villa Torlonia of the 1840s. Iron had been used structurally in 1836 in the campanile, pronaos, and apse of San Leopoldo at Follonica by Carlo Reishammer.

Communications in Italy have always required an enormous expenditure of labor, since there are hardly any level routes except in the plains of Lombardy and Venetia. Even along the coasts an infinitude of tunnels and bridges were required to link up the ports. Road bridges were being improved and metal used in them, as in the chain bridge over the Lima near Lucca by Nottolini in 1839,[2] and the anonymous Egyptian one over the Garigliano of 1832 (Figure 43). Elsewhere more traditional procedures were followed, such as the Roman-looking railway viaduct near Ariccia, badly damaged in World War II (Figure 155). This was designed by Ireneo Aleandri (1795–1885) and built between 1846 and 1853. It crosses the valley in three tiers of arches with strong pilasters between. The arcading resembles that of an arena far more than it resembles the Pont du Gard at Nîmes, except that it is faced in brick instead of stone. Each story is taller and the spans are wider than those below in the canonical manner, though none is as wide as those at Nîmes.

In 1853, the seventh year of the reign of Pius IX, a curiously designed metal bridge, called the Pio Viaduct, was built for the railroad from Rome to Velletri. Its trusses rested on two huge pylons of cast iron decorated with a sequence of orders and arched openings like a palace or a tower.[3] The openings were subsequently filled with brickwork. The use of metal was ingenious and logical,

1. Lavagnino, L'Arte moderna, 2, 1443.
2. See p. 115.
3. Lavagnino, L'Arte moderna, 2, 1454 and fig. 1300.

Figure 155. Ireneo Aleandri: Ariccia, Railway Viaduct, 1846–53

even if no effort at finding a new vocabulary had been made. On the line from Rome to Civitavecchia, about 1868, a smaller bridge over the Tiber had a central section which could be raised like a drawbridge to permit the passage of small ships. It was not an engineering feat nor was it an object of beauty, but was a belated example of Lewis Mumford's eotechnical age.[4]

The most spectacular use of the new techniques was in the great covered galleries, of which some survive, though many of the smaller ones have disappeared. The best known are the colossi at Milan and Naples. In these, the scheme is a roofed street lined with tiers of shops and dwellings. The idea is at least as old as the Markets of Trajan. In the nineteenth century many such "arcades" were built. In Italy they came later but were carried to more spectacular extremes than elsewhere. The giant in Milan was designed in 1861 (Figure 156), the one in Genoa in 1871 (Figure 157), and the Neapolitan one in 1887 (Figures 158, 159). The architect of the first was Giuseppe Mengoni (1829–77), a man who showed here and elsewhere a brilliant, original mind. He had studied at the Academy at Bologna, and in 1861 won the competition for the Milanese gallery and the regularization of the Piazza del Duomo. He was fiercely opposed by Camillo Boito, whose own project was rejected as too romantic and too medieval.[5] Mengoni hoped ultimately to build harmonious galleries along the west end of the piazza, too. The funds used were English, as was some of the metal and glass. An English firm executed it, possibly with advice from Sir Matthew Digby Wyatt, who was on the board.

The program for the arcade in Milan had been settled on only a decade after the spectacular success of the London Crystal Palace Exhibition, with its epoch-making prefabricated building of iron, wood, and glass. The major part of the construction was achieved between 1865 and 1867, but the decoration continued until 1877. In that year the architect made a mis-step on the scaffold and, Frankenstein-like, was hurled to his death at the age of forty-eight, already one of the most famous architects of Italy and one of the few known throughout Europe.[6] The selected style was derived from the local Renaissance. Lavagnino feels that, although undoubtedly spacious and having grandeur, the Milan gallery is on so large a scale that it becomes monotonous and dry, and that the use of elaborate stucco work, particularly in the lunettes under the glass-and-iron dome, is inappropriate.[7] Henry-Russell Hitchcock considers it the ranking Italian work of the period in concept and dimensions—a great urban achievement. He considers that it "makes its impression by its size, its elaboration of detail, and above all its unqualified assurance. . . . All is obvious,

4. Ibid., *2*, 1454.
5. Ibid., *1*, 547.
6. Obituary in *The American Architect, 3* (1878), 37.
7. Lavagnino, *L'Arte moderna, 1*, 547.

Figure 156. Giuseppe Mengoni: Milan, Galleria Vittorio Emanuele II, interior, 1863–67

expensive, and rather parvenu; yet the setting—at once so comfortable and so magnificent—that it provides for urban life, [the] centre as it has always remained of so much Milanese activity, has not been equalled since."[8] It undoubtedly makes a most powerful and agreeable impression on visitors who come to see the Duomo but linger to enjoy the majesty and activity of the Galleria, with its shops, cafés, and restaurants cool and comfortable on the hottest days. It is a novelty not to be found at home and hence all the more enjoyable, however lavish and unpuritanical. The arcades of the Rue de Rivoli are not so refreshing. Mengoni's façade, with its three giant stories and even more colossal two-storied triumphal arch facing the piazza, is a respectable urban solution, orderly yet not monotonous, traditional yet not imitative, fully deserving of its great fame.

The Galleria Mazzini at Genoa (1871), whose architect is unknown, is a more modest affair, although still one of the largest in Europe (Figure 157). It has a less prominent location and hence it is less bustling. Its internal street runs up a hill, with several domed sections masking changes in the level of the façades and vaults, establishing an agreeable rhythm. More modest in dimensions and more simply decorated, only its chandeliers strike a festive note. Both galleries are roofed by perforated, untied iron ribs—a system used at Paddington Station, London, in the 1850s by I. K. Brunel and Sir Matthew Digby Wyatt.

Sixteen years later, Naples followed suit with its very large and admirably located Galleria Umberto I (1887–90, Figures 158, 159) by the architect Ernesto di Mauro, using designs by Emanuele Rocco (born 1852). Many others worked out the decoration, notably Antonio Curri (1850–1917). The iron work is by the engineer Paolo Boubée. The dome rises up more than 180 feet from the pavement. The interior decoration has much of the same lushness that characterizes that at Milan, but the exterior façades have received very little praise. Henry-Russell Hitchcock says that it is a late and inferior imitation of Milan, and that its ornate entrance most ungenerously overpowers Niccolini's San Carlo Theatre across the street.[9] Lavagnino finds the entrance as a whole satisfactory, since it adapts well to the narrowness of the street, but he criticizes severely the mélange of details and scales.[9a] While not inspired, the lower story skillfully uses a triumphal arch motive on a concave surface, and the severe Tuscan orders on their pedestals, some in advance of and some set back in the wall plane, are strong and effectively unusual. At Turin Camillo Riccio (1838–99) and Costantino Gilodi (1853–1918) built the old Galleria Nazionale (Figures 160, 161). It was considerably smaller. Its interior decor used engaged orders, of which the upper one was spirally fluted.

The first Italian passenger stations, like those everywhere else, were highly

---

8. Hitchcock, *Architecture*, pp. 146–47.
9. Ibid., p. 147. Reportedly the work on the façade was still under way in the 1920s.
9a. Lavagnino, *L'Arte moderna, 1*, 587.

Figure 157. Anonymous: Genoa, Galleria Mazzini, interior, 1871

Figure 158. Ernesto di Mauro: Naples, Galleria Umberto I, detail of exterior, 1887–90

Figure 159. Ernesto di Mauro: Naples, Galleria Umberto I, interior, 1887–90

Figure 160. Camillo Riccio and Costantino Gilodi: Turin, Galleria Nazionale, interior, 1890

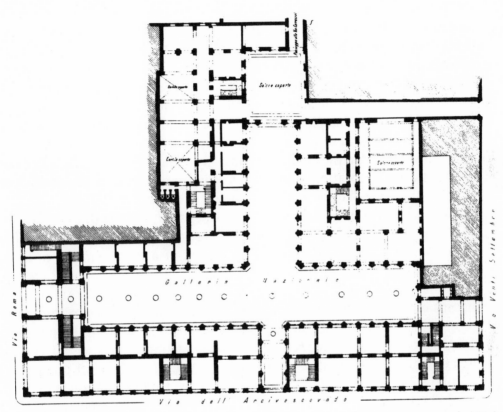

Figure 161. Camillo Riccio and Costantino Gilodi: Turin, Galleria Nazionale, plan, 1890

experimental. In Milan, for instance, the train shed stood out in the middle of the street detached from any other building—a pavilion without walls, its flat roof resting on four rows of columns providing some modicum of shelter for engine and cars. A station of 1839 in Naples at the Porta Nolana provided a low train shed on rows of iron columns between flanking masonry buildings. This contrast between materials was to be found everywhere. There were four portals, one for each of the classes of passengers. The old Maria Antonia station in Florence (built 1848–57), was, like the subsequent ones, the kind of terminal from which even through trains had to back out.[10] The train shed with four lines of tracks was the dominant element. From the piazza the activities within were clearly visible through the four open arcades at its end, as at Leipzig (1840–44).[11] The shed was in a single span carried by queen post-trusses in wood with metal tension rods. The piers on the platform and the clerestory over them were richly decorated with arabesques and tracery. If processions of choristers had been substituted for the puffing engines it would have made a good basilica. Externally, the decoration ranged from *Rundbogenstil,* as at the Munich station of about the same date by Bürklein, to late Cinquecento.[12]

The building of large railroad stations began in the 1860s. That at Bologna by Ratti (1871, Figure 162) is still in use, although the entrance colonnade is not part of the original fabric. It is typical of a large number of European stations of the period. Executed in a modest Quattrocento or *Rundbogenstil* vocabulary, and long and low, they stretch out parallel to the tracks, with numerous entrances into waiting rooms for the various classes, restaurants, baggage, mail, and personnel quarters, all conveniently close to the platforms. At Bologna the entrance court set back between flanking wings served as a parking area for vehicles and made a dignified approach. A much larger and much more original solution was found (1866–68) for the Central Station in Turin (Figure 163) by architect Carlo Ceppi (1829–1921) and the engineer Alessandro Mazzucchetti (1824–94).[13] The enormous curved gable of its principal hall terminates the Via Roma dramatically beyond the place where it has been made into the lovely garden which is the Piazza Carlo Felice. Parallel with its façade runs the important Corso Vittorio Emanuele, with its impressively arcaded sidewalks. Originally, the curved gable marked the end of the train shed, spanning 154 feet. This lofty space is now a *salle des pas perdus* for the new station behind. The whole of the original building was characterized by a lavish use of glass in round-headed windows divided by narrowly set mullions.

The old station in Rome stood well in front of the location of the masterly

10. Ibid., *2,* 1451–52.
11. Meeks, *Railroad,* fig. 22.
12. Ibid., figs. 53, 58.
13. Ibid., p. 98 and fig. 114.

Figure 162. Ratti: Bologna, Railroad Station, 1871

Figure 163. Carlo Ceppi and Alessandro Mazzuchetti: Turin, Porta Nuova Station, 1866–68

new one which has replaced it, but it was by no means a negligible building in its own right and was still in use in the 1930s (Figure 164). Projected in 1867 to centralize the many small ones, it was completed in 1874. The architect, Salvatore Bianchi (1821–84), linked his twin palace façades with the pointed gable end of an iron-and-glass train shed. In plan this was a typical two-sided station, even though it was a terminus and functioned as the Gare de l'Est in Paris had done a few years earlier, with arrival side and departure side clearly separated, and with all tracks and platforms roofed by the metallic shed. The design of the two "palazzi" is unconventional—only two stories in height, the Composite order is placed directly above the Tuscan of the ground floor. The columns are loosely paired and free-standing, but they leave only a shallow balcony or covered walk between them and the façade wall. The tabernacle window frames of the upper floor and the round-headed ones of the lower floor, as well as the use of balustrades, come from Cinquecento Venice more than from Rome. The sharp contrast between the masonry and metallic systems of construction contributes to the unique and dramatic appearance, as do the two changing curves of the truss as expressed in the gable front.

At Naples, the former large central station by Nicola Breglia and Enrico Alvino (1809–72) was begun in 1867 (Figure 165).[14] The twin palazzi and the arcades had a noble Italian breadth and were both monumental and simple. The iron and glass roof of the train shed was much less prominent than at Bianchi's Roman station. The arcades, which ran down the sides and across the front of this, together with the porte cocheres, served admirably to shelter arriving and departing passengers when they changed from one form of transport to another, and indeed invited such traffic, giving maximum freedom of access. These arcades also expressed the public nature of the building. Such solutions of the railroad station problem were restudied at the end of the century under the influence of the new styles, such as *Liberty* or *Floreale* and *Secession,* as shown in the designs for the Central Station in Milan of 1909 (Figure 262) and the Expressionist work of Sant'Elia (Figure 260).[15] The station built in Naples to replace the old one is of course far larger, but is not so impressive nor so inviting.

The new techniques and materials found a logical and economical application in covered markets. The English one at Hungerford in London, featured by Sigfried Giedion, and Les Halles in Paris by Victor Baltard are famous. In Italy, Mengoni was the architect of one near San Lorenzo at Florence which still provides airy protection from sun and rain. At Leghorn a somewhat similar

14. Lavagnino, *L'Arte moderna, 2,* 1453. Elsewhere he gave the date as 1876 (*1,* 585). A nucleus in a Neo-Renaissance style was carried on by Nicola Breglia.
15. See Chapter 5.

Figure 164. Salvatore Bianchi: Rome, Central Station, 1867 ff.

Figure 165. Nicola Breglia and Enrico Alvino: Naples, Railway Station, 1867 ff.

market was built in 1894 by Augusto Battaglioni.[16] Like the Ponte Pio mentioned above, the side walls are pilastered and filled with round-headed windows in a conventional way, and only the clerestory and its roof express the iron and glass. Its dimensions were not remarkable; although it was 95 meters long, the main span was only about 20 meters, a span which had become child's play by this date.

A wholly new nineteenth-century phenomenon—the large department store—also made use of the new materials. The concept of these buildings at this time and for some time afterward was a sort of people's palace, like the Bon Marché and Aux Printemps in Paris, or the former Stewart-Wanamaker Building in New York. A conspicuous Italian one was built in Rome diagonally across from the Piazza Colonna looking out on the important Corso, the Via del Tritone, and the Piazza San Silvestro, terminal of so many tram lines. Now one of the Rinascente stores, it was originally the Magazzini ("Palazzo") Boccioni (Figure 166). It was complete by 1899, and the architect was Giulio de Angelis (1850–1906).[17] Tarchiani considered it to be one of the first early Italian buildings in iron, and indeed it was one of the first semi-monumental Italian buildings in which iron structure was revealed so openly. There are five stories plus penthouse surrounding an open court, so that columns, railings, and so on in metal are all clearly revealed. The exterior is handled as a ground floor and mezzanine surmounted by two high stories, each embracing two actual floors. The lower one is arcaded and the upper one has a sort of strip window over a row of round-headed windows. The huge piers and cornices give an air of stability, which was probably thought necessary in view of the relatively large amount of fenestration. One can see a harmony of scale with the adjoining buildings and a high degree of restraint, compared with the later, more florid buildings which line the Tritone. Nevertheless, one must compare it, not with the progressive stores of Paris, nor the Field Warehouse in Chicago, but rather with the McKim, Mead, and White building of 1906 for Tiffany, with its measured Venetian treatment, or with D. H. Burnham's building for Wanamaker's (1905), both in New York.[18] All of them are in essence disemboweled palaces with the courtyard walls removed and the court roofed over.

A few blocks east of this Roman store stand a few remaining iron-fronted buildings such as one can still find in other cities, where they also date from the nineteenth century, in which the entire façade is built up from cast metal units: columns, window frames, spandrels, and all.

Milan, which became a modern city much more surely and quickly than

16. Lavagnino, L'Arte moderna, 1, 581 and fig. 488.

17. Tarchiani, Ottocento, p. 62. De Angelis restored the Morlacchi theater at Perugia and Villino Bonghi at Rome; see also Edilizia moderna, 8 (1899), 72.

18. "The Unit Method of Design," Arch. Record, 18 (1905), 394–95.

Figure 166. Giulio de Angelis: Rome, Magazzini Boccioni, c. 1895

Figure 167. Giuseppe Bollati: Turin, Piazza dello Statuto, 1864

Rome, had a number of large department-store palaces, some of which are no longer standing. These include the Art Nouveau one at 15 Corso Vittorio Emanuele by Achille Cattaneo (1872–1931) and Giuseppe Santamaria (1904–05) and one for Contratti (Figure 241). The imaginative use of iron, both structurally and decoratively, reached its height in Italy in the *Stile Floreale.*[19] Prior to 1900 there was no serious attempt at a new architecture other than the two currents we have been tracing: Synthetic or Creative Eclecticism using primarily medieval vocabularies, or the relatively timid exploitation of new materials and techniques for new functions, such as the pioneering use of reinforced concrete made by Carlo Ceppi in 1894 in his Via Pietro Micca buildings in Turin (Figure 237). The major line of development was the continuation of an eclecticism which saw in the Cinquecento the ideal of architectural excellence—a style which we have called the *Stile Umberto.*

Urbanism

The emphasis on Cinquecento formulas had one very important effect. The vast number of new offices and apartments which went up harmonized to a remarkable extent with the existing structures, giving Italian cities large areas of pleasing unity. This happy amalgamation is particularly exemplified in Rome.

Each vicissitude in Rome's twenty-five centuries of growth and decay has not only obliterated some of the past, but it has also left a fresh deposit, united by the power of tradition and self-confidence, that has miraculously fused into a continuum. Rome is still capable of performing this remarkable feat.[20] It is spirit working upon marble and travertine parallel with that signalized by Eleanor Clark in *Rome and a Villa;* a combination of tough realism in day-to-day matters with an uninhibited emotionalism in matters of art and architecture.[21]

Think, for example, of Filippo Raguzzini's Piazza Sant' Ignazio of 1727. The exquisitely sinuous irregular blocks stand opposite the gigantic rock cliff of Sant' Ignazio, like a coquette flirting with St. Thomas Aquinas. The apparently incongruous juxtaposition, making its profound statement of two ideological worlds, is today made more challenging by the intrusion of an autopark between the duelists. All day long the subtly molded space is paved with the sleek or chubby bodies of Fiats. But the duelists triumph; the cars are subordinated and inconsequential. Rome can do this. A colonial village green has not this power to conquer such intruders. Its fragile, wooden, domestically-conceived ambient cannot absorb them.

The materials and methods of construction traditional in Rome contribute to

19. See Chapter 5.
20. This section is abridged from Carroll L. V. Meeks, "Rome Ruined?" *Perspecta, 2* (1953), 6 ff.
21. Eleanor Clark, *Rome and a Villa* (Garden City, 1952).

its remarkable unity. Unlike Nordic peoples with a puritanical adoration of the truth, however disagreeable, the Romans have never felt that form *must* be determined by concrete, brick, or wood. The form-idea is predominant; the materials are there to serve the idea. Travertine, marble, and brick, ornamented with mosaic, continue to be constituent elements in Roman construction, so much so that the identical blocks have been reused over and over again. This, together with centuries-old craft experience, goes far toward unifying the capricious molds to which successive generations have bent them.

Integrity of construction is a relative matter in a country which prides itself on its skill in making one material look like another and has centuries of experience at it. The Sicilians covered the beautiful coarse stone of their temples with stucco to imitate marble, the Ostians covered their beautifully molded brick to look like stone, and the nineteenth-century Neapolitans stuccoed their tufa buildings to make them look like brick and travertine. The modern Roman will corrugate his marble to make it look as much as possible like transite. It is a real virtue to let stone look like stone—as Gaetano Koch preferred to do.

There is another force at work or another manifestation of the same force, whatever it is, that has maintained the quality of Roman building. Architects, generations of them, have felt a special responsibility to the city on the seven hills. Almost invariably they have responded to her grandeur. The greatest architects, wherever born, when working in Rome have been worked upon by her. Recall the change in Bramante from his early, provincial work in North Italy to his work after he came to Rome. At once, it seems, he matured and produced designs which re-embodied, as in the Vatican and St. Peter's, her most solemn traditions. Hardly ever has an architect failed to live up to the extraordinary task of building something worthy to be neighbor to the Colosseum or the Palazzo Farnese. Even modern buildings in Rome seem to belong to a continuing family, which can be described as a blocky horizontal mass, terminating with a cornice, surrounding a court, presenting its smooth façade to the street. This family of buildings begins with the apartment houses of antique Rome. The formula has been varied during 2,000 years only by minor modifications of the façade, details of fenestration, rustication, and ornament. Steep mansarded roofs, irregular masses, picturesque effects have been shunned. Each architectural generation has been content, by and large, to recognize the appropriateness of the Roman tradition and to seek only to work within it.[22]

During the early nineteenth century, the French protectors and the popes operating on a relatively small scale did little to change the face of Rome; but, since 1870 when Rome became the capital of Italy, four building waves have washed over it: the *Stile Umberto,* the *Stile Floreale,* "Mussolini Magnificence," and "Organic Eclecticism," each leaving new strata to enrich the whole deposit.

22. Fello Atkinson, "La Rinascente Store, Rome," *Arch. Review, 132* (1962), 269.

These strata are mingled together more than in other capitals which grew with such desperate speed during the last century. Much as we deplore the elimination of the Renaissance villas which had survived, together with ample gardens, within the old walls, the new buildings on their sites have mixed the styles more thoroughly. (In London or New York new building tends to follow a concentric pattern.) The commingling of old and new buildings to give flavor and a sense of continuity to new development, now once more sought after by contemporary city planners and redevelopers, was thus automatically accomplished in Rome. Hence, a line drawn anywhere in Rome intersects an entire historical sequence of buildings. Elsewhere only radial lines are likely to do this.

The *Stile Umberto* seen in the government buildings and palaces which sprang up between 1870 and 1900 is the first of the four recent waves of construction and destruction. As the government of the new state moved to Rome, the bureaus were at first housed in expropriated monasteries, with or without alteration. Gradually new buildings were added, not in one district, but peppered about the city. Parliament met in the old Palazzo Montecitorio in the heart of the city. The enormous National Library shares the Collegio Romano with the University and a museum, and there still seems to be room enough, so vast was the old fabric. There have been grandiose projects to replace these old edifices; but they rarely come to fruition, at best ending with some partial realization. The Senate is still in the Palazzo Madama, with a few additions, including an assembly hall, much in the way the French adapted the Palais de Luxembourg for their Senate. The House meets in a chamber built in the early 1900s by Ernesto Basile, tacked onto the rear of the Palazzo Montecitorio (Figure 253). The Via Nazionale (Figure 151) was planned as an official avenue like Pennsylvania Avenue or Whitehall; but, aside from the Exhibition Hall by Pio Piacentini of 1889 (Figure 184) and Gaetano Koch's Banca d'Italia (Figures 185, 186), the remainder became residential or commercial.

The character of the Italian nineteenth-century public buildings differs from its contemporaries elsewhere. There is less Gothic Revival, less Romanesque, almost nothing picturesque. Instead the Roman architects deliberately clung to their Renaissance and Baroque traditions, which brought their new work into harmony with the existing older buildings in a way that the London Houses of Parliament or the Vienna City Hall did not. To come nearer home, Richardsonian Romanesque buildings never, anywhere, had anything in common with their neighbors. The "Vittoriano" or, more formally, the Monument to Victor Emanuel II, was an exception (Figure 192).

Other cities also grew with varyingly harmonious results, such as Turin, which continued its orderly growth of arcaded boulevards and squares so that today it is one of the most beautiful cities in Europe, the old merging gracefully into the tactful new. The unrivaled series of porticoed streets punctuated by noble piazzas was continued throughout the century with the most commendable adherence to a viable tradition. Some of this was the work of Carlo Promis (1808–72). Among the great piazzas of this period is the vast Piazza dello Statuto opened in 1864. The surrounding palaces by Giuseppe Bollati (1819–69) are brilliantly colored (Figure 167). One end of the piazza leads into the Via Garibaldi, a cross axis of the city, and the other is open-ended. An insignificant station stands there—an anticlimax to the loftier and richer palaces.

At Genoa a group of modern buildings developed around the Piazza de Ferrari with its old theatre and palace. The new banks and Bourse extended the development southward. Another piazza toward the north, Piazza Acquaverde, fronted on the station and drew (convenient to the harbor) a number of hotels as well as the monument to Christopher Columbus.

Florence, the capital of Tuscany, served as the capital of Italy from 1865 to 1870. This short-lived importance accelerated her modernization. Giuseppe Poggi (1811–1901) directed her city planning and designed some individual buildings.

The most important of his city-planning schemes involved the replacement of the old fortifications by a circuit of wide, tree-lined avenues still adequate for the enormously increased traffic of a later century (Figure 168). The same procedure was followed in many cities at this time, such as Paris and Vienna. More spectacularly, Poggi linked the hills left of the Arno by avenues easily negotiated by carriages, and dramatically treated the hill of San Niccolò (Figure 169) with ramps and stairs leading to the Piazzale Michelangelo and further up to San Miniato al Monte. One of Poggi's schemes was to provide a handsome setting for the Antica Porta alla Croce. The powerful order of the proposed structures, if continued as planned, would have unified the oval piazza in spite of the irregularities caused by the old streets (Figure 170). The interior of the building shown as designed by G. Roster shows a similar adroitness. It recalls the intricacies which lie behind the façades of the Place Vendôme. These enterprises took from 1865 to 1877. They contributed greatly to the attractions of the city for its inhabitants as well as for the large foreign colony. After the capital was moved to Rome, non-Florentine architects were employed for a number of buildings, such as the Synagogue and Mengoni's market near San Lorenzo.[23] Later, in the eighties, Poggi collaborated with Mariano Fabrini (1804–85) on the schemes for the Piazza Vittorio Emanuele, now the Piazza della Repubblica and the heart of modern Florence (Figure 171). This piazza was ruthlessly carved from a run-down area rich in ancient buildings. If it was necessary to add

23. See p. 300.

Figure 168. Giuseppe Poggi: Florence, Viale G. Matteotti, 1868 ff.

Figure 169. Giuseppe Poggi: Florence, San Niccolò, improvements, 1865 ff.

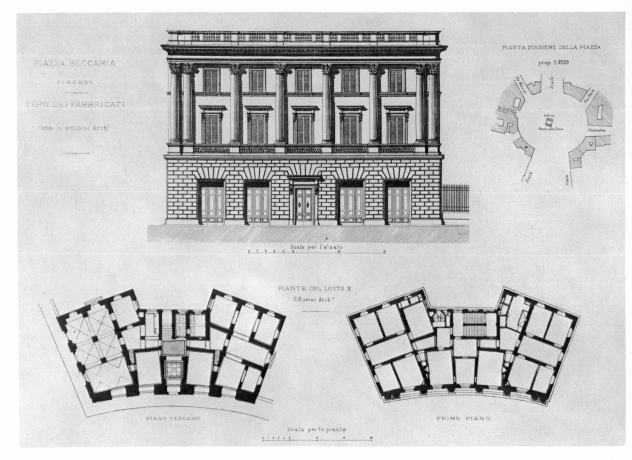

Figure 170. Giuseppe Poggi and G. Roster: Florence, Piazza Beccaria, typical elevation, site plan, and plans of parcel 10, 1860s

Figure 171. Mariano Fabrini (?): Florence, Piazza Vittorio Emanuele, west side, 1893–95

a lung to the city at this point, it was not necessary to surround it with such flatulent buildings.[24] The huge screenlike structure on the west side of the piazza, featuring a triumphal arch, is dated 1895 and is too big for its surroundings. It is an insensitive design: the columns are graceless in proportion, the attic is obviously only thick enough to support the inscription and sculpture. Most of the forms and details come from the Cinquecento although the garlands on the upper frieze of the arch have a *Stile Floreale* look as well as having Roman precedent.

In Naples a certain amount of new building and city planning had taken place from time to time throughout the century.[25] Among the new work was an important street called the *rettifilo,* connecting the station with the area around the Palace. Along it, the fine Piazza Nicola Amore was made at the intersection with a cross street (Figure 172). A number of new multistory palaces for both commercial and residential use were built along it, but the main display at this piazza was entrusted to Piero Paolo Quaglia (1856–98), who designed and built four identical showy buildings on the four corner sites. The essence of the problem was a universal one in the nineteenth century, how to stretch the old palace formula to include the increased number of stories necessary. In this case the number of stories was six, but the clear alternation of main floors and mezzanines directly expressed as such, as Vignola had done in the Palazzo Farnese at Bologna, for instance, was much too simple for this exuberant architect from Varese. Instead he resorted to a lush treatment paralleled in other buildings of this time in Rome and Genoa. The ground floor and one mezzanine are handled as a rusticated basement. Over this is laid another story of intermediate size; above this a main story and mezzanine are combined in a large arcaded layer. This is topped by another story of intermediate size, arcaded and recessed in part. Most of the detailing is Mannerist: prominent rustication at a large scale, and caryatid portals, standing on diamond-faced blocks and supporting huge beam ends, like the type of portal so popular in Genoa in the sixteenth and seventeenth centuries. The more Neoclassical galleries at the top are supported by more beam ends and ganes. The whole surface is deeply modeled with advancing and receding elements. So active and plastic a design was fatally easy to carry out in ductile stucco. Reference has already been made to imitative effects above; Naples is particularly prone to such imitation.[26]

Rome's revived status as a capital required the building of a series of important governmental buildings, and the rapid growth of the population demanded

24. Hitchcock, *Architecture,* p. 145, remarks that the city with a nineteenth-century Neo-Tuscan heart was Munich, not Florence. The arcaded Palazzo Paggi-Tainti by Giovanni Paciarelli which stands one block northwest of the piazza was not finished until 1905. *Edilizia moderna,* *14* (1905), 61.

25. See pp. 121 ff.

26. See p. 305.

Figure 172. Piero Paolo Quaglia: Naples, Piazza Nicola Amore, 1890s

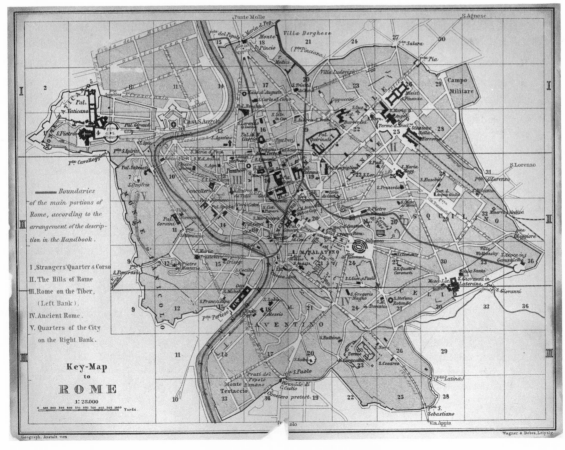

Figure 173. Rome, plan in 1880

new streets, new quarters, and a vast number of new buildings for other purposes. Hence, during the last part of the century, Rome was a center of feverish activity and drew to herself the most distinguished Italian architects. The preferred style was that of the Cinquecento. Medievalism had little success there, as we have seen, apart from religious work done in that style because of its Christian associations. This was partly because *Cinquecentismo* was the dominant style of the period throughout Italy and partly because the Papacy was eclipsed by the secular government. But the most significant factor, as has been said, must have been deference to the great buildings standing there so nobly, which had for so long enjoyed great repute for their quality as well as associations.

Aside from the very skillful work done at the Porta del Popolo by Valadier and others, the systematization of the hillside to the Pincio, and the new entrance to the Villa Borghese with fine gates by Canina, little had been achieved before 1870.[27] Even though in the first half of the century the population had risen to 170,824, the city still occupied only one-third of the area of the ancient imperial city (Figure 173). Coming from the Porta San Sebastiano toward the city by carriage it was said to be half an hour before one encountered habitations. Much of this inhabited third was occupied by villas standing in handsome gardens, which, if preserved, would have provided much-needed parks and piazzas.

Under French and papal control, some planning had taken place. Some work had been done in the Mastai area by Sarti and Busiri-Vici around the Manifattura dei Tabacchi in the 1860s. More important, the Belgian Cardinal de Mérode had been buying up land on the Quirinale and Esquiline and had begun work on connecting the area around the Baths of Diocletian with the Piazza Santissimi Apostoli. He began a street near the Baths which became part of the Via Nazionale.[28] The Cardinal began buying in this location, since it had been suggested by Francesco Gasparoni in 1862 that a street should be laid out there to connect the proposed railroad terminal with the center of the city.

Early in the seventies, General Cadorna appointed a planning commission. The head of the committee was Pietro Camporese the younger. The committee turned in its report in forty days, and it served as the basis of the development plan published in 1873 by Alessandro Viviani, which was never made law but did have considerable influence on subsequent developments. At about this time Quintino Sella invited Baron Haussmann to give his advice. He concluded

27. The principal sources for the study of the development of Rome at this time include Arturo Calza, *Roma moderna* (Milan, 1911); Marcello Piacentini, *Le Vicende edilizie di Roma dal 1870 ad oggi* (Rome, 1952); and Ferdinando Castagnoli, Carlo Cecchelli, Gustavo Giovannoni, and Mario Zocca, *Topografia e urbanistica di Roma,* Storia di Roma, 22 (Bologna, 1958).

28. A tablet on a building at the corners of Via Nazionale and Via Torino states that it is attached to the first of the new buildings, erected 1868–70.

that the future development would lie on and about Monte Mario. Ninety years later his prophecy is beginning to be fulfilled.

The Tiber presented serious problems; its floods repeatedly swept over its banks and into the low-lying districts of the old city. The King resolved that this should be corrected and urged it with sufficient force to have the whole length of the river through the city on both banks cleared, ten kilometers of retaining walls built, and avenues constructed along them planted with trees and animated with trams. This enormous task was put in operation in 1876 and was completed from the Porta del Popolo to the Porta Portese by 1900.

In 1870 there were few usable bridges linking the old city with the adjoining fields and institutions across the Tiber. Some early modern metallic bridges replaced the ruined central parts of the ancient Roman ones, such as the suspension bridge (Figure 174) which long occupied a site near the present Ponte Palatino downriver from the Isola Tiberina, and further up river the Ponte dei Fiorentini (Figure 175), near the site now occupied by the Ponte Amadeo Savoia d'Aosta. The suspension units here ran up over iron columns before being anchored on the shores. Both of these and probably many others were the work of French engineers following Antoine Remi Polonceau and François Léonce Reynaud. The ancient Ponte Salario, which had been wrecked in 1867 to prevent the entrance of troops, was repaired by 1874. The Ponte Flaminio was rebuilt in stone. In 1878 a temporary bridge of iron trusses on tubular iron piers, the Ponte Ripetta, replaced the old wooden ferry by means of which people had traditionally sought solitude and seclusion in the Prati di Castello.[29] This was replaced by the present Ponte Cavour in 1900.

Two new iron bridges were built. The ugly Ponte Palatino of five girdered spans rose on the site of the old wooden bridge of Sublicius just south of the old Pons Aemilius or Ponte Rotto, which had been ruined by a flood in 1598. Its three remaining arches had been linked to the shore with a suspension span by Pius IX (Figure 174). Only one of the old stone arches now survives. Most of the bridgework of this period was done by the Municipal Hydraulic Bureau directed until 1895 by Angelo Vescovali. The second iron bridge is the Ponte Garibaldi, in two-arched spans built by a Viennese firm from 1885 to 1888.

Foundations for a pair of imposing stone bridges were laid in 1884. These are the Ponte Margherita opposite the Piazza del Popolo, opened for traffic in 1891 but not entirely completed until 1895, and the Ponte Umberto opposite the Palazzo di Giustizia, of the same dates. In the meantime controversy arose about widening and making new approaches to the Ponte Sant'Angelo, the ancient Ponte Elio, partly Hadrianic, with famous angels after Bernini. This was ultimately accomplished without serious injury to the general effect. The most elaborate bridge of this era is the Ponte Vittorio Emanuele near the ruins of the

29. Castagnoli, *Topografia*, pl. 139, fig. 1, pl. 143, figs. 1 and 2.

Figure 174. Rome, Ponte Rotto

Figure 175. Rome, Ponte dei Fiorentini

Ponte di Nerone, built to carry the traffic from the new *corso* toward the Vatican and St. Peter's. This was designed by the engineer, Paolo Emilio de Santis, and was not finished until 1910. Close beside it stood a temporary arched bridge in iron. The new one, although richly decorated, is not as admirable as the contemporary Pont Alexandre III in Paris. One more important bridge was constructed before 1914. This is the Ponte del Risorgimento built to connect the two parts of the Exposition of 1911, the permanent art galleries on the Viale delle Belle Arti and the temporary pavilions around the Piazza Giuseppe Mazzini. This is a single span of 100 meters in reinforced concrete, and for some time was one of the boldest spans in that material.

The Isola Tiberina, which had been connected to the mainland from ancient times by a southern bridge, the Ponte Cestio, and a northern one, the Ponte Fabricio or "Quattro Capi" after the four-headed hermae which once stood on the balustrades, also required attention. Two new arches were built to replace the damaged parts of the Ponte Cestio. The Ponte Fabricio, now the oldest bridge in Rome still in use, was repaired.

One of the areas developed at this time (the 1870s) was the Prati di Castello, the low-lying fields across the Tiber back of the Castel Sant'Angelo and toward Monte Mario. These were laid out in gridiron pattern. This area was further extended after the Exposition of 1911, which took place on the old Piazza d'Armi (the nearby barracks are still standing). The plan had radial avenues, some of them very wide, such as the Viale Giuseppe Mazzini and the Via I Settembre.[30]

Similar growth occurred in every direction. The Viminale was covered with discreet buildings, except for the Ministero degli Interni by Manfredo Manfredi (1859–1927), which is too large. The Esquiline around Santa Maria Maggiore developed well, partly because several of Sixtus V's avenues were already there to suggest great vistas. The Palazzo Brancaccio's enormous bulk (Figure 212) determined the character of new building in the area. Nearby an extensive piazza was built—the Piazza Vittorio Emanuele II, 180 by 300 meters (Figure 176). It was surrounded by high buildings with porticoes under them, looking, as Lavagnino has said, like a "chip from Turin," related to that city's Piazza dello Statuto and also to the Rue de Rivoli. It was begun in 1882.[31] A number of architects were assigned the individual buildings. They included Gaetano Koch (1838–1910), who erected the two central palaces on the long sides, among his earliest works, Giulio Podesti (1857–1909) and Riggi (flourished 1880s). The vast piazza itself was intended to feature a monument to

30. Lewis Mumford, *The City in History* (New York, 1961), p. 389. He does not mention the influence of this exposition.

31. Lavagnino, *L'Arte moderna, 1*, 666; and Piacentini, *Vicende edilizie*, p. 22.

Figure 176. Gaetano Koch and others: Rome, Piazza Vittorio Emanuele II, 1870 ff.

Italian Unity, but this was never built and a picturesque informal garden was completed instead in 1890. This, combined with the location and scale of the surrounding palaces and the fact that certain rather untidy markets have taken it over, has meant that it does not enjoy any elegance or fashion. It is doubtful that it ever did so.

The Macao outside the Porta Pia toward the Villa Torlonia and the Piazza Galeno was begun as an area of suburban villas, among the earliest of which was one Giulio de Angelis built for himself before 1877. The area within the walls between the Porta Pia, the Porta Pinciana, and the Via XX Settembre soon became a fashionable residential zone, ignoring the old rule that cities tend to grow in a westerly direction. It is crossed by the Via Veneto and the Via Boncompagni-Ludovisi. Some streets are named for the provinces of Italy, while those that cross the Via Nazionale are named for cities. This area combines mansions standing in their own grounds with apartment blocks. Today some of these are well maintained, some have become famous hotels or cafés, and some which had declined are being carefully restored. There are trees and gardens, and it has maintained much of its upper-class air. Parioli, from the Villa Borghese and the Zoo north and west, shares this luxurious atmosphere. The post-World War II boom has affected this tone adversely as newer buildings further out become more popular.

Some serious mistakes were of course made, notably the building-over of the old villa gardens mentioned above, the destruction of antique ruins and of the urban scale about the "Vittoriano," exemplified by the enlargement of Piazza Venezia. This required the demolition of the old Palazzo Torlonia, originally a building of the Cinquecento which had been remodeled by Valadier early in the nineteenth century. It had a great gallery with Canova's somewhat overpowering Hercules and Lyceas in a niche in one end, a Moorish drawing room, a Gothic chapel, and so on. In taste it was not unlike that exhibited by the structures the Rothschilds erected at the same period.

On the whole, however, new streets and piazzas were managed within the old city with some care and skill. The new Corso Vittorio Emanuele wound its way deftly among important churches and palaces, thus preserving them and setting some of them into interesting perspectives. The imposition on old Rome of a star pattern of wide tree-lined boulevards would have been devastating even if, perhaps, conducive to better traffic flow. But, as we know today, the wider the street the greater the need for widening it soon becomes.

One of the major undertakings was the Traforo Umberto I, a ramped tunnel connecting the new Via del Tritone with the new Via Nazionale. Projected in 1873, the work did not begin until 1900, but was usable in 1902, although the entrance façades were not completed until 1905. That on the Via Milano is by Pio Piacentini (1846–1928), Giulio Tommasi, and Alessandro Viviani (1825–1905). Other streets were created or widened, such as the old Corso, the Via Due Macelli, the Via Cavour, the Via Agostino de Pretis, the Via delle Quattro Fontane, the Via Veneto, and the Via Quattro Novembre. A number of these were made to follow rather difficult contours with apparent ease and naturalness, thus differing from Baron Haussmann's more rigid style. On the whole, in spite of delays, scandals, and irresolution, the job was finally accomplished and with more subtlety than the ruthless triumphal ways later bulldozed by Mussolini.

Some of these new streets required wholly new buildings to be built upon them. Others required new façades to be added to older buildings, such as that added to the Palazzo Odescalchi (1887–89) by Raffaello Oietti (1845–1924) in the Florentine style of the Palazzo Riccardi.

In addition, numerous projects were devised that came to little or nothing. One of the more fervid agitations centered around the idea of building a Galleria, such as those in Milan and Naples, in some central location such as the Piazza Colonna or on the site of the destroyed Palazzo Piombino. It was not until 1923 that the present Y-shaped one north of that piazza, with an arm reaching toward the Piazza San Silvestro and the Tritone, was actually built. From 1872 to 1900 sixty-nine projects for systematizing this area had been offered. The present gallery never achieved the success of its predecessors in other cities.

Rome today is in desperate need of further urban planning, particularly the preservation of open lands. The universal postwar population explosion has led to fantastic overdevelopment of the surrounding countryside. Future slums are being built at an appalling rate.

The Tritone, like the two Corsi, now thronged with shoppers and crowded with traffic, was lined with new multistory buildings of little distinction. Many of the ordinary buildings of the decade from 1895 to 1905 in most Italian cities tended to be relatively ornate and in active competition with their neighbors to attract the attention of the passerby—an Anglo-Saxon weakness which unfortunately had temporarily overcome the better instincts of the Italians.

Haussmann arbitrarily achieved an effect of uniformity in Paris, but Rome's harmonious streets came about more naturally and are consequently less monotonous. It is not always easy to tell the old from the new. This reticence is very general; the work of Gaetano Koch, "*il Padrone di Roma*," only stands out from that of his contemporaries by its greater degree of sobriety and integrity.

One of Koch's most important works was the pair of quadrantal palaces on the Piazza dell'Esedra, occupying the site of the exedra of the Baths of Diocletian and framing the vista down the Via Nazionale toward the Monument

Figure 177. Gaetano Koch: Rome, Palazzi della Piazza dell' Esedra, 1888 ff.

to Victor Emanuel II.[32] These large buildings (begun 1888) have arcades along the ground floor (Figure 177), not a typically Roman feature, and three upper stories. The end pavilions are unusual in Italy. Lavagnino suggests that the instructing committee which sponsored a competition recommended that the contemporary French style, that of Charles Garnier, be followed.[33] There is, indeed, some hint of the Paris Opéra in them, but it is a chastened and static variant, lacking both the sumptuousness and vitality of the original. The pavilions have three bays and suggest at some distance the Trevi Fountain backdrop, but aside from these and the rather crushed caryatids on the uppermost floor, the motives could have come from Sangallo and from the Capitoline, with its use of giant pilasters. Whatever its sources it is a very successful piece of urbanism.

The splendid fountain which occupies the center of the piazza was begun by Alessandro Guerrieri in 1885 to replace the earlier one dedicated in 1870, just before the city fell to the Garibaldian troops. It was subsequently completed between 1901 and 1914, with voluptuous naiads by Mario Rutelli.[34] The old fountain of 1870 was adorned with four noble lions, and the central feature was a single tall jet like the present one, which rises to a magnificent height and is visible from afar.

Ministries and Monuments; Public and Commercial Palaces

One of the most conspicuous nonconforming buildings of this period is the former seat of government in Turin, an addition to Guarini's Palazzo Carignano, in which Victor Emanuel I had been born (Figure 178). The old palace was used by the Subalpine government and then by the government of Italy from 1848. For a while the government, before moving to Florence in 1865, met in a temporary wooden structure, which had been constructed by Antonelli in 1860 in the palace courtyard. It had been previously decided to enlarge the palace. A new eastern façade was designed by Gaetano Ferri (1822–96), a painter from Bologna associated with the engineer Giuseppe Bollati (1819–69). Construction was begun in 1863 in granite and brick and completed in 1874, although by that time the seat of government had moved on to Rome.

The design is thoroughly French, not only because Ferri had been educated in France, but because the whole orientation of Piedmont and its court had

32. Part of the Roman exedra stood until 1887. Castagnoli, *Topografia*, p. 583, suggests a date of about 1885–90 for Koch's work; however Piacentini, *Vicende edilizie*, p. 69, says that Koch was appointed to the task in 1888.

33. Lavagnino, *L'Arte moderna, 1*, 605.

34. Rutelli's bronze groups were considered so daring that the clergy protested and no one ventured to dedicate them. The hoardings were pulled down at night without ceremony. Piacentini, *Vicende edilizie*, p. 68; Castagnoli, *Topografia*, p. 615.

Figure 178. Gaetano Ferri: Turin, Palazzo Carignano, new façade, 1863–71

been traditionally French. Hence Ferri, in a typically nineteenth-century spirit, rejected the Baroque-Rococo aspects of Guarini's palace.

The imposing façade on the Piazza Carlo Alberto is a mélange of motives. The three-storied central pavilion is flanked by bays framed with conventionally superimposed orders ending in segmental pediments, in the manner of Salomon de Brosse at St. Gervais in Paris or of Lescot's pavilions at the Louvre, which begin with free-standing orders and terminate in engaged ones. From St. Gervais may have come the treatment of the column shafts where only the upper two-thirds are fluted and the lower third is rusticated. Other unquestionably Manneristic practices can be found in many details of this façade. The general effect is imposing and the overall scheme original. Such results were not always achieved by revival architects, despite their frequent efforts to find memorable images. The interior of the assembly hall has an eighteenth-century air.[35]

At Trieste, which continued to be Austrian, Niccolò Bruno (or Bruni, died 1899) remodeled the Palazzo Municipale from 1869 to 1876 (Figure 179). This hybrid structure can be taken as representative of a few other buildings of this date which are most notable for their pretentiousness. Granted it is not easy to make a building of this size, five stories in height and seventeen bays in length, anything but monotonous, yet the architect Niccolò Bruno tried hard to avoid this pitfall by designing wings with only three bays and four stories, and his main block with eleven bays and five stories, giving it entirely different ornament and windows. Three of these bays have been further varied through yet another window treatment and through their extension above the cornice with segmental pediments. Finally a picturesque, High Victorian feature has been added, a tower raised above the axial bay with a loggia, a clock framed in a semicircular cornice, and topped off by a crested, steeply sloping rectangular roof. At the piazza level, the arcades alternate in height, some being rusticated and some not. The vocabulary as a whole is derived from Venezia and Lombardy, and is rich with such Mannerist details as rusticated columns, *bifore,* pediments, and caryatids. This building reflects more clearly than most the south European equivalent of High Victorian Gothic with its "Virim" aesthetic.

The Umbertian period did not make as great an imprint on Genoa as did earlier and later periods. A few monumental buildings arose around the Piazza de Ferrari and along the Via XX Settembre, but these are post-Umbertian for the most part. Otherwise, there are only three Umbertian buildings worthy of mention. These are a church, the Immacolata Concezione discussed below,[36] a hospital, and a tomb. The Ospedale di Sant'Andrea Coronato by Cesare Parodi, on a lofty airy site with large-windowed wards and a garden, is quietly

---

35. T.C.I., *Piemonte,* Attraverso l'Italia, *1* (Milan, 1930), p. 54, pl. 65.
36. See p. 386.

Figure 179. Niccolò Bruno: Trieste, Palazzo Comunale, remodelled, 1869–76

Palladian, with its central dome, portico, and widely separated wings. Giuseppe Mazzini's tomb at Staglieno was built in 1872 by Vittorio Gaetano Grosso and is almost expressionist in its exaggeration of normal forms. Basically, it is Greek Doric distyle *in antis.* But the columns are remarkably stubby and taper rapidly toward their capitals. Behind them the massive wall is punctured by a door with battered sides, which Lavagnino calls Egyptian but which is equally plausibly Greek.[37] Everything about the tomb is heavy, bare, and solid, testifying more to Mazzini's leadership than to his physique. Carlyle, who was not very robust himself, found Mazzini markedly weak.

Milan, as the mercantile and industrial capital of Italy, grew rapidly in this period. We have already mentioned above its Neo-Medieval buildings, its numerous restorations, and its greatest modern building, the Galleria.[38]

Toward the end of the century, the most prominent figure was Luca Beltrami (1854–1933) who, in addition to his professorship and his post as chief of antiquities for Lombardy, found time to write prolifically and to undertake a number of important commissions.[39] He was one of those nineteenth-century figures of apparently inexhaustible energy and boundless good health. A Milanese by birth, he had been educated in Paris at the École des Beaux-Arts. He had also studied at the Brera and the Politecnico, and had thus been a pupil of Boito. He is said to have been just and friendly but, although generous, somewhat austere.

In 1890 Beltrami constructed a new façade to Alessi's Palazzo Marino on the Piazza della Scala (Figure 180). The old south façade had fifteen bays, with the portal asymmetrically placed at the seventh bay from the right-hand corner. Beltrami's new western façade on the Piazza della Scala is only twelve bays long. Its two portals occupy the fifth bays from the corners. That on the left is made more prominent by a porch of paired columns not unlike Alessi's portal on the south façade. On both the old and the new façades the sequence of orders, beginning with the ground floor, is Tuscan, Ionic, and a tapered gane. The grand cornice and attic are Neoclassical. The sequence of window frames is unconventional: those on the ground floor are like a battle between evenly matched adversaries, i.e. columns and rustication; those of the second floor are composed of lion-headed ganes supporting broken segmental pediments; and those of the third are descended from Michelangelo's on the Palazzo Farnese. The pairing of pilasters occurs only over one portal and at the ends, suggesting that the south portal had been determined before Beltrami began. The courtyard is extremely rich and Mannerist. The "new façade," while closely derived from Alessi's, is in harmony with the nearby entrance to the Galleria but not at all

---

37. Lavagnino, *L'Arte moderna, 1,* 541 and fig. 443.

38. See pp. 290 ff.

39. Guido Mazzoni, ed., *Bibliografia degli scritti di Luca Beltrami dal marzo 1881 al marzo 1930* (Milan, 1930).

Figure 180. Luca Beltrami: Milan, Palazzo Marino, new façade, 1890

with the severe and timid Scala. Beltrami's work thus shows the occasional nineteenth-century preference for florid display.

The same taste is visible in other buildings by Beltrami, such as the Palazzo Venezia delle Assicurazioni Generali di Milano (1897–99), Piazza Cordusio, which has on its summit the Lion of St. Mark, a cupola, and a dome. The latter two features did not appear on his original project. He contrived to get five stories into the palace formula, and to mingle the elements of the styles of Alessi, the Baroque, and Neoclassicism into a somewhat creative Eclecticism. The obelisks are particularly striking in combination with the huge axial niche.

Like Boito and many other Italian architects, Beltrami was not only a teacher and restorer, but was also active in the field of history and criticism. In addition, he was a Deputy and later a Senator. His architectural work was not as original as he wished. He could not break the chains of tradition, either because the forces of Eclecticism were too powerful or because his clients would not permit it. His work as an historian may have led him to keep his new buildings in harmony with the surroundings. Laudable in itself, such thinking would hinder any powerful impulse toward originality. Taken all together, these were powerful limitations. Nevertheless, at the time and to some critics' eyes, Beltrami's work seemed relatively fresh and expressive of his buildings' function and character. It was a matter of subtleties within an understood range of vocabulary, a much narrower range of form and detail than we are accustomed to, which had the effect of making small differences count for much more then than they do today. Overall, Beltrami's work was never niggling or finicky, but robust and of fairly wide range. Today his rôle as an historian and archaeologist seems more significant than his work as an architect, despite his great professional eminence.[40]

The Palazzo della Cassa di Risparmio at Bologna was begun in 1868 and finished in 1876 (Figure 181). Its architect was Giuseppe Mengoni, the architect of the Galleria in Milan. This bank is an impressively large building which still serves its original purpose, although the interiors have been decisively modernized. It is one of the rare buildings of the period in which fine materials were actually used and not merely imitated. The richness of the window frames, cornice, and paneled surfaces was considered appropriate to its function, according to the prevailing system of associative values which ascribed such a parade of wealth and craftsmanship to the temples of the true faith—money. The arcade within the mass of the building conforms to Bolognese traditions, whereas the ornament owes more to Venice, once the most successful commercial city in Italy.

40. Beltrami's most important work outside of Milan is the Pinacoteca Vaticana of 1932, built near the end of his life. Pope Pius XI had assigned him a difficult task, since works by the greatest masters surrounded the site. Avoiding direct competition with these formidable rivals, Beltrami used an imported Lombardic Renaissance style, unpretentious in material and delicate in scale.

Figure 181. Giuseppe Mengoni: Bologna, Palazzo della Cassa di Risparmio, 1868–76

Piero Quaglia, who had written vehement protests over the conduct of the competitions for the design of the Monument to Victor Emanuel in Rome, *100 Schizzi dei progetti pel monumento a Vittorio Emanuele*, was the architect of the new building for the University of Naples which was executed after his premature death by Guglielmo Melisurgo. The design lacks the exuberance of his buildings on the Piazza Depretis, now Piazza Nicola Amore.

The Neapolitan Bourse had been projected in 1861 (Figure 182). Some ten different schemes had been adopted as the committee repeatedly changed its mind about the site. The final site was irregular, since an old chapel had to be preserved. The architect was Alfonso Guerra (1845–1900) in association with the engineer Luigi Ferrara (1810–94). Work was begun in 1893 and continued to at least 1899. An illustrated monograph describing the building was published in 1909.[41] The French segmental pediment is featured on all façades. The principal window motive is a partially blind Palladian one. The sequence of orders is unconventional: a tall Ionic, a shorter Ionic, and a Corinthian. There are widely spaced caryatids along the attic, and coarse, sans-serif lettering on the base of the flagpole. The interiors are highly ornate and not distinguished. Lavagnino sees in this building a Neapolitan taste for sumptuous display resulting in lavish use of marbles, bronzes, and frescoes, but concludes that it is showy, boring, and gloomy.[42]

The first of the new Roman ministries to be completed was the enormous Ministero delle Finanze on the new Via XX Settembre, built from 1870 to 1877 (Figure 183). It is 300 meters long. Three men were involved, the chief being the hydraulic engineer Raffaele Canevari (1825–1900) who was responsible for the overall scheme. He was assisted by two architects, Martinori Martinozzi and Francesco Pieroni (1829–83). The latter, who had been a pupil of Sarti and Poletti and a collaborator of Letarouilly, designed the huge central court in what some would consider a coldly mechanical manner.[43] The vast building, comparable for its time and place to the Pentagon, was hastily built and requires frequent repair. It has seldom been admired as much as it deserves.[44] Canevari was criticized for undertaking the commission at all, being at the time a government official. His answer was that the building was needed quickly and he alone could get it done expeditiously. Its warm red-and-ochre coloring, its simple articulation into pavilions and stories, and its sparing use of ornament seem restful and practical today. The arrangement into wings, pavilions, and courts effectively breaks up what might otherwise have been a mo-

41. Alfonso Guerra and Luigi Ferrara, *Nuovo Palazzo della Borsa in Napoli* (Napoli, 1909).
42. Lavagnino, *L'Arte moderna, 1*, 587.
43. Ibid., *1*, 601. See also Piacentini, *Vicende edilizie*, p. 31; and *Edilizia moderna, 8* (1899), 85 ff.
44. Hitchcock, *Architecture*, p. 145, considers the Ministero delle Finanze, Rome, less distinguished than the palaces around the Piazza dello Statuto in Turin.

Figure 182. Alfonso Guerra and Luigi Ferrara: Naples, Bourse, 1893 ff.

notonous mass. The devices for gradually increasing interest up to the axis of the main pavilion are skillfully manipulated: bare walls give way to pilastered ones, and these in turn to engaged columns under a very large segmental pediment, a motive which is otherwise used only over certain windows which require accentuation. The corner pavilions have discreet but effective cupolas. The vestibules, arcades, and galleries are suitably impressive and monumental. The dominant source of inspiration was Michelangelo's Senatorial Palace. Among other details, the axial window of the end pavilions comes from the main door of that palace. It is a building which expresses better than many of its successors the best qualities of the new government: dignity and confidence untinged with bombast.

One of the next public buildings to go up in Rome was the Palazzo dell'Esposizione on the Via Nazionale (Figure 184). This was to rival the existing facilities for exhibitions in Turin, Milan, and Florence, and hence was given a high priority. Pio Piacentini (1846–1928) was only thirty-two when he won the competition for this building in 1878. It was begun in 1880, completed in 1882, and opened with great pomp by the King and Queen. It was an immense success with the critics and public. Lavagnino considers that this building was the first to give Rome an example of a new architecture. He admires the planning and the main feature, which, besides being highly monumental, manages to provide an effective transition by means of its forest of columns from the daylight outside to the lower level of light within.[45] The design has originality; although the main feature is a triumphal arch, it is not like any of the classical ones. The differences include the flat-headed lateral openings and the arch springing from the cornice of the order rather than lying below it. This latter feature is Palladian. The attic is limited to the central bay instead of extending over the whole motive. Another Renaissance idea is the framing of the lateral entrances as in the Capitoline palaces. The stairs spreading widely before it, the passages through and up it framed in paired columns, all these are not from ancient Rome and yet have a Roman grandeur and scale. The bare, unpierced wings of five bays marked by pilasters have Palladian garlands at the level of the capitals, and there are Palladian figures standing on the lower parapet.

Gaetano Koch's major government building, the Banca d'Italia on the Via Nazionale in Rome, was a commission won in a closed competition against Francesco Azzurri and Pio Piacentini, although only Koch and Piacentini actually submitted designs.[46] It was being built from 1885 to 1892 (Figures 185, 186). Koch's scheme of two large courtyards surrounded by a colossal three-

45. Lavagnino, *L'Arte moderna, 1,* 609. Hitchcock, *Architecture,* p. 146, calls it "quite academic in a respectable Renaissance way."

46. Francesco Azzurri (1827–1901), President of the Accademia di San Luca, had a considerable practice building institutional buildings as well as hotels. His work was quietly competent.

Figure 183. Raffaele Canevari, Martinori Martinozzi, Francesco Pieroni: Rome, Ministero delle Finanze, 1870–77

story elevation, with two entrance pavilions, one for each court, was excessively admired. Its character was said to be perfect, neither that of a large private palace, nor yet that of an institution, but clearly that of a bank. "Bank" means different things to different races. It is a matter of conditioning. Louis Sullivan did not think the sort of temple that McKim, Mead, and White built was at all expressive of a bank. The Romans would not have recognized the character of a bank in Sullivan's work at Owatonna. Neither McKim nor Sullivan would have thought it possible to express "bank" without a large banking room clearly visible to the passerby. That Koch's was a public building all would have agreed.

Once again the palace formula is stretched, but this time with marked success. The façade is twenty-three bays in length but well composed, employing devices similar to those used by Canevari on the Ministero delle Finanze a few years earlier. There is a gradual increase in plasticity from bare walls at the end via pilasters to engaged columns in the central thirteen bays, which are further manipulated into pavilions of three bays framing the central unit of seven bays. There are entrances under both these pavilions instead of one axial one. The end elevations show mezzanines on the two lower stories, achieved on the basement level by omitting the arched heads of the windows of the front, and on the *piano nobile* by suppressing the architrave and frieze of the entablature and continuing only the cornice. Neither the arcades and rustication of the ground floor, which seem Florentine, nor the attic and sculptural groups are Roman Cinquecento.

His unusual frieze has an eighteenth-century look. He abhorred the alternating pediment. His massive tabernacle window frames on the second and third floors are robust and cold.

The organization of the central block is from the Palazzo Chiericati, Vicenza. The most interesting aspect of this composition is the way in which the plastic central section with its two sculptural groups (since removed because of decay) are modulated into the simpler stucco handling of the ends. As one's eyes move from the center toward the ends, one notices that the balconies and even the balustrading under the windows are gone. The engaged columns also disappear. The pilasters which recall them at the corners are thinner on the sides. The travertine of the front walls of the wings dwindles to simpler effects in stucco. Other modifications of this sort are too numerous to mention.

Italian critics find influences from Garnier and in its decoration in the rustication of the lower floor, which carries all the way around the building until hidden by a congeries of assorted buildings. The interiors unquestionably rival those of the Third Empire in Paris. Koch has been able, while limiting himself to a number of familiar motives, to create a memorable image by means of an ingenious composition.

In 1915, when a memorial bust to the architect was being dedicated, one of the speakers pointed out the many ways in which the bank was still up-to-date,

Figure 184. Pio Piacentini: Rome, Palazzo dell'Esposizione, 1878–82

Figure 185. Gaetano Koch: Rome, Banca d'Italia, exterior, 1885–92

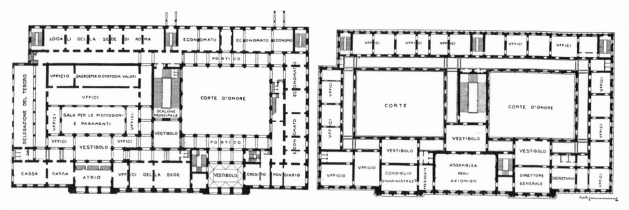

Figure 186. Gaetano Koch: Rome, Banca d'Italia, plans, 1885–92

i.e. *avant-garde* for its day. He mentioned its elevators, internal telephones, electric light, and central heating. The solidity of its construction was considered particularly noteworthy in a city which had recently experienced many deficiencies in this respect. There had been no trace of settlement here and the workmanship was declared equal to that of ancient Rome, by which everything was automatically and proudly measured.

Koch's contemporaries saw in the Banca d'Italia "the most significant building of the period" and could find nothing of servile imitation, but instead found it vigorous and dynamic.[47] We can agree with the first point but not with the second, since what we have come to admire as dynamic in the 1880s and 1890s appeared to the Romans of that time as the experimental follies of would-be innovators.

The Biblioteca del Senato, where, as in his other governmental building, Koch allowed himself to elaborate the detail, is one of the smaller members of the family of classical nineteenth-century libraries which includes the Bibliothèque Sainte Geneviève and the Boston Public Library.

Koch was one of the committee of three architects entrusted with the completion of the "Vittoriano" after the death of Sacconi in 1905. This, the greatest architectural effort of the Italian Government, has a long and complex history. Count Giuseppe Sacconi (1854–1905) came to Rome in 1874 to study architecture with Luigi Rossi, who was the architect of the new façade of the Central Post Office on the Piazza San Silvestro, begun in 1879.[48] He collaborated with Luca Carimini (1830–90) in restoring the basilica at Loreto, and followed his style in his first independent work, the church of San Francesco at Force. This was in a sober Renaissance manner. At almost the same time he won over 292 other contestants the second competition for the Monument to Victor Emanuel II (Figure 187). The Parliament had decreed this international competition in 1880, and the best-known names in architecture and sculpture in Europe made submissions. There were two further stages before the commission was finally awarded in 1884, after bitter wrangling which, in fact, has never entirely ceased. The prize for the first competition had been given to Paul-Henri Nénot (1853–1934), from France, whose submission (Figure 188) was then discovered to be related to his *Grand Prix* design of 1877. Some considered this indefensible, either because it was not a wholly new design or because it was non-Italian. Piero Quaglia, the architect, some of whose work in Naples we have seen, contributed to the polemics.[49]

47. *La Tribuna,* Rome (March 16, 1910), p. 3.
48. See U. Pesci, "Il Nuovo Palazzo della posta," *L'Illustrazione italiana* (Nov. 23, 1879), p. 327.
49. Piero Quaglia, *100 Schizzi dei progetti pel monumento a Vittorio Emanuele* (Rome, 1882). A useful monograph is Primo Acciaresi, *Giuseppe Sacconi e l'opera sua massima* (Rome, 1911).

Figure 187. Giuseppe Sacconi: Rome, Monument to Victor Emanuel II, design, final competition, 1884

Figure 188. Paul-Henri Nénot: Rome, Monument to Victor Emanuel II, design, first competition, 1882

The original decree had called for a design which would resume the history of the country and at the same time be a symbol of the new age. Some interpreted this as the new architectural style of Garnier's Opéra in Paris, which had influenced some other Italian buildings at the time. Corinto Corinti's multi-mansarded Tower of Babel was one of the tower projects (Figure 189). There were further difficulties. Patriotism, then as always at a high pitch in Italy, required that somehow the prize be given to an Italian, and a specific site was finally assigned. The spur north of the Capitoline was now preferred since it would put "modern" Rome in the closest possible conjunction with monuments of Italy's two greatest periods, the Roman Fora and the Renaissance Campidoglio. This was proposed in 1880 by Pio Piacentini and Ettore Ferrari (b. 1849). Some objected to the inevitable destruction of ancient ruins. In 1882 the sentiment for the Capitoline site won out. This decision increased the delays and costs enormously, since, as the preparation of the site went on, what had been believed to be a spur of tufa turned out to be a mass of old quarries incapable of supporting such a *mole* without vast substructures. In the following international competition of 1882, there were seventy entrants. Ultimately a run-off was held between Sacconi, Manfredo Manfredi, and Bruno Schmitz (1858–1916) from Düsseldorf. The young, almost unknown Sacconi was given the commission in 1884 for his Praeneste-based project, and it occupied him the rest of his life.

Many of the grandiose designs submitted in the second competition were published with their authors' comments and some editorial criticism.[50] In this competition, as has been stated, the Campidoglio site had been fixed with the axis of the Corso as an important consideration. The submissions fell into two main types: first, those which raised a great vertical motive skyward from a relatively low setting and placed the equestrian statue of Victor Emanuel up on it or against it; and second, those which placed the statue lower but against an architectural backdrop of some sort. This scheme was derived from the Acropolis of Pergamon or from Praeneste, with special reference to Canina's impressive restoration of the latter. The winning design, that of Sacconi, was of the second type and superior to most others of this class, in that the backdrop did not by its richness or complexity overshadow the memorial statue, as did those by Manfredo Manfredi (Figure 190) and Raimondo d'Aronco (Figure 191). Furthermore, by cutting down and pushing aside the approaches it made the statue visible from nearby. In many instances the foundations and staircases would have obstructed the view of the statue from close at hand. The overly elaborate backgrounds included a curved colonnade (Professor G. Regas) or elaborate screens containing triumphal arches (Martinucci Vincenzo).

There was a scheme which placed the statue against a vast niche like the one in the Cortile of the Belvedere at the Vatican. The niche was to be fifteen meters

50. *L'Italia artistica,* 2 (1884), 3 ff.

Figure 189. Corinto Corinti: Rome, Monument to Victor Emanuel II, design, first competition, 1882

Figure 190. Manfredo Manfredi: Rome, Monument to Victor Emanuel II, design, second competitin, 1884

Figure 191. Raimondo d'Aronco: Rome, Monument to Victor Emanuel II, design, second competition, 1884

wide and thirty-two meters high. This was by Stefano Galletti and Koch. Its authors referred specifically to Bramante and Praeneste.

Bruno Schmitz showed a six-column temple front between pilastered towers, with a quadriga above and the statue in front. This was criticized for following too closely Otto Wagner's project for the Parliament in Berlin and P. Wallot's project for the Bahnhof at Frankfurt. There is also a source in Vanbrugh's entrance portico at Blenheim. The real feeling here, I think, was parallel to that expressed over Nénot's project in the first competition, i.e. that it was not Italian. Innumerable secondary competitions were held for the sculptural accessories. When Sacconi died in 1905 at the age of fifty-one, he left no precise final designs, only rough sketches for a variety of possible schemes. It was necessary to appoint a committee which consisted of Koch, who died shortly, Pio Piacentini, then fifty-five, and Manfredo Manfredi (1859–1927), then forty-six. These men had widely divergent tastes but finally compromised on a scheme for the colonnade and superstructure (Figure 192). They managed, in spite of considerable interference from various officials, to complete most of it in time for the dedication in the Exposition year 1911 on June 4. The first stone had been laid in 1885, twenty-six years earlier. At the time of dedication much of the ornament and sculpture was merely in gesso and was not finally finished in permanent materials until 1922. Many of the interiors were completed still later. The later work was supervised by a commission consisting of Manfredi, Gaetano Vannicola (1859–1923), and Romolo Raffaelli. The rising screen mentioned below was designed by Vannicola.[51] The fact that many details were designed as the work progressed accounts for the variety of styles exhibited, including the *Floreale*. The sums spent were, of course, many times the original estimate.

After all, this building has received little praise. Known affectionately as the "Vittoriano," it is also known less kindly as the "Wedding Cake" and the "Giant Typewriter." Henry-Russell Hitchcock calls it the "most pretentious of all nineteenth-century monuments," representing the total decadence of tradition at the end of the century. It can only be compared with Poelart's Palais de Justice in Brussels, begun twenty years sooner and better for gargantuan assurance. He finds that it is neither Second Empire nor quite Beaux-Arts.[52] That it is overpowering, dominates the city, and blocks the view of the Forum, as I have shown above, was deliberate. Pio Piacentini's son, Marcello, has written about it recently, and Lavagnino on the whole agrees with him.[53] They disapprove of so vast a series of staircases leading up to a colonnade from which there is no exit. This is indeed the case. Once you are up there and have enjoyed the panorama there is nothing to do but come down again. However, this is an inappropriate

51. See p. 456.
52. Hitchcock, *Architecture*, p. 146.
53. Piacentini, *Vicende edilizie*, pp. 44 ff. Lavagnino, *L'Arte moderna, 1,* 526.

Figure 192. Giuseppe Sacconi: Rome, Monument to Victor Emanuel II, 1885–1911

standard by which to judge a purely commemorative monument. They consider that the worst fault, architecturally speaking, is that no distinction was made on the sides between the great base and the upturned flatirons of the ends. They also condemn the placing of a Corinthian temple above terraces supported by excessively decorated walls—an inseparable confusion of line and of ideas.[54] Some regret that glaring white marble was used instead of the traditional Roman travertine so much better adapted to the light of the Campania. In 1880 Italy was nearly twenty years away from a really new style—the *Floreale*—and therefore was unable to create or accept anything more daring than a mixture of traditional classicism and something a little French. This led the younger Piacentini to refer to the architects of that day as "theatrical costumers." Nevertheless, he could praise Sacconi's "noble grandeur of conception," and allowed that he was able to solve well many parts from both structural and decorative standpoints, and granted that he had an unrivaled genius for the interweaving and molding of line and ornament. This I think we, too, can grant. There is an audacity about the conception which leaves this generation gasping. The idea of erecting so colossal a mass without a single significant functional use (there were, inevitably, a number of halls and exhibition galleries within) to guide the architect frightens us, who are accustomed to attack problems as if they required functional or structural solutions. It is like steering a ship without a rudder or sextant, although we are again beginning to give more consideration to character and expression. A revival of interest in the concept of monumentality for its own sake is taking place again today. The recent competition for the F. D. Roosevelt Memorial showed how little aptitude now exists for this sort of imaginative design. Sacconi and his fellow contestants did not have to consider structure or structural economy—they were nearly as free from practical considerations and limitations as the Abstract Impressionist painters of our time; only their strokes and their palette were limited, not their expression.

There can be very little question that this monument achieved its purpose. It is world famous, it commemorates Italy's greatest modern hero, it dominates by color and size the entire capital city much in the way the dome of the Capitol in Washington dominates the District of Columbia. It is breathtaking in its rich intricacy and variety of form, thus testifying in an inescapable manner to the least artistic passerby the vast wealth lavished cheerfully on such a supremely non-utilitarian building. It is a triumphant statement of faith in a material future. A memorable image has been created. The form is unique. Rarely has so tremendous an artificial hill been constructed to support a temple. No traditional theme could have had equal power; no temple, dome, or triumphal arch could have been contrived on this scale, only a ziggurat or a pyramid. But neither of them would have the stamp of the nineteenth century so markedly. Artists and

54. Lavagnino, *L'Arte moderna, 1,* 619–20.

students have often dreamed of such fantasies, but they have remained on paper. It is an astonishing achievement to have realized in three dimensions.

Another of the architectural giants of Koch's day was Guglielmo Calderini (1837–1916), a native of Perugia who studied in Rome and Turin. Ultimately, his style crystallized into a Neo-Baroque one influenced by the success of Sacconi in the "Vittoriano" competition. He was soon able to rival him in ornate exuberance. He always worked at a very large scale and usually with elaborate detail. He dazzled his contemporaries by the fluidity of his imagination and the wealth of his invention, which was expressed in drawings of great power.[55]

Among the competitions to which Calderini submitted designs was that for the Duomo façade in Florence in 1867. In 1877 he lost the competition for the Palazzo Municipale in Naples. In 1879 his project for the Collegiata at Nocera Umbra was published. In the same year he won the competition for the Exhibition Palace at Turin and was awarded the commission. This Palazzo delle Belle Arti was destroyed in World War II. He took part in the first competition for the "Vittoriano." In 1880, as discussed below, he won the competition for and began to execute the façade of the Duomo at Savona.

It was an era of tremendous competitions. In Rome alone there were those for the "Vittoriano," the Palazzo delle Belle Arti, the Policlinico, the new Parliament, and the Banca d'Italia. Calderini won that for the Palazzo di Giustizia, which will be discussed in detail. As has been said, he lost one competition to Piacentini, one to Koch, and one for the Parliament to Talmo. He tried again and was *ex aequus* with Beltrami and Ernesto Basile (1857–1932). He was in charge of the works still in progress at San Paolo f. l. m., and between 1893 and 1910 executed the well-known *quadriportico* to be discussed below.[56] He served as Director of Monuments for Rome, Aquila, and Chieti, and his restorations are said to have been done with meticulous care for the existing remains. These included the cloisters of San Giovanni in Laterano. In 1900 he competed for the projected façade of San Lorenzo in Florence with three designs, all of them relatively but suitably modest compared with his usual taste.[57] In 1906 he lost the competition for the Biblioteca Nazionale in Florence to Cesare Bazzini (Figure 264). He also lost the competition for the Peace Palace at the Hague. But in his very old age, in poor health, he was still able to win another competition, that for the Palazzo Comunale at Messina in 1910. Other

55. Giovanni Battista Milani, *Le Opere architettoniche di Guglielmo Calderini* (Milan, 1916). This portfolio was published during World War I, partly as an act of homage and partly as one of faith in Italy's future. Calderini was one of the most famous architects of his day. He submitted designs of virtuoso brilliance in almost every important competition of the time. These were widely published.

56. T.C.I., *Roma*, p. 322, ascribes the quadriportico to Sacconi.

57. I. B. Supino, *Concorso per la facciata della regia basilica di San Lorenzo in Firenze* (Florence, n.d., c. 1900).

projects continued to be generated on his drafting board until his death in 1916.

His best-known work, the Palazzo di Giustizia in Rome (1880–1910), rivals the "Vittoriano" for sheer bulk and grandeur (Figures 196–199, 263). It is on the Tiber near the Castel Sant'Angelo and thus enjoys a commanding position, as it can be seen from up and down the river for a long way (Figure 197). The large Piazza Cavour makes possible a good view of the rear as well.

The minister Giuseppe Zanardelli had the original idea for this building. He wished it to be a glorious symbol to the third Rome as administrator of justice and peace for united Italy. He sponsored two competitions for it in rapid succession in 1880. He came and went from office, but his rôle as prime mover is clear. In 1884 some forty-eight finalists were selected. These included some of the outstanding architects of the day. Their projects were sumptuous and imposing, more often than not with towering domes, although a certain sentiment in favor of a court of honor was sometimes rumored. In 1886 and 1887 the number of contestants was reduced, and finally a forty-day final run-off competition was held between Calderini and Basile, won by the former. Almost at once the cornerstone was laid, in 1888, and then the usual difficulties followed.

By comparison with Luca Carimini's (1830–90) project, Calderini's capacity for real monumentality is striking; he achieves his effect through largeness of parts, whereas Carimini's is an effort to build up many small parts into a colossal whole (Figure 193). Both use a gigantic arch as the central motive, but Carimini's is weakened by the juxtaposition of four smaller ones; superimposed pairs of them flank the main opening in a Mannerist way. Carimini is more representative of an earlier phase of design; witness his lavish use of towers, four minor and one major, and his determined effort to get plastic variety by bold projections. The minor towers rise in front of the other masses, which include polygonal bastions. Carimini was seven years older than Calderini, and had been a sculptor for many years before he undertook the design of buildings. His use of battlements and crenelations in juxtaposition with palatial and triumphal arch elements recalls Vanbrugh.

Carimini is said to have gotten over his disappointment in losing the competition quite serenely. The handsome model, which had been executed from his design though neglected by him, was photographed, and serves as the basis for the observations above. Basile took a different attitude, and used some features from his rejected design (Figure 195) in his project for the Parliament (Figure 253).

There also had been a surprisingly un-Italian project by F. P. Rivas (Figures 194, 194a). It looked more like something that might have been put up in Washington. Robert Mills would have found it sympathetic, and so would the later architects of the Federal Triangle. The two lower stories were treated as a rusticated basement; the two upper ones were of smooth stone and colossal

Figure 193. Luca Carimini: Rome, Palazzo di Giustizia, model of competition design, 1886

Figure 194. F. P. Rivas: Rome, Palazzo di Giustizia, elevation, preliminary competition

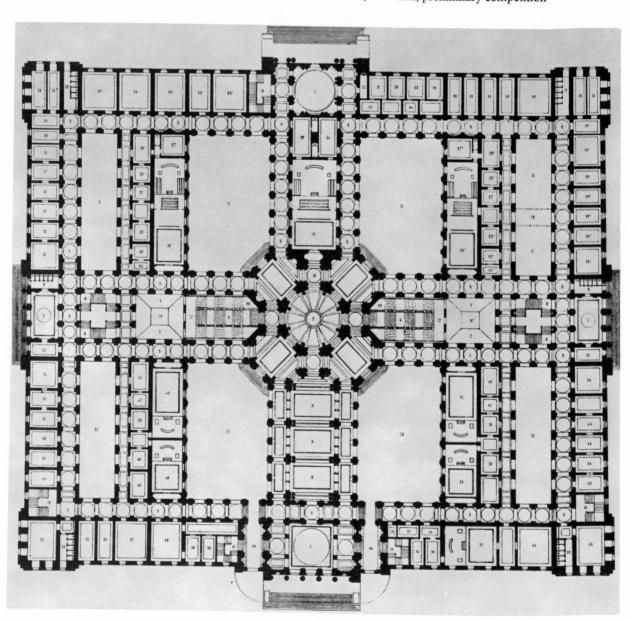

Figure 194a. F. P. Rivas: Rome, Palazzo di Giustizia, plan, preliminary competition

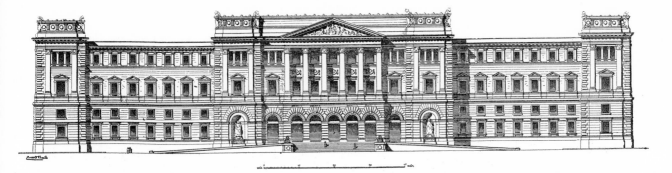

Figure 195. Ernesto Basile: Rome, Palazzo di Giustizia, elevation, preliminary competition, 1885

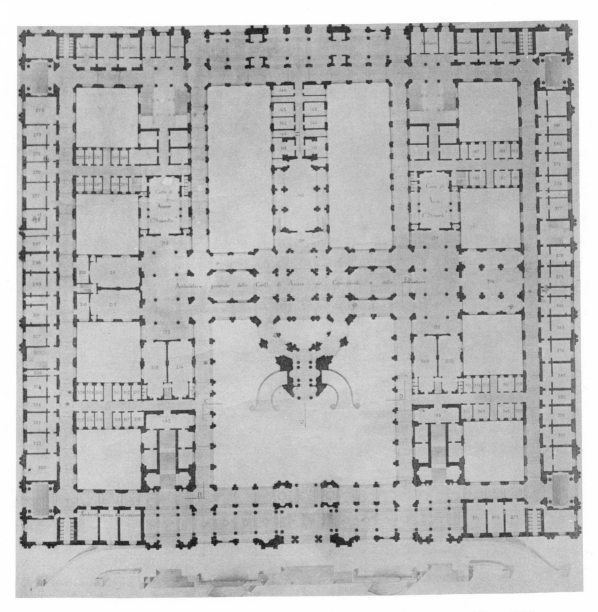

Figure 196. Guglielmo Calderini: Rome, Palazzo di Giustizia, plan of ground floor, 1888

pilasters. The skyline was almost unbroken and the rectangular mass free of jutting pavilions. Within, the great staircases and rotunda at the middle of the complex were not the climax of a courtyard, as in Calderini's project, but were approached under cover. Hence the opportunity for magnificence of exterior effect as seen from the entrance arches was thrown away. This loss seems to have been dictated more by lack of imagination than economy.

Most of the contestants pierced their nearly square plans with numerous interior courts, frequently as many as ten, and sometimes as many as sixteen. The block was generally divided into three principal layers with a dominating feature of some sort over an enormous main entrance. Most designers sought to be monumental and Italian. To some this meant a Renaissance style and to others antique Roman. In Prospero Sarti's design the Roman elements tend to equal the Renaissance ones. Ernesto Basile's project was predominantly Renaissance, with a liberal use of rustication, tabernacle window frames, a giant order, and a six-column temple front (Figure 195). The principal vertical motives, the towers at the corners and those flanking the temple front, ended in attics decorated with a Neoclassical device, triglyphs alternating with disks. His main *salle des pas perdus* ("*sala dei passi perduti*"), as seen in section, was also Neoclassical—a vast hall roofed by five low saucer domes rising above Roman bath windows and columned bays. A Durand-like grid of corridors was woven about the courtrooms, the grand stairs, and ten interior courts. Basile's own description of the scheme emphasizes the circulation system and says nothing about the style of the design.[58]

Some projects maintained an almost unbroken skyline, presumably out of deference to the neighboring Castel Sant'Angelo. Some competitors, while trying to follow the antique Roman style, claimed to be adapting it to modern needs and methods.[59]

Piero Quaglia's project arranged the masses to create numerous vertical accents culminating in a square dome surmounted by a columned and sculptured tower. The large central court, the largest of his thirteen interior courts, would suggest a Renaissance palace scheme except that it is much smaller in proportion to the vast surrounding building. His collaborator on the decorative parts was Raimondo d'Aronco.[60] Calderini, as his earlier career indicates, was ideally prepared for solving the ideological program established by Zanardelli to express the majesty of civil law, as it had been bequeathed by the Imperial Romans, in a building which would recall this glorious tradition to all who beheld it. Spiritual programs like this are a requirement for great public buildings. The

58. Ernesto Basile, "Progetto N. 19," *L'Italia artistica, 4* (1886), 79.

59. Benedetto Andolfi, "Progetto N. 27," *L'Italia artistica, 4* (1886), p. 90. "Giustiniano," "Progetto N. 38," *L'Italia artistica, 4* (1886), p. 87, sought to capture "the true beauty of antiquity and of the pure Renaissance."

60. Piero Quaglia, "Progetto N. 40," *L'Italia artistica, 4* (1886), pp. 94–95.

strict functionalist canon gave less scope, although Le Corbusier, in his projects for Geneva and Moscow, was able to bend the canon triumphantly to his will, and more recently, by being freely creative, he designed symbolic buildings for Chandigarh.

Compared to his contemporaries, Calderini was consistently larger in scale, bolder in mass, and more lavish with circulation areas and multiple corridors (Figure 196). He was particularly grandiose in his handling of stairs. He could not have been very self-conscious, since he used the pseudonym "Imponente" (imposing) for his drawings for one of the Palazzo di Giustizia competitions. He had also used that of "Fieramosca."

Calderini began his designs for this Palace in an era of extravagant optimism, which was warmly congenial to his temperament. The breach in the wall of the city near the Porta Pia had been made only a decade before the first competition for the Palazzo di Giustizia was announced. Rome had returned to her status as capital city. The Third Rome was growing with a rapidity which reminds us of the Florida boom of the twenties. This was accompanied by an atmosphere of unbounded confidence reflected in the pages written in 1911 by Arturo Calza.[61] This project came midway in the series of prodigious new government buildings, a vast program of public works. What a time that was, for Rome, for Italy, and for architects![62]

There were the familiar delays and difficulties, some with the losing contestants, some with the politicians, many over the costs (which, in the usual manner, far exceeded the most lavish estimates), and also some caused by the site (since it was built relatively close to the Tiber on soft, wet ground). Ultimately, like the "Vittoriano," it was completed in 1911 in time for the opening of the Exposition held on the old Piazza d'Armi not far away. Since the work of construction had begun in 1888 it was twenty-three years in progress. This becomes easier to understand when one observes the rich detailing of every part of it, the numerous galleries, the small and large staircases, the balusters, columns, ganes, and vaults, and the elaborate fittings and interior decorations (Figures 198, 263).

Of all the buildings of Italy in the last century, this one has probably come in for more obloquy and objuration than any other, except possibly the "Vittoriano." It was customarily held up to students and public alike as the most licentious, depraved, orgiastic building ever conceived. Such attacks are understandable from the purists of the International Style era, but somewhat more puzzling from the Beaux-Arts men, to whom it might appeal, since their designs for more than a century were built around just such miles of corridors, acres of court-

61. Calza, *Roma moderna*, passim.

62. The love of commemorative monuments in southern countries could be the subject of a valuable study of human motivation.

yards, and interminable flights of grand stairs. The criticism is probably due to the vocabulary chosen by Calderini, which had very little vogue in Paris or anywhere else after 1910, whereas it was quite acceptable at the time it was designed. Heavy rustication was then considered masculine and structurally expressive from Amsterdam to Australia.

The plan of the Palace of Justice is that of a rectangular block surrounding eleven courtyards (Figure 196). The main court is entered through an open arch and a forest of rusticated columns. At the far side rise symmetrically curved flights of stairs leading to a huge domed pavilion. The principal courtroom is at the highest level and at the back. The only other courtrooms in the world to have so grandiloquent an approach are those designed by Poelart for Brussels in the sixties. The scale of everything is gigantic—a man looks like a midget, a cat like a mouse. If ever an architect succeeded in expressing the majesty of the law, Calderini did so in this building. Such spaces as are left after all the ceremonial and processional functions have been so richly provided for are assigned to offices and clerks, much of them in mezzanines opening on the interior courts.

The normal reaction to all this bombast today is expressed by Henry-Russell Hitchcock as follows: "an incredibly brash example of Neo-Baroque loaded down with heavy rustication, doubtless of Piranesian inspiration."[63] On the other hand, Lavagnino says that, whereas enthusiasm for the original project in the case of the "Vittoriano" weakened with time, in this case the nickname "Palazzaccio," originally pejorative, has become affectionate and no longer indicates dislike. He feels that it was placed too near the edge of the embankment. When seen from across the river, however, the embankment serves as a necessary podium. Lavagnino observes its solidity, amplitude, organic character, and good plan. He sees in its lower floor memories of classicism: Palladio and Sansovino eclipsed by memories of Alessi, Tibaldi, and Bibiena. The upper floors are, says Lavagnino, excessively ornate due to Sacconi's influence (Figure 263). There the travertine has been made into low relief rather than architecture, modeled, pierced, and tormented without a moment of repose or quiet, but he does not fail to be impressed by the remarkable power of it, its vitality, and the fact that in spite of its great size it does not sink into monotony. It is consistently majestic within and without (Figure 199).[64]

This seems like a more balanced judgment. It was a real accomplishment to give variety of movement to so vast a building without recourse to significant pediments, towers, or domes. The main façades are twenty-one bays in length with a basic system of a, b, b, b, b, a, b, b, b, c, d, the central bay, and then the reverse (Figure 197). But this is varied within itself. The first and second a's

63. Hitchcock, *Architecture*, p. 146.
64. Lavagnino, *L'Arte moderna, 1*, 622.

Figure 197. Guglielmo Calderini: Rome, Palazzo di Giustizia, exterior, 1888–1910

are not identical, the inner one being three stories high and the second one introducing a commanding Palladian window on its third story. The c, d, c motive in the center pavilion is grouped on the two lower floors under a large semicircular arch, the only important one in the composition. One can see how monotony has been avoided by merely tracing the motives of the first floor, where paired, partly rusticated orders frame some bays and not others, and are sometimes closely coupled and sometimes widely separated. There are a good many other points of interest. As Lavagnino observed, the lower floor has some Alessian "Neoclassical" touches.[65] In this respect it is like Beltrami's Palazzo Marino façade in Milan (Figure 198). The voussoirs under the pediments of the *piano nobile* advance progressively until the sculptured keystone brings the forward movement to a halt. The upper floors make frequent use of two of the motives favored by the *Stile Floreale,* the disk and the heavily weighted garland. These details were designed during the reign of that style. They do not appear in the earlier drawings. The Piranesian character which Professor Hitchcock remarked is largely confined to the rustication of the basement, where the blocks are of formidable size and the barred lunettes have an almost Lodolian severity. Elsewhere the theatrical scale and perspectives of the Bibiena seem operative. What has been said above about the difficulty men of this generation have in appreciating the positive qualities of the "Vittoriano" applies with equal force to this building.

Calderini, however one feels about richly ornamented architecture at a very large scale, did succeed in creating a number of impressively powerful, imaginative works deserving of attention and fame. Ulisse Stacchini's (b. 1871) incredibly colossal station in Milan, designed in 1909, is an example of Calderini's influence.

The competition for the new Parliament in Rome produced another series of grandiose designs. Giulio Magni's (d. 1930), with its courts and vast triple portals, was imposing (Figure 200). Luigi Broggi (1851–1926) and Giuseppe Sommaruga's (1867–1917) heaves up into a single great square dome (Figure 201). There is no trace yet of Sommaruga's more original later phase. Their plan (Figure 202) is of the family of bicameral state capitals arising in the United States, all of them owing a great deal to Beaux-Arts principles. Basile's project (Figure 203) was somewhat more closely related to his design for the Palazzo di Giustizia (Figure 195) than the design he later executed (Figure 253); even so, he proposed a single dominant motive, and gave the whole composition a larger, more monumental handling. His plan (Figure 204), however, derives from Calderini's for the Palazzo di Giustizia, with its inner courtyard and grand staircase.

A number of more utilitarian buildings rose during the last decades of the

65. Ibid., *1,* 623.

Figure 198. Guglielmo Calderini: Rome, Palazzo di Giustizia, detail of exterior, 1888–1910

Figure 199. Guglielmo Calderini: Rome, Palazzo di Giustizia, gallery, 1888–1910

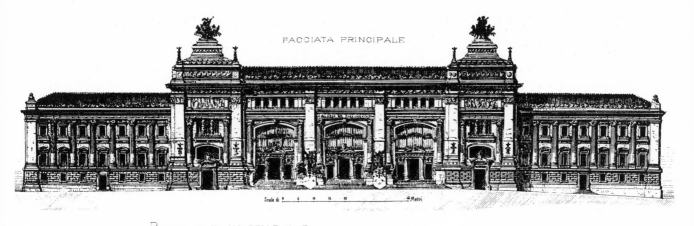

FACCIATA PRINCIPALE

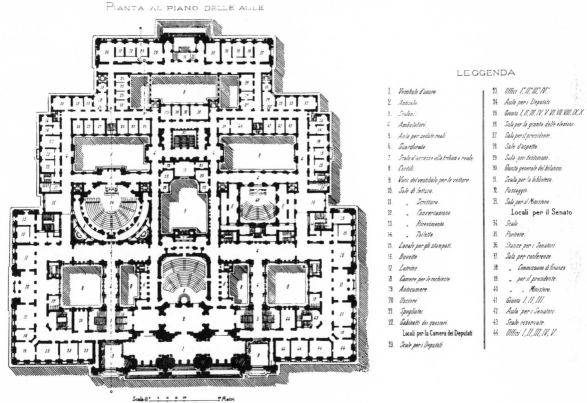

PIANTA AL PIANO DELLE AULE

LEGGENDA

1. Vestibolo d'onore.
2. Anticala.
3. Scaloni.
4. Ambulatori.
5. Aula per sedute reali.
6. Guardaroba.
7. Scala d'accesso alla tribuna reale.
8. Cortili.
9. Vani del vestibolo per le vetture.
10. Sale di lettura.
11.   „   Scrittura.
12.   „   Conversazione.
13.   „   Ricevimento.
14.   „   Toilette.
15. Locale per gli stampati.
16. Buvette.
17. Latrine.
18. Camere per le richieste.
19. Anticamere.
20. Uscieri.
21. Spogliatoi.
22. Gabinetti dei questori.

Locali per la Camera dei Deputati

23. Scale per i Deputati.

23. Uffici I.° II.° III.° IV.°
24. Aula per i Deputati.
25. Giunta I, II, III, IV, V, VI, VII, VIII, IX, X.
26. Sala per la giunta delle elezioni.
27. Sala per il presidente.
28. Sale d'aspetto.
29. Sala per i testimoni.
30. Giunta generale del bilancio.
31. Scala per la biblioteca.
32. Passaggio.
33. Sala per il Ministero

Locali per il Senato

34. Scala
35. Portiere.
36. Stanze per i Senatori.
37. Sala per le conferenze.
38.   „   Commissione di finanze
39.   „   per il presidente.
40.   „   „   Ministero.
41. Giunta I, II, III.
42. Aula per i Senatori.
43. Scale riservate.
44. Uffici I, II, III, IV, V.

Figure 200. Giulio Magni: Rome, Palazzo del Parlamento Nazionale, competition design, elevation and plan, 1890

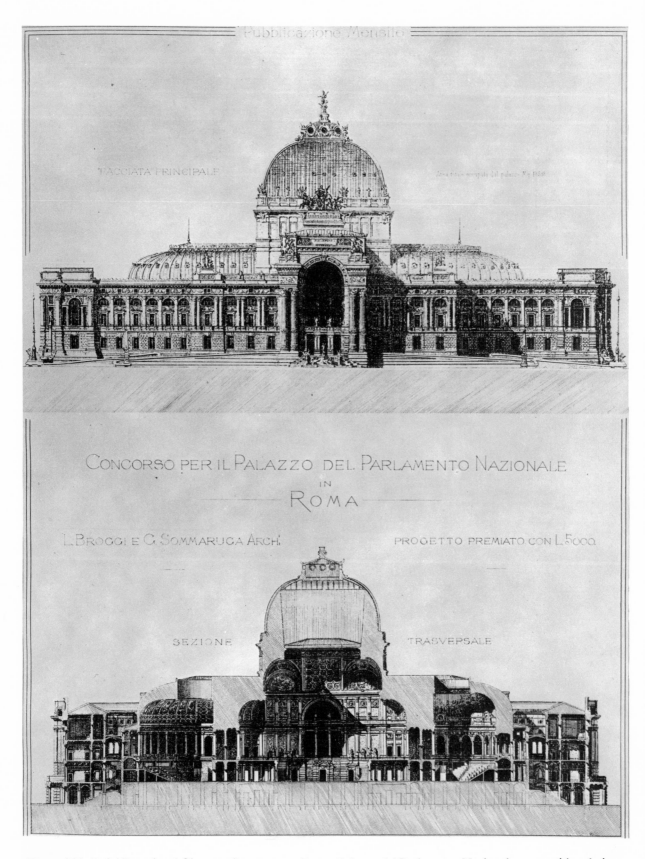

Figure 201. Luigi Broggi and Giuseppe Sommaruga: Rome, Palazzo del Parlamento Nazionale, competition design, elevation and transverse section

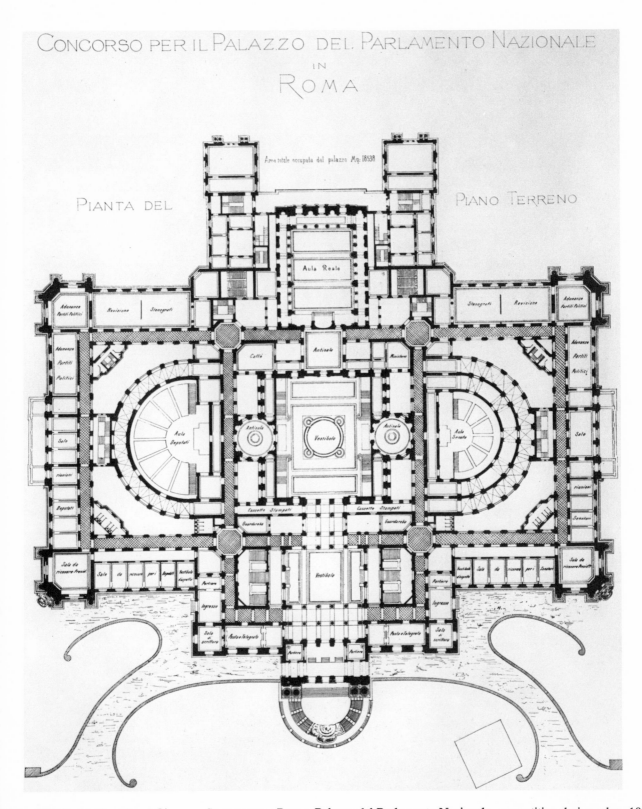

Figure 202. Luigi Broggi and Giuseppe Sommaruga: Rome, Palazzo del Parlamento Nazionale, competition design, plan, 1890

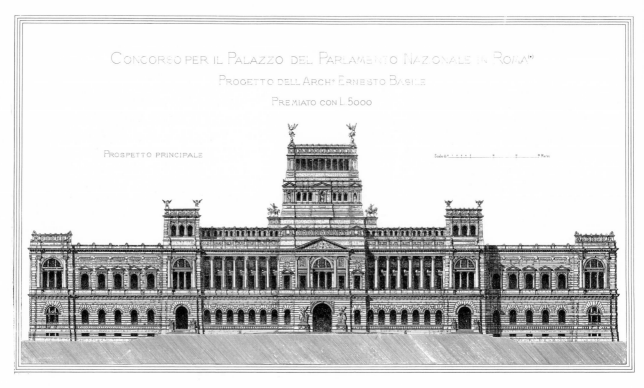

Figure 203. Ernesto Basile: Rome, Palazzo del Parlamento Nazionale, competition design, elevation, 1890

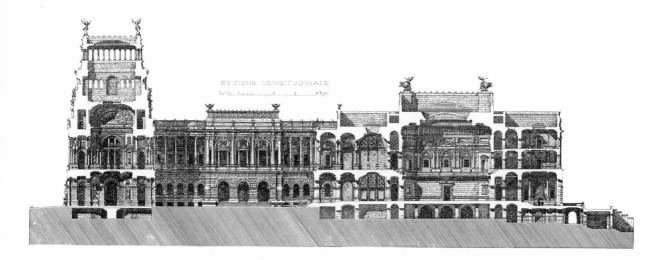

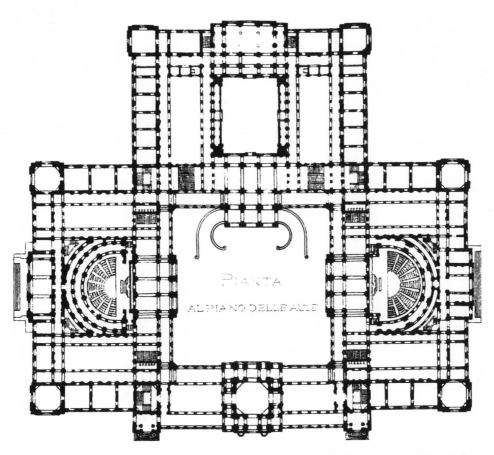

Figure 204. Ernesto Basile: Rome, Palazzo del Parlamento Nazionale, competition design, longitudinal section and plan, 1890

last century, in addition to apartments, villas, and government ministries. In some cases, as with the Biblioteca Nazionale, it was only necessary to remodel part of a gigantic existing building, the Collegio Romano. Others had to be wholly new. These include the Policlinico by Giulio Podesti (1857–1909) who won the competition for it. An earlier competition in 1883 was a failure. Podesti's collaborators were Edgardo Negri and Salvatori. The work began in 1888 and took until 1903. This hospital, modern for its time, was sensibly laid out on a lofty site as a series of airy pavilions in a garden setting. This was the period when, as in Johns Hopkins and London, current theories demanded isolated pavilions with lofty ceilings connected by corridors. Each pavilion contained one or more huge wards. It was universally regarded as a model.

A parallel provision for mankind in the mass, but on a more luxurious basis, produced a number of hotels. Of these Podesti's Grande Albergo of the 1890s near the *Esedra* retains much of its flavor (Figure 205). Many such hotels of varying sizes were required by Rome's status as a double capital and as one of the world's greatest tourist centers. Many of these once-famous hostelries have been torn down or remodeled. Hotels, like automobiles and transatlantic liners, have a limited life before obsolescence undermines them. The Excelsior on the Via Veneto, for instance, is not quite what it was when built in 1905 by Otto Mariani with interiors by Armando Brasini (born 1879), and the Flora on the same avenue has been both up and down. Due to extensive modernization it is once again "up." The planning of these hotels was comfortably ample. This shows again even in such a relatively modest one as the Savoy in Florence (Figure 206) by Vincenzo Michele (1830–95), which simply provides a number of spacious rooms, many of which face out on the Piazza della Repubblica.

Low-cost housing was of course increasingly necessary in Italy as elsewhere, as the urban population mushroomed. An example of this is Corinto Corinti's project for the Via Spontini in Florence (Figure 207). Very plain buildings such as these provided the basic essentials for the poor, but with the small number of rooms per unit they did not provide as much privacy as modern theorists would recommend. They do not show much if any advance over housing for the same class provided in England a generation earlier. The plan can, however, be commended for providing excellent cross ventilation.

Private Palaces and Villas

We find it hard today to be sympathetic to people whose first concern in building is to cover the lot to the building line, in a manner which will disguise or at least minimize any irregularities which happen to be there. It is as though the architect erected a series of flat planes directly above the surveyor's lines and then went to work within that envelope to see what use could be made of the enclosed volume. Today we call this ancient practice "the boring cube." The

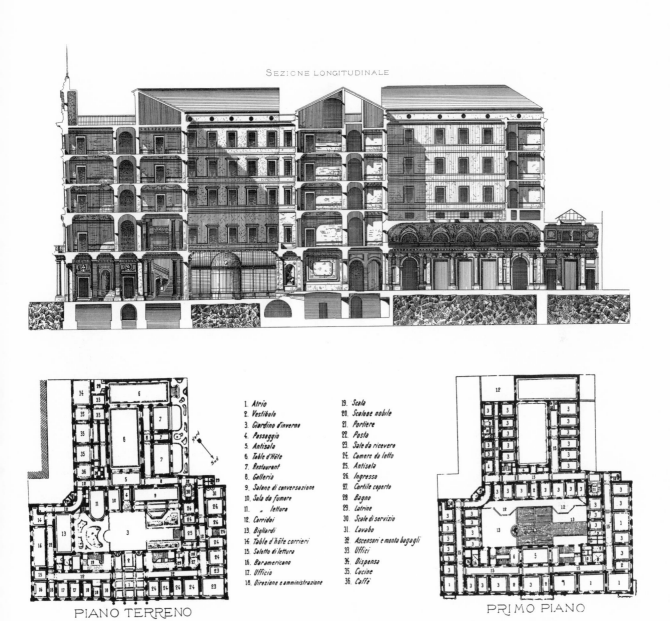

SEZIONE LONGITUDINALE

1. Atrio
2. Vestibulo
3. Giardino d'inverno
4. Passaggio
5. Antisala
6. Table d'Hôte
7. Restaurant
8. Galleria
9. Salone di conversazione
10. Sala da fumare
11.   "   lettura
12. Corridoi
13. Bigliardi
14. Table d'hôte corrieri
15. Saletto di letture
16. Bar americano
17. Ufficio
18. Direzione e amministrazione

19. Scala
20. Scaloae nobile
21. Portiere
22. Posta
23. Sala da ricevere
24. Camere da letto
25. Antisala
26. Ingresso
27. Cortile coperto
28. Bagno
29. Latrine
30. Scale di servizio
31. Lavabo
32. Ascensori e monta bagagli
33. Uffici
34. Dispensa
35. Cucine
36. Caffè

PIANO TERRENO

PRIMO PIANO

Figure 205. Giulio Podesti: Rome, Grande Albergo, longitudinal section and plans, 1890s

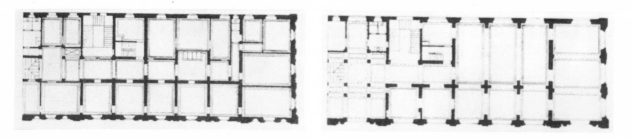

Figure 206. Vincenzo Michele: Florence, Hotel Savoy, exterior and plans, 1890s

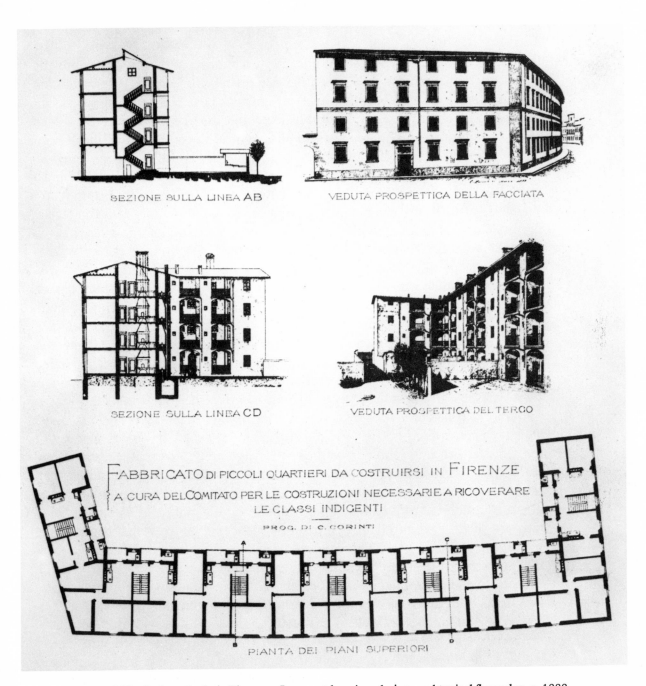

SEZIONE SULLA LINEA AB

VEDUTA PROSPETTICA DELLA FACCIATA

SEZIONE SULLA LINEA CD

VEDUTA PROSPETTICA DEL TERGO

FABBRICATO DI PICCOLI QUARTIERI DA COSTRUIRSI IN FIRENZE
A CURA DEL COMITATO PER LE COSTRUZIONI NECESSARIE A RICOVERARE
LE CLASSI INDIGENTI

PROG. DI C. CORINTI

PIANTA DEI PIANI SUPERIORI

Figure 207. Corinto Corinti: Florence, Low-cost housing, designs and typical floor plan, c. 1888

Italian answer to the hypothetical question was always the same—get into the block by a tunnel centrally placed on the visually most important plane and then cut out as small an air shaft, light well, or court as possible. The space between the inner and outer planes thus established could then be subdivided by a nice play of triangle and T-square. The establishment of floor levels must have been much harder, the only rule being that nothing which could be misconstrued as "cozy" was allowable. This meant apparent story heights of twenty-four to thirty feet and real ones of not less than half this figure, since by mezzanines and similar devices the greater dimension could be reduced to more realistic terms. Dignity was all-important. Man's legs were made to go up and down stairs; the more the vertical circulation of a palace resembled Positano the better.

The term "palazzo" was really significant; no building could be called by anything more humble when built to these dimensions. An ordinary Roman passed his entire life in this grandiose atmosphere. At home he had an apartment made up of some fraction of a palazzo, and he worked in another palazzo. Banks, offices, libraries, and some kinds of industry shared palazzi, and as he came and went he passed through avenues lined with a pleasing assortment of dignified palazzi all pretending to have been built before 1690.

One palazzo in Turin deserves particular mention. It is the exquisite Palazzo Ceriani-Peyron (1878–79) by Count Carlo Ceppi (1829–1921) whose name we have encountered above (Figure 208).[66] It is one of the finest façades of the century. Tarchiani thought well of it; Lavagnino admits that it is a successful mixture of elements from three centuries of Piedmontese tradition and then notes that it heralded the disintegration of design in that region.[67] Decadent or not, it is lovely. Its firmly molded base supports three main stories, and its nine bays are subdivided into triplets framed by rusticated bands which begin above the slightly battered base. The window frames of the *piano nobile* derive from the fantasies of the great Piedmont triumvirate, Guarini, Juvarra, and Vittone. They are set against a finely-scaled brick surface in adherence to another local tradition. The numerous elegant and graceful details include the swinging rinceau of the main frieze which so easily accommodates the oval attic windows; the way in which the balconies of the upper floor lightly touch the cornices of the *piano nobile* windows; the unobtrusive links between the balcony floors and the string course above the ground floor; the boldly projecting twisted columns of the portal which stand obliquely to the plane of the façade on bases that derive from antiquity—lion heads framed by garlands—and support unusual capitals. Other noteworthy details are the ornament of the ground-floor window frames, combining fluted moldings and rustication. The originality is found

66. See p. 298.
67. Tarchiani, *Ottocento*, p. 48; and Lavagnino, *L'Arte moderna, 1*, 537.

Figure 208. Carlo Ceppi: Turin, Palazzo Ceriani-Peyron, 1878–79

first in the revival and combination of such out-of-fashion "incorrect" motives, and second in the harmonious and delicate execution.

Count Ceppi had been a disciple of Carlo Promis and became his successor in the chair of architecture at the Albertina. In 1875 Promis had published his *Fabbriche moderne ad uso degli studenti d'architettura,* which purported to provide solutions in good taste for all the problems of contemporary architecture which the student or practitioner might encounter. These were derived from his teaching at the Albertina.

Poggi in Florence found time to build some private buildings. He was the pupil and son-in-law of the Neoclassicist Pasquale Poccianti, so it is not surprising that some of his early work, such as the Palazzo Poniatowski on the Via Cavour, was Neoclassical. After that he joined the majority and became a Cinquecentoist. Lavagnino says of his style that it was Sangallesque with deviations toward Vignola and Alessi, and that while it was severely correct it was not so in a mechanical way nor did his buildings seem false or hybrid.[68] From this point of view his Villino Favard, now the Facoltà di Scienze Economiche e Commerciali, is an interesting example (Figures 209, 210). Standing in extensive grounds on the Lungarno Amerigo Vespucci, it was built as a private residence in 1857. It was not quite a country villa, but rather a suburban mansion standing in its own grounds. All of the principal elevations are five bays wide, but are differently composed around a basic theme: three arched elements flanked by two rectangular ones under segmental pediments. On the Arno side a colonnade in two stories, Palladian in origin, frames the central group of windows and makes a shallow loggia. On the opposite, entrance side, the central triplet is pulled one bay forward on the upper floor and two bays forward on the ground floor to form a porte cochere. A balustraded parapet conceals the roof, but no urns, statues, or obelisks rise from it. The lateral façades are slightly asymmetrical, due to the projections toward the entrance. The window frames are derived from Michelangelo's at the Senatorial Palace and Sangallo's from the second floor of the Palazzo Farnese, but lack any ornament beyond the basic moldings. The interior is richly decorated in a heavily Neoclassic manner and with much gilt, suggesting the taste of Louis Philippe. In all, it is a correct design of great dignity, remarkably dry and controlled for its date.

Poggi's apartment house, proposed for the former Piazza delle Mulina, is also a restrained design (Figure 211). The variety of rustication and a few moldings gave it the desired dignity. The interior by Narciso Frosali, with its two staircases and inner court, was a conventional one. It was to provide some shops on the ground floor and large apartments on the upper ones.

The loggia designed by Poggi for the Piazzale Michelangelo is a stately and stark use of Palladio's Vicentine Basilica motive.

68. Lavagnino, *L'Arte moderna, 1,* 575.

Figure 209. Giuseppe Poggi: Florence, Villino Favard, exterior, 1857

Figure 210. Giuseppe Poggi: Florence, Villino Favard, vestibule, 1857

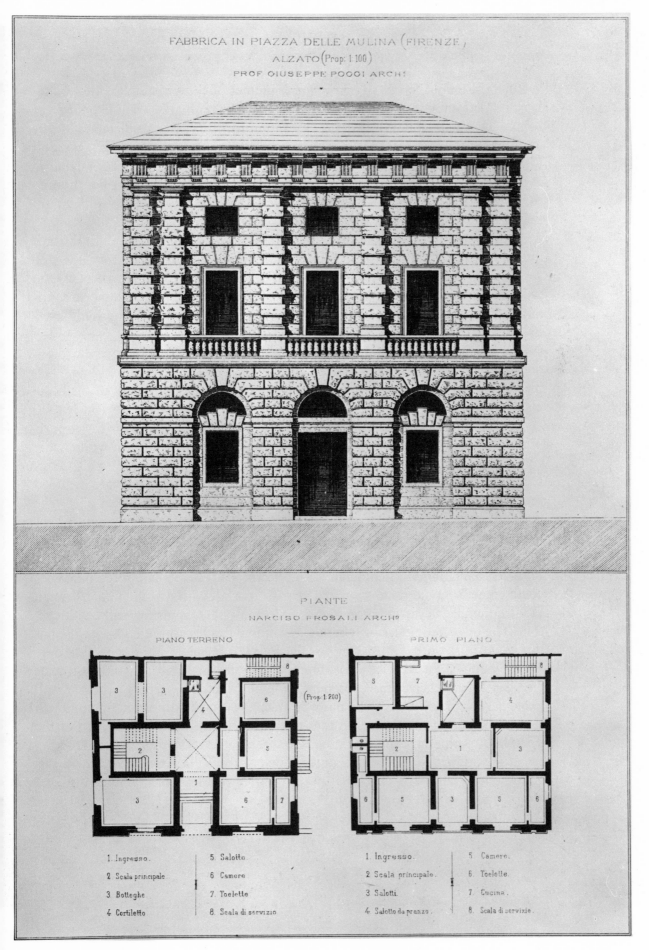

Figure 211. Giuseppe Poggi and Narciso Frosali: Florence, Apartments, Piazza delle Mulina, elevation and plans

Luca Carimini (1830–90) designed a number of churches and modest buildings, but left one really striking monument which dominates a whole quarter of Rome. This is the Palazzo Brancaccio, begun in 1885 and completed six years after his death (Figure 212). It was the project of an American couple, Mr. and Mrs. Henry Field. It is said that when widowed she assisted in the completion of the American Church in return for the rector's assistance in seeing her through the completion of this vast building.[69] Lavagnino says, with some justification, that it is an assemblage of bits and pieces lifted from the books and arranged without any apparent system other than Carimini's own personal and arbitrary ideas. This last observation is a hint at the creative side of eclecticism, the side which tends to escape notice when one is more struck, as Lavagnino was, by the number of "errors." He is willing, however, to concede that, relative to Carimini's other work and the time and place, this gigantic and gloomy building is his masterpiece.[70]

The grading of the new streets in this area left an uneven and irregular piece of ground. Carimini closed this in on three sides by his U-shaped building, leaving an elevated garden within it. This accounts for the great height of the basement compared to the upper floors. The long side is nineteen bays in length, which is six more than the Palazzo Farnese and only six less than the lower parts of the Palazzo Pitti. The mass is correspondingly imposing and drawn out, the detail large in scale and rugged. It is another attempt to stretch the palace formula further than it can easily be made to go. The two lower stories are included in the high basement, with two smaller windows underneath two larger ones. The upper four floors are also grouped in pairs, with the small mezzanine windows in their usual place over the larger ones. The whole of the basement is heavily rusticated in alternate layers of thin and thick cushion-shaped blocks, as in the Palazzo Gagnati in Montepulciano. The enormous brackets under the balconies could come from the same source. The main portal, with its four fluted Roman Doric columns, was a common device in Roman palaces of the eighteenth century. The undeviating use of tabernacle window frames on the *piano nobile* has precedent in the uppermost story of the Palazzo Farnese, although there only half columns are used. The widening and heightening of axial window frames also has Michelangelesque precedent. The coins extend further over the wall plane here than was usual. The main cornice has some features in common with that of the Palazzo Farnese, but the frieze is different. It is close to that of the Temple of Antoninus and Faustina, and recalls the motive of figures fronting the attic window and parted by anthemions at the Villa Farnesina. All of this architectural parade is executed in stucco over a brick core. Interesting as a

69. Carroll L. V. Meeks, "Churches by Street on the Via Nazionale and the Via del Babuino," *Art Quarterly, 16* (1953), 225, n. 5.
70. Lavagnino, *L'Arte moderna, 1,* 603.

Figure 212. Luca Carimini: Rome, Palazzo Brancaccio, 1885–96

reworking in an understated way of Cinquecento elements, it is inferior to the work of the greatest Roman architect of the period—Gaetano Koch.

Koch was born in Rome in 1838. He built his first palace, the Palazzo Voghera on the Via Nazionale, early in the seventies. He died in 1910. He was the most skillful exponent of *Cinquecentismo*. He never entered any of the great competitions of the day, being both shy and proud and having his hands full with a vast number of commissions both public and private. In none of them did he attempt to create a new style, being content to fit his buildings into the environment by using with restraint the style of the middle Cinquecento. Occasionally he introduced a detail or two from the Baroque, and once or twice veered toward the Neoclassical, as in two now-destroyed buildings: the Museo Baracco, a tiny Ionic building housing antique sculpture and looking like a Carnegie Library, and the Palazzo Amici which stood on the Via XX Settembre opposite the church of San Bernardo and which was removed to open up the new avenue linking the Via Veneto to the railroad station, the Via Bissolati.

His first private palace, the Voghera on the Via Nazionale, was comparatively modest. Three stories high and occupying the end of a block, it contained a small courtyard. This was so successful a solution to the problem that it made its author famous. It was mentioned in all of his obituaries as being the first practical solution to the problem of housing the middle class in the Third Rome. It combined dignity without ostentation on the exterior, and, without trying to look like a princely palace, gave the impression of well-bred elegance.[71] The rudiments of his style are apparent in it: the simplicity of motives and massing; the eschewing of alternating pediments, of novelty, or relief; stucco work used frankly, and recourse to the balcony as a device for emphasizing a main or a minor axis.

Koch's palace formulas are largely derived from those of the sixteenth century. The experimentalism of the fifteenth century was Florentine, not Roman. Koch was inclined to design by formula; over half of his work falls into one of three main schemes.

Scheme "A," Albergo de la Paix, Via IV Settembre, combines ground floor and mezzanine in one large element, surmounted by a sequence of diminishing stories, the windows of the lowest simply framed with a bracketed cornice, those of the next one up smaller and without brackets, and those of the uppermost still smaller and simpler. String courses separate the three floors. The main cornice surmounts them. Often there is an additional story above the cornice which is treated with pilasters as a lighter, more loggia-like addition. This formula was used almost verbatim for the Palazzo Boncompagni on the Largo Goldini and in the college at the corner of the Via di Monte della Farina of 1893.

The second formula, "B," is seen in the Palazzo Balestra on the Via Veneto

71. *La Tribuna* (March 16, 1910), p. 3.

(1891). The sequence of the three floors above the plinth motive begins with imposing segmental pedimental frames for the *piano nobile,* the second and third floor windows following the same sequence as in the first formula. The presence of pediments means that the building is more elaborate, and consequently a larger scale is maintained throughout. The portal treatment is more imposing. The window frames of the ground floor may be highly elaborated. This formula was applied to the Palazzo Riganti on the Via XX Settembre, with a portal framed by a pair of Doric columns and an open loggia above the main cornice; in a smaller palazzo on the Piazza dell'Orologio; in the palazzo at the corner of the Lungotevere Prati and the Via Ulpiano facing the Palazzo di Giustizia, with a portal marked by four Ionic columns; in the Palazzo Guglielmi on the Piazza Santissimi Apostoli, with a portal of four Doric columns, standing well forward of the plane of the wall, and richer window frames than usual on the second floor, perhaps in compensation for the omission of the mezzanine in the plinth. It appears again in the lovely Palazzo Pacelli, on the Corso Vittorio (Figure 215).

There are three examples which are freer variations of formula "B": the magnificent Palazzo Margherita (Figure 216), with its obvious dependence on the Palazzo Farnese; the Palazzo della Fondiaria on the Piazza Vittorio Emanuele, with its Florentine arcade, three surprising roof pavilions, and a generally more plastic handling; and third the well known Palazzi della Esedra with their open "Roman" arcade below and main story of pilasters embracing the *piano nobile* and a mezzanine (Figure 177).

Formula "C" uses pilasters extensively to articulate the façade. The Palazzi della Esedra can be considered as transitional examples, with their single Ionic order on the *piano nobile* echoed by Doric ones on the ground floor and attic, and changed to engaged columns in the end pavilions. The Ionic pilasters serve to link the pedimented windows of the *piano nobile* and its mezzanine. On the Palazzo De Parente, Corinthian columns and pilasters are used in precisely the same manner, although there is no echo of them in the basement and the attic uses caryatids freely (Figure 213). This building is the most plastic of any Koch achieved.

In two palaces, the colossal order of pilasters enveloping a main floor and its mezzanine is doubled. A second such order surmounts the first, and thus four stories are piled on a two-story basement. The larger of the two, the Palazzo Marotti on the Via Nazionale, uses the same theme over a rusticated basement. The Palazzo Salviucci in the Via del Tritone, only five bays long, omits much else that Koch used to organize the larger façade. There is another palace, which recalls this third formula, that is, the Palazzo Montani or Niccolini on the Corso Vittorio. When this Corso was laid out, the old Palazzo Niccolini by Jacopo Sansovino had to have a new façade toward the Corso. Koch did not pay much attention to Sansovino's design for the other façades and raised one of his typical

Figure 213. Gaetano Koch: Rome, Palazzo De Parente, Piazza Cavour

six-story, seven-bay palaces. What recalls the third formula is the division of the façade into three main parts in each dimension, nine in all, marked vertically by bands of rustication instead of pilasters. This avoidance of the formal orders was carried into the door treatment as well, where, although a four-column portico is suggested, only two half-columns were used to frame the axial portal.

In the more Neoclassical Palazzo Amici, the third and fourth floors were marked by a recessed Ionic colonnade echoed on the fifth floor by a loggia of free-standing caryatids, a motive which he occasionally used. This building has escaped the formula, as did a number of other buildings of diverse programs requiring special solutions. Its plan provided for horses and carriages on the ground level. The large apartments above (Figure 214) were arranged to permit them to be subdivided into smaller ones if desired. The ample central staircase was supplemented by an elevator.

The same spirit animates, if that is not too strong a word, the little Villino Galli on the Via Maria Adelaide of 1903. Of the uttermost simplicity and regularity, and with all its refinement, it still lacks the vitality of genuine sixteenth-century work.

The difficulties of adjusting formal palazzo compositions to irregular sites could not always be solved neatly. The strain of the effort is clear in the Villino Costanzi, now the Argentine Embassy, just back of Santa Maria Maggiore. The site narrowed toward the church and sloped down from it. It was long enough to permit six bays on the façade, but all the conventional rules require an axial bay, hence the device of setting off one end bay by itself and treating the other five as a unit. But the entrance to the court had to be far to the left because of the arcade. This meant that it would come below the second bay from the left, throwing the building still further off center. The attempted solution, grouping the three central bays of the five-bay part together as a wide axial feature, emphasized by the balcony which runs under them, and the use of blind arcades on the basement level to relate the entrance to the adjoining windows, was partly successful. An occult balance has been achieved, but with too much effort. This is an instance of the failure of ideal composition to adapt itself to an "accidented" site. This design is further remarkable in Koch's oeuvre because of the use of the round-headed opening motive, which is played with throughout the façade, the only case, except for the library mentioned above, where he did this. This is also the only time Koch used the window motives from the *piano nobile* of the Cancelleria, most of his sources coming from a later period.

The Villino Costanzi, Koch's only essay in a late fifteenth-century manner, suggests comparison with the Villard Houses in New York, but one of the original features of the latter was the court open to the street which only occurs once in Rome (at the Palazzo Barberini) and which was followed only once by any nineteenth-century architect in Rome.

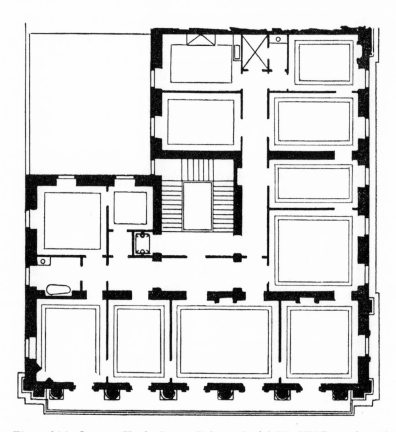

Figure 214. Gaetano Koch: Rome, Palazzo Amici, Via XX Settembre, plan

Koch's schemes for *villini* frequently included what he undoubtedly considered to be a gay and light-hearted feature, superimposed triplets of openings framed by pilasters, one of which would be Palladian. This occurs on the garden fronts of the casinos at the Palazzo Margherita and the Villino Galli. The appropriately cheerful aspect of the casinos is increased by the red and yellow stucco.

One may take as typical of a number of Koch's smaller palaces that for the family of Cardinal Eugenio Pacelli, later Pope Pius XII, on the Corso Vittorio, near the Palazzo Massimi and like it required to curve its façade to conform to the street line (Figure 215). As Lavagnino rightly says, this is an example of the most elegant purity of design.[72] The two lower floors seem to be derived from Koch's favorite, Palazzo Farnese, while the upper two are closer to the Palazzo Sacchetti and a dozen others in the same style illustrated in Letarouilly. The garlands of the frieze lack variety of scale, but combine with the high relief of the coining and cornice to frame clearly and distinctly the lower relief of the detail they enclose. It is only necessary to compare this façade with the adjoining one to realize how restrained, subtle, and harmonious Koch's design is, compared with the run-of-the-mill products of the day.

There are many other distinguished buildings from Koch's hand scattered about Rome. They do not stand out from their neighbors as a rule, except by their greater refinement, blending unobtrusively with the old palaces nearby.

It is, however, worthwhile to single out yet one more of his palaces for attention. This may, in fact, be considered his masterpiece. It is now the American Embassy and stands on ample grounds on a bend of the Via Veneto (Figures 216, 217). It has an interesting history. It was begun in 1886 for Prince Boncompagni-Piombino. This family owned most of the surrounding acres, which formed the grounds of their Villa Ludovisi. With the real-estate boom in Rome after 1870, they sold this very profitably, as well as their old palace on the Piazza Colonna, and from the proceeds began to build this, the grandest private residence of the day. Into it were built and in it were housed parts of their collection of antique and modern sculpture, including Bernini's Rape of Proserpine. Unhappily, the boom collapsed and their fortunes declined, so that it was necessary to sell this great house some ten years after it was completed. By that time Umberto had been assassinated. His widow, the well-beloved Queen Margherita, seeking a town residence for herself, found this to her taste. She occupied it until her death in 1926, hence its current name, the Palazzo Margherita. Subsequently, it was bought by the United States for use as an embassy, together with the two colorful small palaces or villas which stand on the grounds.[73]

72. Lavagnino, *L'Arte moderna, 1,* 606.

73. Hitchcock, *Architecture,* p. 146, agrees with the general opinion that this is a dignified palace and regards it as an exception to the Neo-Baroque which dominated the decade of the 1880s in Italy.

Figure 215. Gaetano Koch: Rome, Palazzo Pacelli, 1880s

Costantini agrees that this palace is one of the best creations of the period, "clear and aristocratic. . . . It resembles all the most beautiful palaces of the sixteenth century."[74]

The Palazzo Margherita is unusual in that there is no interior courtyard (Figure 217). Like the Palazzo Corsini, it is a T-shaped building open on its park. There is a very grand vestibule, atrium, and staircase, recalling those that Koch designed for the Banca d'Italia at about the same time. The main façade owes, as was usual with Koch, a great deal to the Palazzo Farnese, coming even closer this time to imitation. The common features are the three-story, thirteen-bay elevation, the silhouetting of the window frames against a neutral surface (stucco rather than brick here), the enclosing of these in coining and a heavy cornice. The differences are: in proportions—the length is greater relative to the height; the elimination of the alternation of window pediments; and the use of pedimented windows on both the upper floors instead of only on the *piano nobile*. The triple arched portal, with its four free-standing, unfluted, Roman Doric columns and beam-end voussoirs, has no equivalent at the Farnese but had become common, as noted above in connection with Carimini's palace.[75] The cornice is simplified and the frieze bears the original owner's device; the winged dragon and three diagonal bars which are also to be seen above the window frames of the *piano nobile*. The effect of all these changes from the prototype is to tame down the vitality of the original toward a more academic standard of correctness. Sangallo's and Michelangelo's motives usually did suffer from this refining attitude, in spite of the admiration felt for their work. The same sort of thing happened in England at the Reform Club and Dorchester House, and later in the United States in the hands of McKim.[76]

Koch was praised for not making buildings that were "different." This is a point of view so unlike our own that we can hardly believe that it was meant as serious praise. "The semi-anonymous manner" was, as in antiquity, the meritorious one. We have witnessed a return to this point of view. Someone praised McKim, and would have been able to praise Koch in the identical words: "Nothing experimental is visible, you find nothing irrelevant, nothing that is understated or overdone." But McKim was the product of another environment; he was an *aficionado* of Rome, not a Roman. Koch tended to limit himself to the systems of the Renaissance. McKim helped himself with equal freedom to the Rome of the Caesars, a thing which Koch rarely did, except toward the end of

74. Vincenzo Costantini, *Storia dell'arte italiana* (4 vols. Milan, 1945–1949), *4*, 387.
75. See p. 374.
76. Carroll L. V. Meeks, "Wright's Eastern-Seaboard Contemporaries: Creative Eclecticism in the United States Around 1900," in *Studies in Western Art, 2* (New York, 1963), pp. 64 ff.

Figure 216. Gaetano Koch: Rome, Palazzo Margherita (American Embassy), exterior, 1886–90

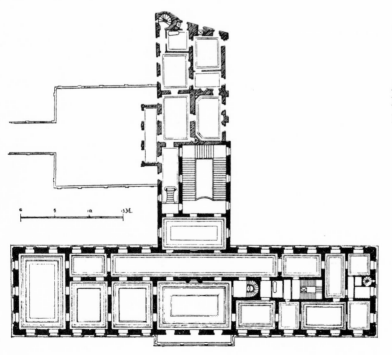

Figure 217. Gaetano Koch: Rome, Palazzo Margherita (American Embassy), plan, 1886

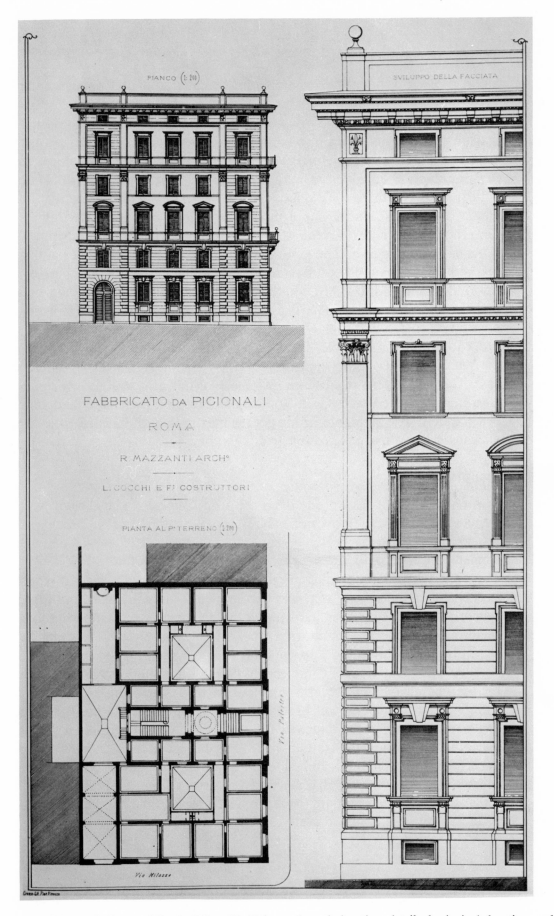

FIANCO (1:200)

SVILUPPO DELLA FACCIATA

FABBRICATO DA PICIONALI

ROMA

R. MAZZANTI ARCH°

L. COCCHI E F.ι COSTRUTTORI

PIANTA AL P.° TERRENO (1:200)

Via Palestra

Via Milazzo

Figure 218. Riccardo Mazzanti: Rome, Office building, Via Palestra, lateral elevation, detail of principal elevation, and plan, c. 1880

his life when he was engaged in completing the greatest of all Roman monuments which another had begun, the "Vittoriano."

Calderini, too, built some private palaces, that of the Bianchi and, in 1908, that of the Cesaroni, both in his native city, Perugia. The latter at one time served as a hotel (Palace Hotel; Hotel Moderno). It was poorly suited to this function since, although large and imposing, with handsome rooms of state and a great staircase, there were relatively few bedrooms. This palace rears its gigantic façade vis-à-vis the more modest, arcaded town hall, the Palazzo del Governo by Alessandro Arienti of 1870, which it arrogantly overshadows.

As has been remarked above, Romans spent their lives in palaces of one sort or another. An example of a palace-office building is the one designed by Riccardo Mazzanti (1850–1910) on the Via Palestra (Figure 218). This building was six stories in height. The stories were grouped in pairs, and rustication, pilasters, cornices, and such Cinquecento devices were used to make it harmonize with the city as a whole, executed, of course, in stucco. The entrance from the Via Milazzo led into a small courtyard, which in turn led to a single staircase. The offices were grouped on either side of this around a pair of lightwells. Corridors permitted access to the offices, which could thus be rented combined or separately. The builder aimed to get the maximum rentable area possible and allocated as little space as possible to circulation.

Churches

A few new churches were built in the *Stile Umberto*. These begin with the Genoese Immacolata Concezione, built between 1856 and 1873, one of the first to return to an Early Renaissance style (Figure 219). It was designed by Domenico Cervetto, and was executed by Maurizio Dufour (1837–97) from Turin and Gioacchino Zandomeneghi (1837–1902) from Venice. It is set on a steeply sloping hillside in what was becoming a fashionable neighborhood, and is lavishly decorated within and without in a Quattrocento Lombardian style of small-scale ornament, such as arabesques, medallions, arcades, and panels. The centrally planned space rises up smoothly into its cupola.

A few years later a more Cinquecento design was supplied by Antonio Spezia for the church of Santa Maria Ausiliatrice in Turin (Figure 220), erected (1865–88) to honor the celebrated Don Giovanni Bosco. Here the influence of Palladio is seen in the interweaving of a low order with a temple front, the pair of small belfries, the transepts with apsidal ends, and the central dome at the crossing. The church is linked to the adjoining blocks by low rusticated arcades which come from Palladian villa prototypes. The original features here, if they can be called such, are the attics which replace the half pediments of the Palladian formula, and the use of lightly scaled ornament, some of it in per-

Figure 219. Domenico Cervetto and others: Genoa, Chiesa dell'Immacolata, 1856–73

Figure 220. Antonio Spezia: Turin, Santa Maria Ausiliatrice, 1865–88

Figure 221. Raffaele Ingami: Rome, San Gioacchino, 1870s

spective relief. Its form and setting are more impressive than its detail. It terminates an axis effectively.

In Rome in the late seventies or early eighties, the rapidly growing district of the Prati di Castelli was supplied with a costly but unlovable church, San Gioacchino (Figure 221), by Raffaele Ingami (1838–1908). This building has the general form of a basilica with narthex, nave, transept, and so on. The remarkable feature is the small dome at the crossing, which is said to have been built of aluminum. Sculpture, marbles, and mosaic were used lavishly but in a meaningless way. There are enough tabernacle windows, pediments, and pilasters to suggest that some Cinquecento precedent was invoked.

From 1880–86 Calderini was engaged on his first important building, the new façade for the Duomo at Savona on the Riviera di Ponente (Figure 222). The commission was awarded to him as the victor in a competition, to which sport he was so addicted.[77] His grandiose pile does not adhere to either of the earlier fashions in church face-lifting, the Neoclassical or the Neo-Medieval. Instead, it is in a typically Umbertian Cinquecento vocabulary in the family of the Gesù and its successors (such as San Carlo al Corso and Sant'Andrea della Valle), but handled with great gusto à la Alessi. The existing three portals and their lunettes had to be retained (Figure 223). The lower part of the elevation he made five bays wide, one story and an attic high, and hid the nave behind an additional story and pediment. The bays are marked off by clusters of pilasters increasing in number toward the central axis. The lateral portals are relatively simple, while the main one kept the old porch of free-standing columns. The lunette motive, a legacy from Neoclassicism, appears three times—once over each of the side doors and once in the upper story over the main portal. The central bay rises up to a heavily decorated pediment supported on ganes and having a top-heavy air, an effect which, as I have pointed out elsewhere, appealed to the taste of the period. This is intensified by the interruption of the lower entablature which is not carried across the central bay. There is an abundance of rich, florid ornament in the form of swags and garlands. The whole façade is executed in marble. The second-prize design by Riccardo Mazzanti (Figure 224) achieved a simpler effect by combining the two lower lunettes with the doors under them, thus eliminating the attic which Calderini stressed. Similarly, Mazzanti's enframement of the axial lunette was much less bulky and elaborate than that by the winner. Calderini made important features of the walls at the extremities of the façade, treating them like narrow bays rather than the minor wings Mazzanti had suggested.

It was also Calderini who completed the *quadriportico* (Figure 225) in front of San Paolo f. l. m. (1893–1910). Typically, he broke away from the simpler colonnades which lined the other three sides of the court. He placed a double

77. The designs were published in *Ricordi, 10* (1888), pls. 1–4.

Figure 222. Guglielmo Calderini: Savona, Cathedral, façade, 1880–86

Figure 223. Savona, Cathedral, old façade

Figure 224. Riccardo Mazzanti: Savona, Cathedral, project for new façade, 1880

Figure 225. Guglielmo Calderini: Rome, San Paolo fuori le mura, Quadriportico, 1893–1910

row of columns under slightly stilted arcading, as though designing a cloister at enormous scale, then with considerable inventiveness ran a tunnel vault at right angles to these little vaults and supported it on the inner side by a third row of columns. Once again, the message is original but the language is familiar, and blends in so harmoniously with the older work that one is hardly aware of the departure. There was no historic precedent for any part of this quadriportico to which an archaeologist might have felt bound. Calderini, therefore, felt free to employ a colossal version of the Cosmatesque cloister of San Giovanni in Laterano, the restoration of which he had previously undertaken.

An elegant new church façade (1891–96) was built by Giovanni Ceruti at Sacro Monte, near Varallo Sésia in Piedmont (Figure 226). This is a dignified and consistent exercise in pilasters and entablatures in low relief, varied by somewhat richer window frames and a small belfry crowned most unexpectedly but not inharmoniously with a Venetian semicircular pediment. It is a neat, quiet, almost undatable work, not what one would expect from the author of the Boitoian-Medieval Museo Civico di Storia Naturale in Milan (Figure 141).

Finally, we have the Roman church of Angeli Custodi on Monte Sacro from another Boitoian, the historian-architect Gustavo Giovannoni (1873–1949). Here, the Palladian formula is again invoked with an interweaving of two orders of pilasters and the use of framing bands, piers, and obelisks. This façade stands on a terrace reached by a broad flight of steps, as at Il Redentore. The drum of the dome has extremely rich window frames.[78] It could be considered a revival of Mannerism if the intention were more obvious.

On the whole then, we must conclude that Umbertian church architecture was not very successful when it made use of the Renaissance themes so successfully employed in other types of buildings, and that the Medievalists came nearer to scoring the high points reached in Neoclassical churches.

Theatres

There was another area of architectural activity in which Italy was keenly active, that is, the opera house.[79] As everyone knows, the nineteenth century was the great century of the opera and, Wagner and Bayreuth or Garnier and Paris notwithstanding, it flourished to a greater extent in Italy than anywhere else. Hence it is not surprising that each Italian city felt the need for as fine a theatre as possible, and that this was regarded as fittingly defrayed by public funds. It would, however, be tedious to discuss them all. The story begins, of

78. Lavagnino, *L'Arte moderna, 1,* 627 says of it that an excessive number of motives have been piled up inorganically in too little space. Ibid., fig. 532.

79. See Daniele Donghi, *Manuale dell'architetto, 2,* part 1, sect. 4 (Turin, 1930), for detailed information on Italian theatres. Some colorful historical details are to be found in Patrick Cains Hughes, *Great Opera Houses; A Traveller's Guide to their History and Traditions* (New York, 1959).

Figure 226. Giovanni Ceruti: Il Sacro Monte, near Varallo Sésia, Chiesa dell' Assunta, 1891–96

course, well before the Umberto decades with such works as have been described above: La Scala, Milan; La Fenice, Venice; Teatro San Carlo, Naples; and Teatro Carlo Felice, Genoa.

Ranked according to size of the auditorium, it will be seen that some of the older theatres were very nearly as large as the Umbertian ones: San Carlo; La Scala; Teatro Costanza (now Teatro dell'Opera), Rome; Teatro Massimo, Palermo; La Fenice; and the Teatro Carlo Felice. A horseshoe-shaped auditorium was standard, as were certain rooms of parade. In every case, immense stages and backstage areas were required, and the renovation and modernization of one or another part frequently occurred. At the San Carlo, for example, after Niccolini's reconstruction in 1816, important work was undertaken in 1844, 1890, 1910, and 1927–29. La Scala was redecorated thirty years after it was opened. It was enlarged and modernized in 1814 by Luigi Canonica and Innocenzo Giusti. Other major works were undertaken there from 1830 to 1860, in 1865 and 1879, and it was drastically rebuilt within in 1921.

There were many others, some of which will be mentioned briefly, such as the Teatro Piccinni (1837–59) by Niccolini at Bari. This Neoclassical façade has a porch recessed behind a portico of six Greek Doric columns which support a taller second floor of Ionic pilasters under a pediment.[80] The ornament of niches, panels, and friezes all suggest a white and gold ballroom. Poletti's theatre at Rimini of 1857 was, however, Palladian, with two orders of Roman arcades, Corinthian above Ionic. Japelli's remodeling of the theatre at Padua (1847), like the contemporary interior of La Fenice at Venice, made rare use of the Rococo, whereas the Neoclassic idea survived into the 1860s with Andrea Scala's (1820–92) Accademia Musicale at Conegliano of 1869 (Figures 227, 228).[81] Scala was a pupil of the Medievalist Selvatico. This area was so long under Austrian domination that it may have influenced the choice of style, since the Austrian Parliament building, another late example of Neoclassicism, was to be built from 1873 to 1883 by Theophil von Hansen (1813–91). It may have been known to Scala in the design stage. Both buildings pile up temple fronts and caryatid porches in a basically picturesque rather than a classical fashion. The plan, however, is as conventional as the site permitted.

Such was Scala's reputation as a builder of theatres that he was called to Catania to work on the opera house there, the Teatro Bellini, which was opened in 1890 with a performance of *Norma*. The scheme was by Carlo Sada the younger (1849–1924) (Figure 229).[82] The motive of the windows of the *piano nobile* could have been derived from those of the Paris Opéra, which was begun in 1861. The segmental pediment of the main block also has a French look. The

80. Lavagnino, *L'Arte moderna, 1,* 134 and fig. 108.
81. Ibid., *1,* 565–66.
82. Ibid., *1,* 536. He says that Sada was faithful to Neoclassicism and showed this in his church of San Massimo in Turin. Sada also designed the new theatre at Alessandria.

Figure 227. Andrea Scala: Conegliano, Accademia
Musicale, elevation, 1860s

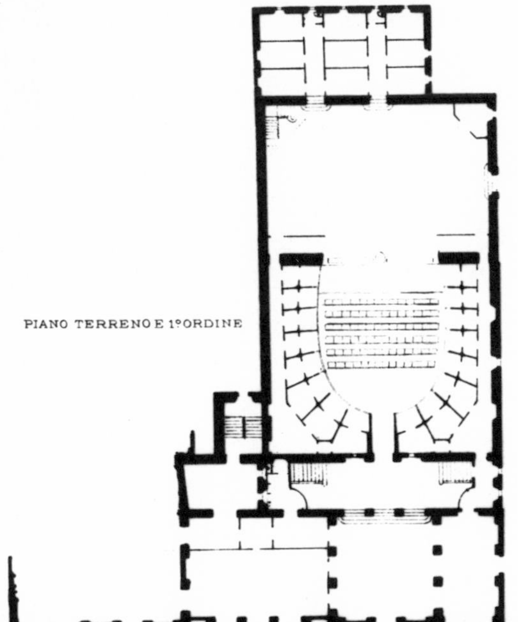

PIANO TERRENO E 1°ORDINE

Figure 228. Andrea Scala: Conegliano, Accademia
Musicale, plan, 1860s

Figure 229. Andrea Scala and Carlo Sada: Catania, Teatro Bellini, 1870–90

quadrants linking the central motive with the wings at the back recall those of the Burgtheater in Vienna, begun in 1874 by Gottfried Semper and Karl von Hasenauer (1833–94). The general idea of a curved, or partly curved façade had been used by Semper in his first and second theatres in Dresden in 1843 and 1878. The source of the *piano nobile* windows is, of course, ultimately Venetian, whether or not they went through Paris on their way to Catania. The sculptural groups on the parapets are also somewhat French, in their lack of formal outline and their excessive naturalism. The ground floor, however, clings to a normal Cinquecento pattern.

Palermo, the capital of Sicily, built two notable theatres at this time. The lesser, the Politeama Garibaldi of 1874, was another belated example of Neoclassicism. Echoes of the Pompeian style can be seen in it. Its architect was Giuseppe Damiani Almeyda (1834–1901). Like Semper's opera houses and theatres, it had convex quadrantal elements. In this case they link a triumphal arch to a cross wing. The quadrants are faced with two stories of loggias. Like so many old theatres, it later became a cinema palace.

The major theatre was called just that, the Teatro Massimo (Figures 230, 231). It was the subject of a competition in 1864, but work was not commenced until 1875, and lasted with interruptions for twenty-two years. Its architect, Giovanni Battista Basile (1825–91), did not live to see it completed by his more famous son, Ernesto. This, the major theatre of Sicily, like that of Rome, provided for 3,000 spectators, but in a building approximately four times as large and many times more monumental. The building of it is one of those murky chapters in the history of Italian architecture. An international competition was announced in 1864. Three years later thirty-five of the projects were exhibited. The jury was distinguished: Gottfried Semper, Mariano Falcini, and one Sicilian, Saverio Cavallari. The award went to Basile, the local architect. Working drawings were prepared and work begun, but a change of government stopped progress for nearly eight years. There is no doubt that every effort was expended over the two decades when it was under construction to make it eclipse the Opéra of Paris in both splendor and stage equipment.

The Teatro Massimo is noteworthy on two counts: its great size (it was one of the largest theatres of the day), and the fact that its plan is workable a century later. This is generally true of the great opera houses of the late nineteenth century; they suit the needs of opera productions adequately, provided only that the stage machinery and the ventilation systems be modernized. The expressive scheme of a dome over the auditorium and a gable over the stage loft, which Charles Garnier had devised for the Paris Opéra three years before, was employed here. It also followed Paris to the extent of having projecting semicircular side vestibules. Basile chose conservative details in which to enclose his up-to-date plan. He used a Roman Corinthian order, in a complete hexastyle

Figure 230. Giovanni Battista Basile: Palermo, Teatro Massimo, 1875–97

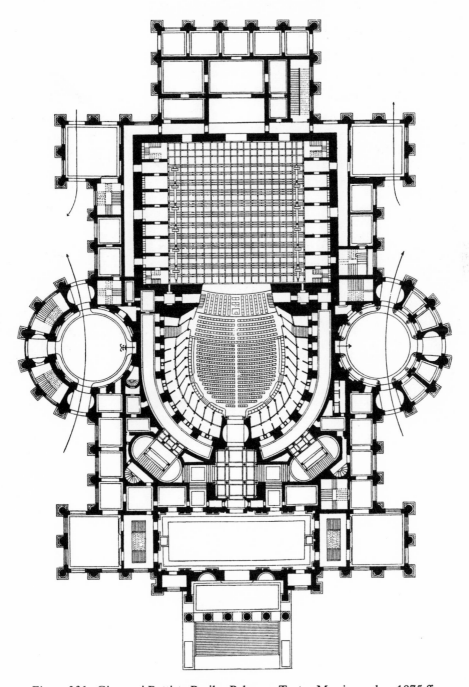

Figure 231. Giovanni Battista Basile: Palermo, Teatro Massimo, plan, 1875 ff.

Figure 232. Achille Sfondrini: Rome, Teatro dell'Opera, 1878–80, as altered in 1928

temple front standing at the top of a little-used flight of steps and continuing as pilasters or engaged columns around the rest of the building. The detailing is consistently Neoclassical on the exterior, including the dome over the auditorium. All of these theatres featured large areas for parade and refreshment and this one is no exception. Such social activities were and still are an important part of attending the opera.

The present opera house in Rome, the Teatro dell'Opera (Figure 232), was begun about 1878 by the architect Achille Sfondrini (1836–1900). It was financed by Domenico Costanzi (died 1898), a speculative builder, who aimed to build the finest theatre in Rome. It was known as the "Teatro Costanzi" until it was bought in 1926 by the City of Rome. Sfondrini encouraged him to build even more grandly than he had at first contemplated. The theatre was nicknamed the "Costantinopoli."[83] It took only a year and one-half to build, and was opened in 1880 with a performance of Rossini's *Semiramide*. It was and is rated as one of the finest in Italy. In 1928 it was remodeled and modernized by Marcello Piacentini, and further work was done in 1960, although the general appearance of the exterior has not been greatly modified. However, considering that it was built in the capital, its appearance is surprisingly modest, due to its being built from private funds; the state had planned to build a far grander opera house at a later date. It is typically Umbertian in its use of applied low-relief pilasters, round-headed windows, and rusticated basement. The segmental pediments from Paris occur here again, used rather more simply than Koch was to use them a few years later at the nearby Esedra. The articulation of the domed auditorium and stage loft is not easily discerned from close at hand. Its changed orientation has made for some oddities. Originally the main entrance was in the more conventional location but was subsequently moved to the Piazza Viminale side, partly in order to make access to the Royal Box more direct. Costanzi was at first accused of having chosen an absurdly remote location, but time has proved him right, as Rome has grown densely around his theatre.

The *Stile Umberto* manifested itself best in Cinquecento-inspired palaces and government buildings such as those by Gaetano Koch. Its second most important legacy was numerous urban improvements. Its major monuments are the two most ponderous buildings in Italy, the "Vittoriano" and the "Palazzaccio," which testify, as well as architecture ever can, to the confident assurance of the bourgeois world of late nineteenth-century Italy. The creative originality of the time was held in check—no one yet daring to invent a new vocabulary— but found some outlet in novel combinations of old forms in new contexts, scales, and materials, some good, some poor. This made easier the introduction of wholly new forms in the following decade.

83. Calza, *Roma moderna*, p. 56.

5

Stile Floreale

Introduction

Architectural Systems of the Art Nouveau

Stile Floreale

The Leaders

Aftermath of the Floreale

Importance of the Floreale

5

Stile Floreale

Introduction

For thirty years it has been customary to winnow the architectural chaff of the nineteenth century in order to find the grains which infrequently ripened into modern architecture.[1] This process has now engaged the Italians.[2] Critics have been finding kernels, not just in Alessandro Antonelli (1798–1888) and Giuseppe Mengoni (1829–77) but in the masters of the Italian Art Nouveau or *Liberty*. Exaggerated claims have been made. The most important, numerically and popularly, and the most peculiarly Italian phenomenon in the Art Nouveau period was the *Stile Floreale,* "La caduca maniera floreale," or "l'agonia floreale," a style which was decorative in intent and results, but in which practically no advances in planning or structure were accomplished. Its manifestations in immense numbers are readily visible, in spite of war and rebuilding, in urban regions or resorts, in every part of Italy from Piedmont and Lombardy through Emilia, Tuscany, and Latium to Calabria and Sicily. An interior, designed by Gaetano Moretti (1860–1938) for the influential International Exposition of Decorative Arts held in Turin in 1902, is an example (Figure 233). The ornament is not only abundant to the point of excess but is realistic and naturalistic to a remarkable degree. It even has the sinister *fin de siècle* overtone of seeming to be on the point of devouring the room and its contents. The *Floreale* ornament is in both high and low relief, in wood, stucco, wool, leather, and glass. The sinuous trunks loaded with fat fruit and heavy leaves are characteristically Italian. The other elements had their counterparts in other countries: the upholstered inglenook is British in derivation, the stained glass is American,

1. This chapter was originally published in the *Art Bulletin, 43* (1961), 113–30, as "The Real *Liberty* of Italy—the *Stile Floreale.*"

2. The principal series of articles is that of the "Eredità dell'ottocento" beginning in *Architettura* in 1955. There have been others in *Casabella*. The principal ones in English have appeared in the *Architectural Review*. One by Reyner Banham, "Italian Retreat from Modern Architecture (Neoliberty)," *125* (1959), 231–35, started a controversy which was summed up in a later issue "Neoliberty: the Debate," *126* (1959), 341–44.

Figure 233. Gaetano Moretti: Turin, Room for Exposition of Decorative Arts, 1902

whereas the rug is Austrian. It is my contention that the room illustrated was far more representative of Italian taste and accomplishment, not only in interior design but also in architecture, than the more exceptional proto-modern buildings.[3]

The *Floreale* was a style of decorative eclectic architecture which flourished most particularly in the residences being built for the prosperous bourgeoisie, and by extension in their places of work, business, and recreation. It did not find a place in religious architecture, with the exception of a few synagogues.

Architectural Systems of the Art Nouveau

In order to place this aspect of the Art Nouveau in its context, it will not be necessary to review the history of the movement in Europe and America in detail, but to point out that it was international, that the years from 1895 to 1914 saw it develop differently in each of the countries where it took hold, and that the line of architectural and decorative development in those fecund years included some ten possibilities or variants, unified by broad general concepts growing out of the Romantic movement. Sir Kenneth Clark has summed these up brilliantly.[4] To paraphrase him, they include violence valued for its own sake; a hunger for adventurous movement; the concepts of nature, liberty, change, power, and emotion as an end in itself; art dealing with thoughts and memories of a kind more usually expressed in words; the sensuous non-literary response to nature, as in landscape painting, or in the worship of natural materials in their raw state and in combination; the cult of the irrational, admiration for violence, and the death wish; the morbidity of the subject matter in both art and architectural decoration, and the unceasing cannibalism of forms in ornament; accepting the continuance of change; the heightened importance given to emotions, tastes, whims, and the desire for individual self-expression without conventional restraint. These forces underlie much of the architecture of this period in Italy as elsewhere, and they provided a nursery in which to develop a new architecture, a nursery, unhappily, over which a nurserymaid rather than an inspired governess commonly presided.

Of the ten possibilities or variants referred to above, linked by the Romantic emotions just mentioned, each found an echo in Italy, but were more often drowned out by the overwhelming *Floreale*. The first variant was an Italian parallel to the Medievalism of the Continent and Great Britain. It contributed to the *Floreale*. This was the romantic Medievalism of Pietro Selvatico (1803–80) who, like Ruskin, preached a doctrine carried on by the more influential Camillo Boito (1836–1914) as professor, writer, and architect. The "Casa Verdi" is an

3. *Edilizia moderna, 12* (1903), 26 ff. This is an extensively illustrated criticism by Luca Beltrami.
4. See p. 5 and fig. 9.

Figure 234. Camillo Boito: Milan, Il Ricovero pei Musicisti ("Casa Verdi"), exterior, 1899

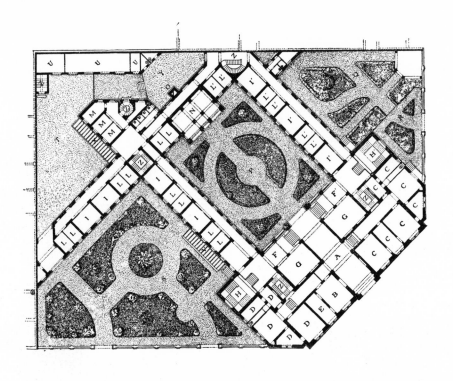

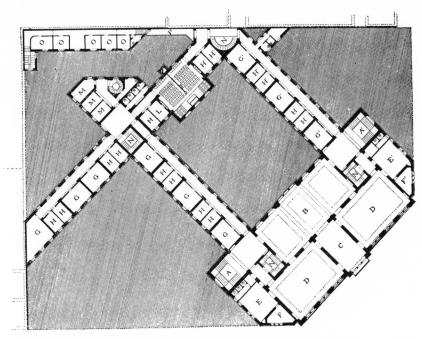

Figure 235. Camillo Boito: Milan, Il Ricovero pei Musicisti ("Casa Verdi"), plans, 1899

example of that master's work which was in so personal a style that it was called *Stile Boito* (Figures 234, 235). To our eyes it has many affinities with the Victorian Gothic, which, via Ruskin and Street, also drew upon the Medieval architecture of Italy. This example is of 1899. Boito's contributions to the *Floreale* include the romanticism of "natural" materials, the free mingling of elements from several historical periods, and the use of constructive coloration, as in the frieze and panels surrounding the windows of the principal floor. One also finds echoes of Eastlakian ornament in the frieze, and of the Pre-Raphaelites in the crowning motive, with its lilies and flowery meads. Lions' heads, a favorite *Floreale* motive, appear on this "frontispiece." Visitors to Milan will find this building standing with an added story and some modifications of detail. The iron grills, not seen in this figure, have the Art Nouveau characteristic of changing from transparent to opaque as the iron-work appears to clot. This can also be seen in the contemporary grill of the Monument to Victor Emanuel in Rome. The most important legacies to the *Floreale* from the *Stile Boito* were the freedom to mix motives and the unabashed zest for ornament.

The second variant, also with English connections, is closely related to the above and to the Arts and Crafts movement. It includes a sort of nursery decoration, in flat friezes and bands, on exteriors as well as interiors. An example of this influence from Walter Crane can be seen in Figure 236. Ornament inspired by William Morris was not rare (the gate in Figure 247) and papers and textiles very close to Morris' were used extensively in the Villino Florio (Figure 255). This second system was sometimes associated with the earlier fashion for Eastlakian ornament—stiff designs originally executed with drills in wood, but in Italy executed in stone or stucco. In the *villino* shown (Figure 236), the two friezes of swans, one a quiet procession, the other of aroused birds with symmetrically spread wings, not only derive from fashionable British motives but are also related to the angels and, to a lesser extent, to the maidens in flowing robes which were also popular in continental decoration and painting of the period (Figures 243, 254, 257, 265). This *villino* also shows an interest in the honest use of materials almost like Philip Webb's: stone, brick, and wood. It also shows a sympathy for the *Stile Boito,* which was not always typical of its architect, Gino Coppedè (1866–1927), who soon ceased to be content with such simplicity (Figures 258, 259).

The *Stile Boito* and the English background had something to do with the distinguished refinement of the Casa delle Imprese Bellia in Turin of 1894–98 (Figure 237) by Carlo Ceppi (1829–1921). His earlier works had shown a similar elegance and simplicity. Even the Medieval touches and the Ottonian columns of the cupolas are in a vein of discreet, material-loving delicacy and subtlety which found few followers.

The third system, a restrained pseudo-traditional one, also contains elements

Figure 236. Gino Coppedè: Genoa, Villino Piaggio, c.1895

Figure 237. Carlo Ceppi: Turin, Casa delle Imprese Bellia, 1894–98

Figure 238. Sebastiano Giuseppe Locati: Milan, Casa Reininghaus, c.1898

from the earlier-mentioned manners (Figure 238). The Casa Reininghaus in Milan, a block of apartments with stores and restaurants on the street floor, by Sebastiano Giuseppe Locati (1861–1945), published in 1898, shows articulation by means of framing bands and straps, which may owe something to such Medievalists as Viollet-le-Duc. The devices used here to link the arcaded lower stories and the stone-trimmed upper ones; the short bands or straps which link the two upper stories; and the linear string courses which tie balconies and lintels together horizontally—all will become more elaborately developed belts in the *Floreale*. Framing bands had, of course, been widely used in the late Renaissance and Baroque.

A rhythmical device, developed in Italy at the end of the nineteenth century to animate the huge new blocks demanded by urban congestion, is shown in both the buildings above (Figures 237, 238). This is achieved by unequal emphasis on the windows. In the long façade of the Turin building, alternate window sills are dropped to permit balconies. The lighter balconies above link with the heavier ones below, and thus establish minor vertical accents that repeat in alternate bays the verticality of the polygonal towers. In the Casa Reininghaus, the elongated elements alternate from floor to floor, producing a skipping rhythm. These rhythmical devices are more elaborate than Baroque alternating window pediments.

A fourth system was like the Belgian style of Van de Velde and his contemporaries, the most elegant of all the variations of the Art Nouveau, since it introduced a graceful curvilinearity into the orthogonal or geometrically curved formulas of traditional architecture. This style, with its remarkable plasticity and fluidity, whether expressed in the whiplash curve or in forms which could have been derived from draped, pulled, or festooned cloth, did not find wide acceptance in Italy. Exceptions occurred here and there, a café near the Cathedral in Vigèvano, the Caffè Due Palmi at Casale Monferrato,[5] or, in Florence, certain houses along the eastern *viale,* and more noticeably a building on the northern side of the Piazza Ognissanti (Figure 239), whose Belgian motives include a window shaped like a "moongate"; frozen drapery effects; batwinged acroteria (the morbid touch) and iron poppies; all are free of the ponderous inertness of the usual Italian *Floreale*. This northern style also dominates the dining room by Ernesto Basile (1857–1932) at the Villa Igiea (Figure 254).

The fifth and sixth manners, both minor, which flourished chiefly at Nancy, are the Art Nouveau versions of the Rococo and of the Flamboyant. But they were not entirely overlooked in Italy. There was a villa by Locati, published in 1898, in which grotesquely distorted Gothic motives appeared, and later in

5. Engineer Torinelli, the local authority, states in an unpublished letter to the author that this café, now used for furniture storage, was designed about 1910 by one of the Novarese school of architects, which was then a center of *Liberty* architecture.

Figure 239. Anonymous: Florence, Building on Piazza Ognissanti, detail, c.1900

1906 his interior decoration of the Festival Hall of the Milan Exposition of that year has obvious affinities with Rococo encrustations.[6] This style also influenced Pietro Fenoglio (born 1865) in his Villa Scott at Turin.[7]

The seventh system is one which we might expect to have had more influence in Italy than, in fact, it did. This is the *Secession* style then developing in Austria under Otto Wagner, J. M. Olbrich, and Josef Hoffmann. The style had certain qualities, possibly derived from the Glasgow school: slenderness, elongation, and delicacy of lines, planes, and curves. This is the Wagner of the subway stations and the Asylum Chapel, the Hoffmann of the Pukersdorf Sanitarium, and the early Loos. These characteristics occasionally appeared in Italy, for some of the Italians had studied in Austria and many had traveled there, but they did not become important elements in the Italian vocabulary. Hence, the graceful buildings erected by Raimondo d'Aronco (1857–1932) for the Turin Exposition of Decorative Arts of 1902 are not at all typical of Italian work (Figure 240). D'Aronco, as chief architect for the Exposition, designed all the buildings, including those occupied by foreign exhibitors. The main building was flanked by low symmetrical wings, the one at the left for England, the one at the right for France. This exhibition rivals the Paris Exposition of 1900 as marking the climax of the Art Nouveau, since outstanding examples of the new decorative arts of Europe were shown there for comparison. The main pavilion shows a wide range of fashionable motives: the eyebrow canopies over the windows at the base of the pointed dome; the maidens whose draperies are almost wings; the curved and curled buttresses; the fringes; the disks both large and small, flat and rounded; the decorative leaf patterns confined in geometric panels; the checkerboard patterns. On the wings, delicately curved elements contrast with flat angular planes: female heads of Egyptoid character; bands of disks; and most prominently, a Glasgow motive—sinuous, asymmetrical young tree trunks culminating in bands of leaves, languid and weightless. The light, thin, graceful, and open effect is quite opposed in character to Italian taste, and hence limited in its influence, but some of the motives in a more solid form were incorporated into the *Floreale*.

The eighth system has, in spite of its infrequent incidence, been built up into one of considerable significance. This is the progressive, adventurous, expressive use of the new materials, metal and reinforced concrete. The Magazzino Contratti in Milan of 1903 by Luigi Broggi (1851–1926) is an example of this manner (Figure 241). The use of metal, usually cast iron for structural purposes, had previously been exhibited in Italy in railroad train sheds, markets, and in the glass-and-iron roofs of the great galleries in Milan and Naples. A few

---

6. Palazzina Franchetti-Prova, Via XX Settembre, Milan, illustrated in *Edilizia moderna, 7* (1898), pls. 6, 7.

7. *Edilizia moderna, 13* (1904), pls. 27, 28.

Figure 240. Raimondo d'Aronco: Turin, Exposition of Decorative Arts, Main Building, 1902

Figure 241. Luigi Broggi: Milan, Magazzino Contratti, 1903

buildings, like this store, showed their structural metal frankly on the exterior. Reinforced concrete did not bulk large in practice yet, though research will undoubtedly uncover more examples. At this stage of our knowledge, we may conclude that the Italian mind lent itself more naturally to experiment in the art rather than in the technique of building. The Contratti store shows a creative use of one of the popular Art Nouveau fonts: the lettering takes its place easily in the overall design. Noteworthy also is the richness and delicacy of the iron work along the edge of the entrance canopy, with its intricately entwined ribbons and upstanding poppies. The fashionable animal heads, ribbons, and floral forms appear elsewhere in the decoration. A strikingly decorative use of iron is shown in the detail of an apartment block on the Via Spadari in Milan of about the same date (Figure 242) by Ernesto Pirovano (born 1866). A number of intricately entwined stems bear few leaves but quantities of snails. This may be considered humorous or morbid. I incline to the latter view, since the stems in places metamorphose surrealistically into winged elements or griffon heads, and elsewhere appear flaccid. The effect of delicacy is apparent, however, and carries over into the detailing of the door frames behind. The metallic medium has been used appropriately and with an imagination that was uncommon in Italy. The ingenious, adventurous work of Alessandro Antonelli (1798–1888) in the nineteenth century, like the work of Gaudí in Spain, did not involve the use of new materials. There were a few other "modern" buildings: the department store in Rome by Giulio de Angelis (1850–1906) of 1899, now the Rinascente (Figure 166), and his nearby commercial building (with much exposed cast iron) on the Via Marco Minghetti of about 1906.[8] The front of the Caffè Due Palmi, mentioned above, was constructed in iron and glass, as was the façade of the larger building at Corso Venezia 15 in Milan.

There is a growing appreciation of these imaginative designs. One of them, the former Albergo Corso, also by Cattaneo and Santamaria in 1905, is being preserved in the façade of a new insurance company building.

Although Sommaruga used the Hennébique system of concrete floor construction in his Palazzo Castiglione in Milan, this was rare (Figures 249, 250). Iron beams and columns occur frequently in the work of this period, but none of this is as significant as similar and earlier work elsewhere in the world.

System nine is a type of composition which must owe much to American sources, directly or indirectly. Giovanni Battista Milani (1876–1940), in his design for a Galleria d'Arte Moderna made in 1900, emphasizes the horizontal in an un-Italian way (Figure 243). The sources for this include H. H. Richardson, Louis Sullivan, and Frank Lloyd Wright. The academic entrance, with its five portals, is wide. Over the first and fifth portals stand familiar motives of the

8. Illustrated in Francesco Sapori, *Architettura in Roma, 1901–1950* (Rome, 1953), p. 41.

Figure 242. Ernesto Pirovano: Milan, House on Via Spadari, detail, c. 1903

PROGETTO PER LA GALLERIA D'ARTE MODERNA · PROSPETTO · SCALA·————

Figure 243. Giovanni Battista Milani: Galleria d'Arte Moderna, project, 1900

period, groups of nudes supporting globes. The windows above the three central portals are clustered to emphasize width. The windows in the wings are similarly composed. The wings themselves are not only extended but are divided into layers to intensify further their horizontality. This method of composition does not become universal in Italy, but is adopted in whole or in part in many buildings (Figures 243, 249, 252, 264, 265).

A motive which does not amount to a system should be mentioned, because it occurs from time to time in conjunction with others. This is the dramatic use of black ornament contrasting with light materials. An example is the iron ornament superimposed on stone in the Guidici Tomb in Milan of 1906 (Figure 248) by Paolo Mezzanotte (born 1878). This device is not particularly architectural. It is most marked in graphic work, particularly that of Aubrey Beardsley and Toulouse-Lautrec, and in the use of black lace over bright light satin in the gowns of the period. In Italy, dark balconies, screens, gates, and grills often produced similar effects.

The tenth and most significant system, the one the Italians took most heartily for their own, was the *Floreale,* the subject of the next section.

Stile Floreale

We have mentioned above many of the characteristic features of the new styles coeval with and contributing to the *Floreale.* Contemporary Italian commentators were opposed to the use of the following devices as mannerisms borrowed from other countries: distorted moldings, tapeworm-like ribbons, and improbable plant forms. The critic Daniele Donghi, writing hostilely of the Turin Exposition of 1902, lists circles, brusque sharp bends, bundles of engraved lines or vertical string courses imitating fringe, horizontal bands imitating bandages, twisted or curled tops of pilasters projecting beyond the eaves, and frequent cornucopias.[9] He dismissed the claims made for them, complaining that they were decorations suitable for toys and knicknacks but not a new style.

No mention is made by most critics of the most ubiquitous type of Italian ornament: the lush heavy bands, garlands, clumps, deposits, and fungi-like growths of flowers and fruit that attach themselves in lumps to Italian buildings of this period. This aspect of the *Floreale* may not have been mentioned because it was basically traditional, hence the failure in observation. The reasons why the *Floreale* was triumphant in Italy include a love for sculpture, which ranks higher as a fine art in Italy than anywhere else in the West, and a devotion to tradition, which in this case meant carrying on familiar ornamental forms and pushing them to new extremes of realism or massiveness. An easy way of being

9. *L'Architettura pratica, 6* (1902), text accompanying pls. 13 and 14.

"modern" was to cling to the customary flat walls and apply "modernized" ornament to them. This was as economical of material as of thought.

The qualities of the *Floreale* reflect the bourgeois era which gave it its opportunity. Bourgeois styles rarely achieve the perfection of aristocratic or court styles; their appeal must be made to a less discriminating public.

The *Floreale* flourished at a moment when Italy was enjoying a prosperity hitherto unknown. From 1899 to 1910 the annual Treasury budget showed a favorable balance of income over expenditure for the only continuous stretch in modern Italian history.[10] A mood of buoyancy accompanied the new affluence, and was reflected in the new *palazzi, palazzetti, ville, villini,* public, and commercial buildings. Although war damage and the newest building boom have obliterated some, many survive. Sometimes the *Floreale* creeps in quietly like a slightly unfamiliar seasoning in a well-known dish.

This voluptuous, naturalistic ornament, the most characteristic Italian motive, has a long history, beginning with Roman funeral pillars like the one in the Terme Museum (Figure 244). In the Renaissance and Baroque, the same subject matter was popular, but usually kept several degrees to the geometrical right of the *Floreale* treatment, though there are close parallels, such as the decorations by Pierin del Vaga in the Cappella del Pallio in the Cancelleria (Figure 245) and on the exterior of many Mannerist buildings. It was the *Floreale* practitioners who let the material run wild, as if nature and not man were responsible. Evidently it was felt that a fecund and limitless vocabulary was at hand. Italy developed its form of the Art Nouveau about 1898, and it had little background compared with the long English and continental periods of preparation. The Art Nouveau movement elsewhere is considered to have been spent by 1906, but in Italy it was then still relatively vigorous. Some buildings designed under *Floreale* influence as late as 1912 to 1914 were built after the war almost without change (Figure 266).

The development of the style in Italy may have been reinforced by the Paris Exposition of 1900, where the Pont Alexandre and the Grand and Petit Palais abound in fruity naturalistic ornament. The Secession Building of the previous year also had some. We should not forget, moreover, that a related ornamental style was already formed by Louis Sullivan in the United States.

Ruskin made a contribution to the *Floreale*. The strength of his influence in Italy may be judged by the violence of the Futurist's sneers at "your deplorable Ruskin . . . with his sick dream of a primitive agrarian life, his nostalgia for Homeric cheeses and the spinning wheels of legend."[11] Furthermore, the fame of Ruskin and his disciple William Morris was at its height in the closing years of the nineteenth century. In Italy the *Aemilia Ars* group was founded at Bologna

10. Denis Mack Smith, *Italy, a Modern History* (Ann Arbor, 1959), p. 246.
11. Quoted by Reyner Banham, *Listener, 62* (1959), 974.

Figure 244. Rome, Museo Nazionale delle Terme, Roman Funerary Stele

Figure 245. Pierin del Vaga: Rome, Palazzo della Cancelleria, Cappella del Pallio, detail

in imitation of the Arts and Crafts Movement, as were the *Wiener Werkstätte* and the *Secession*. Magazines like *The Studio* (1893) were springing up everywhere; the Italian one, *Emporium,* was founded in 1895. Before this there were the influential architect-teachers, Selvatico, Boito, and Beltrami, preaching the renewal of architecture through Medieval traditions. In 1897 the first Italian translations of Ruskin's books appeared, his *Lessons in Design.* The pupil was to draw nature with literal exactness to sharpen his perception, not to produce models for the sculptor. The illustrations from Ruskin's own drawings are exceedingly naturalistic. Beltrami, in criticizing the room designed by Gaetano Moretti in 1902 (Figure 233), complained of its extravagantly naturalistic ornament, and said that the traditional forms were being overthrown to permit the absolute domination of vegetable forms, as though its proponents were saying, "Thanks to God and Ruskin, the arms and the griffons, the scrolls and the cartouches, the tryglyphs and the guttae are buried forever."[12] Neither artists nor critics, including Ruskin himself, had previously supported so grossly naturalistic a style, such uncompromising realism. But in Italy this was being paralelled in painting at the same moment by Giulio Aristide Sartorio (1851–1932), whose decorative friezes in the new wing of the Palazzo di Montecitorio, and whose huge compositions, such as *La Gorgona* in the Galleria Nazionale d'Arte Moderna, are of a startling lubricity. But we cannot lay the force of the whole movement at Ruskin's polyphase portal.

The proponents of the *Stile Floreale* invoked the familiar, banal gods of the nineteenth century: living organism (*organismo vivente*), logic (*logica*), function (*scopo*), and structure (*cosa costruita*). These themes are mentioned in 1908 by Ugo Monneret de Villard in his introduction to a folio of the works of Giuseppe Sommaruga (1867–1917), whose masterpiece, the Palazzo Castiglione in Milan (1901–03), is properly regarded as the archetypal monument of the style (Figures 249, 250).[13] It was alleged that its ornament is in logical harmony with the whole organism. Similar appeals to logic and nature have always been characteristic of architectural propagandists, and have accordingly been invoked to support every vacillation in style for millennia.

For Italy, the opinions of Monneret de Villard are representative of the modernists. He found the styles of the nineteenth century, from the Neoclassic on, to be corrupt, plagiaristic, false, puerile, and vulgar. He claimed that the needs for a style expressive of modern times and modern requirements had been met by the new style, and he referred to the well-known leaders of the Art Nouveau in Belgium, England, Austria, Germany, France, Spain, Sweden, and Russia. The last three were represented by Puig y Cadafalch, Ferdinand Boberg, and Eliel

12. *Edilizia moderna, 12* (1903), 25 ff.
13. U. Monneret de Villard, *L'Architettura di Giuseppe Sommaruga* (Milan, 1908). The frequent references to his views are from the introduction to this book.

Saarinen. Italy was late, he admits, but rapidly attained high stature in works, such as those by Sommaruga, which were not constricted by rules, formulas or antique forms, but were characterized by an intense new life which gave classical forms a truly modern expression, citing Sommaruga's Italian Pavilion for the St. Louis Exposition of 1904 (Figure 251). This spirit, he claimed, was quite opposed to that of the Viennese school of Otto Wagner, which was more archaic, oriental, and simple, whereas the Latin spirit required more opulence, a more varied and intense polychromy, and a new architectural form. Official Italian architecture, he felt, did not express the aspirations of the nation and was more concerned with economics than with the spirit. This aspiration could not be realized by those who simply applied to Italian buildings the more obvious mannerisms borrowed from other countries. Something more serious, dignified, and profound was needed and was supplied by Sommaruga's new architecture, which incorporated from the past such good qualities as the Baroque's love of a ponderous play of plastic masses, expressed through planes, volumes, light, and shade (Figures 249, 251). Sommaruga avoided the "boring cube" in favor of animated movement, employing for this purpose: loggias, balustrades, overhangs, bold flights of stairs, numerous columns, majestic roofs, and rich shadows. His architecture was built from parts, a living organism in which each cell played a vital rôle in harmony with the function of the whole organism. From the masters of the Romanesque, Sommaruga had learned that ornament should intensify the expressiveness and refinement of the forms, and should emphasize their significance and vitality. Hence he made his ornament essentially logical and structural, and made elements, raw and brutal in themselves, beautiful. He always sought a rational harmony between the organism and its decoration. He had been criticized for being heavy, funereal, and excessively solemn, but one does not demand that Hamlet be jolly. These qualities are legitimate in a work of art, and are not defects, even though not easily comprehensible to the superficially fashionable. Like Moretti and Basile, Sommaruga had given Italy an architecture worthy of its traditions and destiny. This last observation of Monneret de Villard's reflects the lengths to which chauvinism was being pushed.

The temperate ideal of having one foot firmly planted in tradition and the other dangling over the abyss of the unknown lacks the power to excite us, since we have seen a much bolder new architecture come and go. We have seen weakness follow that ideal far more often than strength; hence we are much more moved by the fireworks of the Futurists: their thoroughgoing revolutionary programs and their intoxication with machinery, noise, and motion. They were willing to jettison the suffocating burden of tradition, and the *Floreale* men were not. The radical desire to abandon the past was often expressed, and Marinetti's "burn the libraries" was only a more violent way of stating what Antonio Fo-

Figure 246. Raimondo d'Aronco: Udine, D'Aronco Tomb, 1898 (signed and dated)

Figure 247. Giuseppe Sommaruga: Varese, Aletti Tomb, 1898

gazzaro had written concerning the Turin Exposition of 1902.[14] He said that a variant of Dante's phrase should have been inscribed over the portal, "Lasciate ogni memoria voi ch'entrate." The ties of the *Floreale* with tradition fettered it, which is why it was the last of the creative eclectic styles rather than the first of the modern styles. While not achieving the impossible objective of a *tabula rasa,* the atmosphere of liberty and the encouragement to originality and innovation promoted an atmosphere in which more courageous innovations could subsequently be carried out.

Before the *Floreale* had really come to maturity there were signs of it in the work of such unlikely men as Luca Beltrami, whose hostile comments we quoted above. There are a few buildings of his in the late 1890s which, while orthodox in other respects, lavish heavy masses of naturalistic *Floreale* ornament on window frames, such as the Palazzo Venezia, in Milan, on which a monograph was published in 1900.[15]

The Leaders

What were the men who were to become famous exponents of the style doing in 1898? Let us examine a pair of funerary chapel designs, one a project by Raimondo d'Aronco for his family's tomb at Udine, and the other an executed work by Giuseppe Sommaruga, the Aletti Tomb at Varese, also published in that year (Figures 246, 247). These can be profitably compared with a third tomb, published in 1906, the work of Paolo Mezzanotte for the Giudici family in Milan (Figure 248). D'Aronco drives toward novelty by tilting his wall planes, those of the lower tier outward and of the upper, inward. He uses the common coins: disks, lion heads, Egyptoid heads, winged sun disks, uraeus and a number of other realistically handled symbols, but the predominant effect is one of crushing weight intensified by the coarse scale. Sommaruga is less ponderous and more subtle. He employs a number of the *Stile Boito* devices: colonnettes, striping, Gothic detail, and, in the iron grill, a William Morris pattern translated into three dimensions and combined with the ubiquitous ribbons. Two other elements of wider application can be seen here: the use of straps or "bandages" crossed and interwoven in a variety of materials and planes; and the silhouette, with its upturned corners, which appears over and over again. In Mezzanotte's tomb, the massing has become simpler. It is close to the traditional "boring cube"; the use of straps and bands is less plastic, but the *Floreale* ornament appears in some profusion, notably in the dark applications of leafy shrubs high up on the corners, in the ribboned bit in the cornice, and in the panel set high above the door. The details of the grill are characteristic: the

14. Quoted in *Rassegna nazionale, 126* (1902), 517, from *Figaro.*
15. Luca Beltrami, *Il Palazzo Venezia, sede delle Assicurazioni Generali, in Milano* (Milan, 1900).

Figure 248. Paolo Mezzanotte: Milan, Giudici Tomb, 1906

rather listless winged angel, the sun rays, and the web. In this third tomb the separation of the architecture from the ornament is marked, whereas in the first two there is an effort to integrate the two arts and to renew both.

Sommaruga, who had been a pupil of Boito, Beltrami, and Otto Wagner, went on between 1901 and 1903 to build the Palazzo Castiglioni in Milan which, as has been mentioned, is quite properly regarded as the archetype of the *Stile Floreale* (Figures 249, 250). Various motives described above are to be found here, and also some new ones. Most conspicuous are the contorted human figures by Ernesto Bazzaro above the windows and flanking the portal. The latter pair were removed shortly thereafter, and the more discreet ornaments which one sees today took their place. The figures were reinstalled at the Villa Faccononi at Sarnico. They are aggressively realistic. In the lower wall courses are to be observed the delicate triplets of square openings, recalling Austria and the "natural" rock, a legacy from the Baroque. The columns above the secondary door to the right, with their prismatic drums, stubby proportions, and "original" capitals, were a common feature, more lavishly used in villas, and probably Ottonian in origin. As Monneret de Villard stressed, the devices employed here for achieving plasticity are recesses, loggias, projections, deeply cut openings, and ornament in high relief. Three vertical axes are carried up through the façade to end in the characteristic upturned silhouettes. Sommaruga ingeniously wove all these elements together to achieve unity; follow the transmutations of the wide "bandage" just below the lintels of the top floor windows. The juicy *Floreale* ornament, though abundant and often coarse, is kept under geometrical control. Within, the main stair makes long leaps, sustained by its reinforced concrete core, and surrounded by several varieties of luxuriant *Floreale* decoration in several degrees of relief and in metal. The rear façade is less massive than the main front, and there is a greater use of iron and glass.

Sommaruga not only built other important examples of the style, including the Hotel Campo dei Fiori at Varese and one or two which will be mentioned below, but was the leader of a small school of Milanese architects. His closest follower among these was Alfredo Campanini, who developed some of Sommaruga's devices in a manner of his own.[16] He followed the master in his use of large realistic figures at the portal, as in a house at the corner of the Vie Livorno and Bellini, and in his decoration in such houses as the one formerly at Via Senato 28. His own touch shows most clearly in the large scale of all of his decorative devices—figures, ribbons, and foliage—and in his liberal use of "bandages" to tie balconies to door frames and window frames into the adjoining wall surfaces.

In 1904, Sommaruga designed the Italian Pavilion at the St. Louis Exposition of that year (Figure 251), which Monneret de Villard admired for renew-

16. See Mario Scheichenbauer, *Alfredo Campanini* (Milan, 1958) passim.

Figure 249. Giuseppe Sommaruga: Milan, Palazzo Castiglioni, principal façade before alteration, 1901–03

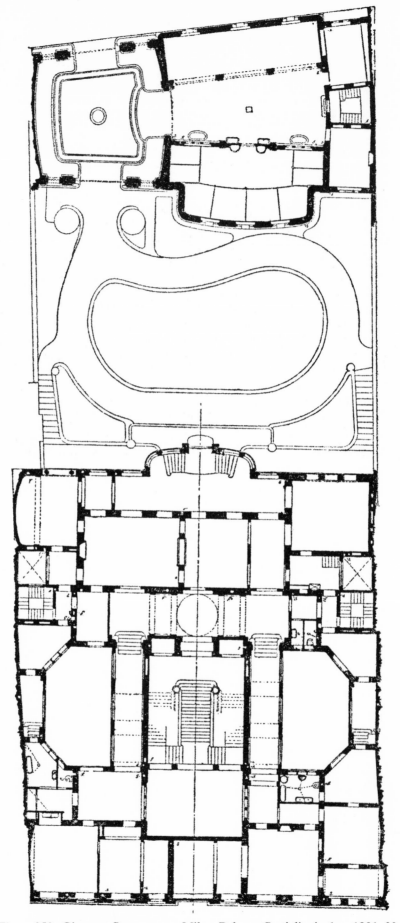

Figure 250. Giuseppe Sommaruga: Milan, Palazzo Castiglioni, plan, 1901–03

Figure 251. Giuseppe Sommaruga: St. Louis, Exposition of 1904, Italian Pavilion

ing classicism. Today the rejuvenation does not seem so noteworthy. The ornament has the *Floreale* fullness, including the odd trellis of garlands which connect the columns of the front screen with the flanking pylons. The columns themselves are treated in a way which enjoyed some success at this time, the channeling being limited to part of the shafts, the balance being left round and smooth, as though awaiting completion. The dark accents furnished by the bronze sculpture and flagstands relate to Mezzanotte's later Giudici Tomb (Figure 248). There has been no occasion so far to mention the mania for wrapping friezes or belts of sculpture in high relief around buildings, often at eye level. In this pavilion, the belts encircle both the main building and the pylons. Such sculpture is usually extremely realistic. Other instances appear in the "Vittoriano" (Figure 192), and, higher on the walls, on the Galleria Nazionale d'Arte Moderna (Figure 265).[17] The Austrian Pavilion by Josef Hoffmann at the same Exposition now seems more creative. Doubtless Sommaruga's ideas were held in check by the more conservative ideas of officialdom.

A third work of Sommaruga's, the Palazzino Comi of 1906 in Milan, exhibits traces of what we have called the ninth system (Figure 252). The influence from the Prairie Style shows in its massing, its horizontal emphasis, and even in the prickly effect of its ornament. The play of textures on the surface is unusually elaborate. They are probably all executed in stucco, from the random ashlar of the bottom layer through the plane and molded bands to the thicker layer of deep vertical corrugations ending in a fringed *Floreale* border. It can be inferred that Wright's Charnley and Winslow Houses had been looked at attentively.

It would distort the picture too much to look further at Sommaruga's work, since he was only one among many. There is Ernesto Basile (1857–1932), son of the architect of the stupendous Teatro Massimo at Palermo. The son became most famous for winning the final competition and the commission, two things which did not necessarily go hand in hand, for the new parliament building in Rome, the vast addition to Bernini's Palazzo Montecitorio (Figure 253). The decision was made in 1902, but construction appears to have begun only in 1906. The illustration shows the main entrance to Basile's structure. In it can be discerned the timorous way in which he blended *Floreale* ornament with more traditional forms. Nevertheless, alone among the grandiose public and commercial buildings of the day, this one retains an air of freshness. For one thing it uses the least pretentious of materials, brick, for the walls of the upper part. For another, it varies the "boring cube" only by slightly projecting corner towers. Third, it avoids the extreme chiaroscuro of so many contemporary build-

17. Henry Millon has suggested to the writer that the interest in such belts may have been aroused by the recently discovered frieze of the altar at Pergamon and the reassembly of the Ara Pacis.

Figure 252. Giuseppe Sommaruga: Milan, Palazzino Comi, 1906

ings by using pilasters exclusively. The corner towers give the mass the upturned silhouette which is underlined by the similar silhouette of each tower. There was a good deal of disappointment over the completed building, because it was simpler and more modest than Italian eyes were accustomed to in ceremonial and symbolic buildings. This simplicity carries through all of the décor within and without, except for Giulio Aristide Sartorio's painted friezes in the council hall, which are so realistic as to appear to be living figures.

The accusation that Basile's design for the Parlamento was merely his rejected design for the Palazzo di Giustizia (Figure 195) does not really stand up. The Parlamento is smaller, its materials more modest, and the Neoclassical effects have disappeared. The two designs do have some common features: the use of giant pilasters, the rusticated arched windows of the basement, and the rise of the flat-topped corner towers. However, all of these have been simplified and lightened. The later building is graphic, while the earlier design is plastic.

A few years before, Basile had completed another large *Floreale* building, the Villa Igiea, an hotel in Palermo. The interior of the main dining room is extremely elaborate (Figure 254), but almost none of the motives is peculiarly Italian, since they are derived from Belgian, French, and English examples. The mural containing maidens and swans appears, perhaps, more three-dimensional and realistic in effect than it would have done in the place of its origin. The poppy so beloved in the north appears here in the column capitals and door frames. Whether or not this is properly an example of the *Floreale,* it is a typically handsome room of the period, which must have contributed decisively to the mood and manners of the *fin de siècle.* Now, alas, it is somewhat altered, but, like the mutilated dining room of the old Hotel Storione in Padua, it serves to remind us of the once widespread elegance now usually associated only with Maxim's.

Basile had a large practice and executed numerous other buildings, sometimes exhibiting not only an awareness of the whole European scene but inventions of his own. The luxurious Villino Florio, of 1900–02, in Palermo (Figure 255) had, as previously mentioned, interiors which owed something to William Morris and a good deal to Victor Horta.[18] The exterior mingles Ottonian and Boitonian elements with the picturesqueness of a chalet. Basile's personal motive can be seen over the windows of the large oriel standing between the two stairs, and also in the window above the entrance porch. This is a quirky bit of tracery which often begins as bare stems running up the window jambs meeting under the lintel to form an intricate pattern of curves and reversed

18. This was scheduled for preservation as an historic monument, but it burned down in 1962. It was illustrated in *Edilizia moderna, 16* (1907), 33–34, and pls. 28–31.

Figure 253. Ernesto Basile: Rome, Palazzo Montecitorio, addition, detail, 1902 ff.

Figure 254. Ernesto Basile: Palermo, Villa Igiea, Dining Room, 1901

Figure 255. Ernesto Basile: Palermo, Villino Florio, 1900–02

curves—a little flamboyant in origin, no doubt, yet instantly recognizable in other buildings of Basile's as his trademark.[19]

It is sometimes claimed that spatial innovations were one of the great merits of the Art Nouveau. It has been asserted that this was the outgrowth of the work of the Impressionist painters.[20] The concrete proofs of this are slight, particularly in Italy where, without more evidence, it is impossible to be sure that spatial oddities result from deliberate aesthetic intent rather than the ingenious treatment of awkward corners. There was no change from the traditional way of life that required changes in planning, aside from the increasing frequency of bathrooms. Little deviation from the habitual closed separateness of each room is discernible. Little in the way of "open planning" or "living halls" seems to have been introduced. Yet, as was the case in the majority of residences in both Europe and America, the architect was free to adjust interior planning to fit his exterior composition. Seldom has the art of architecture suffered from fewer restrictions either of function or economy. This is shown in the Villino Florio, where the contrived irregularities in plan and façades are highly capricious and arbitrary.

It is not possible in a survey of this length to even name all the architects practicing in this style nor to illustrate more than a small sampling of the thousands of buildings bearing its hallmarks. It would be confusing to do so, and hence the same names appear here again and again. Ulisse Stacchini (born 1871), best known for his grandiose main railroad station in Milan (Figure 262), had served his apprenticeship in this style. The apartments he built in Milan on the Via Gioberti show his inventiveness (Figure 256). The contrast with the more conservative adjoining buildings of the same era is striking. Stacchini has tried, like Sommaruga, to avoid the monotony of the usual boxy mass by treating his building as if it were made up of three towers and two connecting links. He opens up the walls of the links and gets an unusual amount of window area in the closely grouped triplets. This becomes part of a complex rhythmical system, in which some windows have balconies and elaborate frames and others do not, thus establishing the skipping effect mentioned above by both vertical and horizontal manipulation of accents. The ornament varies from story to story and from window or door to its neighbor. One or two details may be emphasized: the painted *Floreale* frieze running between two sets of deeply scored horizontal lines; the stiff rather than limp effect of the iron work; the abundant but not excessive use of *Floreale* ornament in relief mingled with poppies and disks; and the fact that the "towers" end with the upturned corner silhouette.

19. Basile's personal signature appears in at least two *villini* in Rome, one at Via Abruzzi 2, and the other on the Piazza Galeno, the residence of the prominent sculptor Ettore Ximenes (1855–1926), who was also from Palermo and who wrapped a rich waistband of realistic sculpture around his villa, as though adding his signature to that of Basile.

20. Discussed in Renato de Fusco, *Il Floreale a Napoli* (Naples, 1959), p. 7.

Figure 256. Ulisse Stacchini: Milan, Via Gioberti 1, Apartments, c. 1906

In 1906 Locati, whose work has been mentioned earlier, became the chief architect for the International Exposition of 1906 held at Milan to celebrate the completion of the Simplon Tunnel. The buildings were banal, pedestrian, and lacking in generative ideas, indicating that the new style was on the wane. An example is the Palazzo delle Belle Arti (Figure 257). Some of the vocabulary used by D'Aronco in the far superior Turin buildings of 1902 (Figure 233) reappears here, but on the whole, the traditional forms are more numerous. The Art Nouveau elements seem undernourished—note the languid air of the ribbons in the spandrels. As a further indication of the ebbing taste of Milan at this time, the ornament of the Transportation Building included locomotive parts.

One of the most extraordinary figures to emerge in Italy at this time was Gino Coppedè (1866–1927). We have seen one of his early, beautifully simple, rather British works above (Figure 236). In Figure 258 we confront an example of the fantastic exuberance which characterized his later work. This apartment block on the Via Anton Maria Maragliano in Genoa bears the date 1907. The details shown in the illustration justify the comment that Coppedè was the most lavish user of ornament of the period. Most of the basic themes were common among his contemporaries, but he had a greater abandon and yet found clients who appreciated him. In this example, the few square feet of plain wall on the second floor contrast startlingly with the lion-head and lion-legged balcony below and the pairs of Egyptoid heads interrupting the pilasters which link this floor with the one above it. The devices used for linkage and separation both vertically and horizontally recall in their ingenuity Buontalenti's Mannerist masterpiece in the Museo dell'Opera del Duomo in Florence. The extravagance shown here is continued in Coppedè's later work in Rome, the apartment blocks on the Via Po (Figure 259), in which the greatest novelty is the variety of scales used in rapid succession and close juxtaposition. This building is signed and dated "Gino Coppedè 1921." It is an example of how persistent some of the characteristics of the *Floreale* were, and of how long they conformed to bourgeois taste. This great double block of apartments, joined by an arch over the street, is ruthlessly asymmetrical and is fitted onto its site as intricately as possible. The interiors are as lavishly decorated as the exterior, and the apartments are still considered luxurious. In spite of the persistence in this work of many *Floreale* motives, and of its mode of composition, it might be more accurate to dub this style the "Stile Coppedè" and to consider it a personal variant. But there is a difficulty: it was also practiced with some success and similar aesthetic consequences by others, including Giulio Arata (born 1885) in Milan.[21]

21. Giulio Arata, who was architect, historian, and restorer, was extravagantly irregular and picturesque in his buildings. The only volume of a projected multivolume monograph of his work

Figure 257. Sebastiano Giuseppe Locati: Milan, Exposition of 1906, Palazzo delle Belle Arti

Figure 258. Gino Coppedè: Genoa, Apartments, Via Maragliano, detail, 1907

Figure 259. Gino Coppedè: Rome, Via Po, Apartments, detail, 1921 (signed and dated)

Aftermath of the Floreale

The aftermath of the *Floreale,* a type of Protocubism, was closely linked to Cubism on one side and to Futurism on the other. By 1911, the original *Floreale* character had been reduced to a blocky massiveness (Figure 260). The designs depended on such late nineteenth-century ones as those of D'Aronco and Sommaruga for tombs (Figures 246, 247) but the legacies from the *Floreale* were composed differently. There had been some intervening experiments, such as Ernesto Pirovano's entrance to the Cemetery at Bergamo (built 1900–13) and the well-known and original hydroelectric plant at Trezzo d'Adda (1906) by Gaetano Moretti. In both, the outstanding impression is ponderousness. Critics have noted many antecedents, such as Egypt, *Liberty,* and *Secession* (or Berlage), and Neoplasticism.[22] In addition, the receding silhouettes have prototypes in Angkor Wat, and there are strongly Niebelungenlieden overtones to the solemn bulks, echoing the work of the great stage designers of these years. A frequently seen form is the diminished, tapered, or stepped crown replacing the traditional dome or tower. Sometimes the profile curves softly (Figures 260, 262). There were similar shapes elsewhere in Europe and also in the United States: in Wright's Mayan period and in Goodhue's later, more progressive work, as in his Nebraska State Capitol. Some examples which show this tendency include the designs submitted in competition for the entrance to the Cemetery at Monza in 1912, Stacchini's, or the youthful Antonio Sant' Elia's (1888–1916) in Figure 260. In both the forms are frozen into lithic masses. The ornament is constrained. Lightness and elegance have been avoided in favor of bulk. The similarity of function shared by this group of buildings and projects does not wholly account for this, because such massiveness was characteristic of residential work by Sommaruga, Stacchini, and Coppedè. Sant'Elia manipulates his bands much as did Sommaruga (Figures 247, 249). Stacchini uses them, too, as well as enormous *Floreale* garlands to drape the supports of the pylon.

By 1912, the revolutionary proclamations of the Futurists had been heard, and a whisper of the concept of architectural Expressionism was audible.[23]

---

that I have seen, Alfredo Melani, *L'Architettura di Giulio Arata, primo volume, ville* (Milan, 1913), consists of extreme examples of romantic eclecticism presented in impassioned sketches. In his executed work he was equally lavish with motives and heedless of economy of space, material, or ornament. It can be inferred that he knew the early work of R. Norman Shaw and possibly that of Frank J. Furness. His most celebrated building is the Palazzo Berri-Meregalli published in Alfredo Melani, "Architettura 'Ars Regina,'" *Vita d'arte, 1* (1914), 47–48.

22. Lavagnino, *L'Arte moderna, 1,* 501, and Bruno Zevi, "Eredità dell' ottocento," *Metron, 37* (1950), 41.

23. Antonio Sant'Elia's famous "Messaggio" was still two years in the future: May 20, 1914. It can be found in *Architettura, 11* (1956), 516. His extreme position followed logically from Marinetti's "Manifesto" of 1910 [*Architectural Review, 126* (1959), 77–80] and shows an equally

Figure 260. Antonio Sant'Elia and Italo Paternostro: Project for Monza Cemetery, 1912

Figure 261. Antonio Sant'Elia: Sketch for a railroad station, c. 1912

Figure 262. Ulisse Stacchini: Milan, Central Station, original design, 1912

These forces, with their more exciting programs, were influencing architectural thinking and designs, as evidenced by those for the railroad stations (Figures 261, 262). Stacchini, at forty-one, won the competition for the Stazione Centrale in Milan in 1912. His design is, as one would expect from a man of his training, a mixture of *Floreale* elements and the newer, more rigid Protocubism which he had shown in his Monza design of the same year. The curved elements are more numerous in the former, and it is significant that, when execution of the revised designs took place after World War I, it was just these elements that were reduced, while the megalomaniac scale and the redundancy of decoration of the newer mode was intensified. It is ironic that in this large, late *Floreale* building, the claim that the style was structurally inventive should be so grossly exposed; the train sheds of surpassing excellence owe far less to the *Floreale* than does the overwhelming inert building which all but conceals them. Sant'Elia, probably at the time that this competition was in the air, made a sketch in which one cannot detect a hint of any ornament; but far more important, one can see how, within the terms of Expressionism, a noble, original, and dynamic expression of the character of a great railroad terminal could have been achieved. The way to such freedom had been in part blazed by the men of the *Floreale*.

The last type of building to be influenced by the *Floreale*, and the one in which it survived longest, was the most conservative, the government building. With the exception of Basile's Palazzo Montecitorio (Figure 253), the *Floreale* had made only the slightest inroads on official buildings, for which Cinquecento or Baroque models were preferred. Nevertheless, so all-pervasive was it that it infiltrated even into these citadels, in a group of conspicuous public buildings.

Two of the most discussed buildings of modern Rome, begun in the 1880s, were under construction so long and subjected to so many vicissitudes that in spite of the early date of the original designs, *Floreale* detailing appeared on them. These are the Monument to Victor Emanuel II, by Giuseppe Sacconi (Figure 192) and the Palace of Justice by Guglielmo Calderini (Figure 263). As described in Chapter Four, Sacconi had died in 1905 and a committee of three architects was appointed to carry on the monument.

The silhouette of the "Vittoriano" is marked by elevated terminal pavilions flanking the crowning colonnade. Previously, one such quadriga-crowned feature would have seemed sufficient to most architects, but this silhouette was popular in nineteenth-century competitions; the germ of it had appeared, for instance, in Nénot's notorious project (Figure 187), and is seen in Paul Wallot's

---

ruthless desire for a complete break with tradition including the recent past with its "tapeworms, columns, stairs, sculpture, cubic and pyramidal shapes, and monumental, commemorative and funerary buildings."

Figure 263. Guglielmo Calderini: Rome, Palazzo di Giustizia, detail, 1888–1910

Reichstagsgebäude in Berlin (1882 ff.).[24] It was a logical outcome of a program which required an equestrian statue as the main feature, with any accessory structure subordinated to form its background. In the "Vittoriano" we can see many *Floreale* devices: the clotted ironwork of the rising screen, mentioned previously; the upturned corners and the open, loosely serrated silhouette; the sharp contrasts between black bronze and gleaming white marble; the wide belt of naturalistic sculpture; the *Floreale* garlands around the base; and such details as the disks and the triplets of square openings. The Palace of Justice, in which the ornament within and without is more redundant, in general outline also has some of the loose composition of the former building. The ornament of the upper part, and particularly of the second floor, is rich with the familiar disks, heads, and *Floreale* garlands, as though, by the time the building reached this level during construction, these fashionable devices were slipped in. Its affinities are with the plasticity and vocabulary of Coppedè rather than with the almost unnoticed building of Basile.

The combined effect of these great buildings and the more marked examples of the *Floreale* influenced other public buildings. Of these, the earliest is Cesare Bazzani's project (1873–1939) for the Biblioteca Nazionale Centrale at Florence. He won the competition in 1906 with the design illustrated (Figure 264), which was begun in 1907 and completed in 1935. The composition belongs to the same family as G. B. Milani's project of 1900 (Figure 243). Bazzani was also the architect of two other important public buildings: the Galleria Nazionale d'Arte Moderna of 1911 (Figure 265), and the Ministero dell'Educazione Nazionale of 1913–28 (Figure 266). The former was a permanent building erected in connection with the Exposition of Fine Arts of 1911 in Rome. The second, designed before World War I, was much delayed in execution. Bazzani has given all three of these buildings wide central blocks, progressively increasing the bays from five to seven and opening up more of them. In each, the wings are set back and extend a considerable distance horizontally. This system of proportioning and massing is characteristic of the early twentieth century; the predominant feeling is that of conservative "Beaux-Arts" buildings, such as were approved by exposition committees and governments everywhere. Into these envelopes, slightly irregular and broken in silhouette, it was easy to inject a little modishness in the form of *Floreale* decoration. In the Library, there is a restrained use of *Floreale* garlands, ribbons, draped maidens, and disks. In the Art Gallery, the ornament is more decisively *Floreale*. The classical elements have been modernized. The bases of the columns are linked in pairs by blocks of *Floreale* ornament, with a lion head perversely placed under the interval. The column capitals are slightly more doughy than a classicist might have made them. The rest of the ornament is unabashedly modish: the garlands,

24. Other related compositions are mentioned on p. 344.

Figure 264. Cesare Bazzani: Florence, Biblioteca Nazionale Centrale, original design, detail, 1906

Figure 265. Cesare Bazzani: Rome, Galleria Nazionale d'Arte Moderna, 1911

Figure 266. Cesare Bazzani: Rome, Ministero dell'Educazione Nazionale, 1913–28

the ribbons, the lions, and the draped maidens, whose raised arms give the outline its jagged upturned silhouette and whose other arms, resting on segmental
pediments, clutch the ends of sagging garlands of ripe vegetation.

In the Ministry (Figure 266), which is the most grandiose of the three, the
ornament is a characteristically flaccid *Floreale,* particularly in the lower parts,
including some play with natural rock forms, all of it on a very large scale.

An exceptional building, and one that shows some slight influence from Basile's 1902 design, is the Palazzo della Marina by Giulio Magni (died 1930).
They have in common the coloration resulting from the use of brick in the
upper layer; the strong corner pavilions, a single bay in width and carried up
above the cornice line; the relative lack of plasticity due in part to the sparing
use of columns; and such characteristics as the irregular silhouette and upturned corners. Not a building of compelling power, not a building exhibiting
much of the conviction of its predecessors or the overpowering stuffiness of its
successors, perhaps it indicates how little real strength there was in the main
current of the Art Nouveau in its Italian form.

Importance of the Floreale

After this review of what constituted the major style of Italian architecture
in the first years of this century, it is proper to inquire to what extent the claims
made for it can be accepted. The state of the discussion has been summed up in
an article in the *Architectural Review,* in which Italian and other critics' views
are quoted and commented on.[25]

In that discussion the term *Liberty* has been used instead of *Floreale,* partly
because it was one of the names used widely in Italy but more particularly because its connotations have been on the whole less pejorative. It has been argued
that much of the character of modern architecture in Italy since 1945 has
been close to that of the *Liberty* of the beginning of the century, and that this is
deplorable. In reply, the Italian critics, and some others who have joined them,
assign to the original *Liberty* or *Floreale* the following virtues: it grows old nobly; it harmonizes with its neighbors; it uses simple, economical materials in
simple, economical structures; it was the first of the modern styles; it exhibits a
creative synthesis; it contains energies to be rescued and canalized; it was the
most precious page of modern architecture; it has been over-abused and condemned in an undiscriminating way along with the earlier and inferior work
of the nineteenth century; its practitioners were artists of the very first rank, not
just forerunners of the modern movement but protagonists of one of its most
fruitful periods; it was less harmful than the work that has been done since; its

25. "Neoliberty: the Debate," *Architectural Review, 126* (1959), 341–44.

true strength was its structural rationalism.[26] None of the enthusiasts who make these claims would assert that what they are stating is true for the whole body of work of the period, but they are implying that the number of works of genius and significance is high, whereas the vast majority of the buildings of the period, as our survey has shown, can lay claim to few of these virtues, even those buildings which come from the drawing boards of highly regarded architects.

There is a separate sub-class of buildings, a handful, built during the same years, but radically different in concept, in which glass walls, metal, and reinforced concrete were exploited. These few, some of which have been mentioned, have in common with "modern architecture" economy and openness. Sant'Elia was mining this thin lode as he wrestled to vanquish tradition. The energies allegedly inherent in the style are to be found chiefly in these pioneer buildings, though other facets, such as self-expression in ornament and decoration, do furnish a precedent for much recent Italian work. Structural rationalism and progressive design—these concepts of lasting value were tolerated in a period which warmly welcomed any kind of innovation, but did not flourish mightily in comparison with the concepts of the more ubiquitous and more superficial ornamentalists. It is even difficult to find a powerful war cry earlier than those of the Futurists.

Growing old nobly, and the associated virtues of fitting in harmoniously and wearing well, are qualities of most Italian architecture prior to the 1920s. This was the case with the eclectic buildings of the nineteenth century, unless some foreigner like G. E. Street tried to be more Italian than the Italians, as in his two Roman churches. The casual visitor may not realize that the buildings he is looking at may range from fifty to five hundred years in age. The harmony comes from shared shapes ("the boring cube"), materials, scale, and the degree of murality as opposed to openness. The urban *Floreale* buildings, which hardly broke with these fundamentals, fit in easily with their older brothers.

26. R. Banham, "Italian Retreat from Modern Architecture (Neoliberty)," *Architectural Review, 125* (1959), 231–35.

Appendix A

CHRONOLOGICAL LIST OF PUBLICATIONS 1700–1800

This appendix demonstrates one of the ways in which new ideas, and new or revived vocabularies, were disseminated throughout the eighteenth century by publication. The arrangement is therefore chronological. It is illustrative and selective rather than comprehensive. It will be noted by the reader that these books nurtured concurrently the persistence of the Renaissance system, the use of antique and exotic vocabularies, and the rise of emotional-romantic concepts. Samplings of pattern books, guide books, and *vedute* are included because of their popularity and influence.

The author regrets that it has not been possible for him to examine in person every volume listed. He realizes that there is therefore an inevitable gathering of errors. While deploring this, he feels that nevertheless this list will be of material aid to other scholars and so offers it for their indulgent consultation even in its imperfect state.

The principal books used in compiling this list, in addition to the catalogues of the British Museum, the Bibliothèque Nationale, the Library of Congress, and Yale University were: *The Fowler Architectural Collection of the Johns Hopkins University, Catalogue compiled by Laurence Hall Fowler and Elizabeth Baer,* Baltimore, 1961; *The Catalog of the Avery Memorial Architectural Library of Columbia University,* 1958; Julius von Schlosser, *La Letteratura artistica,* Florence, 1956; *The Universal Catalogue of Books on Art,* New York, 1964; Leopoldo Cicognara, *Catalogo ragionato dei libri d'arte e d'antichità,* Pisa, 1821; *I Libri di viaggio e le guide della raccolta Luigi Vittorio Fossati Bellani,* edited by Antonio Pescanzoli, Rome, 1957; and Fabia Borroni, *Bibliografia dell'archaeologica classica e dell'arte italiana,* Florence, 1957. Borroni's nine-volume catalogue is by far the most thorough for the early publication history of classical sites. His *Bibliografia* also contains the most complete list of Italian aesthetic writings and a list of bibliographies.

Compilation of this appendix has largely been performed by Helen Searing, David Summers, and John Cameron to whose assiduity a great debt is hereby acknowledged.

(*)—first edition not located
(†)—probably the first edition
(=)—first edition not located but earlier editions
published in the eighteenth century

1700

BRUYN, CORNELIS DE (1652–1726/27), *Voyage au Levant . . . dans l'Asie Mineure, dans les isles de Chio, Rhodes, et Chypre . . . dans . . . villes d'Égypte, de Syrie, et de la Terre Sainte . . .* , Delft, 1700. (1st ed. 1698.)

DANET, PIERRE (d. 1709), *A Complete Dictionary of the Greek and Roman Antiquities . . .* , London, 1700. (1st ed. 1698.)

MONTELATICI, DOMENICO, *Villa Borghese con l'ornamenti che si osservano nel di lei palazzo . . .* , Rome, 1700.

POZZO, ANDREA (1642–1709), *Perspectiva pictorum et architectorum,* Rome, 1700–02.

RAGUENET, FRANÇOIS (1660–1722), *Les Monumens de Rome . . .* , 1st ed. Paris, 1700.

ROSSINI, PIETRO, *Il Mercurio errante delle grandezze di Roma tanto antiche che moderne . . .* , 2d ed. Rome, 1700. (*)

SARNELLI, POMPEO (1649–1724), *La Guide des étrangers, curieux de voir . . . Poussol, Bayes, Cumes . . . traduite par Antoine Bulifon,* Naples, 1700?

SCAMOZZI, VINCENZO (1552–1616), *The Mirror of Architecture . . . ,* London, 1700. (1st English ed. 1669.)

VIGNOLA, GIACOMO BAROZZI DA (1507–73), *Regel der fünff Orden von der Architectur . . . Auffs neue verm. mit etlichen schönen Gebäuen,* Amsterdam, c. 1700.

VIGNOLA, GIACOMO BAROZZI DA, *The Regular Architect: or the General Rule of the Five Orders of Architecture of . . . Vignola, with a new addition of Michael Angelo Buonaroti. Rendred into English . . . and explained by John Leeke, etc.,* London, c. 1700.

1701

BRICE, GERMAIN (1652–1727), *Description nouvelle de la ville de Paris . . . ,* Paris, 1701. (1st ed. 1685.)

COLONIA, DOMINIQUE DE (1660–1741), *Antiquitez profanes et sacrées de la ville de Lyon . . . ,* 1st ed. Lyon, 1701.

DANET, PIERRE (d. 1709), *Dictionarium antiquitatum Romanarum, et Graecarum . . . ,* Amsterdam, 1701. (1st ed. 1698.)

LONGINUS, DIONYSIUS (d. 273), *Traité du sublime ou du merveillieux . . . ,* Paris, 1701.

RAGUENET, FRANÇOIS (1660–1722), *Les Monumens de Rome . . . ,* Amsterdam, 1701. (1st ed. 1700.)

1702

COLONIA, DOMINIQUE DE (1660–1741), *Antiquites . . . de la ville de Lyon . . . ,* Paris and Lyon, 1702. (1st ed. 1701.)

FRÉART, ROLAND, SIEUR DE CHAMBRAY (c. 1606–76), *Parallele de l'architecture antique et de la moderne. Avec un recueil des dix principaux auteurs qui ont écrit des cinq ordres. Scavoir, Palladio & Scammozzi, Serlio & Vignola, D. Barbaro & Cataneo, L. B. Alberti & Viola, Bullant & De Lorme, comparez entr'eux. Les trois ordres grecs, le dorique, l'ionique & le corinthien . . . Et les deux Latins, le Toscan & le Composite . . . ,* Paris, 1702. (1st ed. 1650.)

FRÉMIN, MICHEL DE, *Mémoires critiques d'architecture . . . ,* Paris, 1702. (*)

MONTFAUCON, BERNARD DE (1655–1741), *Diarium Italicum, sive monumentorum veterum bibliothecarum, musaeorum . . . ,* 1st ed. Paris, 1702.

POTTER, JOHN (1674?–1747), *Archaeologia graeca, sive veterum graecorum . . . , Lugduni Batavorum,* 1st Latin ed. 1702.

RAGUENET, FRANÇOIS (1660–1722), *Les Monumens de Rome . . . ,* Paris, 1702. (1st ed. 1700.)

ROSSI, DOMENICO DE (1678?–1742?), *Studio d'architettura civile sopra gli ornamenti di porte e fenestre tratti da alcune fabbriche insigni di Roma . . . ,* 3 vols. Rome, 1702–21. (†)

SARNELLI, POMPEO (1649–1724), *Le Guide des étrangers curieux de voir les choses plus mémorables de Poussol . . . traduite . . . par Antoine Bulifon,* 2d French ed. Naples, 1702. (1st French ed. 1697.)

1703

MAUNDRELL, HENRY (1650–1710), *Journey from Aleppo,* 1st ed. Oxford, 1703.

VIGNOLA, GIACOMO BAROZZI DA (1507–73), *Vignola: or, the Compleat Architect . . . Translated . . . by Joseph Moxon,* 5th ed. London, 1703. (1st ed. 1655; first dated ed. 1665.)

VITRUVIUS POLLIO, MARCUS, *The Theory and·Practice of Architecture; or Vitruvius and Vignola . . . abridged . . . by . . . Mr. Perrault,* London, 1703. (1st English ed. 1692.)

1704

BARTOLI, PIETRO SANTI (1635–1700), *Gli Antichi Sepolcri, ovvero mausolei Romani, ed Etruschi trovati in Roma, ed altri luoghi celebri . . . ,* Rome, 1704. (1st ed. 1697.)

BIANCHINI, FRANCESCO (1662–1729), *Considerazioni teoriche, e pratiche intorno al trasporto della colonna di Antonino Pio collocata in Monte Citorio . . . ,* 1st ed. Rome, 1704.

BLAEU, JEAN, *Nouveau Théâtre d'Italie; ou, description exacte de ses villes, palais, églises . . . ,* Amsterdam, 1704. (1st ed., in Latin, 1633.)

DESEINE, FRANÇOIS JACQUES (d. 1715), *Beschryving von oud en niew Rome . . . ,* 2 vols. Amsterdam, 1704. (1st ed., in French, 1690.)

LA CHAUSSE, MICHEL ANGE DE (fl. 1700), *Lettera in cui si fa parola della colonna* *nuovamente trovate in Roma . . . ed eretta già per l'apoteosi di Antonino Pio,* Naples, 1704. (*)

NARDINI, FAMIANO (d. 1661), *Roma antica . . . ,* 2d ed. Rome, 1704. (1st ed. 1666?)

ORLANDI, PELLEGRINO ANTONIO (1660–1727), *L'Abecedario pittorico . . . ,* Bologna, 1704.

ROSSI, DOMENICO DE (1678?–1742?), *Raccolta di statue antiche e moderni, date in luce . . . da Domenico de Rossi, illustrata colle sposizioni . . . di Paolo Alessandrao Maffei . . . ,* Rome, 1704. (†)

VACCA, FLAMINIO (1538–1600), *Memorie di varie antichità trovate in diverse luoghi dell'alma città di Roma nell'anno 1596,* Rome, 1704. (1st ed. 1666.)

1705

CRESCIMBENI, GIOVANNI MARIO (1663–1729), *Racconte di tutta l'operazione per l'elevazione ed abbassamento della Colonna Antonina . . . ,* 1st ed. Rome, 1705.

FÉLIBIEN, JEAN-FRANÇOIS (c. 1658–1733), *Recueil historique de la vie et des ouvrages des plus célèbres architectes . . . ,* London, 1705. (1st ed. 1687.)

MARTINI, JOSEPHUS, *Theatrum basilicae Pisanae . . . ,* Rome, 1705–23.

MAUNDRELL, HENRY (1650–1710), *Voyage d'Alep . . . traduit de l'anglais,* Utrecht, 1705. (1st English ed. 1699.)

RUBENS, PETER PAUL (1577–1640), *Architecture italienne . . .* [Antwerp], 1705. (1st ed. 1622.)

VIGNOLA, GIACOMO BAROZZI DA (1507–73), *Regel der fünff Orden . . . ,* Augsburg, 1705.

1706

BRETEZ, LOUIS (fl. 1706–39), *La Perspective pratique de l'architecture . . . pour representer en perspective les ordonnances d'architecture . . . ,* 1st ed. Paris, 1706.

CORDEMOY, J. L. DE, *Nouveau Traité de toute l'architecture . . . ,* 1st ed. Paris, 1706.

EVELYN, JOHN (1620–1706), *An Account of Architects and Architecture . . . ,* 1st ed. London, 1706.

FÉLIBIEN, MICHEL (1665–1719), *Histoire de l'Abbaye Royale de Saint Denys en France . . . ,* 1st ed. Paris, 1706.

LA CHAUSSE, MICHEL ANGE DE (fl. 1700), *Le Grand Cabinet romain, ou recueil d'an-*

tiquitez romains . . . , 1st ed. Amsterdam, 1706.

LA CHAUSSE, MICHEL ANGE DE, *Le Pitture antiche delle grotte di Roma . . . ,* Rome, 1706. (*)

MAUNDRELL, HENRY (1650–1710), *Voyage d'Alep . . . traduit de l'anglais . . . ,* Paris, 1706. (1st ed. in English, 1699.)

POTTER, JOHN (1674?–1747), *Archaeologiae Graecae: or the Antiquities of Greece . . . ,* 2d ed. 2 vols. in 8°. London, 1708. (1st ed. 1697.)

1707

FANELLI, FRANCESCO (18th c.), *Atena Attica, descritta da'suoi principi sino all'acquisto fatti dall'armi Venetie nel 1687 . . . ,* 1st ed. Venice, 1707.

FRÉART, ROLAND, SIEUR DE CHAMBRAY (c. 1606–76), *A Parallel of the Ancient Architecture with the Modern . . . ,* London, 1707. (1st ed., in French, 1650; in English, 1664.)

LA CHAUSSE, MICHEL ANGE DE (fl. 1700), *Parisini Romanum Museum . . . ,* Rome, 1707. (*)

MAUNDRELL, HENRY (1650–1710), *A Journey from Aleppo to Jerusalem . . . ,* 2d ed. Oxford, 1707. (1st ed. 1699.)

POSTERLA, FRANCESCO, *Roma sacra e moderna, abellita di nuove figure di rame . . . ,* Rome, 1707.

POZZO, ANDREA (1642–1709), *Rules and Examples of Perspective Proper for Painters and Architects . . . In English and Latin . . . Done into English from the Original Printed at Rome 1693 in Lat. and Ital. By Mr. John James of Greenwich . . . ,* London, 1707.

ROSSI, DOMENICO DE (1678?–1742?), *Gemme antiche figurate . . . ,* 2 vols. Rome, 1707–09. (†)

[ROSSI, FILIPPO DE (fl. 1645)], *Descrizione di Roma antica . . . ,* Rome, 1707. (1st. ed. 1697?)

1708

DE FER, NICOLAS (1646–1720), *Les Beautés de la France,* Paris, 1708. (*)

FONTANA, CARLO (1634–1714), *Discorso . . . sopra l'antico Monte Citatorio . . . con disegno tanto degl'antichi, quanto de' moderni edifici . . . ,* Rome, 1708. (1st ed. 1694.)

FONTANINI, GIUSTO (1666–1736), *De antiquitatibus Hortae, Coloniae Etruscorum* . . . , 1st ed. Rome, 1708.

MURATORI, LODOVICO ANTONIO [pseud., LAMINDO PRITANIO], *Riflessioni sopra il buon gusto intorno le scienze e l'arte* . . . , 1st ed. Venice, 1708.

OVERBEKE, BONAVENTURA VAN (1660–1706), *Reliquiae antiquae urbis Romae* . . . , 1st ed. Amsterdam, 1708.

PALLADIO, ANDREA (1508–80), *The First Book of Architecture by A. Palladio . . . corrected and enlarged, with the new model of the Cathedral of St. Paul's in London* . . . , 7th ed. London, 1708. (2d ed. 1668.)

PERRAULT, CLAUDE (1613–88), *A Treatise of the Five Orders of Columns in Architecture* . . . , London, 1708. (1st ed., in French, 1683.)

POZZO, ANDREA (1642–1709), *Perspectivae pictorum atque architectorum* . . . , Augsburg, 1708–11.

SCAMOZZI, VINCENZO (1552–1616), *The Mirror of Architecture* . . . , London, 1708. (1st English ed. 1669.)

VIGNOLA, GIACOMO BAROZZI DA (1507–73), *Vignola's Five Orders* were translated into Russian and published twice in 1708 at the command of Peter the Great.

1709

FICORINI, FRANCESCO (1664–1747), *Osservazioni . . . sopra l'antichità di Roma descritte nel Diario Italico . . . dal Montfaucon* . . . , 1st ed. Rome, 1709.

KIP, JOHANNES (1652/53–1722), and LEONARD KNIFF (1650–1721), *Britannia illustrata* . . . , London, 1709. (*)

OVERBEKE, BONAVENTURA VAN (1660–1706), *Les Restes de Rome ancienne* . . . , Amsterdam, 1709. (1st ed., in Latin, 1708.)

PALLADIO, ANDREA (1508–80), *L'Antichità di Roma di M. Andrea Palladio . . . Aggiuntovi un discorso sopra li fuochi de gli antichi* . . . , Oxford, 1709.

SARNELLI, POMPEO (1649–1724), *La Guida de forestieri curiosi di vedere, edi riconoscere le cose più memorabili di Pozzuoli, Baja, Cuma* . . . , Naples, 1709. (Italian and French.)

SHAFTESBURY, THE 3RD EARL OF (COOPER, ANTHONY ASHLEY) (1671–1713), *The Moralists* . . . , 1st ed. London, 1709.

1710

AVILER, AUGUSTIN CHARLES D' (1653–1700), *Cours d'architecture* . . . , Paris, 1710. (1st ed. 1691.)

FONTANA, CARLO (1634–1714), *Antio, e sue antichità* . . . , Rome, 1710. (*)

LONGINUS, DIONYSIUS (d. 273), *Dionysii Longini . . . De Sublimatate libellus* . . . , Oxford, 1710, 1718, 1730, 1733.

PERINGSKIÖLD, JOHANN (1654–1720), *Monumentorum Sveo-gothicorum* . . . , 1st ed. Stockholm, 1710–19.

VIGNOLA, GIACOMO BAROZZI DA (1507–73), *Regel der fünff Orden* . . . , Augsburg, 1710.

VIGNOLA, GIACOMO BAROZZI DA, *Regola delli cinque ordini* . . . , Venice, 1710.

1711

AUDIBERTO, CAMILLO MARIA (1643–1717), *Regiae villae agri Taurinensis* . . . , 1st ed. Turin, 1711.

DECKER, PAUL (1677–1713), *Fürstlicher Baumeister* . . . , 1st ed. 2 vols. Augsburg, 1711–16.

GALLI DA BIBIENA, FERDINANDO (1657–1743), *L'Architettura civile* . . . , 1st ed. Parma, 1711.

PALLADIO, ANDREA (1508–80), *L'Architettura di nuovo ristampata. Con L'Aggiunta del quinto libro che tratta delle antichità di Roma dell' autore medesimo non piu veduto,* Venice, 1711.

PALLADIO, ANDREA, *I Quattro Libri dell' architettura* . . . , Venice, 1711. (1st ed. 1570.)

POZZO, ANDREA (1642–1709), *Perspectivae pictorum atque architectorum, II pars . . . Der Mahler and Baumeister Perspectiv.* Theil 2, Augsburg, 1711.

SHAFTESBURY, THE 3RD EARL OF (COOPER, ANTHONY ASHLEY) (1671–1713), *The Moralists* . . . , London, 1711. (1st ed. 1709.)

VITRUVIUS POLLIO, MARCUS, *Compendio dell' architettura generale di vitruvio opera di Mr. Perrault* . . . , Venice, 1711.

1712

LONGINUS, DIONYSIUS (d. 273), *A Treatise of the Sublime* . . . , London, 1712, 1724, 1740, 1743, 1751, 1756, 1770.

MONTFAUCON, BERNARD DE (1655–1741), *The Travels of Father Montfaucon through Italy . . . made English . . . with cuts . . .*, London, 1712. (1st ed., in Latin, 1702.)

TOSCA, TOMAS VICENTE (1651–1723), "Arquitectura civil," *Compendio matemática,* Book 5, 1st ed. Valencia, 1712.

VIGNOLA, GIACOMO BAROZZI DA (1507–73), *Règles des cinq ordres d'architecture . . .*, Leyden, 1712.

1713

DESEINE, FRANÇOIS JACQUES (d. 1715), *L'Ancienne Rome avec toutes ses magnificences . . .*, 4 vols. Leyden, 1713. (Part of a work first published in 1690.)

DESEINE, FRANÇOIS JACQUES, *Rome moderne, première de l'Europe . . .*, 6 vols. Leyden, 1713. (Part of a work first published in 1690.)

FUERSTENBERG, FERDINAND VON (1626–83), *Monumenta Paderbonensia . . .*, Frankfort and Leipzig, 1713. (1st ed. 1669.)

PITISCUS, SAMUEL (1636–1727), *Lexicon antiquitatum Romanarum . . .*, 1st ed. 2 vols. Leovardiae (Leuwarde), 1713.

POPE, ALEXANDER [anonymously] (1688–1744), "Essay on Gardens," *The Guardian,* London, 1713. (*)

ROSSI, DOMENICO DE (1678?–1742?), *Una Raccolta di vasi diversi formata da illustri artefici antichi . . .*, Rome, 1713 (†)

SCAMOZZI, VINCENZO (1552–1616), *Oeuvres d'architecture de Vincent Scamozzi . . .*, traduites en français par M. Augustin Charles d'Aviler . . .*, Leyden, 1713.

1714

BRUYN, CORNELIS DE (1652–1726/27), *Cornelis de Bruins Reizen over Moskovie, door Persie en Indie . . .*, Amsterdam, 1714. (1st ed. 1711.)

BRUYN, CORNELIS DE, *Voyage au Levant . . .*, Paris, 1714. (1st ed. 1698.)

CORDEMOY, J. L. DE, *Nouveau Traité de toute l'architecture . . .*, Paris, 1714. (1st ed. 1706.)

FUERSTENBERG, FERDINAND VON (1626–83), *Monumenta Paderbonensia . . .*, Lemgoviae, 1714. (1st ed. 1669.)

LE CLERC, SEBASTIEN (1637–1714), *Traité d'architecture . . .*, 1st ed. Paris, 1714.

MAUNDRELL, HENRY (1650–1710), *A Journey from Aleppo to Jerusalem . . .*, 3d ed. Oxford, 1714. (1st ed. 1699.)

SCAMOZZI, VINCENZO (1552–1616), *L'Idea della architettura universale di Vincenzo Scamozzi . . .*, Venice, 1714.

1715

CAMPBELL, COLIN (fl. 1715–29), *Vitruvius Britannicus . . .*, 1st ed. 5 vols. London, 1715–71.

CRESCIMBENI, GIOVANNI MARIO (1663–1729), *L'Istoria della basilica . . . di S. Maria in Cosmedin in Roma . . .*, Rome, 1715. (†)

CROUSAZ, JEAN PIERRE DE (1663–1750), *Traité du beau . . .*, 1st ed. Amsterdam, 1715.

LEONI, GIACOMO (1686–1746), *The Architecture of A. Palladio . . .*, 2 vols. London, 1715. (English, Italian, and French text.)

MURATORI, LODOVICO ANTONIO [pseud., LAMINDO PRITANIO], *Delle Riflessioni sopra il buon gusto nelle scienze e nelle arti, . . .*, 1st ed. Colonia, 1715.

PALOMINO DE CASTRO Y VELASCO, ANTONIO (1653–1726), *Museo pictorio y la escala optica,* 2 vols. Madrid, 1715–24.

POST, PIETER (1608–69), *Les Ouvrages d'architecture . . .*, Leyden, 1715. (†)

ROSSINI, PIETRO, *Il Mercurio errante . . .*, Rome, 1715. (*)

SWITZER, STEPHEN (1682?–1745), *The Nobleman, Gentleman, and Gardener's Recreation . . .*, 1st ed. London, 1715.

VIGNOLA, GIACOMO BAROZZI DA (1507–73), *Règle des cinq ordres d'architecture. Abrégée de son grand ouvrage & rev., & augm. . . .*, Amsterdam, 1715.

VIGNOLA, GIACOMO BAROZZI DA, *Reigle des cinq ordres d'architecture . . .*, Paris, c. 1715.

VINCKEBOONS, PHILIPPE (c. 1607–78), *Oeuvres d'architecture contenant les desseins des principaux batimens . . . de la ville d'Amsterdam,* 2 vols. Leyden, 1715. (1st ed., in Dutch, Part I, 1648; Part II, 1674.)

1716

CRESCIMBENI, GIOVANNI MARIO (1663–1729), *Istoria della chiesa di S. Giovanni avanti la Porta Latina . . .*, 1st ed. Rome, 1716.

HEYDENREICH, FRIDERICUS WILHELMUS, *Architectonicam Exercitationem de dispositione fenestrarum et januarum . . .*, Jena [1716]. (*)

MURATORI, LODOVICO ANTONIO [pseud., LA-MINDO PRITANIO], *Delle Riflessioni sopra il buon gusto nelle scienze e nelle arti* . . . , Venice, 1716. (1st ed. 1715.)

1717

BONANNI, GIACOMO, *Delle Antiche Siracuse,* 2 vols. Palermo, 1717. (1st ed. of vol. I, 1624.)

CAPRA, ALLESSANDRO, *La Nuova Architettura famigliare . . . la nuova architettura militare* . . . , 2 vols. Cremona, 1717. (1st ed. of *Architettura famigliare* . . . , 1678.)

MIRABELLA E ALAGONA, VICENZO (1570–1624), *Dichiarazioni della pianta dell'antiche Siracuse* . . . , Palermo, 1717. (1st ed. 1613.)

MURATORI, LODOVICO ANTONIO [pseud., LA-MINDO PRITANIO], *Delle riflessioni sopra il buon gusto nelle scienze e nelle arti* . . . , Venice, 1717. (1st ed. 1715.)

POZZO, ANDREA (1642–1709), *Prospettiva de' pittori, et architetti* . . . , Rome, 1700, 1717. vol. 2 Rome, 1700.

VIGNOLA, GIACOMO BAROZZI DA (1507–73), *Regel der Fünff Orden* . . . , Augsburg, 1717.

1718

BRANCA, GIOVANNI (1571–1645), *Manuale d'architettura con figure delineate da Filippo Vasconi,* Rome, 1718. (1st ed. 1629.)

BRUYN, CORNELIS DE (1652–1726/27), *Voyages . . . par la Moscovie, en Perse, et aux Indes Orientales* . . . , 2 vols. Amsterdam, 1718. (1st ed. 1711.)

MADRISIO, NICCOLÒ, *Viaggi per l'Italia, Francia e Germania descritti in versi* . . . , 2 vols. Venice, 1718. (*)

POZZO, BARTOLOMEO FR., dal, *Le Vite de' pittori, de gli scultori, et architetti Veronesi* . . . , Verona, 1718.

SWITZER, STEPHEN (1682?–1745), *Ichnographia rustica or the Nobleman, Gentleman and Gardener's Recreation* . . . , London, 1718.

1719

CRESCIMBENI, GIOVANNI MARIO (1663–1729), *Stato della basilica . . . di S. Maria in Cosmedin di Roma* . . . , Rome, 1719. (1st ed. probably 1715.)

LONGINUS, DIONYSIUS (d. 273), *Verhandeling over de Verheventheit en Deftigheit des styles* . . . , Amsterdam, 1719.

MONTFAUCON, BERNARD DE (1655–1741), *L'Antiquité expliquée . . . et représentée en figures* . . . , 1st ed. 10 vols. Paris, 1719.

MUSGRAVE, WILLIAM (1655?–1721), *Antiquitates Britanno-Belgicae praecipue Romanae* . . . , 1st ed. Exeter, 1719.

ORLANDI, PELLEGRINO ANTONIO (1660–1727), *Abecedario pittorico* . . . , Bologna, 1719.

PITISCUS, SAMUEL (1636–1727), *Lexicon antiquitatum Romanarum* . . . , 3 vols. Venice, 1719. (1st ed. 1713.)

POZZO, ANDREA (1642–1709), *Perspectivar pictorum atque architectorum 1ª pars . . . Der Mahler und Baumeister Perspectiv,* Theil 1, Augsburg, 1719.

ROSSI, FILIPPO DE (fl. 1645), *Descrizione di Roma antica* . . . , Rome, 1719. (1st ed. 1697?)

1720

FÄLSCH, JOHANN RUDOLPH (d. 1787), *Des Jacobi Barozzi von Vignola Grund Regeln über Die Fünff Säulen.* . . . , Nuremberg, [c. 1720].

1721

BUCHOTTE, *Les Règles du dessein* . . . , Paris, 1721. (*)

ERLACH, JOHANN BERNHARD FISCHER VON (1656–1723), *Entwurff Einer Historischen Architectur* . . . , 1st ed. Vienna, 1721.

MAUNDRELL, HENRY (1650–1710), *A Journey from Aleppo to Jerusalem,* . . . , 4th ed. Oxford, 1721. (1st ed. 1699.)

MONTFAUCON, BERNARD DE (1655–1741), *Antiquity Explained, and Represented in Sculptures . . . Translated into English by D. Humphreys* . . . , 5 vols. London, 1721–25. (1st ed., in French, 1719.)

MURATORI, LODOVICO ANTONIO [pseud., LA-MINDO PRITANIO], *Riflessioni sopra il buon gusto nelle scienze e nelle arti* . . . , Colonia, 1721.

PALLADIO, ANDREA (1508–80), *The Architecture of A. Palladio . . . , by Giacomo Leoni* . . . , 2d ed. 2 vols. London, 1721. (1st English ed. 1715.)

SCAMOZZI, VICENZO (1552–1616), *The Mirror of Architecture* . . . , 6th ed. London, 1721.

1722

BUCHOTTE, *Les Règles du dessein* . . . , Paris, 1722. (*)

CRESCIMBENI, GIOVANNI MARIO (1663–1729), *L'Istoria della basilica di S. Anastasi titolo Cardinalizio* . . . , 1st ed. Rome, 1722.

FRONTINUS, SEXTUS JULIUS (40–103), *De Aquaeductibus urbis Romae* . . . , Padua, 1722. (1st published in 15th c.)

MONTFAUCON, BERNARD DE (1655–1741), *L'Antiquité expliquée* . . . , 10 vols. Paris, 1722. (1st ed. 1719.)

PERRAULT, CLAUDE (1613–88), *A Treatise of the Five Orders of Columns in Architecture* . . . , London, 1722. (1st English ed. 1708.)

POTTER, JOHN (1674?–1747), *Archaeologia Graeca* . . . , 4th ed. London, 1722.

RICHARDSON, JONATHAN, *An Account of the Statues and Bas-reliefs, Drawings and Pictures in Italy, France, etc.* . . . , 1st ed. London, 1722.

1723

CRESCIMBENI, GIOVANNI MARIO (1663–1729), *Ristretto delle cose più notabili della . . . chiesa papale Lateranese* . . . , [Rome], 1723. (*)

FONTANINI, GIUSTO (1666–1736), *De Antiquitatibus Hortae, Coloniae Etruscorum* . . . , Rome, 1723. (1st ed. 1708.)

FRÉART, ROLAND, SIEUR DE CHAMBRAY (c. 1606–76), *A Parallel of the Antient Architecture with the Modern . . . Made English* . . . , 3d ed. London, 1723.

LE CLERC, SEBASTIEN (1637–1714), *A Treatise of Architecture* . . . , 2 vols. London, 1723–24.

LIGORIO, PIRRO (1530–80), *Descriptio . . . villae tiburtinae hadrianiae* . . . , Leyden, [1723].

MIRABELLA E ALAGONA, VICENZO (1570–1624), *Ichnographicae Syracusarum antiquarum explicatio* . . . , Leyden, 1723. (1st ed. 1613.)

MURATORI, LODOVICO ANTONIO [pseud., LAMINDO PRITANIO], *Delle Riflessioni sopra il buon gusto nelle scienze e nelle arti* . . . , Venice, 1723.

NICASTRO, GIOVANNI DI, *Descrizione del celebre arco eretto in Benevento* . . . , Benevento, 1723.

POZZO, ANDREA (1642–1709), *Perspectiva pictorum et architectorum* . . . , Rome, 1723.

SARNELLI, POMPEO (1649–1724), *Antiquitates Puteolorum, cum balneorum Agnani* . . . , Lugduni Batavorum, 1723.

SUARESIUS, JOSEPHUS MARIA (1599–1677), *. . . Praenestes antiquae libri duo* . . . , Lugduni Batavorum, 1723. (1st ed. 1655.)

1724

BALDI, BERNADINO (1553–1617), *Memorie concernenti la città d'Urbino . . . descrizione del Palazzo Ducale* . . . , Rome, 1724. (†)

CROUSAZ, JEAN PIERRE DE (1663–1750), *Traité du beau* . . . , 2 vols. Amsterdam, 1724. (1st ed. 1715.)

DE FER, NICOLAS (1646–1720), *Les Beautés de la France* . . . , Paris, 1724. (*)

KLEINER, SALOMON (1703–61), *Vera et Accurata Delineato omnium templorum et coenobiorum* . . . , 1st ed. 2 vols. Augsburg, 1724–37.

LE CLERC, SEBASTIEN (1637–1714), *A Treatise of Architecture* . . . , [London, 1724?].

LONGINUS, DIONYSIUS (d. 273), *De Sublimitate libellus* . . . , London, 1724.

MONTFAUCON, BERNARD DE (1655–1741), *L'Antiquité expliquée* . . . , 5 vols. Paris, 1724. (1st ed. 1719.)

PALLADIO, ANDREA (1508–80), *Le Antichità di Roma con le sue figure* . . . , Rome, 1724. (1st ed. 1554.)

SWITZER, STEPHEN (1682?–1745), *Ichnographia rustica* . . . , London, 1724. (1st ed. 1715.)

TARUFFI, GIOVANNI ANDREA (1667–1744), *Breve Discorso intorno l'architettura*, Bologna, 1724.

1725

BRUYN, CORNELIS DE (1652–1726/27), *Voyage au Levant . . . Voyages par la Moscovie* . . . , 5 vols. Paris, 1725. (1st composite ed. of works of 1698 and 1711.)

COURTONNE, JEAN (1671–1739), *Traité de la perspective pratique, avec des remarques sur l'architecture* . . . , 1st ed. Paris, 1725.

ERLACH, JOHANN BERNHARD FISCHER VON (1656–1723), *Entwurff einer Historischen Architektur* . . . , Leipzig, 1725. (1st ed. 1721.)

FONTANA, CARLO (1634–1714), *L'Anfitea-tro Flavio descritto, e delineato . . .* , 1st ed. The Hague, 1725.

FRANZINI, GIROLOMO (16th c.), *Les Merveilles de la ville de Rome . . .* , Rome, 1725. (1st ed. 16th c.)

GALLI DA BIBIENA, FERDINANDO (1657–1743), *Direzioni a giovani studenti nel disegno dell'architettura civile . . .* , 1st ed. Bologna, 1725.

GRAEVIUS, JOHANNES GEORGIUS (1622–1703), ed., *Thesaurus antiquitatum et historiarum Italiae, Neapolis, Siciliae . . .* , 45 vols. Leyden, 1725.

HUTCHESON, FRANCIS (1694–1747), *Inquiry . . . into our Ideas of Beauty and Virtue . . .* , 1st ed. London, 1725.

MONTFAUCON, BERNARD DE (1655–1741), *The Antiquities of Italy . . . revised . . . by J. Henley . . .* , 2d ed. London, 1725. (1st English ed. 1712.)

MURATORI, LODOVICO ANTONIO [pseud., LAMINDO PRITANIO], *Delle Riflessioni sopra il buon gusto nelle scienze e nelle arti . . .* , Venice, 1725.

ROSSINI, PIETRO, *Il Mercurio errante . . .* , Rome, 1725. (*)

VICO, GIOVANNI BATTISTA, *Principi di una scienza nuova . . .* , 1st ed. Naples, 1725.

VIGNOLA, GIACOMO BAROZZI DA (1507–73), *Regel der Fünff Orden . . .* , Augsburg, 1725.

1726

AMICO, GIOVANNI, *L'Architetto pratico . . .* , 1st ed. Palermo, 1726–50.

BREVAL, JOHN DURANT (1680?–1738), *Remarks on Several Parts of Europe: relating chiefly to the History, Antiquities and Geography . . .* , 1st ed. 2 vols. London, 1726.

HUTCHESON, FRANCIS, *Inquiry into . . . Our Ideas of Beauty and Virtue . . .* , London, 1726. (1st ed. 1725.)

LEONI, GIACOMO (1686–1746), *The Architecture of Leon Battista Alberti in Ten Books. Of Painting in Three Books and of Statuary in One Book,* 1st English ed. 4 vols. London, 1726.

LEONI, GIACOMO, *Architecture de Palladio, divisée en quatre livres . . . , avec des notes d' Inigo Jones . . .* , 2 vols. The Hague, 1726.

N., M. A. V., *Antiquitates sacrae et civiles Romanorum explicatae . . .* , The Hague, 1726.

1727

BARTOLI, PIETRO SANTI (1635–1700), *Gli antichi sepolcri . . .* , Rome, 1727. (1st ed. 1697.)

BIANCHINI, FRANCESCO (1662–1729), *Camera ed iscrizioni sepolcrali de' liberti, servi, ed ufficiali della casa de Augusto scoperte nella via Appia . . .* , 1st ed. Rome, 1727.

GORI, ANTONIO FRANCESCO (1691–1757), *Monumentum, sive columbarium libertorum, et servorum Liviae Augustae et Caesarum . . .* , 1st ed. Florence, 1727.

LANGLEY, BATTY (1696–1751), *The Builder's Chest Book . . .* , 1st ed. London, 1727.

KENT, WILLIAM (1684–1748), *The Designs of Inigo Jones . . .* , 1st ed. [London], 1727.

MARIETTE, JEAN (1654?–1742), *L'Architecture françoise . . .* , 1st ed. 2 vols. Paris, 1727.

TOSCA, THOMAS VICENTE (1651–1723), "Arquitectura Civil," *Compendio Mathematico,* Book 5, Valencia, 1727. (1st ed. 1712.)

VITRUVIUS POLLIO, MARCUS, *De Architectura libri decem,* Amsterdam, 1727.

1728

BARTOLI, PIETRO SANTI (1635–1700), *Veterum Sepolcra . . . mausolea Romanorum et Etruscorum . . . cum explicationibus J. P. Bellorii . . .* , Leyden, 1728. (1st ed. 1697.)

BERGIER, NICOLAS (1567–1623), *Histoire des grands chemins de l'Empire Romain . . .* , 2 vols. Brussels, 1728. (1st ed. 1622.)

BRISEUX, CHARLES ÉTIENNE (c. 1660–1754), *L'Architecture moderne . . .* , 1st ed. 2 vols. Paris, 1728.

CALOGIERÀ, ANGELO (1699–1768), ed., *Raccolta d'opuscoli . . .* , 1st ed. Venice, 1728–57.

CASTELL, ROBERT (d. 1729), *The Villas of the Ancients Illustrated . . .* , 1st ed. London, 1728.

COURTONNE, JEAN (1671–1739), *Architecture moderne . . .* , 1st ed. Paris, 1728.

GIBBS, JAMES (1682–1754), *A Book of Architecture . . .* , 1st ed. London, 1728.

GORI, ANTONIO FRANCESCO (1691–1757), *Descrizione della capella di S. Antonino . . . nella chiesa di San Marco di Firenze . . .* , 1st ed. Florence, 1728.

HALFPENNY, WILLIAM (fl. 1722–55), *Magnum in parvo: or the Marrow of Architecture* . . . , London, 1728.

LANGLEY, BATTY (1696–1751), *New Principles of Gardening* . . . , 1st ed. London, 1728.

MAFFEI, FRANCESCO SCIPIONE (1675–1755), *Deglie Anfiteatri, e singolarmente del Veronese* . . . , 1st ed. Verona, 1728.

MORRIS, ROBERT (fl. 1750s), *An Essay in Defence of Ancient Architecture* . . . , 1st ed. London, 1728.

POTTER, JOHN (1674?–1747), *Archaeologia Graeca* . . . , 5th ed. London, 1728.

SALVIATI, ALAMANNO (1663–1733), *Descrizione della Cappella di S. Antonino Arcivescovo di Firenze* . . . , Florence, 1728.

1729

CAMPBELL, COLIN (fl. 1715–29), *Andrea Palladio's Five Orders of Architecture* . . . , London, 1729.

FRANZINI, GIROLOMO (16th c.) *Las Cosas maravillosas de* . . . *Roma* . . . , Rome, 1729. (1st Spanish ed. 1589.)

MANCINI, NICCOLÒ, *Orazioni, e discorsi istorici sopra l'antica città di Fiesole* . . . , 1st ed. Florence, 1729.

NATIVELLE, PIERRE, *Nouveau Traité d'architecture contenant les cinq ordres* . . . , 1st ed. 2 vols. Paris, 1729.

VIGNOLA, GIACOMO BAROZZI DA (1507–73), *Vignola: or, the Compleat Architect,* [London], 1729.

VITRUVIUS POLLIO, MARCUS, *The Theory and Practice of Architecture; or Vitruvius* . . . *abridged* . . . *by* . . . *Mr. Perrault,* [London], 1729.

1730

BURLINGTON, 3RD EARL OF (BOYLE, RICHARD) (1694–1753), *Fabbriche' antiche' disegnate' da Andrea Palladio* . . . , London, 1730.

FICORINI, FRANCESCO, *Le Memorie più singolari di Roma e sue vicinanze* . . . , 1st ed. Rome, 1730.

ERLACH, JOHANN BERNHARD FISCHER VON (1656–1723), *Entwurff einer Historischen Architektur* . . . , London, 1730.

MAFFEI, FRANCESCO SCIPIONE (1675–1755), *A Compleat History of the Ancient Amphitheatres* . . . , London, 1730. (1st ed., in Italian, 1728.)

ORLANDI, PELLEGRINO ANTONIO (1660–1727), *Repertorium sculptile-typicum* . . . *Translated from the Abecedario pittorico of P. A. Orlandi* . . . , London, 1730.

PASCOLI, LIONE (1674–1744), *Vite de pittori, scultori, ed architetti moderni* . . . , 2 vols. Rome, 1730–36.

VITRUVIUS POLLIO, MARCUS, *M. Vitruvii Pollionis de architectura libri decem* . . . *The Architecture of M. Vitruvius Pollio translated into English with the Commentaries of Inigo Jones and others, and the Latin text, by Robert Castell,* 2 vols. London, 1730.

WRIGHT, EDWARD, *Some Observations Made in Travelling through France and Italy in the Years 1720, 1721 and 1722* . . . , 1st ed. London, 1730.

1731

GALLI DA BIBIENA, FERDINANDO (1657–1743), *Direzioni ai giovini studenti del disegno dell' architettura civile* . . . , 2 vols. Bologna, 1731–32. (1st ed. 1725.)

GHEZZI, PIETRO LEONE (1674–1755), *Camere sepolcrali de'liberti, e liberte di Livia Augusta ed i altri Cesari* . . . , 1st ed. Rome, 1731.

MAFFEI, FRANCESCO SCIPIONE (1675–1755), *Verona illustrata* . . . , 1st ed. 4 vols. Verona, 1731–32.

ORLANDI, PELLEGRINO ANTONIO (1660–1727), *L'Abecedario pittorico* . . . , Florence, 1731.

PAUSANIAS (2d half of 2d c. B.C.), *Pausanias ou voyage historique de la Grèce* . . . , 2 vols. Paris, 1731.

TARUFFI, GIOVANNI ANDREA (1667–1744), *Breve Compendio di diverse misure delle strade* . . . *e piazze, descrizione delle chiese, e palazzi di Bologna,* 1st ed. Bologna, 1731.

1732

GIBBS, JAMES (1682–1754), *Rules for Drawing the Several Parts of Architecture* . . . , 1st ed. London, 1732.

GRAEVIUS, JOHANNES GEORGIUS (1622–1703), *Thesaurus antiquitatum Graecarum et Romanarum* . . . , Venice, 1732–37. (1st ed. 1694–99.)

LE CLERC, SEBASTIEN (1637–1714), *A Treatise of Architecture, with Remarks and Observations* . . . , London, 1732. (1st ed., in French, 1714.)

MAUNDRELL, HENRY (1650–1710), *A Journey from Aleppo to Jerusalem* . . . , 5th ed. Oxford, 1732. (1st ed. 1699.)

PASCOLI, LIONE (1674–1744), *Vite de' pittori, scultori, ed architetti Perugini . . .* , Rome, 1732.

VIGNOLA, GIACOMO BAROZZI DA (1507–73), *Architettura di Giacomo Barozzio da Vignola cioè regola delli cinque ordini di dett'architettura,* Rome, 1732.

1733

BAGLIONE, GIOVANNI (1571–1644), *Le Vite de' pittori, scultori, architetti, ed intagliatori . . .* , Naples, 1733. (1st ed. 1642.)

BROEBES, JEAN BAPTISTE (1660?–1720?), *Vues des palais et maisons de plaisance de Sa Majesté le Roy de Prusse . . .* , Augsburg, 1733. (*)

COLONIA, DOMINIQUE DE (1660–1741), *Antiquités de la Ville de Lyon . . .* , Lyon, 1733. (1st ed. 1701.)

FRÉART, ROLAND, SIEUR DE CHAMBRAY (c. 1606–76), *A Parallel of the Ancient Architecture with the Modern . . . Made English . . .* , 4th ed. London, 1733.

MAFFEI, FRANCESCO SCIPIONE (1675–1755), *Galliae Antiquitates quaedam selectae . . .* , 1st ed. Paris, 1733.

MONTENARI, GIOVANNI, *Del Teatro Olimpico di Andrea Palladio in Vicenza . . .* , Padua, 1733.

MURATORI, LODOVICO ANTONIO [pseud., LAMINDO PRITANIO], *Delle Riflessioni sopra il buon gusto nelle scienze e nelle arti . . .* , Venice, 1733.

ORLANDI, PELLEGRINO ANTONIO (1660–1727), *Abecedario Pittorico . . .* , Naples, 1733.

PALLADIO, ANDREA (1508–80), *The First Book of Architecture . . .* , 1733.

PAUSANIAS (2d half of 2d c. B.C.), *Pausanias ou voyage historique de la Grèce . . .* , Amsterdam, 1733.

POTTER, JOHN (1674?–1747), *Archaeologia graeca . . .* , Venice, 1733.

SGRILLI, BERNARDO SANSONE (fl. 1733–55), *Descrizione e studj dell'insigne fabbrica di S. M. del Fiore, metropolitana fiorentina . . .* , 1st ed. Florence, 1733.

VIGNOLA, GIACOMO BAROZZI DA (1507–73), *Règles des cinq ordres d'architecture . . .* , Paris, [c. 1733–45].

1734

AQUINO, CARLO D' (1654–1737), *Vocabularium architecturae aedificatoriae . . .* , 1st ed. Rome, 1734.

GRANARA, GIOVANNI STEFANO (1697–1735), *Dell'Antichità, ed origine, di Roma . . .* , 1st ed. Venice, 1734.

MAFFEI, FRANCESCO SCIPIONE (1675–1755), *Galliae Antiquitates quaedam selectae . . .* , Verona, 1734. (1st ed. 1733.)

MORRIS, ROBERT (fl. 1750s), *Lectures on Architecture . . .* , 1st ed. London, 1734.

NOLLI, CARLO (d. 1770), *The Triumphal Arch of Trajan at Ancona . . .* , Naples, 1734.

POTTER, JOHN (1674?–1747), *Archaeologia graeca . . .* , Latin ed. Venice, 1734.

PREISLER, JOHANNES JUSTIN (1698–1771), *Ornamenti d'Architettura. Architectonische Verzierungen aus verschiedenen fürnehmen Gebäuden in und ausser Rom . . .* , 1st ed. Nuremberg, 1734.

SCAMOZZI, VINCENZO (1552–1616), *The Mirror of Architecture . . .* , 7th ed. London, 1734. (1st English ed. 1669.)

SALMON, WILLIAM, *Palladio Londonensis . . .* , 1st ed. London, 1734.

1735

GRAZIOLI, PIETRO (1700–53), *De Praeclaris Mediolani aedificiis . . .* , Milan, 1735. (†)

KENT, WILLIAM (1684–1748), *The Designs of Inigo Jones . . .* , London, 1735. (1st ed. 1727.)

MAFFEI, FRANCESCO SCIPIONE (1675–1755), *A Compleat History of the Ancient Amphitheatres . . .* , 2d ed. London, [1735]. (1st English ed. 1730.)

MONTENARI, GIOVANNI, and GIOVANNI POLENI (1683–1761), *Degli Antichi Teatri, e anfiteatri . . .* , Vicenza, 1735.

OLIVIERI DEGLI ABATI, ANNIBALE (1708–89), *Spiegazione di alcuni monumenti degli antichi Pelasgi . . .* , Pesaro, 1735.

SANMICHELI, MICHELE (1485–1559), *Cinque Ordini dell' architettura civile . . .* , 1st ed. Verona, 1735.

VIGNOLA, GIACOMO BAROZZI DA (1507–73), *Regel der Fünff Orden . . .* , Augsburg, 1735.

WARE, ISAAC (d. 1766), *Designs of Inigo Jones and Others . . .* , 1st ed. [London, c. 1735].

1736

AVILER, AUGUSTIN CHARLES D' (1653–1700), *Oeuvres d'architecture de Vincent Scamozzi . . .* , The Hague, 1736. (1st ed. 1685.)

BERGIER, NICOLAS (1567–1623), *Histoire des grands chemins de l'Empire Romain,* 2 vols. Brussels, 1736. (1st ed. 1622.)

GADDI, GIOVANNI BATTISTA, *Roma nobilitata nelle sue fabbriche dall santità di N.S. Clemente XII,* 1st ed. Rome, 1736.

HOPPUS, EDWARD (d. 1739), *Andrea Palladio's Architecture . . .* , London, 1736.

MURATORI, LODOVICO ANTONIO [pseud., LAMINDO PRITANIO], *Delle Riflessioni sopra il buon gusto nelle scienze e nelle arti . . .* , Venice, 1736.

PALLADIO, ANDREA (1508–80), *Andrea Palladio's Architecture . . .* , London, 1736.

SAN NICOLÁS, FR. LORENZO DE (1595–1679), *Arte y uso de arquitectura,* 2 vols. Madrid, 1736. (1st ed. 1633.)

SCAMOZZI, VINCENZO (1552–1616), *Oeuvres d'architecture de Vincent Scamozzi . . . traduites en françois par Mr. Augustin Charles D'Aviler . . . On y a joint aussi plusieurs nouveaux desseins des plus beaux edifices de Rome . . .* , The Hague, 1736.

VENUTI, RIDOLFINO (1705–63), *Collectanea antiquitatum Romanarum quas 100 tabulis incisas eta Rid. Venuti notis illustratas exhibet Ant. Borioni,* Rome, 1736.

VIGNOLA, GIACOMO BAROZZI DA (1507–73), *Regles des cinq ordres d'architecture de J. B. de Vignole, avec les augmentations de Michel Ange Buonaroti . . .* , Utrecht, 1736.

VIGNOLA, GIACOMO BAROZZI DA, *Regola delli cinque ordini d'architettura di M. Jac. Barozzio da Vignola . . .* , Bologna, [1736].

VINCKEBOONS, PHILIPPE (c. 1607–78), *Oeuvres d'architecture contenant les desseins des principaux bâtimens . . . de la ville d'Amsterdam . . .* , The Hague, 1736. (1st ed., in Dutch, 1648–74.)

1737

BLONDEL, JACQUES-FRANÇOIS (1705–74), *De la Distribution des maisons de plaisance, et de la décoration des édifices en général . . .* , 1st ed. 2 vols. Paris, 1737.

ERLACH, JOHANN BERNHARD FISCHER VON (1656–1723), *Entwurff einer Historischen Architektur . . .* , London. (1st ed. 1721.)

FRÉZIER, AMÉDÉE-FRANÇOIS (1682–1733), *Théorie . . . de la coupe des pierres,* 1st ed. 3 vols. Strasbourg and Paris, 1737–39.

GORI, ANTONIO FRANCESCO (1691–1757), *Museum Etruscum exhibens insignia veterum Etruscorum monumenta . . .* , 1st ed. 3 vols. Florence, 1737–43.

GUARINI, GUARINO (1624–83), *Architettura civile . . .* , 1st ed. Turin, 1737.

HOPPUS, EDWARD (d. 1739), *The Gentleman's and Builder's Repository . . .* , 1st ed. London, 1737.

LONGINUS, DIONYSIUS (d. 273), *Trattato del Sublime . . .* , Florence, 1737.

LONGINUS, DIONYSIUS, *Vom Erhabenen, gr. u. deutsch, nebst dessen Leben, einer Nachricht von seinen Schriften, und einer Untersuchungen, was Longin durch das Erhabene verstehe, von Carl Heinr.* Heineken, Dresden, 1737.

PITISCUS, SAMUEL (1636–1727), *Lexicon antiquitatum romanarum . . .* , The Hague, 1737.

POLENI, GIOVANNI (1683–1761), *Utriusque Thesauri antiquitatum Romanarum Graecarumque nova supplementa,* 5 vols. Venice, 1737.

POZZO, ANDREA (1642–1709), *Perspectiva pictorum et architectorum . . . pars secunda . . .* , Rome, 1737.

1738

AVILER, AUGUSTIN-CHARLES D' (1653–1700), *Cours d'architecture . . .* , new ed. Paris, 1738. (1st ed. 1691.)

BIANCHINI, FRANCESCO (1662–1729), *Del Palazzo de' Cesari . . .* , 1st ed. Verona, 1738.

BREVAL, JOHN DURANT (1680?–1738), *Remarks on several parts of Europe, relating chiefly to their antiquities . . .* , London, 1738. (1st ed. 1726.)

FRÉZIER, AMADÉE-FRANÇOIS (1682–1773), *Dissertation historique et critique sur les ordres d'architecture . . .* , 1st ed. Strasbourg, 1738.

HOPPUS, EDWARD (d. 1739), *The Gentleman's and Builder's Repository . . .* , London, 1738. (1st ed. 1737.)

LA CHAUSSE, MICHEL ANGE DE (fl. 1700), *Picturae antiquae cryptarum Romanarum . . .* , Rome, 1738. (*)

PALLADIO, ANDREA (1508–80), *The Four Books of Andrea Palladio's Architecture . . .* , 1st ed. London, 1738.

TARUFFI, GIOVANNI ANDREA (1667–1744), *Antica fondazione della città di Bologna,* Bologna, 1738. (1st ed. 1731.)

ZARAGOZA Y EBRI, AUGUSTIN BRUNO ["ATHANASIO GENARO BRIAGUZ Y BRU"], *Escuela de arquitectura civil,* 1st ed. Valencia, 1738.

1739

ALBERTI, LEON BATTISTA (1404–72), *The Architecture of Leon Battista Alberti . . . Translated . . . into English . . . by James Leoni . . .*, London, 1739.

BERTOLI, GIANDOMINICO (b. 1676), *Le Antichità de Aquileja, profane e sacre . . .*, 1st ed. Venice, 1739.

BOCCHI, OTTAVIO, *Osservazioni sopra un antico teatro scoperto in Adria,* 1st ed. Venice, 1739.

CAMPIGLIA, GIOVANNI DOMENICO (1692–1770), *Il Secondo Libro del nuovo teatro delle fabriche et edifij fatte fare in Roma dalla santità di nostro Signore Papa Clemente XII . . .*, 1st ed. Rome, 1739.

GIBBS, JAMES (1682–1754), *A Book of Architecture . . .*, London, 1739. (1st ed. 1728.)

[MORIGIA, PAOLA (1525–1604)], *Distinto Ragguaglio dell'ottava maraviglia del mondo, o sia . . . il duomo di Milano,* Milan, 1739. (1st ed. 1642.)

OVERBEKE, BONAVENTURA VAN (1660–1706), *Stampe degli avanzi dell'antica Roma . . .*, London, 1739. (*)

POLENI, GIOVANNI (1683–1761), *Exercitationes Vitruvianae primae . . .*, 1st ed. Padua, 1739 [1741].

ROSSI, FILIPPO DE (fl. 1645), *Descrizione di Roma antica . . .*, Rome, 1739. (1st ed. 1697?)

ROSSI, GIUSEPPE IGNAZIO (d. before 1739), *La Libreria Mediceo-Laurenziana [di Michelangelo Buonarroti] . . .*, 1st ed. Florence, 1739.

VENUTI, RIDOLFINO (1705–63), *Antiqua Numismata maximi modulii ex Museo Alex Cardin Albani . . .*, 2 vols. Rome, 1739–44.

VIGNOLA, GIACOMO BAROZZI DA (1507–73), *Architettura di Giacomo Barozzi da Vignola . . .*, Rome, 1739.

VIGNOLA, GIACOMO BAROZZI DA, *Aufs neue verm. mit etlichen herrlichen Gebäuen des Michaël Angelo Bonaroti, durch den Herrn Muet . . .*, Nüremberg, 1739.

1740

ALBRIZZI, G. B., *Forestiero illuminato . . .*, 1st ed. Venice, 1740.

BARDET DE VILLENEUVE, P.-P.-A., *Traité d'architecture civile à l'usage des ingénieurs,* 1st ed. The Hague, 1740.

FOSSATI, GIORGIO (1706–78), *Architettura di Andrea Palladio . . . , con la traduzione francese . . .*, 8 vols. Venice, 1740–48.

GALLI DA BIBIENA, GIUSEPPE (1696–1757), *Architetture, e prospettive . . .*, 1st ed. Augusta, 1740.

JUVENEL DE CARLENCAS, FELIX DE (1669–1760), *Essais sur l'histoire des belles-lettres, des sciences et des arts . . .*, 1st ed. 2 vols. Lyon, 1740–44.

LANGLEY, BATTY (1696–1751), *The City and Country Builder's Treasury of Designs,* 1st ed. London, 1740.

MAUNDRELL, HENRY (1650–1710), *A Journey from Aleppo to Jerusalem . . .*, 6th ed. Oxford, 1740. (1st ed. 1699.)

PALLADIO, ANDREA (1508–80), *Architettura di Andrea Palladio . . . , con la traduzione francese . . .*, 1st ed. 3 vols. Venice.

POTTER, JOHN (1674?–1747), *Archaeologia Graeca . . .*, 6th ed. London, 1740.

[ZUCCHI, FRANCESCO] (1698?–1764) *Teatro delle fabbriche più cospicue in prospettiva della città di Venezia . . .*, [Venice, 1740].

1741

ALVAREZ DE COLMENAR, JUAN, *Annales d'Espagne et de Portugal,* Amsterdam, 1741. (†)

ANDRÉ, YVES DE L'ISLE [Le Père] (1675–1764), *Essai sur le beau . . .*, 1st ed. Paris, 1741.

LANGLEY, BATTY (1696–1751), *Ancient Architecture Restored and Improved . . .*, 1st ed. London, 1741–42.

MARIESCHI, MICHELE (1696–1743), *Magnificentiores selectioresque urbis Venetiarum prospectus . . .*, 1st ed. Venice, 1741.

NORDEN, FRIDERICK LUDVIG (1708–42), *Drawings of Some Ruins and Colossal Statues at Thebes in Egypt . . .*, 1st ed. [London], 1741.

POZZO, ANDREA (1642–1709), *Perspectiva pictorum et architectorum . . .*, Rome, 1741.

SEBASTIANI, LEOPOLDO, *Descrizione del real palazzo di Caprarola . . .*, Rome, 1741.

TEMANZA, TOMMASO (1705–89), *Delle Antichità di Rimini . . .*, 1st ed. Venice, 1741.

WOOD, JOHN (1704–54), *The Origin of Building: or, The Plagiarism of the Heathens Detected,* 1st ed. Bath, 1741.

1742

DOMINICI, BERNARDO DE' (1684–1750), *Vite de' pittori, sculture, et architetti napoletani . . .*, 1st ed. Naples, 1742–43.

ERLACH, JOHANN BERNHARD FISCHER VON (1656–1723), *Entwurff einer historischen Architektur* . . . , Leipzig, 1742.

HALFPENNY, WILLIAM (fl. 1722–55), and others, *The Modern Builder's Assistant* . . . , 1st ed. London, [1742].

LANGLEY, BATTY (1696–1751), *Gothic Architecture, Improved* . . . , 1st ed. London, 1742.

MURATORI, LODOVICO ANTONIO [pseud., Lamindo Pritanio], *Delle riflessioni sopra il buon gusto nelle scienze e nell'arti* . . . , Venice, 1742.

PALLADIO, ANDREA (1508–80), *The Architecture of A. Palladio; in four books . . . Revis'd . . . by G. Leoni . . . Translated by N. Du Bois . . . with notes . . . of Inigo Jones . . . an appendix containing the Antiquities of Rome* . . . , 3d ed. London, 1742.

POLENI, GIOVANNI (1683–1761), *Dissertazione sopra il Tempio di Diana di Efeso* . . . , Rome, 1742.

SGRILLI, BERNARDO SANSONE (fl. 1733–55), *Descrizione della regia villa, fontane, e fabbriche di Pratolino* . . . , 1st ed. Florence, 1742.

SWITZER, STEPHEN (1682–1745), *Ichnographia rustica* . . . , 2d ed. London, 1742.

WOOD, JOHN (1704–54), . . . *A Description of Bath* . . . , 2 vols. London, 1742–43.

1743

BRISEUX, CHARLES ÉTIENNE (c. 1660–1754), *L'Art de bâtir des maisons de campagne* . . . , 1st ed. 2 vols. Paris, 1743.

BUCHOTTE, *Les Règles du dessein* . . . , Paris, 1743. (*)

LEONARDI, DOMENICO FELICE, *Le Delizie della villa di Castellazzo descritte in verso* . . . , Milan, 1743. (*)

LONGINUS, DIONYSIUS (d. 273), *On the Sublime. Translated with notes and observations . . . by W. Smith* . . . , London, 1743.

MARANGONI, CHANOINE GIOVANNI (1673–1753), *Delle Memorie sacre e civili dell' antica città de Novana, oggi Civitanova* . . . , Rome, 1743.

PIRANESI, GIOVANNI BATTISTA (1720–78), *Prima Parte di architetture, e prospettive* . . . , 1st ed. Rome, 1743.

POCOCKE, RICHARD (1704–65), *A Description of the East and Some Other Countries,* 1st ed. 2 vols. London, 1743–45.

VIGNOLA, GIACOMO BAROZZI DA (1507–73), *Regola della prospettiva prattica* . . . [ed. by Francesco Veniero], 4th ed. Venice, 1743. (1st ed. 1582.)

WARE, ISAAC (d. 1766), *Designs of Inigo Jones and Others* . . . , London, 1743. (1st ed. 1735.)

1744

FICORINI, FRANCESCO (1664–1747), *Le Vestigie e rarità di Roma antica* . . . , 1st ed. Rome, 1744.

MURATORI, LODOVICO ANTONIO [pseud., LAMINDO PRITANIO], *Delle riflessioni sopra il buon gusto nelle scienze e nelle arti* . . . , Venice, 1744.

NERALCO, PASTORE ARCADE (pseud. for GIUSEPPE MARIA ERCOLANI) (1672–1759), *I Tre Ordini d'architettura . . . presi dalle fabbriche più celebri dell'antica Roma* . . . , 1st ed. Rome, 1744.

ZOCCHI, GIUSEPPE (1711–67), *Scelta di XXIV vedute . . . delle città di Firenze* . . . , Florence, 1744.

ZOCCHI, GIUSEPPE, *Vedute delle ville e d'altri luoghi della Toscana,* Florence, 1744.

1745

BOFFRAND, GERMAIN (1667–1754), *Livre d'architecture* . . . , 1st ed. Paris, 1745.

CASSINI, GIOVANNI MARIA, *Roma antica e moderna* . . . , 1st ed. 3 vols. Rome, 1745.

FICORINI, FRANCESCO (1664–1747), *Le Memorie ritrovate nel territorio della prima, e seconda città di Labico* . . . , 1st ed. Rome, 1745.

LANGLEY, BATTY (1696–1751), . . . *Treasury of Designs,* London, 1745. (1st ed. 1740.)

PRATILLI, FRANCESCO MARIA (1689–1763), *Delle Via Appia riconosciuta, da Roma a Brindisi* . . . , Naples, 1745.

RIVAULTELLA, ANTONIO (1708–53), and GIOVANNI PAOLO RICOLVI (1723–48), *Il Sito dell'antica città d'industria scoperto, ed illustrato* . . . , Turin, 1745. (*)

SALMON, WILLIAM, *The London and Country Builders' Vade Mecum* . . . , 1st ed. London, 1745.

SWAN, ABRAHAM (fl. 1745–65), *The British Architect* . . . , 1st ed. London, 1745.

1746

BATTEUX, CHARLES (1713–80), *Les Beaux Arts réduits à un même principe,* 1st ed. Paris, 1746.

COSTA, GIANFRANCESCO (1711–72), *I Cinque Ordini di architettura di Andrea Palladio . . .* , 1st ed. Venice, 1746.

LA CHAUSSE, MICHEL ANGE DE (fl. 1700), *Romanum Museum, sive thesaurus eruditae antiquitatis . . .* , Rome, 1746. (1st ed., in French, 1706.)

MANNI, DOMENICO MARIA (1690–1788), *Notizie istoriche intorno al parlagio ovvero anfiteatro di Firenze . . .* , Bologna, 1746.

MARANGONI, GIOVANNI (1673–1753), *Delle Memorie sacre, e profane, dell'anfiteatro flavio . . .* , Rome, 1746.

[MARSY, FRANÇOIS MARIE DE (1714–63)], *Dictionnaire abrégé de peinture et architecture . . .* , 1st ed. 2 vols. Paris, 1746.

[THURAH, LAURIDS LAURIDSEN DE (1706–59)], *Den danske Vitruvius . . .* , 1st ed. Copenhagen, 1746–49.

ZUZZERI, GIOVANNI LUCA, *D'Un' Antica Villa scoperta sul dosso del Tusculo, e d'un antico orologio . . .* , Venice, 1746.

1747

BATTEUX, CHARLES (1713–80), *Les Beaux Arts réduits à un même principe,* Paris, 1747. (1st ed. 1746.)

BIANCHINI, FRANCESCO (1662–1729), *La Istoria universale provata con monumenti, e figurata con simboli degli antichi . . .* , Rome, 1747. (1st ed. 1697.)

BLONDEL, JACQUES-FRANÇOIS (1705–44), *Discours sur la manière d'étudier l'architecture . . .* , 1st ed. [Paris, 1747].

CIAMPINI, JOANNES (1633–98), *Vetera Monumenta . . .* , 3 vols. Rome, 1747. (1st ed. 1690–99.)

FOSSATI, GIORGIO (1706–78), ed., Félibien, *Storia dell'architettura nella quale, oltre le vite degli architetti, si esaminane l'origine e i progressi dell'arte . . .* , Venice, 1747. (1st ed., in French, 1687.)

GIBBS, JAMES (1682–1754), *Bibliotheca Radcliviana,* 1st ed. London, 1747.

LANGLEY, BATTY (1696–1751), *Gothic Architecture, improved . . .* , London, 1747.

PERRAULT, CLAUDE (1613–88), *L'Architettura generale di Vitruvio . . .* , Venice, 1747.

VASI, GIUSEPPE (1710–82), *Delle Magnificenze di Roma antica, e moderna . . .* , 1st ed. 10 vols. [Rome], 1747–61.

VIGNOLA, GIACOMO BAROZZI DA (1507–73), *Règles des cinq ordres d'architecture de Jacques Barozzio de Vignole . . .* , Paris, 1747.

1748

BORRA, GIOVANNI BATTISTA, *Trattato della cognizione pratica delle resistenze ad uso degli edificj coll'aggiunta delle armature . . .* , 1st ed. Turin, 1748.

BUONAMICI, GIOVANNI FRANCESCO (1692–c. 1759), *Metropolitana di Ravenna . . .* , 1st ed. Bologna, 1748–54.

GORI, ANTONIO FRANCESCO (1691–1757), *Notizie del memorabile scoprimento dell' antica città d'Ercolano . . .* , 1st ed. Florence, 1748.

GORI, ANTONIO FRANCESCO, ed., *Symbolae literariae opuscola varia philologica scientifica antiquaria . . .* , 1st ed. 10 vols. Florence, 1748–53.

HOPPUS, EDWARD (d. 1739), *The Gentleman's and Builder's Repository . . .* , London, 1748. (1st ed. 1737.)

LONGINUS, DIONYSIUS (d. 273), *Trattato del sublime . . .* , Bologna, 1748.

MAFFEI, FRANCESCO SCIPIONE (1675–1755), *Tre Lettere . . .* , Verona, 1748.

NOLLI, GIAMBATTISTA (1692?–1756), *Nuova Pianta di Roma . . .* , [Rome], 1748.

PIRANESI, GIOVANNI BATTISTA (1720–78), *Antichità Romane de' tempi della repubblica, e de' primi imperatori . . .* , Rome, 1748.

PIRANESI, GIOVANNI BATTISTA, *Le Vedute di Roma,* Rome, 1748.

POLENI, GIOVANNI (1683–1761), *Memorie storiche della gran cupola del tempio Vaticano . . .* , 1st ed. Padua, 1748.

VENUTI, NICCOLÒ MARCELLO (1700–55), *Descrizione della prime scoperte dell'antica città d'Ercolano . . .* , Rome, 1748.

VIGNOLA, GIACOMO BAROZZI DA (1507–73), *L'architettura ridotta a facile metodo, aggiuntovi un trattato di meccanica,* 8 vols. Venice, 1748.

1749

GORI, ANTONIO FRANCESCO (1691–1757), *Storia antiqua etrusca . . .* , Florence, 1749. (*)

HALFPENNY, WILLIAM (fl. 1722–55), *A New and Compleat System of Architecture,* 1st ed. London, 1749.

JUVENEL DE CARLENCAS, FELIX DE (1669–1760), *Essais sur l'histoire . . . des arts . . .* , 4 vols. Lyon, 1749. (1st ed. 1740–44.)

MAUNDRELL, HENRY (1650–1710), *A Jour-*

ney from Aleppo to Jerusalem . . . , Oxford, 1749. (1st ed. 1699.)

MONTENARI, GIOVANNI, *Del Teatro Olimpico* . . . , Padua, 1749.

VENUTI, NICCOLÒ MARCELLO, *Descrizione delle prime scoperte* . . . *d'Ercolano* . . . , Venice, 1749. (1st ed. 1748.)

VIGNOLA, GIACOMO BAROZZI DA (1507–73), *Li cinque ordini di architettura* . . . , Venice, 1749.

1750

BANDINI, ANGELI MARIA (1726–1800), *De Obelisco Caesarie Augusti e Campi Martii* . . . , 1st ed. Rome, 1750.

BAUMGARTEN, ALEXANDER GOTTLIEB, *Aesthetica* . . . , *traiectis viadrum,* 1750.

BESOZZI, RAIMONDO, *La Storia della basilica di S. Croce in Gerusalemme* . . . , 1st ed. Rome, 1750.

CARLI, GIOVANNI RINALDO [COUNT] (1720–95), *Relazione delle scoperte fatte nell' anfiteatro di Pola* . . . , 1st ed. Venice, 1750.

ESCHINARDI, FRANCESCO (1623–c. 1700), *Descrizione di Roma, e dell'agro Romano* . . . , 1st ed. Rome, 1750.

FORDYCE, WILLIAM, *Memoirs Concerning Herculaneum* . . . , London, 1750. (*)

[FRANZINI, GIROLOMO (16th c.)], *Les Merveilles de la ville de Rome* . . . , Rome, 1750. (*)

HALFPENNY, WILLIAM (fl. 1722–55), *New Designs for Chinese Temples* . . . , London, 1750–52.

DE CORNY, EMMANUEL HÉRÉ (1705–63), *Recueil des plans, élévations, et coupes des châteaux, jardins, et dependances que le roy de Pologne occupe en Lôraine* . . . , 2 vols. Paris, [1750–56?]. (*)

LUCATELLI, GIANPIETRO, *Del Porto d'Ostia, e della maniera* . . . *dei Romani nel fabbricare i porti nel Mediterraneo* . . . , Rome, 1750.

MORRIS, ROBERT (fl. 1750s), *Rural Architecture* . . . , 1st ed. London, 1750.

PALLADIO, ANDREA (1508–80), *Le Antichità della città di Roma,* Rome, 1750. (1st ed. 1554.)

PIRANESI, GIOVANNI BATTISTA (1720–78), *Camere sepolcrali degli antichi Romani* . . . , Rome [c. 1750].

PIRANESI, GIOVANNI BATTISTA, *Invenzioni capric de carceri* . . . , Rome, c. 1750.

PIRANESI, GIOVANNI BATTISTA, *Opere varie di architettura* . . . , Rome, c. 1750.

ROUSSEAU, JEAN-JACQUES (1712–78), *Discours* . . . , *"Si le rétablissement des sciences et des arts a contribué à épurer les moeurs,"* 1st ed. Geneva, 1750.

SECONDO, GIUSEPPE MARIA (1715–98), *Relazione storica dell'antichità, rovine, e residui di Capri* . . . , 1st ed. Naples, 1750.

SIDONE, RAFFAELE, and ANTONIO MARTINETTI, *Della sacrosanta Basilica di S. Pietro in Vaticano* . . . , Rome, 1750.

STUART, JAMES (1713–88), *De obelisco Caesaris Augusti* . . . , 1st ed. Rome, 1750.

SWAN, ABRAHAM (fl. 1745–65), *The British Architect* . . . , London, 1750. (1st ed. 1745.)

TAIA [or TAJA], AGOSTINO SANESE, *Descrizione del palazzo apostolico Vaticana* . . . , Rome, 1750. (*)

VASI, GIUSEPPE (1710–82), *Il Palazzo di Caprarola* . . . , Rome, [c. 1750].

VENUTI, NICCOLÒ MARCELLO (1700–55), *A Description of Heraclea* . . . , 1st English ed. London, 1750.

VIGNOLA, GIACOMO BAROZZI DA (1507–73), *Grund regeln über die fünff Säulen* . . . , Nuremberg, [c. 1750].

VIGNOLA, GIACOMO BAROZZI DA, *Règle des cinq ordres d'architecture* . . . , Paris, c. 1750.

VIGNOLA, GIACOMO BAROZZI DA, *Regul der fünf Ordnungen von der Architectur* . . . , Augsburg, [c. 1750].

WALCH, JOHANN ERNST IMMANUEL (1725–78), *Antiquitates Herculanenses* . . . , 1st ed. [Jena, 1750].

WOOD, JOHN (1704–54), *Dissertation upon the Orders of Columns* . . . , London, 1750. (†)

1751

CONTINI, FRANCESCO (fl. 1650), *Ichonographia villae tiburtinae Hadriani Caesaris* . . . , Rome, 1751. (1st ed. 1668?)

DALTON, RICHARD (c. 1715–91), *A Series of Engravings representing Views* . . . *in Sicily, Greece, Asia Minor and Egypt,* [London, 1751–52].

GORI, ANTONIO FRANCESCO (1691–1757), ed., *Symbolae literariae opuscula varia* . . . , 10 vols. Rome, 1751–54. (1st ed. 1748–53.)

[MARRA, FRANCESCO DELLA] (1710–80), *Descrizione istorica del monastero di Monte Cassino* . . . , 1st ed. Naples, 1751.

MORRIS, ROBERT (fl. 1750), *The Architec-*

tural Remembrancer . . . , 1st ed. London, 1751.

PANCRAZI, GIUSEPPE MARIA (d. c. 1764), *Antichità Siciliani spiegate* . . . , 2 vols. Naples, 1751–52.

PIRANESI, GIOVANNI BATTISTA (1720–78), *Le Magnificenze di Roma* . . . , Rome, [1751?].

POTTER, JOHN (1674?–1747), *Archaeologia Graeca* . . . , 7th ed. London, 1751.

RIVAULTELLA, ANTONIO (1708–53), and GIOVANNI PAOLO RICOLVI (1723–48), *Il Sito dell'antica città d'industria* . . . , 2d ed. Rome, 1751.

VISENTINI, ANTONIO (1688–1782), *Urbis Venetiarum prospectus celebriores ex tabulis 38 Antonii Canal* . . . , Venice, 1751.

WALCH, JOHANN ERNST IMMANUEL (1725–78), *Antiquitates Herculanensis literariae* . . . , Jena, 1751. (1st ed. 1750.)

1752

BAYARDI, OTTAVIO ANTONIO (1690–1765), *Prodromo delle antichità d'Ercolano,* 1st ed. 5 vols. Naples, 1752.

BLONDEL, JACQUES-FRANÇOIS (1705–74), *Architecture françoise* . . . , 1st ed. 4 vols. Paris, 1752–56.

BRISEUX, CHARLES ÉTIENNE (c. 1660–1754), *Traité du beau essentiel dans les arts appliqué particulièrement à l'architecture* . . . , 1st ed. 2 vols. Paris, 1752.

CAYLUS, COMTE DE (1692–1765), *Recueil d'antiquités Egyptiennes, Etrusques, Grecques, et Romaines* . . . , 1st ed. 7 vols. Paris, 1752–67.

GORI, ANTONIO FRANCESCO (1691–1757), *Admiranda Antiquitatum Herculanensium descripta et illustrata ad annum 1750* . . . , Padua, 1752. (*)

HALFPENNY, WILLIAM (fl. 1722–55), and JOHN HALFPENNY, *Chinese and Gothic Architecture* . . . , 1st ed. London, 1752.

HALFPENNY, WILLIAM, and JOHN HALFPENNY, *Rural Architecture in the Gothic Taste* . . . , 1st ed. London, 1752.

LACOMBE, JACQUES (1724–1811), *Dictionnaire portatif des beaux arts* . . . , 1st ed. Paris, 1752.

NERINI, FELICIS MARIE (1705–87), *De Templo, et Caenobio SS. Bonifacii, et Alexii historica monumenta* . . . , Rome, 1752.

PÉRAU, GABRIEL LOUIS CALABRE (1700–67), *Description de la ville de Paris* . . . , new ed. 4 vols. Paris, 1752. (*)

PIRANESI, GIOVANNI BATTISTA (1720–78), *Raccolte di varie vedute di Roma* . . . , Rome, 1752. (1st ed. 1748.)

SCAMOZZI, VINCENZO (1552–1616), *The Mirror of Architecture* . . . , London, 1752.

TEMANZA, TOMMASO (1705–89), *Vita di Jacopo Sansovino fiorentino scultore et architetto* . . . , 1st ed. Venice, 1752.

VIGNOLA, GIACOMO BAROZZI DA (1507–73), *Règles des cinq ordres d'architecture de Vignole, revues, corrigées et reduites par M. Blondel* . . . , Paris, 1752.

1753

ALGAROTTI, FRANCESCO (1712–64), *Saggio sopra l'architettura,* 1st ed. Pisa, [1753 or 1756].

ANDRÉ, YVES DE L'ISLE (1675–1764), *Versuch von dem Schönen* . . . , Königsberg, 1753. (1st ed. 1741.)

BELLICARD, J. C. (1726–c. 1786) [and C. N. COCHIN (le fils) (1715–1790)], *Observations upon the Antiquities of the Town of Herculaneum* . . . , 1st ed. London, 1753.

BIANCHI, GIOVANNI ANTONIO [pseud., LAURISO TRAGIENSE] (1686–1758), *Di I Vizj, e de i difetti del moderno teatro* . . . , 1st ed. Rome, 1753.

ESTÈVE, PIERRE (fl. c. 1750), *L'Esprit des beaux arts ou histoire raisonnée du gout,* 1st ed. 2 vols. Paris, 1753.

GALLI DA BIBIENA, FERDINANDO (1657–1743), *Direzioni ai giovani studenti del disegno* . . . , [Bologna (?)], 1753. (1st ed. 1725).

HALFPENNY, WILLIAM (fl. 1722–55) and JOHN HALFPENNY, *The Country Gentleman's Pocket Companion* . . . *Containing Thirty-two New Designs* . . . *in the Augustine, Gothick and Chinese Taste* . . . , 1st ed. London, 1753.

DE CORNY, EMMANUEL HÉRÉ (1705–63), *Plans et élévations de la Race Royale de Nancy, et d'autres edifices* . . . , Paris, 1753.

HOGARTH, WILLIAM (1697–1764), *The Analysis of Beauty* . . . , 1st ed. London, 1753.

LACOMBE, JACQUES (1724–1811), *Dictionnaire portatif des beaux arts* . . . , Paris, 1753. (1st ed. 1752.)

LAUGIER, MARC-ANTOINE (1713–69), *Essai sur l'architecture,* 1st ed. Paris, 1753.

MESCHINELLO, GIOVANNI, *La Chiesa ducale di San Marco* . . . , n.p., 1753–54.

NELLI, GIOVANNI BATTISTA (1661–1725), *Discorsi di architettura* . . . , Florence, 1753.

ORLANDI, PELLEGRINO ANTONIO (1660–1727), *Abecedario pittorico* . . . , Venice, 1753.

PIRANESI, GIOVANNI BATTISTA (1720–78), *Trofei di Ottaviano Augusto innalzati per la vittoria ad Actium* . . . , Rome, 1753.

VALESI, DIONISIO (fl. 1737–66), *Varie Fabbriche antiche e moderne della citta di Verona* . . . Verona, 1753. (*)

VENUTI, RIDOLFINO (1705–63), *Osservazioni sopra il fiume Clitunno, e antico suo tempio* . . . , Rome, 1753.

WOOD, ROBERT (1717?–71), and JAMES DAWKINS (1722–57), *The Ruins of Palmyra, Otherwise Tedmar, in the Desart,* 1st ed. London, 1753.

1754

BLONDEL, JACQUES-FRANÇOIS (1705–74), *Discours sur la nécessité de l'étude de l'architecture* . . . , 1st ed. Paris, 1754.

BORLASE, WILLIAM (1695–1772), *Observations on the Antiquities, Historical and Monumental of the County of Cornwall* . . . , 1st ed. Oxford, 1754.

BOTTARI, GIOVANNI GAETANO (1689–1775), *Dialoghi sopra le tre arti del disegno,* 1st ed. Lucca, 1754.

BOTTARI, GIOVANNI GAETANO, *Raccolta di lettere sulla pittura, scultura, architettura* . . . , 1st ed. 7 vols. Rome, 1754–73.

BUCHOTTE, *Les Règles du dessein* . . . , Paris, 1754. (*)

BUONAMICI, GIOVANNI FRANCESCO (1692–c. 1759), *Fabbriche fatte sul porto di Pesaro* . . . , Bologna, 1754. (†)

COCHIN, CHARLES NICOLAS [le fils] (1715–90) and J. C. BELLICARD (1726–c. 1786), *Observations sur les antiquités de la ville d'Herculaneum* . . . , 1st French ed. Paris, 1754. (1st ed., in English, 1753.)

DRUMMOND, ALEXANDER (d. 1769), *Travels through Different Cities of Germany, Italy, Greece, and Several Parts of Asia* . . . , 1st ed. London, 1754.

HOGARTH, WILLIAM (1697–1764), *Zergliederung der Schönheit* . . . , London, 1754. (1st ed., in English, 1753.)

MAFFEI, FRANCESCO SCIPIONE (1675–1755), *Dei Teatri antichi e moderni* . . . , Verona, 1754.

PATTE, PIERRE (1732–1814), *Discours sur l'architecture* . . . , Paris, 1754.

REQUIER, JEAN BAPTISTE (1715–99), *Recueil général historique* . . . *sur la ville d'Hêrculane* . . . , Paris, 1754. (†)

RICHA, GIUSEPPE (1693–1761), *Notizie storiche delle chiese Fiorentine* . . . , Florence, 1754–62.

VENUTI, FILIPPO, *Dissertations sur les anciens monumens de la ville de Bordeaux* . . . , Bordeaux, 1754.

VIGNOLA, GIACOMO BAROZZI DA (1507–73), *Regola delli cinque ordini* . . . *con la nuova agionta di Michelangelo Buonaroti* . . . , Rome, 1754.

VITA, GIOVANNI DE (1708–74), *Thesaurus antiquitatum Beneventarum,* 2 vols. Rome, 1764.

ZOCCHI, GIUSEPPE (1711–67), *Vedute delle ville e d'altri luoghi della Toscana,* Florence, 1754.

1755

ALBERTI, LEON BATTISTA (1404–72), *The Architecture of Leon Battista Alberti* . . . , Leoni, editor, London, 1755.

AVILER, AUGUSTIN CHARLES D' (1653–1700), *Dictionnaire* . . . *d'architecture civile et hydraulique* . . . , 1st ed. Paris, 1755.

BUCHOTTE, *Les Règles du dessein* . . . , Paris, 1755. (*)

CALOGIERÀ, ANGELO (1699–1768), ed., *Nuova Raccolta d'opuscoli scientifici e filologici* . . . , 1st ed. Venice, 1755–84.

CASSIO, ALBERTO, *Memorie istoriche della vita di Santa Silvia* . . . *e castelli nel Lazio* . . . , Rome, 1755. (*)

COCHIN, CHARLES NICOLAS [le fils] (1715–90), and J. C. BELLICARD (1726–c. 1786), *Observations sur les antiquités de la ville d'Herculanum* . . . , 2d ed. Paris, 1755. (1st French ed. 1754.)

HALFPENNY, WILLIAM (fl. 1722–55), *Rural Architecture in the Chinese Taste* . . . , 3d ed. London, 1755?

LAUGIER, MARC-ANTOINE (1713–69), *An Essay on Architecture* . . . , London, 1755. (1st ed., in French, 1753.)

LAUGIER, MARC-ANTOINE, *Essai sur l'architecture, nouvelle édition revue, corrigée et augmentée* . . . , Paris, 1755. (1st ed. 1753.)

LONGINUS, DIONYSIUS (d. 273), *De Sublimitate, Græce* . . . , Ratisbonne, 1755.

MÉHÉGAN, GUILLAUME-ALEXANDRE DE (1721–66), *Considérations sur les révolutions des arts* . . . , 1st ed. Paris, 1755.

MORRIS, ROBERT (fl. 1750s), *Architecture Improved* . . . , 1st ed. London, 1755.

NORDEN, FRIDERICK LUDVIG, *Voyage d'Égypte et de Nubie* . . . , 1st ed. Copenhagen, 1755.

PASSERI, GIOVANNI BATTISTA (1694–1780), *Discorso della ragione dell'architettura* . . . , n.p., 1755.

ROSSI, GIUSEPPE IGNAZIO (d. before 1739), *La Libreria Mediceo-Laurenziana* . . . , Florence, 1755. (1st ed. 1739.)

RUBENS, PETER PAUL (1577–1640), *Architecture italienne . . . palais et edifices de la Ville Gênes* . . . , 3d ed. Amsterdam and Leipzig, 1755. (1st ed. 1622.)

RUGGIERI, FERNANDO, *Scelta di architetture antiche e moderne della città di Firenze* . . . , 2d ed. 2 vols. Florence, 1755. (1st ed., under title *Studio di architettura,* 1722–28.)

VIGNOLA, GIACOMO BAROZZI DA (1507–73), *Nouveau livre des cinq ordres d'architecture par Jacque Barozzio Vignole enrichi* . . . , Paris, c. 1755.

VIGNOLA, GIACOMO BAROZZI DA, *Le Nouveau Vignole ou règles des cinq ordres* . . . , Paris, 1755.

VIGNOLA, GIACOMO BAROZZI DA, *Regeln des 5 Saulenordnungen von d. Architektur* . . . , Nuremberg, 1755.

WINCKELMANN, JOHANN JOACHIM (1717–68), *Gedanken über die Nachahmung der grieschischen Werke in der Mahlerey und Bildhauer-Kunst,* 1st ed. Dresden, 1755.

1756

AVILER, AUGUSTIN CHARLES D' (1653–1700), *Cours d'architecture* . . . , new ed. Paris, 1756. (1st ed. 1691.)

BELLICARD, J. C. (1726–c. 1786), and C. N. COCHIN [le fils] (1715–90), *Observations upon the antiquities . . . of Herculaneum* . . . , 2d ed. London, 1756. (1st ed. 1753.)

CASSIO, ALBERTO, *Corso delle acque antiche portate da lontane* . . . , 2 vols. Rome, 1756–57. (*)

COCHIN, CHARLES NICOLAS [le fils] (1715–90), *Voyage pittoresque d'Italie,* Paris, 1756. (*)

HALFPENNY, WILLIAM (fl. 1722–55), *The Country Gentleman's Pocket Companion* . . . , London, 1756.

LAUGIER, MARC-ANTOINE (1713–69), *An Essay on the Study and Practice of Archi-*tecture . . . , London, 1756. (1st English ed. 1755.)

LAUGIER, MARC-ANTOINE, *Versuch über die Baukunst,* Frankfurt and Leipzig, 1756. (1st ed., in French, 1753.)

MURATORI, LODOVICO ANTONIO [pseud., LAMINDO PRITANIO], *Delle riflessioni sopra il buon gusto nelle scienze e nell' arte* . . . , Venice, 1756.

PIRANESI, GIOVANNI BATTISTA (1720–78), *Le Antichità Romane* . . . , 4 vols. Rome, 1756.

RIEGER, CHRISTIANUS, *Universae architecturae civilis elementa* . . . , 1st ed. Venice, Prague, and Trieste, 1756.

VANVITELLI, LUIGI (1700–73), *Dichiarazione dei disegni del reale palazzo di Caserta* . . . , 1st ed. Naples, 1756.

VENUTI, RIDOLFINO (1705–63), *Marmora Albana sive in duas inscriptiones gladiatorias Collegii Silvani Aureliani inter rudera Urbis Romae nuper repertas conjecturae* . . . , Rome, 1756.

VENUTI, RIDOLFINO, *Spiegazione de' bassi-rilievi* . . . , Rome, 1756.

VITRUVIUS POLLIO, MARCUS, *Des Grossen und Weltberühmten Vitruvii Architectura* . . . , Nuremberg, Würzburg, and Prague, 1756.

WARE, ISAAC (d. 1766), *A Complete Body of Architecture . . . Some Designs of Inigo Jones, Never before Published* . . . , 1st ed. London, 1756.

WINCKELMANN, JOHANN JOACHIM (1717–68), *Gedanken über die Nachahmung der griechischen Werke* . . . , Dresden, 1756.

1757

ALLEGRANZA, GIUSEPPE (1713–85), *Spiegazione e riflessioni sopra alcuni sacri monumenti antichi di Milano,* 1st ed. Milan, 1757.

BARTOLI, PIETRO SANTI (1635–1700), *Recueil de peintures antiques, imitées fidèlement* . . . , Paris 1757–60. (1st ed., in Italian, 1680.)

BELLICARD, J. C. (1726–c. 1786), and CHARLES NICOLAS COCHIN [le fils] (1715–90), *Observations sur les antiquités de la ville d'Herculanum* . . . , Paris, 1757. (1st French ed. 1754.)

BLONDEL, JACQUES-FRANÇOIS (1705–74), *De La Distribution des maisons de plaisance, et de la décoration des édifices en general* . . . , 1st ed. 2 vols. Paris, 1737.

BRANCA, GIOVANNI (1571–1645), *Manuale di architettura, breve e risoluta pratica di Giovanni Branca . . .* , new ed. Rome, 1757. (1st ed. 1629.)

BURKE, EDMUND (1730–97), *A Philosophical Enquiry into the Origin of our Ideas of the Sublime and Beautiful,* 1st ed. London, 1757.

CHAMBERS, SIR WILLIAM (1723–96), *Designs of Chinese Buildings . . .* , 1st ed. London, 1757.

JUVENEL DE CARLENCAS, FELIX DE, *Essais sur l'histoire des arts . . .* , 4 vols. Lyon, 1757. (1st ed. 1740–44.)

MÉHÉGAN, GUILLAUME-ALEXANDRE DE (1721–66), *L'Histoire considérée vis-à-vis de la religion, de l'état et des beaux-arts . . .* , Paris, 1757. (†)

MONTFAUCON, BERNARD DE (1655–1741), *Antiquitates graecae et romanae . . .* , 2 vols. Nuremberg, 1757. (*)

MONTFAUCON, BERNARD DE, *L'Antiquité expliquée . . .* , 5 vols. Paris, 1757. (1st ed. 1719.)

MORRIS, ROBERT (fl. 1750s), *Select Architecture . . .* , London, 1757. (*)

NEUFFORGE, JEAN-FRANÇOIS (b. 1714), *Recueil élémentaire d'architecture,* 10 vols. Paris, 1757–80.

NORDEN, FRIDERICK LUDVIG (1708–42), *A Compendium of the Travels of F. L. Norden through Egypt and Nubia . . .* , Dublin, 1757. (1st ed., in French, 1755.)

NORDEN, FRIDERICK LUDVIG, *Travels in Egypt and Nubia translated . . . and enlarged . . . by P. Templeman . . .* , 1st English ed. London, 1757 in-folio, and another edition 1757 in 8°.

PIRANESI, GIOVANNI BATTISTA (1720–78), *Lettere di giustificazione scritte a Milord Charlemont . . .* , Rome, 1757.

TOSCA, TOMAS VICENTE (1651–1723), "Arquitectura civil," *Compendio matemático,* Book 5, Valencia, 1757.

VIGNOLA, GIACOMO BAROZZI DA (1507–73), *Livre nouveau ou règles des cinq ordres d'architecture . . .* , Paris, 1757.

VITRUVIUS POLLIO, MARCUS, *Des Grossen und Weltberühmten Vitruvii Architectura . . .* , Nuremberg, Würzburg, and Prague, 1757.

WOOD, ROBERT (1717?–71), *The Ruins of Balbek, Otherwise Heliopolis in Coelosyria . . .* , 1st ed. London, 1757.

ZOCCHI, GIUSEPPE (1711–67), *Vedute delle ville e d'altri luoghi della Toscana,* Florence, 1757.

1758

CELANO, CARLO, *Notizie del bello, dell' antico e del curioso della città di Napoli . . .* , 6 vols. Naples, 1758. (1st ed. 1692.)

COCHIN, CHARLES NICOLAS [le fils] (1715–90), *Voyage d'Italie . . .* , 3 vols. Paris, 1758. (†)

GOGULET, ANTOINE Y. (1716–58), and A.-C. FUGÈRE, *De l'Origine des loix, des arts, et des sciences, et de leurs progrès chez les anciens peuples . . .* , 1st ed. 3 vols. Paris, [1758].

LACOMBE, JACQUES (1724–1811), *Dizionario portabile delle belle arti . . .* , 1st Italian trans. Venice, 1758.

LACOMBE, JACQUES, *Le Spectacle des beaux-arts . . .* , 1st ed. Paris, 1758.

LAUGIER, MARC-ANTOINE (1713–69), *Versuch in der Baukunst . . .* , Frankfurt and Leipzig, 1758. (1st German ed. 1756.)

LE ROY, JULIEN DAVID (1724–1803), *Les Ruines des plus beaux monuments de la Grèce . . .* , 1st ed. Paris, 1758.

OVER, CHARLES, *Ornamental Architecture in the Gothic, Chinese and Modern Taste . . .* , London, 1758. (*)

PAUSANIAS (2d half of 2d c. B.C.), *An Extract out of Pausanias, of the Statues, Pictures, and Temples in Greece . . .* , London, 1758.

SWAN, ABRAHAM, *The British Architect . . .* , [London], 1758. (1st ed. 1745.)

VENUTI, RIDOLFINO (1705–63), *La favola di Circe rappresentata in antico Greco basso-rilievo di marmo . . .* , Rome, 1758.

VITRUVIUS POLLIO, MARCUS, *L'Architettura di M. Vitruvio . . . commento del Marchese Berardo Galiani . . .* , 1st Galiani ed. Naples, 1758.

WRIGHT, THOMAS (1711–86), *Louthania: or, an Introduction to the Antiquities of Ireland . . .* , 1st ed. London, 1758.

ZANETTI, GIROLAMO FRANCESCO (1713–82), *Dell' origine di alcune arti principali appresso i Veneziani . . .* , 1st ed. Venice, 1758.

1759

ANDRÉ, YVES DE L'ISLE (1675–1764), *Essai sur le beau . . .* , Amsterdam, 1759. (1st ed. 1741.)

BURKE, EDMUND (1730–97), *A Philosophical Enquiry* . . . , 2d ed. London, 1759. (1st ed. 1757.)

CHAMBERS, SIR WILLIAM (1723–96), *A Treatise on Civil Architecture* . . . , 1st ed. London, 1759.

DECKER, PAUL (1677–1713), *Chinese Architecture, Civil and Ornamental, A Collection of Designs* . . . , 1st ed. London, 1759.

DECKER, PAUL, *Gothic Architecture Decorated* . . . , 1st ed. London, 1759.

LACOMBE, JACQUES (1724–1811), *Dictionnaire portatif des beaux arts* . . . , new ed. Paris, 1759. (1st ed. 1752.)

LE CLERC, SEBASTIEN (1637–1714), *Neue Abhandlung von der Civil-Baukunst* . . . , Nuremberg, 1759. (1st ed., in French, 1714.)

LE ROY, JULIEN DAVID (1724–1803), *The Ruins of Athens, with . . . Antiquities in Greece,* London, 1759. (1st ed., in French, 1758.)

MILLER, JOHN, and WILLIAM HALFPENNY (fl. 1722–55), *Andrea Palladio's Elements of Architecture* . . . , London, 1759.

PASSERI, GIOVANNI BATTISTA (1694–1780), *In Monumenta sacra Eburnea* . . . , Florence, 1759.

VASARI, GIORGIO (1512–74), *Vite de' più eccellenti pittori scultori e architetti . . . corrette da molti errori* . . . , 3 vols. Rome, 1759–60.

VIGNOLA, GIACOMO BAROZZI DA (1507–73), *Anhang zu der ausführlichen Anleitung der ganzen Civil-Baukunst,* 1759.

YOUNG, EDWARD (c. 1683–1765), *Conjectures on Original Composition,* 1st ed. [London], 1759.

1760

AVILER, AUGUSTIN CHARLES D' (1653–1700), *Cours d'architecture* . . . , new ed. Paris, 1760. (1st ed. 1691.)

HALFPENNY, WILLIAM (fl. 1722–55), *Useful Architecture* . . . , 3d ed. London, 1760. (1st ed. 1752.)

HOPPUS, EDWARD (d. 1739), *The Gentleman's and Builder's Repository* . . . , London, 1760. (1st ed. 1737.)

MONCHABLON, E. J., *Dictionnaire abrégé d'antiquités* . . . , 1st ed. Paris, 1760.

MURATORI, LODOVICO ANTONIO [pseud., LAMINDO PRITANIO], *Delle Riflessioni sopra il buon gusto nelle scienze e nelle arti* . . . , Naples, 1760.

VIGNOLA, GIACOMO BAROZZI DA (1507–73), *Nouveau Livre des cinq ordres d'architecture . . . On y a joint aussi l'ordre françois* . . . , Paris, 1760.

VIGNOLA, GIACOMO BAROZZI DA, *Règles des cinq ordres d'architecture. Nouvellement rev., corr. et réduites de grand en petit par Blondel* . . . , Paris, [c. 1760].

VITTONE, BERNARDO ANTONIO (1705–70), *Istruzioni elementari per indirizzo de' giovani allo studio dell' architettura civile,* 1st ed. 3 vols. Lugano, 1760.

1761

BARBAULT, JEAN (1705–66), *Les Plus Beaux Monuments de Rome ancienne ou recuëil des plus beaux morceaux de l'antiquité romaine qui existent encore* . . . , 1st ed. Rome, 1761.

BERTOTTI-SCAMOZZI, OTTAVIO (1719–90), *Il Forestiere istruito* . . . , 1st ed. Vicenza, 1761.

BRETTINGHAM, MATTHEW (1699–1769), *The Plans, Elevations, and Sections of Holkham in Norfolk* . . . , 1st ed. London, 1761.

BURKE, EDMUND (1730–97), *A Philosophical Enquiry* . . . , 3d ed. London, 1761. (1st ed. 1757.)

DUMONT, GABRIEL-PIERRE-MARTIN (c. 1720, still active in 1790), *Suite de profils et détails d'architecture levés et mesurés . . . à l'académie de France à Rome en 1744* . . . , Paris, 1761. (*)

HOGARTH, WILLIAM (1697–1764), *L'Analisi della bellezza.* Leghorn, 1761. (1st ed., in English, 1753.)

MONTAGU, D., *Nuova Raccolta delle più belle vedute di Roma, dissegnate, e intagliale da celebri autori* . . . , Rome, 1761.

PACIAUDI, PAOLO MARIA (1710–85), *Monumenta Peloponnesia commentariis explicata* . . . , 2 vols. Rome, 1761.

PERRAULT, CLAUDE (1613–88), *Compendio de los diez libros de arquitectura de Vitruvio* . . . , Madrid, 1761.

PIRANESI, GIOVANNI BATTISTA (1720–78), *Il Campo Marzio dell'antica Roma* . . . , Rome, [1761].

PIRANESI, GIOVANNI BATTISTA, *Carceri d'invenzione* . . . , Rome, c. 1761.

PIRANESI, GIOVANNI BATTISTA, *Della Magnificenza et architettura de' Romani* . . . , Rome, 1761.

PIRANESI, GIOVANNI BATTISTA, *Opere varie di architettura* . . . , Rome, c. 1761.

PIRANESI, GIOVANNI BATTISTA, *Le Rovine dell Castello dell' Acqua Giulia . . .* , Rome, 1761.

ROUSSEAU, JEAN-JACQUES (1712–78), *Eloisa . . .* , 4 vols. London, 1761.

ROUSSEAU, JEAN-JACQUES, *Julie ou la nouvelle Héloïse . . .* , 6 vols. Amsterdam, 1761.

ROUSSEAU, JEAN-JACQUES, *La Nouvelle Héloïse . . .* , 6 vols. Leipzig, 1761.

SANCTIS, DOMENICO DE, *Dissertazione sopra la villa d'Orazio Flacco . . .* , 1st ed. Rome, 1761.

VENNI, GIUSEPPE, *Elogio storico alle gesta del B. Oderico . . . colla storia dei suoi viaggi asiatici illustrata . . .* , Venice, 1761.

VIGNOLA, GIACOMO BAROZZI DA (1507–73), *Livre nouveau ou règles des cinq ordres d'architecture . . .* , 2d ed. Paris, 1761.

VIGNOLA, GIACOMO BAROZZI DA, *Vignola Revived, Wherein Is Shewn the True and Most Elegant Proportions of the Five Orders . . .* , London, 1761.

VITRUVIUS POLLIO, MARCUS, *Compendio de los diez Libros de Architectura de Vitruvio, Escrito en Francés por Cl. Perrault Traducido all Castellano por J. Castaneda . . .* , in 8°, Madrid, 1761.

WINCKELMANN, JOHANN JOACHIM (1717–68), *Anmerkungen über die Baukunst der Alten . . .* , 1st ed. Leipzig, 1761.

[ZATTA, ANTONIO], *L'Augusta Ducale Basilica dell'Evangelista San Marco . . .* , Venice, 1761.

1762

ARNALDI, ENEA (1716–94), *Idea di un teatro . . . simile a' teatri antichi . . .* , 1st ed. Vicenza, 1762.

CHATTARD, GIOVANNI PIETRO, *Nuova Descrizione del Vaticano, o sia della sacrosanta basilica di S. Pietro . . .* , 1st ed. 3 vols. Rome, 1762–67.

DUPUIS, CHARLES (18th c.), *Nouveau Traité d'architecture . . .* , 1st ed. Paris, 1762.

MENGS, ANTON RAPHAEL (1728–79), *Gedanken über die Schönheit und über den Geschmak in der Malerey . . .* , Zürich, 1762.

MURATORI, LODOVICO ANTONIO [*pseud.*, LAMINDO PRITANIO], *Delle Riflessioni sopra il buon gusto nelle scienze e nelle arti . . .* , Venice, 1762.

PIRANESI, GIOVANNI BATTISTA (1720–78),

Campus Martius antiquae urbis . . . , . . . , Rome, [1762–64].

PIRANESI, GIOVANNI BATTISTA, *Descrizione e disegno dell' emissario del Lago Albano . . .* , Rome [1762–64].

PIRANESI, GIOVANNI BATTISTA, *Di Due Spelonche ornate dagli antichi alla riva del Lago Albano,* Rome, [1762–64].

PIRANESI, GIOVANNI BATTISTA, *Lapides Capitolini . . .* , Rome, 1762.

ROUSSEAU, JEAN-JACQUES (1712–78), *Du Contrat social; ou principes du droit politique . . .* , 1st ed. Amsterdam, 1762.

STUART, JAMES (1713–88), and NICHOLAS REVETT (1721–1804), *The Antiquities of Athens . . .* , 1st ed. vol. I, London, 1762.

TEMANZA, TOMMASO (1705–89), *Vita Di Andrea Palladio . . .* , 1st ed. Venice, 1762.

VENUTI, RIDOLFINO (1705–63), *A Collection of Some of the Finest Prospects in Italy, with Short Remarks on Them . . . Engraved by Various Celebrated Engravers at Rome . . .* , vol. 1, London, 1762. (In Italian, English, and French.)

WINCKELMANN, JOHANN JOACHIM (1717–68), *Anmerkungen über die Baukunst der Alten,* Leipzig, 1762. (1st ed. 1761.)

1763

ALGAROTTI, FRANCESCO (1712–64), *Saggio sopra l'Accademia di Francia, che è in Roma . . .* , 1st ed. Leghorn, 1763.

ANDRÉ, YVES DE L'ISLE (1675–1764), *Essai sur le beau . . .* , 2 vols. Paris, 1763. (1st ed. 1741.)

BARBAULT, JEAN (1705–66), *Edifices de Rome moderne . . .* , 1st ed. Rome, 1763.

CHAMBERS, SIR WILLIAM (1723–96), *Plans, Elevations, Sections, and Perspective Views of the Gardens and Buildings at Kew . . .* , 1st ed. London, 1763.

DUMONT, GABRIEL-PIERRE-MARTIN (c. 1720, still active in 1790), *Détails des plus intéressantes parties d'architecture de la basilique de S. Pierre de Rome . . .* , 1st ed. Paris, 1763.

LACOMBE, JACQUES (1724–1811), *Le Spectacle des beaux-arts . . .* , Paris, 1763. (1st ed. 1758.)

ORLANDI, PELLEGRINO ANTONIO (1660–1727), *Abecedario pittorico . . .* , Naples, 1763.

ROUSSEAU, JEAN-JACQUES (1712–78), *Julie ou la nouvelle Héloïse . . .* Volumes IV, V, VI of *Oeuvres diverses, 1762–1764,* 3 vols. Amsterdam, 1763.

VENUTI, RIDOLFINO (1705–63), *Accurata, e Succinta Descrizione topographica dell'antichita di Roma* . . . , 1st ed. 2 vols. Rome, 1763.

VIGNOLA, GIACOMO BAROZZI DA (1507–73), *Regola delli cinque ordini* . . . , Rome, 1763.

WINCKELMANN, JOHANN JOACHIM (1717–68), *Abhandlung von der Fähigkeit der Empfindung des Schönen in der Kunst* . . . , 1st ed. Dresden, 1763.

1764

ADAM, ROBERT (1728–92), *Ruins of the Palace of the Emperor Diocletian, at Spalatro, in Dalmatia* . . . , 1st ed. London, 1764.

ALGAROTTI, FRANCESCO (1712–64), "Lettere sopra l'architettura, 1742–63" in *Opere* . . . , 1st ed. Leghorn, 1764–65.

BELLORI, GIOVANNI PIETRO (c. 1615–96), *Ichnographia veteris Romae* . . . , Rome, 1764. (*)

BRISEUX, CHARLES ÉTIENNE (c. 1660–1754), *L'Architecture moderne* . . . , Paris, 1764. (1st ed. 1728.)

CAROTO, GIOVANNI (1488/95–1563/66), *Antichità di Verona disegnate* . . . , Verona, 1764. (1st ed. 1540.)

DUMONT, GABRIEL-PIERRE-MARTIN (c. 1720, still active in 1790), *Suite de plans, coupes, profils, élévations géométrales et perspectives de trois temples antiques, de Poesto* . . . *mésurés par J.-G. Soufflot* . . . , 1st ed. Paris, 1764.

GALLI DA BIBIENA, ANTONIO (1700–74), *Pianta e spaccato del nuovo teatro di Bologna aperto in 1763* . . . , 1st ed. Venice, 1764.

IKEN, CONRAD (1689–1753), *Antiquitates Hebraicae* . . . , Bremen, 1764. (*)

IZZO, JOHANN BAPTIST (1721–93), *Elementa architecturae civilis* . . . , Vienna, 1764. (†)

JOMBERT, CHARLES-ANTOINE (1712–84), *Architecture moderne* . . . , 2 vols. Paris, 1764. (1st ed. see C. E. Briseux, 1728.)

JOMBERT, CHARLES-ANTOINE, *Bibliothèque portative d'architecture élémentaire* . . . , 1st ed. 2 vols. Paris, 1764–66.

KANT, IMMANUEL (1724–1804), *Beobachtungen über das gefühl des schönen und erhabenen* . . . , 1st ed. Königsberg, 1764.

MAROT, JEAN (c. 1619–79), *Le Petit Marot, ou recueil de divers morceaux d'architecture* . . . , Paris, 1764. (*)

ORVILLE, JACQUES PHILIPPE D' (1696–1751), *Sicula, quibus Siciliae veteris rudera* . . . , 1st ed. 2 vols. Amsterdam, 1764.

PIRANESI, GIOVANNI BATTISTA (1720–78), *Antichità d'Albano e di Castel Gandolfo* . . . , Rome, 1764.

PIRANESI, GIOVANNI BATTISTA, *Antichità di Cora* . . . , Rome, [1764].

POTTER, JOHN (1674?–1747), *Archaeologia Graeca* . . . , 8th ed. London, 1764.

POZZO, ANDREA (1642–1709), *Perspectiva pictorum et architectorum* . . . , Rome, 1764.

ROUSSEAU, JEAN-JACQUES (1712–78), *Eloisa* . . . , London, 1764.

ROUSSEAU, JEAN-JACQUES, *La Nouvelle Héloïse* . . . , 4 vols. Paris, 1764.

SCAMOZZI, VINCENZO (1552–1616), *Oeuvres d'architecture de Vincent Scamozzi* . . . , Paris, 1764.

VIGNOLA, GIACOMO BAROZZI DA (1507–73), *Règles des cinq ordres d'architecture* . . . , new ed. Paris, 1764.

VITA, GIOVANNI DE (1708–74), *Thesaurus alter Antiquitatum Beneventanarum medii ævi* . . . , 2d ed. Rome, 1764. (1st ed. 1754.)

WINCKELMANN, JOHANN JOACHIM (1717–68), *Geschichte der Kunst des Alterthums,* Thiel 2. Dresden, 1764.

WINCKELMANN, JOHANN JOACHIM, *Lettre à M. le comte de Brühl sur les découvertes d'Herculanum* . . . , [Paris], 1764.

WINCKELMANN, JOHANN JOACHIM, *Nachrichten von den neusten Herculanischen Entdeckungen,* Dresden and Leipzig, 1764.

WRIGHT, EDWARD, *Some Observations Made in Travelling through France and Italy* . . . , 2d ed. 2 vols. London, 1764. (1st ed. 1730.)

XIMENES, ANDRES, *Descripción del real monastero de S. Lorenzo de l'Escorial* . . . , 1st ed. Madrid, 1764.

1765

BALDINUCCI, FILIPPO (1624–96), *Raccolta di alcuni opuscoli sopra varie materie di pittura, scultura e architettura* . . . , Florence, 1765. (†)

BURKE, EDMUND (1730–97), *Recherches philosophiques sur l'origine des idées que nous avons du beau et du sublime* . . . , 1st French ed. London, 1765.

CASSINI, GIOVANNI MARIA, *Rome antique et moderne* . . . , 3 vols. Paris, 1765. (1st ed. 1745.)

COCHIN, CHARLES NICOLAS [le fils] (1715–90), *Projet d'une salle de spectacle pour un théâtre de comédie* . . . , 1st ed. Paris, 1765.

GAMBA GHISELLI, PAOLO, *Lettera sopra l'antico edificio di Ravenna detto volgarmente La Rotonda* . . . , 1st ed. Rome, 1765.

HUBE, JEAN MICHEL (1737–1807), *Réflexions sur l'architecture* . . . , 1st ed. Königsberg and Leipzig, 1765.

JOMBERT, CHARLES ANTOINE (1712–84), *Répertoire des artistes, ou recueil des compositions d'architecture* . . . , 1st ed. 2 vols. Paris, 1764.

LAUGIER, MARC-ANTOINE (1713–69), *Observations sur l'architecture* . . . , 1st ed. The Hague, 1765.

MENGS, ANTON RAPHAEL (1728–79), *Gedanken über die Schönheit, und über den Geschmack in der Mahlerey* . . . , Zurich, 1765.

PATTE, PIERRE (1732–1814), *Monumens érigés en France à la gloire de Louis XV* . . . , 1st ed. Paris, 1765.

PEYRE, MARIE-JOSEPH (1730–85), *Oeuvres d'architecture* . . . , 1st ed. Paris, 1765.

PIRANESI, GIOVANNI BATTISTA (1720–78), *Osservazioni di Gio. Battista Piranesi* . . . , with *Parere sull'architettura* . . . , Rome, 1765.

PITISCUS, SAMUEL (1636–1727), *Dictionnaire des antiquités romaines* . . . , Paris, Lyon, Bordeaux, and Rouen, 1765.

RAGUENET, FRANÇOIS (1660–1722), *Observations nouvelles sur les ouvrages de peinture, de sculpture, et d'architecture, qui se voyent à Rome* . . . , London, 1765. (†)

ROUSSEAU, JEAN-JACQUES (1712–78), *Julie ou la nouvelle Héloyse* . . . , 6 vols. Amsterdam, 1765.

SANVITALE, FEDERIGO (1704–61), *Elementi d'architettura civile* . . . , 1st ed. Brescia, 1765.

SPALLETTI, GIUSEPPE, *Saggio sopra la bellezza* . . . , Rome, 1765.

VIGNOLA, GIACOMO BAROZZI DA (1507–73), *Architettura di . . . Vignola* . . . , Rome, 1765.

WINCKELMANN, JOHANN JOACHIM (1717–68), *Reflections on the Painting and Sculpture of the Greeks* . . . , translated . . . by *H. Fuselli,* 1st English ed. London, 1765.

WOOD, JOHN (1704–54), *A Description of Bath* . . . , 2 vols. London, 1765. (1st ed. 1742–43.)

1766

DUMONT, GABRIEL-PIERRE-MARTIN (c. 1720, still active in 1790), *Études d'architecture de differents maitres Italiens* . . . , [Paris, 1766]. (*)

FRÉART, ROLAND, SIEUR DE CHAMBRAY (c. 1606–76), and CHARLES ERRARD (1606–89), *Parallèle de l'Architecture antique avec la moderne* . . . , Paris, 1766.

HUGUES, PIERRE FRANÇOIS [called D'HANCARVILLE] (1719–1805), *Collection of Etruscan, Greek and Roman antiquities from the Cabinet of the Hon. W. Hamilton* . . . , 1st ed. 4 vols. Naples, 1766–67.

KANT, IMMANUEL (1724–1804), *Beobachtungen über das gefühl des schönen und erhabenen* . . . , Königsberg, 1766.

LACOMBE, JACQUES (1724–1811), *Dictionnaire portatif des beaux-arts* . . . , Paris, 1766.

LESSING, GOTTHOLD EPHRAIM (1728–81), *Laokoon* . . . , 1st ed. Berlin, 1766.

MORGHEN, FILIPPO (b. 1730), *Environs de Pouzzoles* . . . , 1766.

MURATORI, LODOVICO ANTONIO [pseud., LAMINDO PRITANIO], *Delle Riflessioni sopra il buon gusto nelle scienze e nell'arti* . . . , Venice, 1766.

PAUSANIAS, *Des Pausanias ausfürleche Reisebeschreibung* . . . , Berlin and Leipzig, 1766.

PITISCUS, SAMUEL (1636–1727), *Dictionnaire des antiquités romaines* . . . , Paris, 1766.

SPAGNIO, ANDREA, *De Bono, de malo, de pulcro* . . . , 1st ed. Rome, 1766.

VENUTI, RIDOLFINO (1705–63), *Topographica ed istorica di Roma moderna* . . . , 2 vols. Rome, 1766.

VENUTI, RIDOLFINO, and GIOVANNI CRISTOFORO AMADUZZI (1740–92), *Vetera Monumenta* . . . , 3 vols. Rome, 1776–79.

VITTONE, BERNARDO ANTONIO (1705–70), *Istruzioni diversi concernanti l'officio dell'architetto civile* . . . , 1st ed. 2 vols. Lugano, 1766.

WINCKELMANN, JOHANN JOACHIM (1717–68), *Histoire de l'art chez les anciens* . . . , Amsterdam, 1766.

WINCKELMANN, JOHANN JOACHIM, *Reflections concerning the Imitation of the Grecian Artists in Painting and Sculpture* . . . , Glasgow, 1766.

1767

ANDRÉ, YVES DE L'ISLE (1675–1764), *Essai sur le beau* . . . , Amsterdam, 1767. (1st ed. 1741.)

ARNALDI, ENEA (1716–94), *Delle Basiliche antiche . . . di Vicenza* . . . , 1st ed. Vicenza, 1767.

[BERKENHOUT, JOHN] (c. 1730–91), *The Ruins of Paestum or Posidonia* . . . , 1st ed. [London], 1767.

BRENNA, VICENZO (1745–1820), *Del Tempio Tibertino, volgarmente detto della sibilla* . . . , Rome, 1767. (*)

GALLACCINI, TEOFILO (1564–1641), *Trattato di Teofilo Gallaccini sopra gli errori degli architetti* . . . , 1st ed. Venice, 1767.

GUARNACCI, MARIO [pseud., CIPOLLONE LAVACECI] (1710–85), *Origini italiche, ossia memorie istorico-etrusche* . . . , 1st ed. 3 vols. Lucca, 1767–82.

LE ROY, JULIEN DAVID (1724–1803), *Observations sur les édifices des anciens peuples* . . . , Paris, 1767.

PAINE, JAMES (1716–89), *Plans, Elevations and Sections of Noblemen and Gentlemen's Houses* . . . , 1st ed. London, 1767–83.

POTAIN, NICOLAS MARIE (1713–96), *Traité des ordres d'architecture* . . . , 1st ed. Paris, 1767.

ROUSSEAU, JEAN-JACQUES (1712–78), *Julie ou la nouvelle Héloïse* . . . [Volumes IV, V, VI of *Oeuvres de Rousseau*, 1769] . . . , 3 vols. Amsterdam, 1767.

STEPHENS, PETER, *Raccolta di alcune delle più belle vedute d'Italia* . . . , 1 vol. in 8°. [London], 1767.

VASARI, GIORGIO (1512–74), *Vite de' più eccellenti pittori, scultori e architetti* . . . , Leghorn, 1767–72.

VENUTI, RIDOLFINO (1705–63), *Accurata e succinta descrizione . . . di Roma moderna* . . . , Rome, 1767.

VIGNOLA, GIACOMO BAROZZI DA (1507–73), *Livre nouveau ou règles des cinq ordres d'architecture,* Paris, 1767.

WINCKELMANN, JOHANN JOACHIM (1717–68), *Anmerkungen über die Geschichte der Kunst des Althertums* . . . , Dresden, 1767.

WINCKELMANN, JOHANN JOACHIM, *Monumenti antichi inediti spiegati ed illustrati* . . . , 2 or 3 vols. Rome, 1767.

WRIGHT, WILLIAM, *Grotesque Architecture* . . . , 1st ed. London, 1767.

1768

ANTOINE, JEAN, *Traité d'architecture, ou proportions des trois ordres grecs* . . . , 1st ed. Trier, 1768.

BARTOLI, PIETRO SANTI (1635–1700), *Gli Antichi Sepolcri* . . . , Rome, 1768. (1st ed. 1697.)

CHAMBERS, SIR WILLIAM (1723–96), *Treatise on Civil Architecture* . . . , 2d ed. London, 1768. (1st ed. 1759.)

CONTINI, FRANCESCO (fl. 1650), *Dichiarazione generale della pianta della villa Adriana* . . . , Rome, 1768. (1st ed. 1668.)

DELAFOSSE, JEAN CHARLES (1734–89), *Nouvelle Iconologie historique* . . . , 1st ed. Paris, 1768.

DUPUIS, CHARLES (18th c.), *Nouveau Traité d'architecture* . . . , Paris, 1768. (1st ed. 1762.)

GIOFFREDO, MARIO (1718–85), *Dell'Architettura, parte prima* . . . , 1st ed. Naples, 1768.

LAUGIER, MARC-ANTOINE (1713–69), *Anmerkungen über die Baukunst.* . . . , Leipzig, 1768. (1st ed., in French, 1765.)

MAJOR, THOMAS (1720–99), *Les Ruines de Paestum* . . . , London, 1768. (1st ed., in English also, 1768.)

MAJOR, THOMAS, *The Ruins of Paestum* . . . , 1st ed. London, 1768.

MILIZIA, FRANCESCO (1725–98), *Le Vite de' più celebri architetti . . . precedute da uno saggio sopra l'architettura,* 1st ed. Rome, 1768.

PAOLI, PAOLO ANTONIO (1720?–90?), *Antichità di Pozzuoli* . . . , [Naples], 1768.

RAWLINS, THOMAS (fl. 1747–76), *Familiar Architecture* . . . , 1st ed. [London], 1768.

RIOU, STEPHEN, *The Grecian Orders of Architecture, Delineated and Explained from the Antiquities of Athens, also Parallels of the Orders of Palladio, Scamozzi and Vignola* . . . , London, 1768.

SANCTIS, DOMENICO DE, *Dissertazione sopra la villa d'Orazio Flacco* . . . , Rome, 1768.

SARNELLI, POMPEO (1649–1724), *La Guida . . . di Pozzuoli, Baja, Cuma* . . . , Naples, 1768.

VITRUVIUS POLLIO, MARCUS, *Architecture générale de Vitruve reduite en abrégé par Perrault,* Paris, 1768.

ZANCHI, CARLO, *Il Vejo illustrato* . . . , Rome, 1768.

1769

ALGAROTTI, FRANCESCO (1712–64), *Essai sur la peinture, et sur l'Académie de France, établie à Rome . . . traduit de l'italien . . .*, Paris, 1769. (1st French ed. of earlier work in 1763.)

ALGAROTTI, FRANCESCO, *Versuch über die Architectur, Malerey und musicalische Opera . . .*, 1st German ed. Cassel, 1769.

ARNALDI, ENEA (1716–94), *Delle Basiliche antiche . . .*, Vicenza, 1769. (1st ed. 1767.)

BORLASE, WILLIAM (1695–1772), *Observations on the Antiquities, Historical and Monumental, of the County of Cornwall . . .*, London, 1769. (1st ed. 1754.)

COCHIN, CHARLES NICOLAS [le fils] (1715–90), *Voyage d'Italie . . .*, Paris, 1769. (*)

DUMONT, GABRIEL-PIERRE-MARTIN, *Les Ruines de Paestum . . . traduction libre de l'anglois . . . par M. B. [Berkenhout]*, Paris and London, 1769. (1st ed., in English, by Berkenhout, 1767.)

LA LANDE, JÉRÔME DE (1732–1807), *Voyage d'un français en Italie fait dans les années 1765 et 1766 . . .*, 1st ed. 8 vols. Venice and Paris, 1769.

MAJOR, THOMAS (1720–99), *Les Ruines de Paestum . . .*, Paris, 1769. (1st ed. 1768.)

MORGHEN, FILIPPO (b. 1730), *Le Antichità di Pozzuoli, Baja e Cuma . . .*, 1st ed. Naples, 1769.

PATTE, PIERRE (1732–1814), *Mémoires sur les objêts les plus importants de l'architecture . . .*, 1st ed. Paris, 1769.

PIRANESI, GIOVANNI BATTISTA (1720–78), *Diverse Maniere d'adorname i cammini . . . dell'architettura Egizia, Etrusca, e Greca con un ragionamento apologetico in difesa dell'architettura Egizia, e Toscana . . .*, Rome, 1769.

REVETT, NICHOLAS (1721–1804), RICHARD CHANDLER (1738–1810), and WILLIAM PARS (1742–1782), *Ionian Antiquities . . ., Part One,* 1st ed. London, 1769.

SARNELLI, POMPEO (1649–1724), *La Guida . . . di Pozzuoli, Baja, Cuma . . .* Italian and French . . ., Naples, 1769.

1770

ANDRÉ, YVES DE L'ISLE (1675–1764), *Essai sur le beau . . .*, Paris, 1770. (1st ed. 1741.)

BARBAULT, JEAN (1705–66), *Recueil de divers monumens anciens . . .*, 1st ed. Rome, 1770.

BURKE, EDMUND (1730–97), *A Philosophical Enquiry . . .*, 6th ed. London, 1770. (1st ed. 1757.)

FOUGEROUX DE BONDAROY, AUGUSTE DENIS (1732–89), *Recherches sur les ruines d'Herculanum . . .*, Paris, 1770. (†)

GORI, ANTONIO FRANCESCO (1691–1757), *Antiquitates Etruscae . . .*, [Nuremberg], 1770. (*)

KENT, WILLIAM (1684–1748), *The Designs of Inigo Jones . . .*, London, 1770. (1st ed. 1727.)

LE ROY, JULIEN DAVID (1724–1803), *Les Ruines des plus beaux monuments de la Grèce . . .*, Paris, 1770. (1st ed. 1758.)

LONGINUS, DIONYSIUS (d. 273), *El Sublime . . . traducido . . . por Don M. Perez Balderrabano . . .*, Madrid, 1770.

PATERNÒ, GIACINTO MARIA, *Del Ginnasio e anfiteatro di Catania . . .*, Palermo, 1770.

PATTE, PIERRE (1732–1814), *Mémoire sur la construction de la coupole projectée pour couronner la nouvelle église de Ste. Geneviève à Paris,* Paris, 1770. (†)

ROLAND LE VIRLOYS, CHARLES FRANÇOIS (1716–1772), *Dictionnaire d'architecture civile . . .*, 1st ed. 3 vols. Paris, 1770–71.

ROUSSEAU, JEAN-JACQUES (1712–78), *Julie ou la nouvelle Héloïse . . .*, Amsterdam, 1770.

SARNELLI, POMPEO (1649–1724), *La Guida . . . di Pozzuoli, Baja, Cuma . . .*, Naples, 1770.

SEIGNEUX DE CORREVON, GABRIEL (1695–1776), *Lettres sur la decouverte de l'ancienne ville de Herculane . . .*, 2 vols. Yverdon, 1770.

SPAMPANI, GIAMBATTISTA (b. 1745), and CARLO ANTONINI (c. 1750–1784), *Il Vignola illustrato . . .*, Rome, 1770.

TEMANZA, TOMMASO (1705–89), *Vita di Vincenzio Scamozzi . . .*, 1st ed. Venice, 1770.

WHATELY, SIR THOMAS (d. 1772), *Observations on Modern Gardening . . .*, 1st ed. London, 1770.

1771

BARTOLI, FRANCESCO (1745–1806), *Le Pitture, sculture, ed architetture delle chiese, e d'altri luoghi publicci di Bergamo . . .*, Vicenza, 1771. (†)

BENTHAM, JAMES (1708–94), *The History and Antiquities of the Conventual and Ca-*

thedral Church of Ely from . . . A.D. *673 to . . . 1771,* 1st ed. Cambridge, 1771.

BIANCHI, ISODORO (1733–1807), *Delle Scienze e delle arti . . .* , Palermo, 1771. (*)

BLONDEL, JACQUES-FRANÇOIS (1705–74), *Cours d'architecture . . .* , 1st ed. 6 vols. Paris, 1771–77.

DESGODETS, ANTOINE BABUTY (1653–1728), *The Ancient Buildings of Rome . . .* , 2 vols. London, 1771, 1795. (1st. ed. 1682.)

GALLI DA BIBIENA, ANTONIO (1700–74), *Pianta e spaccato del nuovo teatro di Bologna . . .* , Bologna, 1771. (1st ed. 1764.)

GIRARDIN, RÉNÉ LOUIS (1735–1808), *De la Composition des paysages . . .* , 1st ed. Paris, 1771.

JAGEMANN, GAUDENZIO, *Saggio sul buon gusto nelle belle arti . . .* , 1st ed. Florence, 1771.

KANT, IMMANUEL (1724–1804), *Beobachtungen über das gefühl des schönen und ehabenen . . .* , Riga, 1771.

LE GOUX DE BERLAN, BÉNIGNE (1695–1774), *Dissertations sur l'origine de la ville de Dijon . . .* , 1st ed. Dijon, 1771.

LONGINUS, DIONYSIUS (d. 273), *Dionysio Longino tratado do subime . . .* , *traduzido . . . por C. J. Oliveira . . .* , Lisbon, 1771.

MAFFEI, FRANCESCO SCIPIONE (1675–1755), *Verona illustrata . . .* , Verona, 1771. (1st ed. 1731–32.)

MILIZIA, FRANCESCO (1725–98), *Del Teatro . . .* , 1st ed. Rome, 1771.

MILIZIA, FRANCESCO, *Vies des architectes anciens et modernes . . .* , 2 vols. Paris, 1771.

NARDINI, FAMIANO (d. 1661), *Roma antica . . .* , 3d ed. Rome, 1771. (1st ed. 1666.)

NEWTON, WILLIAM (1735–90), *The Architecture of M. Vitruvius Pollio: Translated from The Original Latin, By W. Newton, Architect . . .* , vol. 1, London, 1771.

NOLLI, CARLO (d. 1770), *L'Arco trionfale eretto all'imp. Nerva Trajano in Benevento . . .* , [Naples, after 1770].

PALLADIO, ANDREA (1508–80), *I Quattro Libri dell' architettura di Andrea Palladio . . .* , Venice, [1771–80?].

PESSANI, PIETRO, *Dei Palazzi reali, che sono stati nella città e territorio di Pavia . . .* , Pavia, 1771.

ROUSSEAU, JEAN-JACQUES (1712–78), *Julie ou la nouvelle Héloïse . . .* , Amsterdam, 1771.

SULZER, JOHANN GEORG (1720–99), *Allgemeine Theorie der schönen Künste . . .* , 1st ed. 2 vols. Leipzig, 1771–74.

VENUTI, RIDOLFINO (1705–63), *Veteris Latii Antiquitatum amplissima collectio; cum figuris . . .* , 1st ed. Rome, 1771.

VISENTINI, ANTONIO (1688–1782), *Osservazioni . . . sopra gli errori degli architetti . . .* , 1st ed. Venice, 1771.

WINCKELMANN, JOHANN JOACHIM (1717–68), *Abhandlung von der Fahigkeit der Empfindung des Schönen in der Kunst . . .* , Dresden, 1771.

WINCKELMANN, JOHANN JOACHIM, *Critical Account of the Situation and Destruction by the First Eruptions of Mount Vesuvius, of Herculaneum, Pompeii, and Stabia . . .* , London, 1771.

1772

ALBRIZZI, G. B., *Forestiero illuminato . . .* , Venice, 1772. (1st ed. 1740.)

ALGAROTTI, FRANCESCO (1712–64), *Oeuvres du Comte Algarotti . . . traduit de l'italien . . .* , 7 vols. Berlin, 1772. (1st ed., in Italian, 1764–65.)

BOTTARI, GIOVANNI GAETANO (1689–1775), *Dialoghi sopra le tre arti del disegno corretti ed accresciuti . . .* , Naples, 1772. (1st ed. 1754.)

BRANCA, GIOVANNI (1571–1645), *Manuale d'architettura con figure delineate da Filippo Vasconi,* Rome, 1772. (1st ed. 1629.)

CAMERON, CHARLES (1740–1812), *The Baths of the Romans Explained and Illustrated . . .* , 1st ed. London, 1772.

CARLETTI, NICCOLÒ (c. 1720–96), *Instituzione d'architettura civile . . .* , 2 vols. Naples, 1772. (†)

CHAMBERS, SIR WILLIAM (1723–96), *A Dissertation on Oriental Gardening,* 1st ed. London, 1772.

DUMONT, GABRIEL-PIERRE-MARTIN (c. 1720, still active in 1790), *Projet d'une salle de spectacle pour la ville de Brest . . .* , Paris, 1772. (*)

HALFPENNY, WILLIAM (fl. 1722–55), *A New and Complete System of Architecture . . .* , London, 1772. (1st ed. 1749.)

IZZO, JOHANN BAPTIST [S.J.], *Élémens de l'architecture civile . . .* , Vienna, 1772. (*)

MILIZIA, FRANCESCO (1725–98), *Del Teatro . . .* , Rome, 1772. (1st ed. 1771.)

MURATORI, LODOVICO ANTONIO [pseud., LAMINDO PRITANIO], . . . *von dem Guten Geschmacke in den schönen Künsten und Wissenschaften* . . . , Augsburg, 1772.

PASSERI, GIOVANNI BATTISTA (1694–1780), *Discorso della ragione dell'architettura,* [Venice], 1772.

PASSERI, GIOVANNI BATTISTA, *Vite de' pittori, scultori ed architetti che anno lavorato in Roma* . . . , Rome, 1772.

POCOCKE, RICHARD (1704–65), *Voyages . . . en Orient . . . dans l'Egypte* . . . , Neuchatel, 1772–73. (1st ed., in English, 1743–45.)

ROUSSEAU, JEAN-JACQUES (1712–78), *Julie ou la nouvelle Héloïse* . . . , 3 vols. Amsterdam, 1772.

1773

ADAM, ROBERT (1728–92), and JAMES ADAM (1730–94), *The Works in Architecture of Robert and James Adam* . . . , 1st ed. 3 vols. London, 1773–1822.

BATTEUX, CHARLES (1713–80), *Les Beaux Arts réduits à un même principe,* Paris, 1773. (1st ed. 1746.)

BRETTINGHAM, MATTHEW (1699–1769), *The Plans, Elevations, and Sections of Holkham in Norfolk* . . . , London, 1773. (1st ed. 1761.)

BURKE, EDMUND (1730–97), *A Philosophic Enquiry* . . . , 7th ed. London, 1773. (1st ed. 1757.)

BURKE, EDMUND, . . . *philosophische Untersuchungen über den Ursprung unserer Begriffe vom Erhabnen und Schönen* . . . , 1st German ed. Riga, 1773.

CHAMBERS, SIR WILLIAM (1723–96), *A Dissertation on Oriental Gardening* . . . , London, 1773. (1st ed. 1772.)

COCHIN, CHARLES NICOLAS [le fils] (1715–90), *Voyage d'Italie* . . . , new ed. 3 vols. Paris, and Lausanne, 1773. (*)

GALLI DA BIBIENA, ANTONIO (1700–74), *I Disegni del nuovo teatro de quattro cavaliere eretto in Pavia* . . . , Pavia, 1773. (*)

GOETHE, JOHANN WOLFGANG VON (1749–1832), *"Von deutscher Baukunst,"* published in J. G. von Herder (1744–1803), ed., *Von deutscher Art und Kunst,* 1st ed. Hamburg, 1773. (Goethe essay appeared in 1772.)

GROSSON, J. B., *Receuil des antiquités et monuments marseillais* . . . , 1st ed. Marseilles, 1773.

GUASCO, OTTAVIO (1712–81), *Dell'Edificio di Pozzuolo, volgarmente detto il tempio di Serapide* . . . , Rome, 1773. (†)

LABACCO, ANTONIO (c. 1495–1559), *Libro d'Antonio Labacco appartenente a l'architettura nel qual si figurano alcune notabili antiquita di Roma* . . . , Rome, 1773. (1st ed. 1552.)

MILIZIA, FRANCESCO (1725–98), *Del Teatro* . . . , Venice, 1773.

MONCHABLON, E. J., *Dictionnaire abrégé d'antiquités* . . . , Paris, 1773.

POLCASTRO, GIANDOMENICO, *Notizia della scoperta fatta in Padova d'un ponte antico* . . . , Padua, 1773.

[ROSSI, G. B. DE], *Palazzi diversi nel'alma città di Roma, et altre* . . . , Rome, 1773. (1st ed. 1668?)

ROUSSEAU, JEAN-JACQUES (1712–78), *Julie ou la nouvelle Héloïse* . . . , Amsterdam, 1773.

ROUSSEAU, JEAN-JACQUES, *Julie or the New Héloïse* . . . , 3 vols. Edinburgh, 1773.

1774

AFFÒ, IRENEO (1741–97), *Antichità, e pregj della chiesa Guastallese* . . . , 1st ed. Parma, 1774.

GORI, ANTONIO FRANCESCO (1691–1757), *Museum Guarnaccii antiqua monumenta Etrusca* . . . , Florence, 1774. (*)

MENGS, ANTON RAPHAEL (1728–79), *Gedanken über die Schönheit, un über den Geschmack in der Mahlerey* . . . , Zurich, 1774.

WATELET, CLAUDE-HENRI (1718–86), *Essai sur les jardins,* 1st ed. Paris, 1774.

ROUSSEAU, JEAN-JACQUES (1712–78), *Julie ou la nouvelle Héloïse* . . . , 2 vols. London, 1774.

1775

BARBAULT, JEAN (1705–66), *Vues des plus beaux restes des antiquités romaines* . . . , Rome, 1775. (1st composite ed. of works of 1761 and 1770.)

CAMERON, CHARLES (1740–1812), *The Baths of the Romans* . . . , London, 1775. (1st ed. 1772.)

CASSINI, GIOVANNI MARIA (late 18th c.), *Raccolta delle migliori vedute . . . di Roma* . . . , 1st ed. Rome, 1775–76.

CHANDLER, RICHARD (1738–1810), *Travels in Asia Minor,* 1st ed. Oxford, 1775.

DUMONT, GABRIEL-PIERRE-MARTIN (c. 1720, still active in 1790), *Suite des projets détaillés de salles de spectacles . . .* , Paris [1775?].

MAFFEI, FRANCESCO SCIPIONE (1675–1755), *Verona illustrata . . .* , Verona, 1775. (1st ed. 1731–32.)

MARRA, FRANCESCO DELLA (1710–80), *Descrizione istorica del monastero di Monte Cassino . . .* , 2d ed. Naples, 1775. (1st ed. 1751.)

PIRANESI, GIOVANNI BATTISTA (1720–78), *Trofeo o sia magnifica colonna . . . fatte da Trajano . . .* , Rome, [1775–76].

POTTER, JOHN (1674?–1747), *Archaeologia graeca . . .* , 9th ed. 2 vols. London, 1775.

POTTER, JOHN, *Griechische Archaeologie . . .* , 3 vols. Halle, 1775–78.

ROUSSEAU, JEAN-JACQUES (1712–78), *Julie ou la nouvelle Héloïse . . .* , 6 vols. Amsterdam, 1775.

SWAN, ABRAHAM (fl. 1745–65), *The British Architect . . .* , Philadelphia, 1775. (1st ed. London, 1745.)

VENUTI, RIDOLFINO (1705–63), *Spiegazione de' bassirilievi che si osservano nell'urna sepolcrale detta volgarmente d'Alessandro Severo . . .* , Rome, 1775.

1776

BARTOLI, FRANCESCO (1745–1806), *Notizie delle pitture, sculture, ed architetture . . .* , 1st ed. 2 vols. Venice, 1776.

BERTOTTI-SCAMOZZI, OTTAVIO (1719–90), *Les Bâtimens et les desseins de André Palladio . . .* , 4 vols. Vicenza, 1776–83.

BURKE, EDMUND (1730–97), *A Philosophical Enquiry . . .* , 8th ed. London, 1776.

CHAMBERS, SIR WILLIAM (1723–96), *Traité des édifices des Chinois . . .* , Paris, 1776. (1st ed. 1757.)

CHANDLER, RICHARD (1738–1810), *Travels in Asia Minor . . .* , London, 1776. (1st ed. 1775.)

CHANDLER, RICHARD, *Travels in Greece,* 1st ed. Oxford, 1776.

FONTENAY, LOUIS-ABEL DE BONAFOUS, ABBÉ DE (1737–1806), *Dictionnaire des artistes . . .* , 1st ed. 2 vols. Paris, 1776–77.

MIRRI, LODOVICO (1747–1824), *Le Antiche Camere delle Terme di Tito . . .* , 1st ed. Rome, 1776.

ORLANDI, PELLEGRINO ANTONIO (1660–1727), *Supplemento alla sia Abecedario pittorico . . .* , Florence, 1776.

PIRANESI, GIOVANNI BATTISTA (1720–78), *Colonna Antonina,* Rome, [1776–77].

ROUSSEAU, JEAN-JACQUES (1712–78), *Eloisa . . .* , 4 vols. London, 1776.

ROUSSEAU, JEAN-JACQUES, *Julie ou la nouvelle Héloïse . . .* , 6 vols. Amsterdam, 1776.

VENUTI, RIDOLFINO (1705–63), *Veteris Latii antiquitatum . . . collectio . . . Editio altera auctior* [Edited, vol. 2 added by V. Monaldini], 2 vols. Rome, 1776.

VIGNOLA, GIACOMO BAROZZI DA (1507–73), *Nouveau Livre des cinq ordres d'architecture . . . , On y a joint aussi l'ordre français . . .* , Paris, 1776.

WINCKELMAN, JOHANN JOACHIM (1717–68), *Geschichte der Kunst des Alterthums . . .* , Vienna, 1776.

1777

CHAULNES, DUC DE (1741–c. 1789), *Mémoire sur la véritable entrée du monument Égyptien que se trouve à quatre lieues du Caire . . .* , Paris, 1777. (†)

EARLOM, RICHARD (1742–1822), *Liber Veritatis,* 1st ed. London, 1777.

GALLI DA BIBIENA, FERDINANDO (1657–1743), *Direzione a' giovani studenti nel disegno . . .* , Bologna, 1777–83. (1st ed. 1725.)

GIRARDIN, RENÉ LOUIS (1735–1808), *De La Composition des paysages . . .* , Paris, 1777. (1st ed. 1771.)

HAMILTON, WILLIAM (1730–1803), *Account of the Discoveries at Pompeii . . .* , London, 1777. (*)

MONCHABLON, E. J., *Dictionnaire abrégé d'antiquités . . .* , Paris, 1777.

ROUBO, ANDRÉ JACQUES (1739–91), *Traité de la construction des théâtres, et des machine théâtrales . . .* , 1st ed. Paris, 1777.

SULZER, JOHANN GEORG (1720–99), *Allgemeine Theorie der schönen Kunste . . .* , 2 vols. [Leipzig?], 1777. (1st ed. 1771–74.)

VIGNOLA, GIACOMO BAROZZI DA (1507–73), *Anleitung zur ganzen Civilbaukunst . . .* , Augsburg, 1777.

VITRUVIUS POLLIO, MARCUS, *The Architecture of M. Vitruvius Pollio, trans.* William Newton (*1735–90*), London, 1777.

WINCKELMAN, JOHANN JOACHIM (1717–68), *Winckelmanns Briefe an seine Freunde . . .* , Dresden, 1777–80.

WHATELEY, SIR THOMAS (d. 1772), *Observations on Modern Gardening* . . . , London, 1777. (1st ed. 1770.)

1778

ALGAROTTI, FRANCESCO (1712–64), *Opere* . . . , Cremona, 1778–84. (1st ed. 1764–65.)

CLÉRISSEAU, CHARLES LOUIS (1722–1820), *Antiquités de la France* . . . , 1st ed. Paris, 1778.

DANIELE, FRANCESCO (1740–1812), *Le Forche Caudine illustrate* . . . , 1st ed. Caserta, 1778.

MENGS, ANTON RAPHAEL (1728–79), *Die antiken Wand-und Deckengemälde des Landhauses Negroni* . . . , Rome, 1778.

MONCHABLON, E. J., *Dizionario compendioso d'antichità tradotto dal francese* . . . , [Venice?], 1778.

PIRANESI, GIOVANNI BATTISTA (1720–78), *Alcune Vedute di archi trionfali* . . . , Rome, c. 1778–92.

PIRANESI, GIOVANNI BATTISTA, *Vasi, candelabri, cippi, sarcofagi* . . . , Rome, 1778.

ROUSSEAU, JEAN-JACQUES (1712–78), *Julie ou la nouvelle Héloyse* . . . , Amsterdam, 1778.

SOANE, SIR JOHN (1753–1837), *Designs in Architecture* . . . , 1st ed. London, 1778.

TEMANZA, TOMMASO (1705–89), *Vite de' piu eccellenti architetti e scultori veneziani* . . . , 1st ed. Venice, 1778.

ZAMBONI, BALDASSARE (1730?–97), *Memorie intorno alle pubbliche fabbriche più insigne della città di Brescia* . . . , 1st ed. Brescia, 1778.

1779

ARNALDI, ENEA (1716–94), *Descrizione delle architetture, pitture e sculture di Vicenza* . . . , 1st ed. 2 vols. Vicenza, 1779.

CASSINI, GIOVANNI MARIA (late 18th c.), *Nuova Raccolta delle migliori vedute* . . . *di Roma,* Rome [c. 1779]. (1st ed. 1775–76.)

DESGODETS, ANTOINE BABUTY (1653–1728), *Les Edifices antiques de Rome* . . . , Paris, 1779. (1st ed. 1682.)

LAMY, C., *Description de deux monumens antique qui subsistent près la ville de Saint Remy, à Provence* . . . , Paris, 1779. (*)

PIRANESI, GIOVANNI BATTISTA (1720–78), *Colonna eretta in memoria dell' apoteosi di Antonio Pio e Faustina* . . . , Rome, [1779–80].

SWINBURNE, HENRY (1752–1803), *Travels through Spain in the Years 1775 and 1776* . . . , 1st ed. London, 1779.

VALCARCEL PIO DE SABOYA Y MOURA, ANTONIO (1740–1808), *Barros Saguntinos, Disertacion sobre estos monumentos antiguos,* 1st ed. Valencia, 1779.

VENUTI, RIDOLFINI (1705–63), and GIOVANNI CRISTOFORO AMADUZZI (1740–92), *Vetera Monumenta* . . . , 3 vols. Rome, 1779.

WINCKELMAN, JOHANN JOACHIM (1717–68), *Storia delle arti del disegno presso gli antichi* . . . , 2 vols. Milan, 1779.

1780

BERTOTTI-SCAMOZZI, OTTAVIO (1719–90), *Il Forestiere istrutto* . . . , Vicenza, 1780. (1st ed. 1761.)

GALLARATI, FRANCESCO MARIA, *Delle Cagione per le quali nel nostro secolo pochi riescono eccellenti disegnatori* . . . , 1st ed. Milan, 1780.

LAUTERBACH, JEAN BALTHASAR, *Kort Begrip van de burgerlyke bouwkunst volgens de proportie van het antique en het moderne* . . . , The Hague, 1780. (*)

LE CAMUS DE MÉZIÈRES, NICOLAS (1721–89), *Le Génie de l'architecture, ou l'analogie de cet art avec nos sensations,* 1st ed. Paris, 1780.

LEWIS, JAMES (1751–1820), *Original Designs in Architecture* . . . , 1st ed. London, 1780–97.

MENGS, ANTON RAPHAEL (1728–79), *Obras* . . . , 1st Spanish ed. Madrid, 1780.

MENGS, ANTON RAPHAEL, *Opere* . . . , 2 vols. in 4°. Parma, 1780.

MORELLI, COSIMO (1732–1812), *Pianto e spaccato del nuovo teatro d'Imola* . . . , Rome, 1780.

NEWTON, WILLIAM (1735–90), *Commentaires sur Vitruve éclaircis par les fig. et propres à être joints aux différentes traductions de cet auteur* . . . , London, 1780.

PAUSANIAS (2d half of 2d c. B.C.), *An Account of the Statues, Pictures and Temples in Greece* . . . *translated* . . . *by U. Price* . . . , London, 1780.

PIRANESI, FRANCESCO (1748–1810), *Raccolta de'tempj antichi* . . . *in Tivoli* . . . , Rome, [1780].

PIRANESI, GIOVANNI BATTISTA (1720–78), *Trofei di Ottaviano Augusto* . . . , Rome, 1780.

PRETI, FRANCESCO MARIA (1701–74), *Elementi d'architettura* . . . , 1st ed. Venice, 1780.

SULZER, JOHANN GEORG (1720–99), *Bemerkungen auf einer Reise im Jahre 1775 und 76, aus Deutschland nach der Schweiz und Ober Italien* . . . , Bern, 1780.

VIGNOLA, GIACOMO BAROZZI DA (1507–73), *Manuale di architettura di Giacomo Borozzio da Vignola con l'aggiunta di dodici facciate delle più belle chiese di Roma* . . . , Rome, 1780.

VIGNOLA, GIACOMO BAROZZI DA, *Nouveau Livre des cinq ordres d'architecture* . . . , Paris, [c. 1780–90].

VIGNOLA, GIACOMO BAROZZI DA, *Il Vignola illustrato* . . . , 2d ed. Rome, 1780.

WALPOLE, HORACE (1717–97), *On Modern Gardening,* 1st ed. Strawberry Hill, 1780.

1781

ADLER, GEORG CHRISTIAN (1734–1804), *Ausfürliche Beschreibung der Stadt Rom,* 1st ed. Altona, 1781.

ANTONINI, CARLO (late 18th c.), *Manuale de varj ornamenti* . . . , 1st ed. Rome, 1781–90.

BIANCONI, GIOVANNI LODOVICO (1717–1781), *Biographie des Ritters Anton Raphael Mengs* . . . , Vienna, 1781. (1st ed., in Italian, 1780.)

FALCONET, ÉTIENNE MAURICE, *Oeuvres* . . . *contenantes plusiers écrits relatifs aux beaux arts* . . . , 1st ed. 6 vols. Lausanne, 1781.

LACOMBE, JACQUES (1724–1811), *Dizionario portabile delle belle arti* . . . , Bassano, 1781. (1st ed., in French, 1752.)

LE CLERC, SEBASTIAN (1637–1714), *Neue Abhandlung von der Civil-Baukunst* . . . , Nuremberg, 1781. (1st German ed. 1759.)

LONGINUS, DIONYSIUS (d. 273), *Longin vom Erhabenen* . . . , Leipzig, 1781.

MAJOR, THOMAS (1720–99), *Die Ruinen von Paestum oder Posidonia* . . . , 1st German ed. Würzburg, 1781. (1st English ed. 1768.)

MENGS, ANTON RAPHAEL (1728–79), *Oeuvres de M. le Chevalier Antoine Raphael Mengs* . . . , 1st French ed. Amsterdam and Paris, 1781.

MILIZIA, FRANCESCO (1725–98), *Dell' Arte di vedere nelle belle arti* . . . , 1st ed. Venice, 1781.

MILIZIA, FRANCESCO, *Memorie degli architetti antichi e moderni,* 3d ed. 2 vols. Parma, 1781.

MILIZIA, FRANCESCO, *Principj di architettura civile* . . . , 1st ed. 3 vols. Finale, 1781.

N. N., *Notizie istoriche dell'antica, e presente magnifica cattedrale d'Orvieto* . . . , Rome, 1781.

ORTIZ Y SANZ, JOSÉ FRANCISCO (1739–1822), *Abaton Reseratum* . . . *cap. ult. lib. tert. architecturae M. Vitruvii Pollionis* . . . , 1st ed. Rome, 1781.

PATERNÒ-CASTELLÓ, IGNAZIO (1719–86), *Viaggio per tutte le antichità delle Sicilia descritto* . . . , Naples, 1781.

ROUSSEAU, JEAN-JACQUES (1712–78), *La Nouvelle Héloïse* . . . , 4 vols. Geneva, 1780–81.

SAINT-NON, JEAN-CLAUDE RICHARD DE (1727–91), *Voyage pittoresque et description des royaumes de Naples et de Sicile* . . . , 1st ed. 4 vols. Paris, 1781–86.

TEMANZA, TOMMASO (1705–89), *Antica pianta dell'inclita città di Venezia* . . . , Venice, 1781.

VIGNOLA, GIACOMO BAROZZI DA (1507–73), *Kunst die fünf architektonische Saulenordnungen* . . . , Augsburg, 1781.

WALPOLE, HORACE (1719–97), *On Modern Gardening,* London, 1782. (1st ed. 1780).

WINCKELMANN, JOHANN JOACHIM (1717–68), *Histoire de l'art de l'antiquité* . . . , 3 vols. Leipzig and Yverdon, 1781.

WINCKELMANN, JOHANN JOACHIM, *Lettres familières (Éloge de M. Winckelmann par M. Heyne),* Amsterdam, 1781.

1782

ALBERTI, LEON BATTISTA (1404–72), *Della Architettura, della pittura e della statua. Traduzione di Cosimo Bartoli* . . . , Bologna, 1782.

ALBERTOLLI, GIOCONDO (1742–1839), *Ornamenti diversi* . . . , 1st ed. Milan, 1782.

ANTOINE, PIERRE-JOSEPH (1730–1814), *Série des colonnes,* Dijon, 1782.

BARBAULT, JEAN (1705–66), *Denkmäler des alten Roms* . . . , Augsburg, 1782. (1st ed., in French, 1761.)

BAROZZI, SERAFINO (1750s–c. 1800), *Pianta e spaccato della celebre chiesa di San Vitale di Ravenna* . . . , 1st ed. Bologna, 1782.

BURKE, EDMUND (1730–97), *A Philosophical Enquiry* . . . , 9th. ed. London, 1782.

CHOISEUL-GOUFFIER, COMTE DE (1752–1817), *Voyage pittoresque de la Grèce*, Paris, 1782.

DUPUIS, CHARLES (18th c.), *Traité d'architecture* . . . , Paris, 1782. (*)

GRANDIDIER, PHILIPPE ANDRÉ (1752–87), *Essais historiques et topographiques sur l'Église Cathédrale de Strasbourg* . . . , 1st ed. Strasbourg, 1782.

HOUEL, JEAN-PIERRE-LOUIS-LAURENT (1735–1813), *Voyage pittoresque des isles de Sicile, de Malte et de Lipari* . . . , 1st ed. 4 vols. Paris, 1782–87.

LE CLERC, SEBASTIAN (1637–1714), *Traité d'architecture* . . . , Nuremberg, 1782.

LONGINUS, DIONYSIUS (d. 273), *L'Aureo Trattao . . . intorno al sublime modo* . . . , Venice, 1782.

MENGS, ANTON RAPHAEL (1728–79), *Oeuvres* . . . , Ratisbon, 1782.

MURATORI, LODOVICO ANTONIO [pseud., LAMINDO PRITANIO], *Reflexiones sobre el buen gusto en las ciencias y en las artes* . . . , Madrid, 1782.

PATTE, PIERRE (1732–1814), *Essai sur l'architecture théâtrale* . . . , 1st ed. Paris, 1782.

RANGHIASCI-BRANCALEONI, SEBASTIANO (1747–1822), *Del Tempietto di Marte Ciprio e de' suoi monumenti* . . . , Perugia, 1782.

SARNELLI, POMPEO (1649–1724), *La Guida . . . di Pozzuoli, Baja, Cuma* . . . , Naples, 1782.

VIGNOLA, GIACOMO BAROZZI DA (1507–73), *Bürgerliche Baukunst nach den Grund Regeln der fünff Säulenordnung* . . . , Nuremberg, 1782.

1783

BARBAULT, JEAN (1705–66), *Monumens antiques, ou collection choisie d'anciens bas-relief* . . . , 1st ed. Rome, 1783.

BARTOLI, PIETRO SANTI (1635–1700), *Recueil de peintures antiques trouvées à Rome* . . . , Paris, 1783–87. (1st French ed. 1757–60.)

CASSINI, GIOVANNI MARIA (late 18th c.), *Pitture antiche ritrovate nello scavo* . . . , Rome, 1783. (†)

CHAULNES, DUC DE (1741–c. 1789), *Mémoire sur la véritable entrée du monument Egyptien que se trouve à quatre lieues du Caire* . . . , Rome and Paris, 1783. (1st ed. 1777.)

GAUTTANI, GIUSEPPE ANTONIO (1748–1830), *Della Gran Cella solare nelle terme di Antonino Caracalla* . . . , Rome, 1783. (†)

GIRARDIN, RENÉ LOUIS (1735–1808), *An Essay on Landscape* . . . , 1st English ed. London, 1783. (1st ed. 1771.)

MENGS, ANTON RAPHAEL (1728–79), *Opere* . . . , 2 vols. in 8°. Bassano, 1783.

MONCHABLON, E. J., *Dizionario compendioso d'antichità tradotto dal francese* . . . , 2d Italian ed. Venice, 1778. (1st ed. 1760; 1st Italian ed. 1778.)

PAUSANIAS (2d half of 2d c. B.C.), *Pausanias . . . ou voyage historique de la Grèce, traduit par Gédoyn* . . . , Paris, 1783.

PIRANESI, FRANCESCO (1748–1810), *Teatro d'Ercolano* . . . , n.p., [1783].

ROUSSEAU, JEAN-JACQUES (1712–78), *La Nouvelle Héloïse* . . . , Geneva, 1783.

SWINBURNE, HENRY (1752–1803), *Travels in the Two Sicilies in . . . 1777, 1778, 1779, and 1780* . . . , 1st ed. London, 1783–85.

WINCKELMANN, JOHANNES JOACHIM (1717–68), *Remarques sur l'architecture des anciens* . . . , Paris, 1783.

WINCKELMANN, JOHANN JOACHIM, *Storia delle arti del disegno presso gli antichi* . . . , 3 vols. in 4. Rome, 1783–84.

1784

ALGAROTTI, FRANCESCO (1712–64), *Saggio sopra l'architettura,* Venice, 1784. (1st ed. 1753 or 1756.)

BARTOLI, COSIMO (c. 1503–1572), *I Dieci Libri di architettura di Leon Battista Alberti* . . . , Rome, 1784.

CERATO, DOMENICO VICENTINO (1720–92), *Nouvo Metodo per insegnare li cinque ordini d'architettura civile* . . . , 1st ed. 2 vols. Padua, 1784.

CONTI DI CALEPIO, NICOLINI DE, *Elementi d'architettura civile* . . . , Bergamo, 1784. (*)

COSTA, GIANFRANCESCO (1711–72), *I Cinque Ordini di architettura di Andrea Palladio* . . . , Venice, 1784. (1st ed. 1746.)

DANIELE, FRANCESCO (1740–1812), *I Regali Sepolcri del Duomo di Palermo* . . . , 1st ed. Naples, 1784.

MAGNONI, PASQUALE, *. . . De Veris Posidoniae et Paesti* . . . , Naples, 1784.

MENGS, ANTON RAPHAEL (1728–79), *Antologia dell' arte pittorica* . . . , Augusta, 1784.

MILIZIA, FRANCESCO (1725–98), *Principj di architectura civile* . . . , Leipzig, 1784–86. (1st ed., Finale, 1781.)

PALLADIO, ANDREA (1508–80), *Gli Ordini di architettura di A. P. designati de incisi da A. Balzafiori* . . . , Vicenza, 1784.

PAOLI, PAOLO ANTONIO (1720?–90?), *Rovine della Città di Pesto detta ancora Posidonia* . . . , 1st ed. Rome, 1784.

PIRANESI, GIOVANNI BATTISTA (1720–78), *Le Antichità romane* . . . , Rome, 1784.

RANGHIASCI-BRANCALEONI, SEBASTIANO (1747–1822), *Del Tempietto di Marte Ciprio e de' suoi' monumenti* . . . , Perugia, 1784.

ROUSSEAU, JEAN-JACQUES (1712–78), *Eloisa . . . to Which Is Now First Added the Sequel of Julia or the New Eloisa* . . . , 4 vols. London, 1784.

SANCTIS, DOMENICO DE, *Dissertazione sopre I, La Villa d'Orazio Flacco; II, Il Mausoleo dei Plauzii in Tivoli; III, Antino, città municipale de Marsi* . . . , Ravenna, 1784.

SARNELLI, POMPEO (1649–1724), *La Guida . . . di Pozzuoli, Baja, Cuma* . . . , Naples, 1784.

STERN, GIOVANNI (1734–94), *Piante, elevazioni, profili, e spaccati degli edificj della villa suburbana di Giulio III, fuori di Porta Flaminia* . . . , Rome, 1784.

WINCKELMANN, JOHANN JOACHIM (1717–68), *. . . Briefe an einem Freund in Liefland. Mit einem Anhang (Anmerkungen über die Alterthümer in Rom)* . . . , Coburg, 1784.

WINCKELMANN, JOHANN JOACHIM, *Lettres familières de M. Winckelmann* . . . , Yverdon, 1784.

WINCKELMANN, JOHANN JOACHIM, *Recueil de lettres de M. Winckelmann, sur les découvertes faites à Herculaneum, à Pompeii, à Stabia, à Caserte et à Rome* . . . , Paris, 1784.

1785

ANTOLINI, GIOVANNI (1754–1842), *L'Ordine dorico, ossia il Tempio d'Ercole nella città di Cori* . . . , Rome, 1785. (†)

BERTOTTI-SCAMOZZI, OTTAVIO (1719–90), *Le Terme dei romani disegnate da Andrea Palladio* . . . , 1st Italian ed. Vicenza, 1785.

BIAGI, CLEMENTE [le père] (1740–1804), *Monumenta Graeca ex museo* . . . , 1st ed. 2 vols. Rome, 1785–87.

DENON, DOMINIQUE VIVANT (1747–1825), *Voyage de Henri Swinburne dans les Deux Siciles* . . . , 5 vols. Paris, [1785–87]. (Translated from the English with notes of Swinburne, 1783–85.)

GERLI, AGOSTINO (18th c.), *Opuscoli in materia d'architettura* . . . , 1st ed. Parma, 1785.

[GOUGH, RICHARD (1735–1809)], *A Comparative View of the Ancient Monuments of India* . . . , London, 1785. (*)

HUGUES, PIERRE FRANÇOIS [called D'HANCARVILLE] (1719–1805), *Antiquités etrusques, grecques et romaines* . . . , 5 vols. Paris, 1785–88. (1st ed. 1766.)

HUGUES, PIERRE FRANÇOIS [called D'HANCARVILLE], *Recherches sur l'origine, l'esprit, et les progres des arts de la Grèce* . . . , 1st ed. 3 vols. London, 1785.

MILIZIA, FRANCESCO (1725–98), *Dell'Arte di vedere nelle belle arti del disegno* . . . , Halle, 1785.

MILIZIA, FRANCESCO, *Memorie degli architetti antichi e moderni,* 4th ed. Bassano, 1785.

MILIZIA, FRANCESCO, *Principj di architettura civile,* 3 vols. Bassano, 1785.

MURATORI, LODOVICO ANTONIO [pseud., LAMINDO PRITANIO], *Delle Riflessioni sopra il buon gusto nelle scienze e nell'arti* . . . , Naples, 1785.

PIRANESI, FRANCESCO (1748–1810), *Monumenti degli Scipioni* . . . , [Rome], 1785.

TARQUINI, GIUSEPPE (18th c.), *Fedele Descrizione circa il piantato, elevazione e volta del nuovo teatro di Tor di Nona* . . . , 1st ed. Rome, 1785.

WALPOLE, HORACE (1717–97), *On Modern Gardening,* Strawberry Hill, 1785. (1st ed. 1780.)

WHATELEY, SIR THOMAS (d. 1772), *Observations on Modern Gardening,* London, 1785. (1st ed. 1770.)

1786

BARTOLUCCI, VINCENTI (1753–1823), *Dissertatio de viis publicis* . . . , Rome, 1786. (*)

[BELGRADO, JACQUES] (1704–89), *Dell'Architettura egiziana* . . . , 1st ed. Parma, 1786.

BENE, BENEDETTO DEL (1749–1825), *Osservazioni sopra l'origine ultimamente attribuita all'anfiteatro di Verona . . .* , Verona, 1786. (†)

BERTOTTI-SCAMOZZI, OTTAVIO (1719–90), *Les Bâtimens et les desseins de André Palladio . . .* , Vicenza, 1786.

COLUCCI, GIUSEPPE (b. 1752), *Delle Antichità picene . . .* , 1st ed. 31 vols. Fermo, 1786–94.

DELAGARDETTE, CLAUDE MATHIEU (1762–1805), *Règles des cinq ordres d'architecture de Vignole, avec un détail d'un ordre dorique de Poestum . . .* , 1st ed. Paris, 1786.

FEA, CARLO (1753–1834), *Risposta alle osservazioni del Cav. Onofrio Boni sul tomo III. della storia delle arti del disegno di Gio. Winckelmann . . .* , Rome, 1786.

GOUGH, RICHARD (1735–1809), *Sepulchral Monuments in Great Britain . . . from the Norman Conquest to the 17th century . . .* , 1st ed. 3 vols. London, 1786–96.

LANDE, JÉRÔME DE LA (1732–1807), *Voyage en Italie . . .* , 2d ed. 8 vols. Paris, 1786. (1st ed. 1769.)

MEMMO, ANDREA (1729–93), *Elementi dell'architettura Lodoliana . . .* , 1st ed. Rome, 1786.

MENGS, ANTON RAPHAEL (1728–79), *. . . Hinterlassene Werke . . .* , Halle, 1786.

MENGS, ANTON RAPHAEL, *Oeuvres complètes, traduites de l'Italien . . .* , 2 vols. Paris, 1786.

MILIZIA, FRANCESCO (1725–98), *Dell'Arte di vedere nelle belle arti . . .* , 2d ed. Genoa, 1786.

PASSERI, GIOVANNI BATTISTA (1694–1780), *Leben der Maler, Bildhauer und Baumeister welche zu Rom im 16. Jahrhundert gearbeitet haben . . .* , 1st German ed. Dresden and Leipzig, 1786.

ROUSSEAU, JEAN-JACQUES (1712–78), *La nouvelle Héloïse . . .* , 6 vols. Geneva, 1786.

SULZER, JOHANN GEORG, *Allgemeine Theorie der schönen Kunste . . .* , 4 vols. Leipzig, 1786–87. (1st ed. 1771–74.)

VIGNOLA, GIACOMO BAROZZI DA (1507–73), *Règles d'architecture . . .* , Paris, 1786.

WALPOLE, HORACE (1717–97), *On Modern Gardening*, London, 1786. (1st ed. 1780).

WINCKELMANN, JOHANN JOACHIM (1717–68), *Recueil de différentes pièces sur les arts . . .* , Paris, 1786.

1787

ALBERTOLLI, GIOCONDO (1742–1839), *Alcune Decorazioni di nobile sale, ed altri ornamenti . . .* , Milan, 1787. (*)

BAILS, BENITO (b. 1743), *Arquitectura civil*, vol. 9 of *Elementos de Matemáticas*, 10 vols. Madrid, 1787–93. (†)

BARBAULT, JEAN (1705–66), *Vues des plus beaux restes des antiquités romaines . . .* , Rome, 1787. (1st ed. 1781.)

BURKE, EDMUND (1730–97), *A Philosophical Enquiry . . .* , new ed. London, 1787.

FALCONET, ÉTIENNE MAURICE, *Oeuvres . . .* , new ed. 3 vols. Paris, 1787. (1st ed. 1781.)

GIBELIN, ANTOINE ESPRIT (1739–1814), *Lettres sur les tours antiques qu'on démolies à Aix en Provence . . .* , 1st ed. Aix, 1787.

MENGS, ANTON RAPHAEL (1728–79), *Oeuvres complètes . . .* , Paris, 1787.

MENGS, ANTON RAPHAEL, *Opere . . .* , Rome, 1787.

MILIZIA, FRANCESCO (1725–98), *Roma, delle belle arti del disegno: parte prima: dell' architettura civile*, 1st ed. Bassano, 1787.

QUARENGHI, GIACOMO (1774–1817), *Théâtre de l'Hermitage de S.M. l'Imperatrice de toute les Russies . . .* , 1st ed. St. Petersburg, 1787.

REYNOLDS, SIR JOSHUA, *Delle Arti del disegno . . .* , Bassano, 1787.

RIEM, ANDREAS (1749–1807), *Über die Malerie der Alten . . .* , Berlin, 1787. (*)

ROSSO, GIUSEPPE DEL (1760?–1831), *Ricerche sull'architettura egiziana, e su ciò che i Greci pare abbiano preso da quella nazione . . .* , 1st ed. Florence, 1787.

ROUSSEAU, JEAN-JACQUES (1712–78), *La Nouvelle Héloïse . . .* , Geneva, 1787.

SALIMBENI, LEONARDO (late 18th c.), *Degli Archi e delle volte . . .* , Verona, 1787. (*)

STUART, JAMES (1713–88), and NICHOLAS REVETT (1721–1804), *The Antiquities of Athens*, London, 1787 [1789?]. (1st ed. Vol. I, 1762.)

VIGNOLA, GIACOMO BAROZZI DA (1507–73), *Neue Ausgabe der Lehre von den Säulenordnungen . . .* , Augsburg, 1787.

VIGNOLA, GIACOMO BAROZZI DA, *Regras das cinco ordens de architectura de Jacomo Barozio de Vinhola, . . .* , Lisbon, 1787.

VITRUVIUS POLLIO, MARCUS, *Los Diez Libros de architectura de M. Vitruvio Polión traducidos del Latin, y comentados por Don Joseph Ortíz Y Sanz . . .* , Madrid, 1787.

1788

BULLET, PIERRE, *Architecture pratique . . .* , Paris, 1788. (1st ed. 1691.)

CARLI, GIOVANNI RINALDO (1720–95), *Degli Anfiteatri, e particolarmente del Flavio . . .* , Milan, 1788. (†)

CARLI, GIOVANNI RINALDO, *Delle Antichità italiche . . .* , 1st ed. Milan, 1788–91.

COMOLLI, ANGELO, *Bibliografia storico-critica dell'architettura civile, ed arti subalterne . . .* , 1st ed. 4 vols. Rome, 1788–92.

CORDINER, CHARLES (fl. 1790s), *Remarkable Ruins, and Romantic Prospects of North Britain . . .* , 2 vols. London, 1788. (*)

DENON, DOMINIQUE VIVANT (1741–1825), *Voyage en Sicile . . .* , Paris, 1788. (1st French ed. 1785–87.)

FEA, CARLO (1753–1834), *Progetto per una nuova edizione dell'architettura di Vitruvio . . .* , Rome, 1788.

LESSING, GOTTHOLD EPHRAIM (1728–81), *Laokoon . . .* , Berlin, 1788. (1st ed. 1766.)

MASI, GIROLAMO, *Teoria e pratica di architettura civile . . .* , Rome, 1788.

MEMMO, ANDREA (1729–93), *Riflessioni sopra alcuni equivoci . . . intorno l'architettura, in difesa del fù F. Carlo Lodoli,* Padua, 1788.

ORLANDI, PELLEGRINO ANTONIO (1660–1727), *Abecedario pittorico . . .* , Florence, 1788.

QUATREMÈRE DE QUINCY, ANTOINE CHRYSOSTOME (1755–1849), *Encyclopédie méthodique d'architecture . . .* , 1st ed. 3 vols. Paris, 1788–1825.

ROUSSEAU, JEAN-JACQUES (1712–78), *Amori di Milord Boniston. Novella morale . . .* , Naples, 1788.

ROUSSEAU, JEAN-JACQUES, *La Nouvelle Héloïse . . .* , 3 vols. Geneva, 1788.

ROUSSEAU, JEAN-JACQUES, *La Nouvelle Héloïse . . .* , 2 vols. Leipzig, 1788.

SOANE, SIR JOHN (1753–1837), *Plans . . . of Buildings . . .* , 1st ed. London, 1788.

1789

ALDRICH, HENRY (1648–1710), *The Elements of Civil Architecture . . .* , Oxford, 1789.

BIANCONI, GIOVANNI LODOVICO, and CARLO FEA (1753–1834), *Descrizione dei cirche particolaremente di quello di Caracalla . . .* , 1st ed. Rome, 1789.

CIPRIANI, GIOVANNI BATTISTA (1727–85), *A collection of Prints . . . engraved by Richard Earlom . . .* , London, 1789.

DENON, DOMINIQUE VIVANT (1747–1825), *Travels in Sicily and Malta . . .* , London, 1789. (1st ed., in French, 1785–87.)

DURAND, JEAN-NICOLAS-LOUIS (1760–1834), *Views of the Principal Buildings in Paris and its Environs . . .* , 1st ed. [Paris, 1789?].

GUARNIERI OTTONI, AURELIO (1748–88), *Dissertazione intorno al corso dell'antica Via Claudia dalla città d'Altino sino al Danubio . . .* , 1st ed. Bassano, 1789.

LANZI, LUIGI (1732–1810), *Saggio di lingua etrusca . . .* , 1st ed. 2 vols. Rome, 1789.

LANZI, LUIGI, *Storia pittorica dell' Italia dal' risorgimento delle belle arti fin presso al fine del XVIII secolo . . .* , 1st ed. Bassano, 1789.

MILIZIA, FRANCESCO (1725–98), *Del Teatro . . .* , Venice, 1789.

MILIZIA, FRANCESCO, *Trattato completo, formale e materiale del teatro . . .* , Madrid, 1789.

PEYRE, MARIE-JOSEPH (1730–85), *Disertacion de Arquitectura . . .* , Madrid, 1789. (†)

PIERMARINI, GIUSEPPE (1734–1808), *Architettura del Teatro della Scala in Milano . . .* , 1st ed. n.p., 1789.

ROUSSEAU, JEAN-JACQUES (1712–78), *Aventures d'Edward Bomston . . .* , Lausanne and Paris, 1789.

ROUSSEAU, JEAN-JACQUES, *Julie ou la Nouvelle Héloïse . . .* , 3 vols. Prague, 1788–89.

VASARI, GIORGIO (1512–74), *Vita di M. Jacopo Sansovino scultore e architetto . . .* , 2d ed. Venice, 1789.

1790

ALISON, ARCHIBALD (1757–1839), *Essays on the Nature and Principles of Taste,* 1st ed. London, 1790.

FEA, CARLO (1753–1834), *Miscellanea filogica, critica, e antiquaria . . .* , 1st ed. Rome, 1790.

KANT, IMMANUEL (1724–1804), *Kritik der Urteilskraft . . .* , 1st ed. Berlin and Libau, 1790.

MURATORI, LODOVICO ANTONIO [pseud., LAMINDO PRITANIO], *Delle Riflessioni sopra il buon gusto nelle scienze e nell'arti* . . . , Venice, 1790.

PIRANESI, FRANCESCO (1748–1810), *Seconda Parte di tempi antichi che contiene il celebre Panteon* . . . , Rome, 1790.

PISTOCCHI, GIUSEPPE (1744–1814), *Prospetto d'un teatro* . . . , 1st ed. Faenza, 1790.

RICCATI, FRANCESCO (1718–91), *Delle Costruzione de' teatri secondo il costume d'Italia* . . . , 1st ed. Bassano, 1790.

RONDELET, JEAN BAPTISTE (1734–1829), *Mémoire sur l'architecture considérée généralment* . . . , Paris, 1790. (*)

SCHMIDT, FRIEDRICH CHRISTIAN (1755–1830), *Der bürgliche Baumeister* . . . , 1st ed. Gotha, 1790–99.

SOANE, SIR JOHN (1753–1837), *Designs in Architecture* . . . , London, 1790. (1st ed. 1778.)

VITRUVIUS POLLIO, MARCUS, *L'Architettura di Marco Vitruvio . . . commentata dal Marchese Berardo Galiani* . . . , 2d ed. Siena and Naples, 1790.

WALPOLE, HORACE (1717–97), *Essai sur l'art des jardins modernes* . . . , Paris, [c. 1790].

WINCKELMANN, JOHANN JOACHIM (1717–68), *Histoire de l'art chez les anciens* . . . , 2 vols. in 3. Paris, 1790–1803.

WRIGHT, WILLIAM, *Grotesque Architecture* . . . , 2d ed. London, 1790. (1st ed. 1767.)

1791

ALGAROTTI, FRANCESCO (1712–64), *Opere* . . . , new ed. Venice, 1791–94.

CHAMBERS, SIR WILLIAM (1723–96), *A Treatise on the Decorative Part of Civil Architecture* . . . , 3d ed. (considerably augmented) London, 1791. (1st ed. 1759.)

DALTON, RICHARD (c. 1715–91), *Antiquities and Views in Greece and Egypt* . . . , London, 1791. (=)

HIRT, ALOYS LUDWIG (1759–1837), *Osservazioni istorico-architettoniche sopra il Panteon* . . . , Rome, 1791. (*)

KEERL, JOHANN H., *Über die Ruinen Herkulanums und Pompeii* . . . , Gotha, 1791. (*)

MALASPINA DI SANNAZARO, LUIGI (1754–1834), *Delle Leggi del bello applicate all pittura, e architettura* . . . , Pavia, 1791.

NEWTON, WILLIAM (1735–90), *The Architecture of M. Vitruvius Polio* . . . , London, 1791.

QUATREMÈRE DE QUINCY, ANTOINE CHRYSOSTOME (1755–1849), *Considerations sur les arts du dessin en France* . . . , Paris, (1791). (†)

ROUSSEAU, JEAN-JACQUES (1712–78), *Julie ou la nouvelle Héloïse* . . . , Amsterdam, 1791.

VALLE, GUGLIEMO DELLA (1740?–94?), *Storia del duomo di Orvieto* . . . , Rome, 1791.

VASARI, GIORGIO (1512–74), *Vite di più eccellenti pittori, scultori e architetti* . . . , Siena, 1791–94.

WINCKELMANN, JOHANN JOACHIM (1717–68), *Alte Denkmäler der Kunst* . . . , 2 vols. Berlin, 1791–92.

1792

BURKE, EDMUND (1730–97), *A Philosophical Enquiry* . . . , new ed. London, 1792.

CELANO, CARLO, *Notizie del bello* . . . , 4th ed. Naples, 1792. (1st ed. 1692.)

COLUCCI, GIUSEPPE (b. 1752), *Antichità ascolani illustrate* . . . , Fermo, 1792. (†)

CORNIDE DE SAAVEDRA, JOSEF, *Investigaciones sobre la fundacion y fabbrica de la torre . . . de Hercules . . . de la coruna* . . . , Madrid, 1792. (*)

FRONTINUS, SEXTUS JULIUS (40–103), *De Aqueductibus Romae . . .* [edited by Georg Christian Adler], Altona, 1792. (1st ed. by Adler; see also ed. of 1722.)

[FUMIGALLI, A. (1728–1804), and others] *Delle Antichità Longobardico-Milanesi* . . . , 1st ed. 4 vols. Milan, 1792–93.

GILPIN, WILLIAM (1724–1804), *Three essays . . . on Picturesque Beauty; on Picturesque Travel; and on Sketching Landscape,* London, 1792. (=)

KANT, IMMANUEL (1724–1804), *Kritik der Urteilskraft* . . . , Frankfurt and Leipzig, 1792.

MALTON, THOMAS (1748–1804), *A Picturesque Tour through the Cities of London and Westminster* . . . , 2 vols. London, 1792. (*)

MILIZIA, FRANCESCO (1725–98), *Dell' Arte di vedere nelle belle arti di disegno* . . . , Venice, 1792.

MOORE, JAMES, *Monastic Remains and Ancient Castles in England and Wales,* London, 1792. (*)

NORDEN, FRIDERIK LUDVIG, *The Antiquities, Natural History, Ruins, and other Curiosities of Egypt* . . . , London, 1792. (*)

PAUSANIAS (2d half of 2d c. B.C.), *Pausania viaggio istorico* . . . , 5 vols. Rome, 1792–93.

ROUSSEAU, JEAN-JACQUES (1712–78), *Julie ou la nouvelle Héloïse* . . . (*Précédée du: Voyage à Ermenonville, par Le Tourneu*), Lausanne, 1792.

SMITH, JOHN (1749–1831), *Select Views in Italy with Topographical and Historical Descriptions* . . . , 1st ed. 2 vols. London, 1792–96.

SULZER, JOHANN GEORG (1720–99), *Allgemeine Theorie der schönen Kunste* . . . , 4 vols. Leipzig, 1792–94. (1st ed. 1771–74.)

VIGNOLA, GIACOMO BAROZZI DA (1507–73), *Le Nouveau Vignole ou règles des cinq ordres* . . . , Paris, 1792.

WATELET, CLAUDE-HENRI (1718–86), and PIERRE CHARLES LÉVESQUE (1736–1812), *Dictionnaire des arts* . . . , 1st ed. 5 vols. Paris, 1792.

WINCKELMANN, JOHANN JOACHIM (1717–68), *Sendschreiben von den Herculanischen Entdeckungen,* Dresden, 1792.

1793

BIANCHI, ISODORO (1733–1807), *Antichi Monumenti della gente magia* . . . , Cremona, 1793. (*)

CARLI, GIOVANNI RINALDO (1720–95), *Delle Antichità italiche* . . . , 2d ed. 4 vols. Milan, 1793–95. (1st ed. 1788–91.)

HADRAWA, NORBERT, *Ragguagli di varj scavi e scoverti di antichità fatte nell'Isola di Capri* . . . , 1st ed. Naples, 1793.

KANT, IMMANUEL (1724–1804), *Kritik der Urteilskraft* . . . , Berlin, 1793.

MENGS, ANTON RAPHAEL (1728–79), *Die Antiken Wand-und Deckengemälde des Landhauses Negroni* . . . , Rome, 1793.

PALOS Y NAVARRO, ENRIQUE, *Disertación sobre el teatro y circo de Sagunto* . . . , Valencia, 1793.

PAUSANIAS (2d half of 2d c. B.C.), *The Description of Greece* . . . , 3 vols. London, 1793.

ROUSSEAU, JEAN-JACQUES (1712–78), *Begebenheit Edvard Bomstons in Italien* . . . n.p. n.d. [c. 1793].

ROUSSEAU, JEAN-JACQUES, *La Nouvelle Héloïse* . . . , 6 vols. Avignon, 1793.

SOANE, SIR JOHN (1753–1837), *Sketches in Architecture* . . . , 1st ed. London, 1793.

WATELET, CLAUDE-HENRI (1718–86), and PIERRE CHARLES LÉVESQUE (1736–1812), *Aesthetisches Worterbuch über die bildenden Kunst* . . . , Leipzig, 1793. (1st ed., in French, 1792.)

1794

FOSSATI, CARLO GIUSEPPE (b. 1737), *La Temple de Malateste de Rimini* . . . , 1st ed. Fuligno, 1794.

GILPIN, WILLIAM (1724–1804), *Three Essays* . . . *on Picturesque Beauty* . . . , London, 1794. (1st ed. 1792.)

HADRAWA, NORBERT, *Briefe über* . . . *der Insel Capri* . . . , Dresden, 1794. (1st ed., in Italian, 1793.)

HADRAWA, NORBERT, *Ragguagli di varj scavi* . . . *di Capri* . . . , Dresden, 1794. (1st ed. 1793.)

KANT, IMMANUEL (1724–1804), *Kritik der Urteilskraft* . . . , Frankfort and Leipzig, 1794.

KNIGHT, RICHARD PAYNE (1750–1824), *The Landscape* . . . , 1st ed. London, 1794.

MILIZIA, FRANCESCO (1725–98), *Trattato completo, formale e materiale del teatro* . . . , 5th ed. Venice, 1794.

PAUSANIAS (2d half of 2d c. B.C.), *The Description of Greece* . . . , 3 vols. London, 1794.

PAUSANIAS, *Graeciae descriptio* . . . , 4 vols. Leipzig, 1794–96.

PIROLI, TOMMASO (1750–1824), *Gli Edificj antichi di Roma* . . . , [Rome, 1794].

PRICE, SIR UVEDALE (1747–1829), *An Essay on the Picturesque,* 1st ed. London, 1794–98.

REPTON, HUMPHREY (1752–1818), *Sketches and Hints on Landscape Gardening,* 1st ed. London, 1794.

ROUSSEAU, JEAN-JACQUES (1712–78), *Julia or The New Eloïsa* . . . , 3 vols. Edinburgh, 1794.

ROUSSEAU, JEAN-JACQUES, *Julie ou la nouvelle Héloïse* . . . , 6 vols. Paris, 1794.

SWAN, ABRAHAM (fl. 1745–65), *The British Architect: or, The Builder's Treasury of Stair-cases* . . . , Boston, 1794. (1st ed., London, 1745.)

TONCI, SALVATORE (1756–1844), *Descrizione ragionata della Galleria Doria* . . . , 1st ed. Rome, 1794.

TOSCA, TOMAS VICENTE (1651–1723), *"Ar-*

quitectura civil," *Compendio Matemático,* 5, Valencia, 1794.

WINCKELMANN, JOHANN JOACHIM (1717–68), *Histoire de l'art chez les anciens . . . ,* 2 vols. Paris, 1794.

ZANI, PIETRO (1748–1821), *Enciclopedia metodica delle arti . . . ,* 1st ed. Parma, 1794.

1795

DANIELL, THOMAS (1749–1840), *Oriental Scenery,* London, 1795–1807. (†)

DESGODETS, ANTOINE BABUTY (1653–1728), *The Ancient Buildings of Rome . . . ,* 2 vols. London, 1795. (1st ed. 1682.)

GALLICCIOLI, GIOVANNI BATTISTA, *Delle Memorie venete antiche . . . ,* Venice, 1795. (*)

GIORGI, FELICE, *Descrizione istorica del teatro di Tor di Nona . . . ,* Rome, 1795. (*)

GUATTANI, GIUSEPPE ANTONIO (1748–1830), *Roma antica . . . ,* 1st ed. Bologna, 1795.

KNIGHT, RICHARD PAYNE (1750–1824), *The Landscape . . . ,* London, 1795. (1st ed. 1794.)

LANZI, LUIGI (1732–1810), *Storia pittorica dell' Italia dal risorgimento delle belle arti . . . ,* 3 vols. Bassano, 1795–96. (†)

MALTON, JAMES (d. 1803), *Essay on British Cottage Architecture,* 1st ed. London, 1795.

MARQUEZ, PIETRO GIUSEPPE (1741–1820), *Delle Case di città degli antichi Romani, secondo la dottrina di Vitruvio . . . ,* Rome, 1795.

MONCHABLON, E. J., *Dizionario compendioso d'antichità tradotto dal francese . . . ,* 3d ed. Venice, 1795.

NORDEN, FRIDERICK LUDVIG (1708–42), *Voyage d'Égypte et de Nubie . . . ,* new ed. 3 vols. Paris, 1795–98. (1st ed. 1755.)

PALOMINO DE CASTRO Y VELASCO (ANTONIO) (1653–1726), *El Museo pictorico y escala optica . . . ,* Madrid, 1795–97. (1st ed. 1715.)

PEYRE, MARIE-JOSEPH (1730–85), *Oeuvres d'architecture . . . ,* 2d ed. Paris, 1795. (1st ed. 1765.)

POTTER, JOHN (1674?–1747), *Archaeologia graeca . . . ,* new ed. 2 vols. London, 1795.

PRETI, FRANCESCO MARIA (1701–74), *Ragionamento sopra i principj d'architettura . . . ,* 1st ed. Padua, 1795.

ROUSSEAU, JEAN-JACQUES (1712–78), *Elo-* isa *. . . and the adventures of Lord Bomston at Rome . . . ,* 3 vols. London, 1795.

ROUSSEAU, JEAN-JACQUES, *La Nouvelle Héloïse . . . ,* Rouen, 1795.

STRATICO, SIMONE (1773–1824), *Dell'Antico teatro di Padova . . . ,* Padua, 1795.

STUART, JAMES (1713–88), and NICHOLAS REVETT (1721–1804), *The Antiquities of Athens,* WILLEY REVELY (d. 1798), ed., 1st ed. vol. 3. London, 1795.

VALLE, GUGLIEMO DELLA (1740?–94?), *Vite dei pittori antichi greci e latini . . . ,* Siena, 1795.

VIGNOLA, GIACOMO BAROZZI DA (1507–73), *Bürgerliche Baukunst nach den Grundregeln der fünf Säulenordnung . . . ,* Nuremberg, 1795.

VIGNOLA, GIACOMO BAROZZI DA, *Le Regole de cinque ordini di architettura civile . . . ,* Naples, 1795.

VINCI, GIOVANNI BATTISTA, *Saggio di architettura civile con alcune cognizioni comuni a tutte le belle arti . . . ,* Rome, 1795.

1796

ALBERTOLLI, GIOCONDO (1742–1839), *Miscellanea per i giovani studiosi del disegno . . . ,* 1st ed. Milan, 1796.

ALBRIZZI, G. B. *Forestiero illuminato . . . ,* Venice, 1796. (1st ed. 1740.)

BERTOTTI-SCAMOZZI, OTTAVIO (1719–90), *Les Bâtimens et les desseins de André Palladio . . .* (also in Italian), 6 vols. Vicenza, 1796–97.

BURKE, EDMUND (1730–97), *A Philosophical Enquiry . . . ,* new ed. Oxford, 1796.

CIPRIANI, GIOVANNI BATTISTA (1727–85), *Monumenti di fabbriche antichi estratti dai disegni dei più celebri autori . . . ,* 3 vols. Rome, 1796–1803. (*)

GALLI DA BIBIENA, FERDINANDO (1657–1743), *Direzioni a' giovani studenti nel disegno dell'architettura civile . . . ,* 2 vols. Venice, 1796. (1st ed. 1725.)

KANT, IMMANUEL (1724–1804), *Observations sur le sentiment du beau et du sublime . . . ,* Paris, 1796.

MARQUEZ, PIETRO GIUSEPPE (1741–1820), *Delle Ville di Plinio il giovine . . . ,* Rome, 1796.

MENGS, ANTON RAPHAEL (1728–79), *The Works of Anthony Raphael Mengs . . . ,* 2 vols. London, 1796.

PAULINUS A SANCTO BARTHOLOMEO [JOANNES PHILIPPUS WERDIN] (1748–1806),

Viaggio alle Indie Orientali . . . , Rome, 1796.

PRICE, SIR UVEDALE (1747–1829), *An Essay on the Picturesque* . . . , London, 1796–98. (1st ed. 1794.)

ROUSSEAU, JEAN-JACQUES (1712–78), *Eloisa . . . together with the sequel of Julia or the new Eloisa . . .* , 3 vols. Philadelphia, 1796.

ROUSSEAU, JEAN-JACQUES, *La Nouvelle Héloïse . . .* , 4 vols. Basle, n.d. [1796].

VITRUVIUS POLLIO, MARCUS, *Des M. Vitruvius Pollio Baukunst . . .* , Leipzig, 1796.

1797

BERTOTTI-SCAMOZZI, OTTAVIO (1719–90), *Les Thermes des Romains dessinées par André Palladio . . .* , Vicenza, 1797.

DELAGARDETTE, CLAUDE MATHIEU (1762–1805), *Règles des cinq ordres d'architecture de Vignole . . .* , Paris, 1797. (1st ed. 1786.)

FEA, CARLO (1753–1834), *Discorso intorno alle belle arti in Roma . . .* , 1st ed. Rome, 1797.

KANT, IMMANUEL (1724–1804), *Beobachtungen über das Gefühl des Schönen und Erhabenen . . .* , Graz, 1797.

KANT, IMMANUEL, *Kritik der Urteilskraft . . .* , Graz, 1797.

LE CLERC, SEBASTIEN (1637–1714), *Neue Abhandlung von der Civil-Baukunst . . .* , Nuremberg, 1797.

MENGS, ANTON RAPHAEL (1728–79), *Obras . . .* , Madrid, 1797.

MILIZIA, FRANCESCO (1725–98), *Dizionario delle belle arti del disegno . . .* , 2 vols. Bassano, 1797.

PALLADIO, ANDREA (1508–80), *Los quatro libros de Arquitectura civil . . .* , vol. 1. Madrid, 1797.

PAUSANIAS (2d half of 2d c. B.C.), *Pausanias, ou voyage historique, pittoresque et philosophique de la Grèce . . .* , Paris, 1797.

REVETT, NICHOLAS (1721–1804), and others, *Ionian Antiquities . . .* , Part Two, London, 1797. (Part One, 1769.)

RONDELET, JEAN BAPTISTE (1734–1829), *Mémoire historique sur le dôme du Panthéon français . . .* , 1st ed. Paris, 1797.

VIGNOLA, GIACOMO BAROZZI DA (1507–73), *Règles . . . Suivies d'une seconde partie, contenant des leçons élémentaires des ombres. Par C. M. Delagardette . . .* , Paris, 1797.

ZOEGA, GEORGES (1755–1809), *De Origine et usu obeliscorum . . .* , 1st ed. Rome, 1797.

1798

[BENTHAM, JAMES (1708–94), and BROWNE WILLIS (1682–1760)], *The History of Gothic and Saxon Architecture in England . . .* , London, 1798.

DELAGARDETTE, CLAUDE MATHIEU (1762–1805), *Essai sur la restauration des piliers du dôme du Panthéon français . . .* , Paris, [1798]. (†)

DELAGARDETTE, CLAUDE MATHIEU, *Les Ruines de Paestum . . .* , 1st ed. Paris, [1798].

MILIZIA, FRANCESCO (1725–98), *De l'Art de voir dans les beaux-arts,* Paris, 1798.

MILIZIA, FRANCESCO, *Dell' Arte di vedere nelle belli arti del disegno . . .* , Venice, 1798.

MOORE, JAMES, *A List of the Principal Castles and Monasteries in Great Britain,* London, 1798. (*)

PAULINUS A SANCTO BARTHOLOMEO [JOANNES PHILIPPUS WERDIN] (1748–1806), *Reise des Fra Paolino da San Bartolomeo nach Ostindien . . .* , Berlin, 1798. (1st ed. in Italian 1796.)

PAUSANIAS (2d half of 2d c. B.C.), *Des Pausanias ausfürliche Reisebeschreibung . . .* , 4 vols. Berlin, 1798–99.

PERCIER, CHARLES (1764–1838), and P. F. L. FONTAINE (1762–1853), *Palais, maisons, et autres edifices modernes dessinés à Rome . . .* , 1st ed. Paris, [1798].

POZZO, ANDREA (1642–1709), *Perspectiva pictorum et architectorum . . .* , Rome, 1798.

WALPOLE, HORACE (1717–97), *On Modern Gardening,* London, 1798. (1st ed. 1780.)

1799

CIPRIANI, GIOVANNI BATTISTA (1727–85), *Vedute principale e più interessanti di Roma . . .* , Rome, 1799.

DANIELL, THOMAS (1749–1840), and WILLIAM DANIELL (1769–1837), *Antiquities of India,* London, 1799–1800.

DELAGARDETTE, CLAUDE MATHIEU (1762–1805), *Les Ruines de Paestum . . .* , Paris, [1799]. (1st ed. 1798.)

GILPIN, WILLIAM (1724–1804), *Trois Essais sur le beau pittoresque . . .* , Breslau, 1799. (1st ed., in English, 1792.)

KANT, IMMANUEL (1724–1804), *Kritik der Urteilskraft . . .* , Berlin, 1799.

ROUSSEAU, JEAN-JACQUES (1712–78), *La Nouvelle Héloïse* . . . , 6 vols. Paris, 1799.

TATHAM, CHARLES HEATHCOTE (1772–1842), *Etchings Representing the Best Examples of Ancient Ornamental Architecture* . . . , 1st ed. London, 1799.

1800

BRENNA, VICENZO (1745–1820), *Disegni dell'imperial palazzi S. Michele e sue adiancenze eretto in S. Pietroburgo* . . . , [n.p., 1800?]. (*)

CIPRIANI, GIOVANNI BATTISTA (1727–85), *Indice di figure relative ai principj d'architettura civile da Francesco Milizia* . . . , Rome, 1800. (*)

MAUNDRELL, HENRY (1650–1710), *A Journey from Aleppo to Jerusalem* . . . , Perth, 1800. (1st ed. 1699.)

PAULINUS A SANCTO BARTHOLOMEO [JOANNES PHILIPPUS WERDIN (1748–1806), *A Voyage to the East Indies* . . . , London, 1800. (1st ed. in Italian 1796.)

POZZO, ANDREA (1642–1709), *Maler und Baumeister Architectur und Perspective* . . . , Augsburg, 1800.

ROSSO, GIUSEPPE DEL (1760?–1831), *Ricerche sull' architettura eguiziana* . . . , Siena, 1800. (1st ed. 1787.)

VITRUVIUS POLLIO, MARCUS, *De Architectura libri dicem* . . . , Berlin, 1800.

WARTON, THOMAS (1728–90), and others, *Essays on Gothic Architecture* . . . , 1st ed. London, 1800.

Appendix B

VISITORS TO ITALY IN THE EIGHTEENTH CENTURY

This list of persons, while far from complete, demonstrates that Italy and Rome exercised a strong pull upon architects, artists, and writers, not to mention their patrons, during the eighteenth century; most of the influential creators of the century were exposed to the *Mezzogiorno,* its shapes, spirits, and personalities.

There follows a shorter list of those who apparently did not have this direct experience, here called "absentees."

DATES	VISITORS
1699–1703	Houasse, René Antoine (1644/45–1710)
1699–1706 1738–52	Troy, Jean-François de (1679–1752)
1703–06	Hardouin, Jules-Michel-Alexandre (?–1737)
1704–23	Poirson
c. 1707–09	Gibbs, James (1683–1754)
1710–19	Kent, William (1684–1748)
1712–18	Coke, Thomas (1697–1759)
1712	Herbert, Henry (1693–1750)
1714–15 1719	Lord Burlington (1694–1753)
c. 1715–16	Caylus, Anne Claude Philippe de (1692–1765)
1715–21 1727–37	Lestache, Pierre de (1688/89–1774)
1716–21	Saussard, Auguste Malo
c. 1720	Deriset, Antoine (1697–1760)
c. 1721	Buache, Philippe (1700–73)
c. 1722	Chivolet (Chevotet), Jean-Michel (1698–1772)
1723–29 1751–74	Natoire, Charles Joseph (1700–77)
c. 1723	Orville, Jacques Philippe d' (1696–1751)
c. 1723	Pinard (1700–61)
c. 1724	Boncourt (1700–?)
1724–26 1737	Vleugels, Nicolas (1669–1737)
c. 1725	Lebon, Pierre-Étienne (1700–54)
prior to 1727	Ware, Isaac (?–1766)
c. 1727	Gallot (1700–?)
c. 1728	Desmarest (Demarets) (1703–70)
c. 1729	Bourge, Antoine de (1705–72)
c. 1730	Daviler, Charles-Louis (1700–64)
c. 1731	Marteau, Jean-Baptiste (1704–70)
1731–38 1749–51	Soufflot, Jacques-Germain (1713–80)
c. 1733	Haneuse (1710–65)
c. 1734	Vattebled (1711–60)
c. 1735	Laurent, Paul-Nicolas
1735–54	Vernet, Claude Joseph (1714–89)
c. 1736	Pollevert (1716–60)
1736–38 1755–57	Ramsay, Allan (1713–84)
c. 1737–44	Dumont, Gabriel-Pierre-Martin (1720–91)
1737–42	Legeay, Jean (1708–90)
c. 1738–46	Potain, Nicolas-Marie (1713–96)
c. 1739	Dorbay, Jean-Pierre (1716–fl. 46)
c. 1740	Brébion, Maximilien (1716–96)

1740s–52 1754–91	Hamilton, Gavin (1724–98)
1740–41	Walpole, Horace (1717–98)
1740–41	Gray, Thomas (1716–71)
1740–48	Saly, Jacques (1717–76)
1741–42 1756–58	Dalton, Richard (c. 1715–91)
1741–44 1746–49 1752–61	Mengs, Anton Raphael (1728–79)
1742–46	Challe, Charles-Michel-Ange (1718–78)
1742–51	Revett, Nicholas (1720–1804)
1742 ff.	Wood, Robert (1717?–71)
c. 1743 1754–56	Moreau-Desproux, Pierre- Louis (1727–93)
1743–50 1775–81	Vien, Joseph-Marie (1716–1809)
1744–48	Jardin, Nicolas-Henri (1720–1802)
c. 1745	Petitot, Ennemond-Alexandre (1720–72)
c. 1746	Brebion (le jeune) (1721–76)
1746	Villanueva, Diego de (1715–74)
1747–54	Brettingham, Matthew, II (1725–1803)
c. 1748–54	Bellicard, Jérôme-Charles (1726–86)
c. 1748	Marchy, Pierre de (1723– 1807)
c. 1748	Parvis (1723–80)
1748–51 1751–53	Stuart, James (1713–88)
c. 1749	Bareau de Chefdeville, François-Dominique (1725–80)
1749–50	Borra, Giovanni Battista (not. 1747–86)
1749–67	Clérisseau, Charles-Louis (1721–1820)
1749–51	Cochin, Charles Nicolas (1715–90)
1749–50	Dawkins, James (1722–57)
1749–51	Le Blanc, Jean-Bernard, Abbé (1707–81)
1749–51	Marigny, Marquis de (Abel- François Poisson) (1727–81)
1749–52	Reynolds, Joshua (1723–92)
1750 ff.	Barbault, Jean (c. 1705–66)
1750–55	Chambers, Sir William (1723–96)
c. 1750 1781–87	Lagrenée (l'ainé), Louis Jean François (1725–1805)
1750–54	Le Roy, Julien David (1724–1803)
1750 ff.	Nagel, George Adam (1712–79)
1750s–62	Parker, John (1730?–65?)
1752–55 1772 1777–78	De Wailly, Charles (1729–98)
1752–56	Harper, Adolph Friedrich (1725–1806)
c. 1752+ 1765–67	Peyre, Marie-Joseph (l'ainé) (1730–85)
1752–55	Wilton, Joseph (1722–1803)
1754–58	Adam, Robert (1728–92)
c. 1754	Hélin, Pierre (1730–85)
1754–65	Robert, Hubert (1733–1808)
1754–57 1783	Trouard, Louis-François (1729–97)
1755	Als, Peter (1726–76)
c. 1755	Caulfield, James (1728–99)
1755–64	Dance, Nathaniel (1735–1811)
1755–61	Fragonard, Jean-Honoré (1732–1806)
1755	Greuze, Jean-Baptiste (1725–1805)
c. 1755 1757–58	Maréchaux, Charles
1755–59	Mylne, Robert (1734–1811)
1755–68	Winckelmann, Johann J. (1717–68)
1756–59	Louis, Victor-Louis-Nicolas (1731–1800)
1757–58	Laugier, Marc-Antoine (1713–69)
1758–65	Dance, George, Jr. (1741–1825)

1759–63	Chalgrin, Jean-François-Thérèse (1739–1811)
1759	Cherpitel, Mathurin (1736–1809)
1759–63? 1775	Gondoin, Jacques (1737–1818)
c. 1759	Leroy, Étienne (1737–80)
1759–65	Villanueva, Juan de (1739–1811)
1760–63	Adam, James (1730–94)
1760s 1776–84	Desprez, Jean-Louis (1743–1804)
c. 1760	Lefebvre, [Jacques-François-Joseph (1744–1810)]
1760–61	Pillement, Jean-Baptiste (1728–1808)
1760–63	Richardson, George (1736?–c. 1813)
1760–63	West, Benjamin (1738–1820)
c. 1761	Debourge, Antoine-Joseph (1735–1811)
1762–64	Bazhenov, Vassily (1737–99)
c. 1762	Peyre, Antoine-François (1739–1823)
1762–68	Wyatt, James (1746–1813)
1763–66	Chandler, Richard (1738–1810)
c. 1763	Darnaudin, Charles François (1741–1805)
1763–66 1781 ff.	Kauffmann, Angelica (1741–1807)
1763–68 1781–86	Lagrenée, Jean-Jacques (1739–1821)
1763–80	Quarenghi, Giacomo (1744–1817)
1764	Gibbon, Edward (1737–94)
1764	Morgan, John
1764	Powell, Samuel
c. 1765	Heurtier, Jean-François (1739–1822)
c. 1765	Starov, Ivan (1743–1808)
1766–71	Barry, James (1741–1806)
c. 1766	Hamilton, William (1730–1803)
c. 1766 1787–91 1792–1800	Menageot, François Guillaume (1744–1816)
1766–67	Mouton, Adrien (1741–1820)
1766–67	Newton, William (1735–90)
1767 –c. 1770 1777 ff. 1785 ff.	Knight, Richard Payne (1750–1824)
1767–70	Weinlig, Christian (1739–99)
1768	Cameron, Charles (1740/41–1812)
1768–69	Langhans, Karl Gotthard (1732–1808)
1769–76	Harrison, Thomas (1744–1829)
1769 1776–79	Houel, Jean-Pierre-Louis-Laurent (1735–1813)
1769– prior to 1781	Paine, James, Jr. (1745–1829)
1769 ff.	Poyet, Bernard (1742–1824)
1769–1777	Raymond, Jean-Armond (1742–1811)
1770–72	Lewis, James (c. 1751–1820)
c. 1771	Huvé, Jean-Jacques (1742–1808)
1771–74 1783	Paris, Pierre-Adrien (1745–1819)
1772–78 1792–1806	Suvée, Joseph Benoît (1743–1807)
1773–93	More, Jacob (1740?–93)
1774	Legrand, Jacques-Guillaume (1743–1807/08)
1774–84	Renard, Jean-Augustine (1744–1807)
c. 1775	Hallé, Noël (1711–81)
1776 1784–86 1787–92	Cassas, Louis François (1756–1827)
1776	Grimm, Friedrich Melchior (1723–1807)
c. 1776–79	Lemoine, Paul Guillaume (1755–?)
1776–80 1783–84	Quatremère-de-Quincy, Antoine-Chrysostome (1755–1849)

1777–78	Antoine, Jacques-Denis (1733–1801)	1786–88	Goethe, Johann Wolfgang von (1749–1832)

1777–78   Antoine, Jacques-Denis (1733–1801)

1777–79   Northcote, James (1746–1831)

1778–80   Soane, Sir John (1753–1837)

c. 1779   Delannoy, Jacques (1755–1835)

c. 1779   Gisors, Alexandre Jean-Baptiste-Guy de (1762–1835)

c. 1780   Thomon, Thomas de (1754–1813)

early 1780s   Lequeu, Jean-Jacques (1757–c. 1824)

1780–83   Trouard, Louis-Alexandre (fils)

c. 1781–84   Combes, Louis-Guy (1758–1818)

1781–83   Bellisard, Claude Billard de

c. 1781–98   Head, Guy (1753–1800)

c. 1782–85   Bernard, Pierre (1761–?)

1782–95   DuFourny, Léon (1754–1818)

1783–84   Latrobe, Benjamin Henry (1764–1820)
1786

1783 ff.   Rondelet, Jean-Baptiste (1734–1829)

1783–88   Vaudoyer, Antoine-Laurent-Thomas (1756–1846)

1784–87   Chinard, Joseph (1756–1813)
1791

c. 1784   Hubert, Auguste-Cheval (1755–98)

1784   Molinos, Jacques (1743–1831)

1784–89   Reveley, Willey (1760–99)

c. 1784–90   Voronikhin, Andrei (1760–1814)

1785–98   Deare, John (1759–98)

1785–87   Genelli, Hans Christian (1763–1823)

1785–90   Fontaine, Pierre-François-Léonard (1762–1853)

1785   Hansen, Christian Frederik (1756–1845)

1785   Moreau, Jean-Charles-Alexandre (1762–1810)

1786   Bulfinch, Charles (1763–1844)

1786–88   Goethe, Johann Wolfgang von (1749–1832)

c. 1786–87   Zakharov, Adrian (1761–1811)

1786–91   Percier, Charles (1764–1838)

1787   Jefferson, Thomas (1743–1826)

1788–89   Baltard, Louis-Pierre (1764–1846)

c. 1789–91   Bonnard, Jacques-Charles (1766–1818)

1789–93   Faivre, Jean-Baptiste-Louis (1766–98)

1789–91   Tardieu, Jean-Jacques (1762–1833)

1790   Couture, Guillaume Martin (1732–99)

1790–95   Gentz, Heinrich (1766–1811)

1790s   Vigée-Lebrun, Elisabeth (1755–1842)

1791   Delagardette, Claude-Mathieu (1762–1805)

c. 1792   Normand, Charles-Pierre-Joseph (1765–1840)

1792–97   Weinbrenner, Friedrich (1766–1826)

1795   Tatham, Charles Heathcote

c. 1797   Coussin, Jean-Antoine (1770–1849)

c. 1797   Dubut, Louis-Ambroise (1769–1846)

c. 1798   Clémence, Joseph (1776–1827)

c. 1799   Grandjean de Montigny, Henri Augustin Victor (1776–1850)

c. 1799   Hope, Thomas (c. 1770–1831)

SOME NOTABLE ABSENTEES

Belanger, François-Joseph (1744–1818)
Boffrand, Germain (1667–1754)
Boullée, Étienne-Louis (1728–99)
Brongniart, Alexander-Théodore (1739–1813)
Campbell, Colin (d. 1729)
De Corny, Emmanuel Héré (1705–63)
Durand, Jean-Nicolas-Louis (1760–1834)
Gilly, Friedrich (1772–1800)
Ledoux, Claude-Nicolas (1736–1806)
Mique, Richard (1728–94)

Bibliography

The number of periodicals dealing with Italian architecture in the period covered by this book is limited; furthermore, they are scarce outside Italy. In most cases they begin rather late in the nineteenth century. They include:

> *Il Politecnico* (Milan), 1839–1937; *Annuario scientifico ed industriale* (Milan), 1863–1927; *L'Arte in Italia* (Turin), 1869–73; *Illustrazione popolare italiana* (Milan), 1869–1907?; *Ricordi di architettura* (Florence), 1878–1900; *Italia artistica illustrata* (Rome), 1882–86; *Arte italiana decorativa e industriale* (Rome-Venice), 1890–1911; *Edilizia moderna* (Milan), 1891–1917; *Emporium* (Bergamo), 1895 ff.; *L'Arte* (Rome, Milan), 1898 ff.; *L'Architettura pratica* (Turin), 1898 ff.; *Rassegna contemporanea* (Rome), 1908 ff.; *Rassegna d'arte,* (Milan), 1901–22; *Architettura italiana* (Turin), 1905 ff.; *Casabella* (Milan), 1927 ff.; *Paragone* (Florence), 1949 ff.; *L'Architettura* (Milan), 1955 ff.

There are only two significant monographs on the subject covered by this book: the brief, but sound, account by Nello Tarchiani, *L'Architettura italiana dell'ottocento,* Florence, 1937; and the much more detailed account by Emilio Lavagnino in his *L'Arte moderna dai neoclassici ai contemporanei,* two volumes, Turin, 1956, with an enlarged edition in 1961. This is lavishly illustrated, well-indexed, and emphasizes architecture. There is an extensive bibliography in Bruno Zevi's *Storia dell'architettura moderna,* Turin, 1950. The Touring Club Italiano (T.C.I.), formerly La Consociazone Turistica Italiana (C.T.I.), issues two series of invaluable works: the *Guida d'Italia,* in many volumes, frequently reissued and revised, and the illustrated series *Attraverso l'Italia,* originally begun in 1930 and comprising twenty-one volumes, now being reissued in enlarged, revised volumes.

The rest of the bibliographical material is arranged under the following headings:

SOURCES

Many sources and special works dealing with the eighteenth century are in Appendix A, where a chronological arrangement shows the entrances of the sources and the dissemination of the architectural systems of the eighteenth century in both their theoretical and repertorial aspects.

Accademia della Pace, *Raccolta di X progetti architettonici inventati da alcuni membri della A. della Pace, contenuti in XXIV tavole,* Florence, n.d., c.1825.

Allason, Thomas, *Antiquities of Pola,* London, 1819.

Amati, Carlo, *Gli Ordini di Barozzi,* Milan, 1805.

———, *Memoria sullo stato della architettura civile nel medioevo,* Milan, 1825.

Architectural Publication Society, *Dictionary of Architecture,* 8 vols. in 5. London, 1853–92.

L'Artista moderno, *Il Ferro battuto e il fabbro moderno,* 1st series, 2nd series, Turin, Crudo, n.d., c.1905.

Barozzi, J., *Gli Ordini d'architettura civile,* Milan, 1825.

Beccega, Tomaso Carlo, *Sull'Architettura greco-romano applicata alla costruzione del teatro moderno italiano,* Venice, 1817.

Berti, Giovan Battista, *Elementi d'architettura,* Venice, 1811.

———, *Studio elementare degli ordini di architettura di Palladio,* Milan, 1818.

———, *Sul Monumento a Palladio,* Vicenza, 1845.

Bessone-Aurelj, Antonietta Maria, *Dizionario degli scultori ed architetti italiani,* Genoa, Società Anonima Editrice Dante Alighieri, 1947.

Bettini, André, *Guide de Florence . . . ,* 5th ed. Florence, 1870.

Calderari, Ottone, *Disegni e scritti d'architettura . . . ,* 2 vols. Vicenza, 1808–15.

Clochar, Pierre, *Palais, maisons et vues d'Italie,* Paris, 1809.

D'Althan, Nino, *Gli Artisti italiani e le loro opere,* Turin, Gio. Gallizio, 1902.

De Gubernatis, Angelo, *Dizionario degli artisti italiani viventi pittori, scultori e architetti,* Florence, 1892.

Delaire, E., *Les Architects élèves de l'École des Beaux-Arts,* 2nd ed. Paris, Librarie de la Construction Moderne, 1907.

De Vico, Andrea. *Trenta Tavole di ornamenti architettonici greci romani e italiani . . . ,* Rome, 1862.

Dussieux, Louis Étienne, *Les Artistes français à l'étranger,* Paris, 1856; 3rd ed. Paris, 1876.

Espouy, Hector d', *Fragments d'architecture du moyen âge et de la renaissance . . . ,* 2 vols. Paris, 1897.

Gherardesca, Alessandro, *La Casa di delizia: il giardino e la fattoria . . . ,* Pisa, 1826.

Grandjean de Montigny, Auguste Henri Victor, *Architecture toscane . . . ,* Paris, 1815.

Hittorff, Jacob Ignaz, *Architecture moderne de la Sicile . . . ,* Paris, 1835.

Holt, Elizabeth G., ed., *A Documentary History of Art,* 2 vols. Garden City, Doubleday, 1958.

Honour, Hugh, *Chinoiserie, The Vision of Cathay,* New York, E. P. Dutton, 1962.

Lapauze, H., *Histoire de l'Académie de France à Rome,* Paris, Plon, 1924.

Lavori e progetti di valenti architetti moderni, Milan, Saldini, 1862.

Letarouilly, Paul Marie, *Édifices de Rome moderne . . . ,* 3 vols., Paris, 1868–74.

Lewis, Douglas, "The Image of Greece in 18th Century English Architecture," Master's thesis, Yale University, 1963.

Moglia, Domenico, *Collezione di sogetti ornamentali ed architettonici inventati e disegnati da D. M.,* Milan, 1837.

Montecchini, P. L., *Sulla Possibilità e la convenienza di un nuovo stile nazionale d'architettura . . . ,* Turin, 1865.

Pizzagalli, Felice, Giulio Aluisetti, and Agostino Comerio, *Opera dei grandi concorsi premiati dall' I. R. Accademia delle Belle Arti in Milano,* Milan, 1824.

Rossini, Luigi, *Magnificenze di Roma,* Rome, 1823.
———, *I Sette Colli di Roma antica e moderna, con piante e restauri dei medesimi . . . ,* Rome, 1828–29.
———, *Scenografia degl' interni delle più belle chiese e basiliche antiche di Roma . . . ,* Rome, 1843.
———, *Scenografia di Roma moderna, che comprende le più belle vedute delle principali strade, piazze, e fontane . . . ,* Rome, 1850.

Schlosser-Magnino, J., *La Letteratura artistica,* Florence, La Nuova Italia Editrice Firenze, and Vienna, Schroll, 1956.
Selvatico, Pietro, *Sulla architettura e scultura in Venezia,* Venice, 1847.
———, *Scritti d'arte,* Florence, 1859.
Sganzin, Mattia Giuseppe, *Pubbliche costruzioni,* 4 vols. Venice, 1847–53.
Silva, Ercole, *Dell'Arte dei giardini inglesi,* Milan, 1802.
Sironi and Benni, *Case e palazzi in Italia . . . ,* Milan, Bestetti e Tumminelli, n.d., c.1912.
———, *Ville e villini in Italia . . . ,* Milan, Bestetti e Tumminelli, n.d., c.1912.
Stendhal, *A Roman Journal,* ed. and trans. by Haakon Chevalier, New York, Orion, 1957.

Woods, Joseph, *Letters of an Architect from France, Italy and Greece,* 2 vols. London, 1828.

Zanetti, Giuseppe, *Studi architettonico-ornamentali,* 2 vols. Venice, 1843.

GENERAL STUDIES

Banham, Reyner, "Italian Retreat from Modern Architecture (Neoliberty)," *Architectural Review, 125* (1959), 231–35.
———, "Neoliberty: the Debate," *Architectural Review, 126* (1959), 341–44.
Barzun, Jacques, *Classic, Romantic and Modern,* 2nd ed. New York, Doubleday, 1961.
Bianchi, Carlo, *Le Ville moderne in Italia,* Turin, Crudo, 1909.
Boito, Camillo, *Architettura del medio evo in Italia, con una introduzione: sullo stile futuro dell'architettura italiana . . . ,* Milan, 1880.
———, *Questioni pratiche di belle arti . . . ,* Milan, 1893.

Calligaris, A., *I Ferri battuti . . . ,* Turin, Crudo, n.d., c.1900.
Carbonara, Pasquale, *Architettura pratica, le chiese, gli edifici teatrali,* Turin, Unione Tipografico, 1958.
Carrott, Richard, "The Egyptian Revival: Its Sources, Monuments and Meaning, 1808–1858," unpublished Ph.D. dissertation, Yale University, 1962.
Ceradini, Mario, *L'Architettura italiana alla prima esposizione d'architettura in Torino,* Turin-Palermo, 1890.
Cevese, Renato, ed., "Il Neoclassicismo nel Veneto," *Bolletino del Centro . . . di Studi Andrea Palladio,* 5 (1963), Vicenza.
Chierici, Gino, *Il Palazzo italiano dal secolo XVII al secolo XIX,* 3 vols. Milan, Antonio Vallardi, 1952–57.
Clark, Sir Kenneth, "Introduction" in: The Arts Council of Great Britain, *The Romantic Movement,* London, 1959.

Colvin, H. M., *A Biographical Dictionary of English Architects, 1660–1840,* Cambridge, Mass., Harvard University Press, 1954.

Costantini, Vincenzo, *Storia dell'arte italiana,* 4 vols. Milan, Cheschina, 1945–49.

Croce, Benedetto, *Storia d'Italia dal 1871—al 1915,* Bari, Laterza, 1953.

Le Costruzioni moderne in Italia, facciate di edifizi in stile moderno: Milano, Genova, Torino, 4 vols. Turin, Crudo, 1908.

De Castro, Vincenzo, *L'Italia monumentale; o galleria delle principali fabriche antiche e moderne,* 2 vols. 2nd ed. Milan, 1870.

Delogu, Giuseppe, *L'Architettura italiana del seicento e del settecento . . . ,* 2 vols. Florence, Novissima Enciclopedia, 1935.

Donghi, Daniele, *Manuale dell'architetto,* 2 vols. in 8. Turin, Unione Tipografico–Editrice Torinese, 1925–35, *2,* part I, sect. 4 (1930).

Drewry, Charles S., *A Memoir on Suspension Bridges,* London, 1832.

Ewen, David, *Encyclopedia of the Opera,* New York, Hill & Wang, 1963.

Fasolo, Vicenzo, and G. B. Milani, *Le forme architettoniche,* 3 vols. Milan, Vallardi, 1931–40; *2, Dal Quattrocento ai neoclassica* (1934); *3, Dall' Ottocento ai nostri giorni* (1940).

Franklin, J. W., *The Cathedrals of Italy,* New York, Hastings House, 1958.

Geiati, C., *Nozioni pratiche ed artistiche di architettura per il corso di architettura,* Turin, 1899.

Giampaoli, Carlo, *Dizionario storico delle vite e opere degli architetti, scultori, e pittori Italiani,* Naples, Studio di Propaganda Editoriale, 1942, *1, Architetti.*

Giannelli, E., *Artisti napoletani viventi, pittore, scultori e architetti,* Naples, Libreria dello Stato, 1916.

Giovannoni, Gustavo, *Architetture di pensiero e pensieri sull'architettura,* Rome, Apollon, 1945.

Golzio, V., *Il Seicento e il settecento,* Turin, Unione Tipografico–Editrice Torinese, 1950.

Hamilton, George Heard, *The Art and Architecture of Russia,* Baltimore, Penguin Books, 1954.

Hautecoeur, Louis, *Rome et la renaissance de l'antiquité à la fin du XVIIIe siècle,* Paris, Fontemoing, 1912.

——, *Histoire de l'architecture classique en France,* 7 vols. in 9. Paris, Picard, 1943–57.

Herrmann, Wolfgang, *Laugier and Eighteenth Century French Theory,* London, Zwemmer, 1962.

Hitchcock, Henry-Russell, *Architecture: Nineteenth and Twentieth Centuries,* 2nd ed. Baltimore, Penguin Books, 1963.

Hoffstadt, F., *Principi dello stilo gotico . . . ,* translated by F. Lazzari, Venice, 1858.

Hughes, Patrick Cairns, *Great Opera Houses; a Traveller's Guide to Their History and Traditions,* New York, McBride, 1959.

Kaufmann, Emil, *Architecture in the Age of Reason,* Cambridge, Mass., Harvard University Press, 1955.

Kimball, Fiske, "Romantic Classicism in Architecture," *Gazette des Beaux-Arts,* Series 6, *25* (1944), 95–112.

Kirchmayr, Mario, *L'Architettura italiana dalle origini ai giorni nostri* . . . , 2 vols. Turin, Società Editrice Internazionale, 1946.

Lees-Milne, James, *Earls of Creation,* London, Hamish Hamilton, 1962.
Lovejoy, Arthur, *Essays in the History of Ideas,* New York, Putnam, 1948.

Manwaring, Elizabeth W., *Italian Landscape in Eighteenth Century England,* New York, Oxford University Press, 1925.
Meeks, Carroll L. V., "Books and Buildings, 1449–1949, 100 Great Architectural Books . . .," *Journal of the Society of Architectural Historians, 8* (1949), 55–67.
——, "Rome Ruined?," *Perspecta, 2* (1953), 6–9.
——, "Romanesque before Richardson," *Art Bulletin, 35* (1953), 17–33.
——, *The Railroad Station, An Architectural History,* New Haven, Yale University Press, 1956.
——, "Pantheon Paradigm," *Journal of the Society of Architectural Historians, 19* (1960), 135–44.
——, "The Real *Liberty* of Italy—the *Stile Floreale,*" *Art Bulletin, 43* (1961), 113–30.
——, "Wright's Eastern-Seaboard Contemporaries: Creative Eclecticism in the United States around 1900," *Studies in Western Art,* New York, Twentieth International Congress of the History of Art, 1963, *2,* 64–77.
——, Review of Herrmann, *Laugier and Eighteenth Century French Theory* in JSAH, *22* (1963), 234 ff.
Melani, Alfredo, "Modern Architecture in Italy," *Arch. Record, 14* (1903), 393 ff.
——, and Luigi Conforti, *Il Secolo XIX nella vita e nella cultura dei popoli,* Milan, n.d., c. 1900.
Middleton, R. D., "The Abbé de Cordemoy . . . ," *Journal of the Warburg and Courtauld Institutes, 25* (1962), 278 ff.
Milani, Giovanni Battista, *I Concorsi di architettura in Italia,* Milan, Bestetti & Tumminelli, n.d., c.1913.
——, and V. Fasolo, *Le Forme architettoniche,* 3 vols. Milan, Vallardi, 1931–40.
Monneret de Villard, Ugo, *Opera d'architettura moderna,* Milan, Le Costruzioni Moderne, 1909.

Ojetti, Ugo, *I Palazzi e le ville che non sono più del re* . . . , Milan, Treves, 1921.

Pauli, G., *Die Kunst des Klassizismus und der Romantik,* Berlin, Propyläen, 1925.
Petrocchi, M., *Razionalismo architettonico e razionalismo storiografico; due studi sul settecento italiano,* Rome, Edizioni di Storia e Letteratura, 1947.
Pevsner, Nikolaus, *An Outline of European Architecture,* 6th ed. Baltimore, Penguin Books, 1960.
Piacentini, Marcello, *Il Volto di Roma, e altre immagini,* Rome, Edizione della Bussola, 1944.
Praz, Mario, *Gusto neoclassico,* 2nd ed. Naples, Edizioni Scientifiche Italiane, 1959.
Price, Martin, "The Picturesque Moment," in: *Essays From Sensibility to Romanticism; Presented to Frederick A. Pottle,* ed. Frederick W. Hilles and Harold Bloom, New York, Oxford University Press, 1965, pp. 259 ff.
Promis, Carlo, *Fabbriche moderne ad uso degli studenti d'architettura,* Turin, 1871.

Rosenau, Helen, ed., *Boullée's Treatise on Architecture,* London, Tiranti, 1953.
———, "The Engravings of the Grands Prix of the French Academy of Architecture," *Architectural History, 3* (1960), 15–180.

Sacchi, Archimede, *Architettura pratica, le abitazioni, alberghi . . . ,* 2 vols. 3rd ed. Milan, 1886.
Sartoris, Alberto, *Encyclopédie de l'architecture nouvelle,* Milan, Ulrico Hoepli, 1948.
Selz, Peter and Mildred Constantine, ed., *Art Nouveau,* New York, Museum of Modern Art, 1959.
Smith, Denis Mack, *Italy: A Modern History,* Ann Arbor, University of Michigan Press, 1959.
———, and Janet Trevelyan, *A Short History of the Italian People . . . ,* London, Allen and Unwin, 1956.
Smith, G. E. Kidder, *Italy Builds,* New York, Reinhold, 1955.
Sonzogno, Edoardo, ed., *L'Esposizione italiana del 1884,* Turin, 1884.
Sutton, Denys, ed., *Apollo, 78,* 334 ff. (1963, "Aspects of Neo-Classicism" issue).
Sypher, Wylie, *Four Stages of Renaissance Style . . . ,* Garden City, Doubleday, 1955.
———, *Rococo to Cubism in Art and Literature,* New York, Random House, 1960.

Tirelli, Guido, *Palazzine e ville signorili,* Turin, Crudo, 1923.

Viollet-le-Duc, E. E., *Dictionnaire raisonné de l'architecture française du XIe au XVIe siècle,* 10 vols. Paris, 1854–68 (*5–6,* 1875).
———, *Discourses on Architecture,* trans. William Bucknall, 2 vols. Boston, 1889.

Willard, Ashton Rollins, *History of Modern Italian Art,* London, 1895, 1896, 1898, New York, 1900.
Wischnitzer, Rachel, *Synagogue Architecture in the United States,* Philadelphia, Jewish Publication Society, 1955.
Wittkower, Rudolf, *Architectural Principles in the Age of Humanism,* London, Tiranti, 1952.
———, *Art and Architecture in Italy, 1600 to 1750,* 2nd ed. Baltimore, Penguin Books, 1958.

CITIES AND PROVINCES

BOLOGNA, EMILIA, AND ROMAGNA

Beseghi, Umberto, *Palazzi di Bologna,* Bologna, Tamari, 1956.
———, *Introduzione alle chiese di Bologna,* Bologna, Tamari, 1956.

Golfiere, E., *Artisti neoclassici in Faenza,* Faenza, 1929.

Raule, Angelo, *Architetture bolognesi,* Bologna, A.B.E.S., 1952.
Ricci, Corrado, and Guido Zucchini, *Guida di Bologna,* 6th ed. Bologna, N. Zanichelli, 1930.

Zucchini, Guido, *Edifici di Bologna, repertorio bibliografico e iconografico,* Rome, R. Istituto d'Archeologia e Storia dell'Arte, 1931.

FLORENCE, TUSCANY, AND UMBRIA

Beltrami, Luca, *Storia della facciata di S. Maria del Fiore in Firenze,* Milan, Allegretti, 1900.

Carocci, Guido, *I Dintorni di Firenze,* 2 vols. Florence, Galletti e Cocci, 1906–07.
Cavallucci, C. J., *S. Maria del Fiore e la sua facciata; narrazione storica,* Florence, 1887.

Conti, Augusto, *Illustrazione delle sculture e dei mosaici sulla facciata del Duomo di Firenze* ..., Florence, 1887.

Conti, Giuseppe, *Firenze vecchia,* 2 vols. Florence, Vallecchi, 1928.

Crispolti, Virgilio, *Santa Maria del Fiore alla luce dei documenti,* Florence, Vallechi, 1937.

De Fabris, Emilio, *Del Sistema tricuspidale per il coronamento della facciata di S. Maria del Fiore e delle sue linee organiche,* Florence, 1886.

Fumi, L., *Il Duomo di Orvieto e i suoi restauri,* Rome, 1891.

Funghini, Vincenzo, *Voti e Pareri sulla facciata del Duomo di Firenze contro il sistema tricuspidale,* Arezzo, 1875.

Giovannozzi, Vera Daddi, "I Modelli dei secoli XVI e XVII per la facciata de Santa Maria del Fiore," *L'Arte, 17* (1936), 33 ff.

Guasti, Cesare, *Santa Maria del Fiore; la costruzione della chiesa e del campanile secondo i documenti tratti dall'Archivo dell'Opera secolare e da quello di Stato* ..., Florence, 1887.

Guérinet, Armand, *Florence monumental,* Paris, n.d.

Limburger, Walther, *Die gebäude von Florenz* ..., Leipzig, Brockhaus, 1910.

Mazzanti, Enrico, and Torquato Del Lungo, *Raccolta delle migliori fabbriche di Firenze,* Florence, 1876.

Meeks, Carroll L. V., "Mannerist Churches in Florence," *College Art Journal, 1* (1942), 73.

Moro, Luigi del, *La Facciata di S. Maria del Fiore* ..., Florence, 1888.

Nardini Despotti Mospignotti, Aristide, *Il Sistema tricuspidale e la facciata del Duomo di Firenze,* Leghorn, 1871.

Paatz, Walter, and Elisabeth Paatz, *Die Kirchen von Florenz, ein Kunstgeschichtliches Handbuch* ..., 6 vols. Frankfurt am Main, Klostermann, 1940–54.

Perilli, Scipione, *Relazione storica sul risorgimento della Basilica degli Angeli presso Assisi,* 2nd ed. Rome, 1842.

Pesci, U., *Firenze capitale (1865–70),* Florence, Libreria di Stato, 1904.

Poggi, Giovanni, *Il Duomo di Firenze; documenti sulla decorazione della chiesa e del campanile* ..., Berlin, Cassirer, 1909.

Ricci, Corrado, *Cento Vedute di Firenze antica,* Florence, Alinari, 1906.

Saalman, Howard, "Santa Maria del Fiore: 1294–1418," *Art Bulletin, 46* (1964), 471 ff.

Supino, I. B., *Concorso per la facciata delle regia Basilica di San Lorenzo in Firenze,* Florence, n.d., c.1906.

GENOA AND LIGURIA

Banchero, Giuseppe, *I Monumenti pubblici di Genova,* Genoa, 1846.

Castagna, D., and M. V. Masini, *Genova, guida storico artistica,* Genoa, 1929.

Cicala, Vittorio, *Ville e castelli d'Italia; Riviere, Ligure,* Milan, G. Modiano, 1917.

De Simoni, L., *Le Chiese di Genova,* Genoa, Ceretti, 1948.

Gauthier, M. P., *Les Plus Beaux Edifices de la ville de Goenes* ..., 2 vols. in 1. Paris, 1830–32.

Giunta municipale, *Intorno ad alcuni progetti di ingrandimento . . . di Genova . . .* , Genoa, 1906.

Grosso, Orlando, *Dimore genovesi; i palazzi, le ville, i castelli,* Milan, Alfieri, 1956.

——, *Portali e palazzi di Genova,* Milan, Bestetti & Tumminelli, n.d.

——, and Giuseppe Pessagno, *Il Palazzo del Comune di Genova,* Genoa, Edito a Cura della Società Ligure di Storia Patria, 1933.

Resasco, Ferdinando, *La Necropoli di Staglieno,* Genoa, 1892.

MILAN AND LOMBARDY

Anselmo, Arduino, *Milano storica nelle sue vie, nei suoi monumenti,* Milan, Hoepli, 1933.

Arrigoni, P., *Milano e la Lombardia antiche e moderne,* Turin, Finzi, 1925.

Artaria, F., *Il Duomo di Milano,* Milan, 1831.

Bagatti-Valsecchi, Fausto, *Qui Si Contengono Le Tavole rappresentanti li disegni de la casa de li fratelli Bagatti Valsecchi che ritrovasi in Milano . . .* , Milan, 1898.

Bagatti-Valsecchi, Giuseppe, *La Casa Bagatti-Valsecchi . . .* , Milan, Hoepli, 1918.

Bagnoli, Raffaele, *Le Chiese di Milano nella storia e nell' arte,* Milan, 1942, 1950.

——, *Il Duomo di Milano,* Milan, Maestri Arti Grafiche, 1950.

Beltrami, Luca, *La Facciata del nostro duomo,* Milan, 1883.

——, *Per La Facciata del Duomo di Milano,* Milan, 1887.

——, *Il Modello per la nuova facciata del Duomo di Milano e il disegno per la torre campanaria,* Milan, 1892.

——, *Guida storica del Castello di Milano, 1368–1894,* Milan, 1894.

——, *Il Coronamento nella fronte del Duomo di Milano,* Milan, Allegretti, 1900.

——, *Il Palazzo Venezia, sede delle Assicurazioni Generali, in Milano,* Milan, Estratto dall' "Edilizia moderna," 1900.

——, and Gaetano Moretti, *Resoconto dei lavori di restauro eseguiti al Castello di Milano,* Milan, 1898.

Boito, Camillo, *Il Duomo di Milano e i disegni per la sua facciata, di Camillo Boito,* Milan, 1889.

Broggi, Luigi, *L'Edificio del Teatro alla Scala in Milano, memoria dell'architetto Luigi Broggi,* Milan, 1878.

——, *Progetto di un nuovo quartiere per caseggiati e villini e della sua congiunzione col centro della città contrapposto a quello dell' ing. Maraini,* Milan, 1880.

Carotti, Giulio, *Il Duomo di Milano e la sua facciata,* Milan, 1888.

Cassina, Ferdinando, *Le Fabbriche piu cospicue di Milano . . .* , Milan, 1840.

Cicala, Vittorio, *Ville e castelli d'Italia; Lombardia e Laghi,* Milan, Tecnografica, 1907.

Cima, Otto, *Milano di ieri . . .* , Milan, Varese, 1955.

Cimitero Monumentale di Milano, Turin, L'Artista Moderno, n.d., c.1920.

D'Adda, Gioachimo, *La Metropolitana di Milano e dettagli rimarcabili di questo edificio . . .* , Milan, 1824.

Della Chiesa, Angela Ottino, *L'Età neoclassica in Lombardia,* Como, Nani, 1959.

Hodges, Frederick, *Description of the Cathedral of Milan,* Milan, 1884.

Manzi, Lodovico, *Osservazioni di Lodovico Manzi in ordine al progetto di una piazza intorno al Duomo di Milano,* Milan, 1863.

Marescotti, E. A. and Ximenes, E., *Milano e l'esposizione internazionale del Sempione,* Milan, Treves, 1906.

Massarani, Tullo, *Le Ville Crespi: Villa Pia a Orta e Castello Crespi a Crespi d'Adda,* Milan, Bassani, 1905.

Mezzanotte, Paolo, and Giacomo Bascapè, *Milano nell'arte e nella storia,* Milan, Bestetti, 1948.

Nardini Despotti Mospignotti, Aristide, *Del Duomo di Milano e della sua nuova facciata . . . ,* Milan, 1889.

Nardini-Saladini, Raffaello, *La Cappella espiatoria di Monza,* Bergamo, Istituto Italiano d'Arte Grafiche, 1912.

Ojetti, Ugo, *L'Arte nell'esposizione di Milano . . . ,* Milan, Treves, 1906.
———, *Il Monumento a Vittorio Emanuele II,* Milan, Treves, 1907.

Paravicini, Tito Vespasiano, *Il Palazzo Marino . . . ,* Dresden, 1880.

Pareto, R., *Italie monumentale: vol. 2, Collection monuments de Milan . . . ,* Paris, 1879, Milan, 1881.

Ponzoni, Carlo, *Le Chiese di Milano,* Milan, Arti Grafiche Milanesi, 1930.

Portaluppi, Piero, and Marco Semanza, *Milano com'è ora, come sarà,* Milan, Arti Grafiche Milanesi, 1955.

Reggiori, Ferdinando, *Milano 1800–1943,* Milan, Edizione del Milione, 1947.

Reina, G., *Description of the Arch of Peace in Milan,* Milan, 1844.

Rocco, Giovanni, *Pellegrino Pellegrini, "L'Architetto di San Carlo" e le sue opere nel Duomo di Milano,* Milan, Hoepli, 1939.

Romussi, Carlo, *Il Duomo di Milano nella storia e nell'arte,* Milan, Hoepli, n.d., c.1902.
———, *Intorno alla facciata del Duomo di Milano,* Milan, Sonzogno, 1903.
———, *Milano ne' suoi monumenti,* 3rd ed. 2 vols. Milan, Sonzogno, 1912–13.

Vallardi, Giuseppe, *Il Duomo di Milano,* Milan, 1863 (in French, Milan, 1881).

Verga, Ettore, *L'Archivio della fabbrica del Duomo di Milano,* Milan, Allegretti, 1908.

NAPLES AND THE SOUTH

Alajamo, A. G., *Gli Architetti regi in Sicilia: L'Architetto della Catania settecentesca G. B. Vaccarini . . . ,* Palermo, Di. Ma., 1950.

Calandra, E., *Breve Storia dell'architettura in Sicilia,* Bari, Laterza, 1938.

Caracciolo, E., "Architettura dell'ottocento in Sicilia," *Metron, 8* (1952), 29–40.

Celano, C., *Notizie del bello, dell'antico e del curioso della città di Napoli,* ed. G. B. Chiarini, Naples, 1856–60.

Chierici, Gino, *La Reggia Caserta,* Rome, Libreria dello Stato, 1937.

De Fusco, Renato, *Il Floreale a Napoli,* Naples, Edizioni Scientifiche Italiane, 1959.

Fichera, F. G. B., *Vaccarini e l'architettura del settecento in Sicilia,* Rome, Reale Accademia d'Italia, 1934.

Giannelli, E., *Artisti napoletani viventi, pittori, scultori, e architetti,* Naples, Libreria di Stato, 1916.

Guerra, Alfonso, and Luigi Ferrara, *Nuovo Palazzo della Borsa in Napoli,* Naples, 1909.

Murray, Edward Croft, "The Palazzina Cinese at Palermo," *Country Life, 102* (Oct. 10, 1947), 724–25.

Pane, Roberto, *Architettura dell'età barocca in Napoli,* Naples, Editrice Politecnica, 1939.

Pevsner, Nikolaus, "Review of *Architettura neoclassica a Napoli,*" *Architectural Review, 131* (1962), 307.

Sasso, Camillo Napoleone, *Storia de'monumenti di Napoli e degli architetti . . . ,* 2 vols. in 1 Naples, 1856–58.

Venditti, Arnaldo, *Architettura neoclassica a Napoli,* Naples, Edizione Scientifiche Italiane, n.d., c.1961.

Villa, Pietro, *Storia della vita urbanistica di Palermo,* Palermo, 1941.

Ziino, V., *Contributi allo studio dell'architettura del'700 in Sicilia,* Palermo, A. Priulla, 1950.

ROME

Amadei, E., *I Ponti di Roma,* Rome, Palombi, 1948.

Angeli, Diego, *Roma, barocca e moderna,* Bergamo, Istituto Italiano d'Arti Grafiche, 1933.

Armellini, M., *Le Chiese di Roma,* 2 vols. Rome, Ruffolo, 1948.

Atkinson, Fello, "La Rinascente Store, Rome," *Architectural Review, 132* (October 1962), 268–74.

Bruhns, L., *Der Kunst der Stadt Rom,* 2 vols. Vienna, Schroll, 1951.

Callari, Luigi, *Storia dell'arte contemporanea,* Rome, Loescher, 1909.

———, *Le Ville di Roma,* Rome, Bardi, 1934.

———, *I Palazzi di Roma,* 3rd ed. Rome, Apollon, 1944.

———, *Le Fontane di Roma,* Rome, Apollon, 1945.

Calza, Arturo, *Roma moderna,* Milan, Treves, 1911.

Canina, Luigi, *Le Nuove Fabbriche della Villa Borghese . . . ,* Rome, 1828.

———, *Pianta topografica di Roma antica . . . ,* Rome, 1832.

———, *Gli Edifizj* (sic) *di Roma antica . . . ,* 6 vols. Rome, 1848–56.

———, *Vedute dei principali monumenti di Roma antica,* Rome, 1851.

Castagnoli, Ferdinando, Carlo Cecchelli, Gustavo Giovannoni, and Mario Zocca, *Topografia e urbanistica di Roma,* Bologna, Cappelli, 1958.

Clark, Eleanor, *Rome and a Villa,* Garden City, Doubleday, 1952.

Colasanti, A., *Case e palazzi barocchi di Roma,* Rome, Calzone, 1913.

Concorso architettonico pel progetto di massima del palazzo del parlamento da erigersi in Roma . . . , Rome, n.d., c.1900.

Cuccioni, Tommaso, ed., *Raccolta delle principali vedute di Roma e suoi contorni,* Rome, 1837.

Della Pergola, Paola, *Villa Borghese,* Rome, Istituto Poligrafico dello Stato, 1962.

———, *Villa Borghese,* Itinerari dei musei, gallerie e monumenti d'Italia, Rome, Istituto Poligrafico dello Stato, 1964.

———, *The Borghese Gallery in Rome,* Guide-Books to the Museums and Monuments of Italy, trans. M. E. Stanley, Rome, La Libreria dello Stato, 1951.

Donati, U., *Artisti ticinesi a Roma,* Bellinzona, Istituto Editoriale Ticinese, 1942.

Dubourg, M., *Views of Rome,* London, 1820.

Egger, Hermann, *Römische Veduten . . .*, 2 vols. Vienna and Leipzig, Wolfrum, 1911–31.

Elling, Christian, *Rom Arkitekturens Liv,* Copenhagen, Gyldendal, 1956.

Escher, Konrad, *Barock und Klassizismus; Studien zur Geschichte der Architektur Roms,* Leipzig, Klinkhardt, 1910.

Fasolo, F., *Le Chiese di Roma nel '700,* Rome, Danesi, 1949, *1, Trastevere.*

Gaunt, William, *Rome, Past and Present,* ed. Geoffrey Holme, London, The Studio, 1926.

La Padula, A., *Roma 1809–1814, Contributo alla storia dell'urbanistica,* Rome, Palombi, 1958.

Lavagnino, Emilio, *Mostra del settecento a Roma,* ed. De Lucca, Rome, Grafico Tiberino, 1959.

Letarouilly, Paul Marie, *Edifices de Rome moderne . . .*, 3 vols. Paris, 1868–74.

Lowrie, Rev. Walter, *Fifty Years of St. Paul's American Church, Rome,* Rome, 1926.

Lugli, Giuseppe, *Roma nei suoi monumenti,* Rome, Signorelli, 1950.

Matthiae, Guglielmo, *Piazza del Popolo,* Rome, Palombi, 1946.

Missirini, Melchiorre, *Memorie per servire alla storia della romana Accademia di S. Luca,* Rome, 1823.

Meeks, Carroll L. V., "Churches by Street on the Via Nazionale and the Via del Babuino," *Art Quarterly, 16* (1953), 215–27.

Muñoz, Antonio, *Basilica di S. Lorenzo fuori le mura,* Rome, Palombi, 1944.

Nevin, Rev. R. J., *St. Paul's within the Walls: an account of the American Chapel at Rome, Italy,* New York, 1878.

Onofrio, C. d', *Le Fontane di Roma, con documenti e disegni inediti,* Rome, Staderini, 1957.

Orbaan, J. A. F., *Documenti sul barocco in Roma,* Rome, Nella Sede Della Società, 1920.

Passeri, G. B., *Vite de'pittori, scultori ed architetti,* Vienna, Keller, 1934.

Piacentini, Marcello, *Le Vicende edilizie di Roma dal 1870 ad oggi,* Rome, Palombi, 1952.

Pietrangeli, C., *Palazzo Braschi,* Rome, Quintily, 1958.

Quaglia, Piero, *100 Schizzi dei progetti pel monumento a Vittorio Emanuele,* Rome, 1882.

Rossi, Renzo, *Il Palazzo di Giustizia,* Rome, Voghera, 1908.

Sacripanti, Maurizio, *La Villa Borghese in Roma,* Rome, Palombi, 1953.

Sapori, Francesco, *Il Vittoriano,* Rome, Libreria dello Stato, 1946.

———, *Architettura in Roma, 1901–1950,* Rome, Belardetti, 1953.

Schiavo, Armando, *Villa Doria Pamphilj,* Rome, Ente Nazionale Industrie Turistiche Ferrovie Dello Stato, 1942.

Stettiner, Pietro, *Roma nei suoi monumenti,* Rome, Officina di Fotoincisione, 1911.

Sutton, Gertrud, "Architecture in Eighteenth-Century Rome," *Gazette des Beaux-Arts,* series 6, *59* (1962), 21–28.

Tesorone, G., *Il Padiglione . . . all'Esposizione di Roma del 1911 . . .*, Milan, Alfieri & La-croix, 1913.

Vicchi, Leone, *Villa Borghese,* Rome, 1885.

Vighi, Roberto, *The Pantheon,* trans. G. B. Ward Perkins, Rome, Tipografia Artistica, 1957.

Wasse, Canon Watson, *An Account of the . . . Church for the Anglican Communion . . . in Rome,* Aylesbury, 1885.

Wilson, Muriel Talbot, *The History of the English Church in Rome from 1816–1916,* Rome, Tipografica la Speranza, 1916.

TURIN AND PIEDMONT

Barlassina, G., and A. Picconi, *Le Chiese di Novara,* Novara, Gaudensio, 1933.

Boselli, P. and others, *Torino, guida della città . . .*, Turin, 1928.

Brizio, A. M., *L'Architettura barocca in Piemonte,* Turin, 1953.

Canina, Luigi, *Ricerche sull'architettura più propria dei temp; cristiani e applicazione della medesima ad una idea di sostituzione della Chiesa Cattedrale di S. Giovanni in Torino,* Rome, 1843.

Daverio, Arialdo, *La Cupola di S. Gaudenzio . . .*, Novara, Centro di Studi Antonelliani, 1940.

L'Esposizione di Torino del 1884, Genoa, 1884.

Ferria, G. G., *La Cupola della Mole Antonelliana . . .*, Turin, 1888.

Giraude, Fedele, *Il Santuario di Maria SS. Ausiliatrice,* Turin, S. E. I., 1948.

Michela, Ignazio, *Descrizione e disegni del Palazzo dei Magistrati Supremi di Torino . . .*, Turin, 1841.

Nacht, Leo, *Torino, 1902; Esposizione d'arte moderna,* Berlin, Wasmuth, 1902.

Olivero, E., *L'Architettura in Torino durante la prima metà dell'ottocento,* Turin, 1935.
——, *Miscellanea di architettura piemontese del settecento,* Turin, Palatina, 1937.

Passanti, M., *Architettura in Piemonte,* Turin, 1945.

Ricci, C., *Elenco degli edifici monumentali di Novara,* Rome, 1911.

Rossi, L. M., *The Santuario of the Madonna di Vico,* London, Macmillan, 1907.
——, *Il Tempio della Pace in Val d'Ermena,* Milan, Alfiere & Lacroix, 1914.

Tornielli, Vittorio, *Architetture di otto secoli del Monferrato,* Casale Monferrato, 1957.

VENICE, THE VENETO, AND THE VENEZIAS

Barbieri, F., R. Cevese, and L. Magagnato, *Guida di Vicenza,* Guide artistiche delle città d'Italia "Serie Veneta," *1,* 2nd ed. Vicenza, Eretinia, 1956.

Barbieri, Giuseppe, *Cimitero della regia città di Verona,* Verona, 1833.

Bassi, Elena, *Architettura del sei e settecento a Venezia,* Naples, Edizioni Scientifiche Itali-ane, 1962.

Beltrami, Luca, *Settantadue Giorni ai lavori del campanile di S. Marco,* Milan, Allegretti, 1903.

Cicala, Vittorio, *Ville venete,* Turin, Casa editrice "Italia ars," 1924.

Crescini, J., and G. Stefani, ed., *Il Teatro di Padova* . . . , Padua, n.d., c. 1850.

Lorenzetti, Giulio, *Venezia e il suo estuario,* Venice, Bestetti & Tumminelli, 1928.

Mazzotti, Giuseppe, *Le Ville venete,* Rome, Carlo Bestetti, 1958.

McCarthy, Mary Therese, *Venice Observed,* New York, Reynal, 1956.

Missirini, Melchiorre, *Del Tempio eretto in Possagno da Antonio Canova* . . . , Venice, 1833.

Murat, Augusto Cavallari, and others, "Il Neoclassicismo nel Veneto," *Bollettino del Centro Internazionale di Studi di Architettura Andrea Palladio, 5* (1963), 99–257.

Negrin, A. C., *Il Tempio di Lonigo* . . . , Vicenza, 1895.

Pevsner, Nikolaus, "Pedrocchino and some Allied Problems," *Architectural Review, 122* (August 1957), 112–15.

Ronchi, Oliviero, and others, *Il Caffè Pedrocchi, 1831–9 giugno–1931,* Padua, Tipografia del Messaggiero, 1931.

ARCHITECTS

Note: This portion of the bibliography does not attempt to be inclusive; references to encyclopedias, *Thieme-Becker,* biographical dictionaries, and articles in journals are given when nothing else is readily available. References to individual publication of architectural designs or executed buildings have been omitted for lack of space. Many architects have been omitted, either because they are of second rank, or for lack of information. *Thieme-Becker (Künstler-Lexikon)* has generally been given preference over the *Enciclopedia italiana,* since it is more complete and gives more extensive bibliographies. This lack is being remedied by the *Dizionario biografico degli italiani* (Rome, Istituto della Enciclopedia Italiana, 1960 ff.), referred to hereafter as *D.b.d.i.,* of which Volume 6, through "Bartolozzi," appeared in 1964.

ALBERTOLLI, GIOCONDO (1742–1839)
"G. A.," *D.b.d.i., 1.*
Della Chiesa, Angela, *L'Età neoclassica* . . . , Como, 1959, pp. 56 ff.
Kauffmann, A., *Giocondo Albertolli* . . . , Strasburg, 1911.
Albertolli, Giocondo, *Ornamenti diversi,* Milan, 2 series, 1782 ff.
———, *Miscellanea per i giovanni studiosi del disegno* . . . , Milan, 1796.
ALEANDRI, IRENEO (1795–1885)
"I. A.," *Thieme-Becker, Enciclopedia italiana.*
ALGAROTTI, FRANCESCO (1712–1764)
"F. A.," *D.b.d.i., 2.*
Michelessi, Domenico, *Memorie intorno alla vitta ed agli scritti del conte Francesco Algarotti,* Venice, 1770.
Algarotti, Francesco, *Lettere sopra l'architettura,* Venice, 1756.
———, *Lettere sopra la pittura,* Venice, 1762.

ALVINO, ENRICO (1809–1872)
"E. A.," *D.b.d.i., 2.*
Alvino, Enrico, *Memoria illustrata del progetto per la facciata della Cattedrale di Firenze,* Florence, 1864.
AMATI, CARLO (1776–1852)
"C. A.," *D.b.d.i., 2*
Amati, Carlo, *Antichità di Milano* . . . , Milan, 1804 and 1821.
ANTOLINI, GIOVANNI ANTONIO (1756–1841)
"G. A. A.," *D.b.d.i., 3.*
Della Chiesa, Angela, *L'Età neoclassica* . . . , Como, 1959, pp. 61 ff.
Antolini, Giovanni Antonio, *Progetto sul foro che doveva eseguirsi in Milano* . . . , Milan, n.d., c. 1820.
———, *Idee elementari di architettura civile,* Bologna, 1813; also Milan, 1829.
———, *Osservazioni ed aggiunte ai principii d'architettura civile di Francesco Milizia,* Milan, 1817–1818.

——, *Il Tempio di Ercole in Cori,* Milan, 1785, 1828.

ANTONELLI, ALESSANDRO (1798–1888)
"A. A.," *D.b.d.i., 3.*
Arialdo, Daverio, "Attualità di Antonelli," *Metron, 25* (1948), 24–28.
Caselli, C., *Cenni sulla vita e le fabbriche dell'architetto A. A.,* Turin, 1889.
Gregotti, Vittorio, and Aldo Rossi, "L'Influenza del romanticismo europeo nell' architettura di A. A.," *Casabella, 214,* 62–81.

ARATA, GIULIO (b. 1885)
Melani, Alfredo, *L'Architettura di Giulio Arata,* Milan, n.d., c. 1913.
Arata, Giulio, *L'Arte rustica in Sardegna,* Milan, 1925.
——, *L'Architettura arabo-normanna e il rinascimento in Sicilia,* Milan, 1914.

ARMANNI, OSVALDO (1855–1929)
"O. A.," *Enciclopedia italiana, D.b.d.i., 4.*

ASPRUCCI, ANTONIO (1723–1808)
"A. A.," *Thieme-Becker, Enciclopedia italiana, D.b.d.i., 4.*

ASPRUCCI, MARIO (1764–1804)
"M. A.," *Thieme-Becker.*

AZZOLINI, TITO (1837–1907)
"T. A.," *D.b.d.i., 4.*
Azzolini, Tito, *Natura ed arte, 2* (1895–96), 529–35.

AZZURRI, FRANCESCO (1827–1901)
"F. A.," *D.b.d.i., 4*
"Obituary," *L'Architettura pratica, 6* (1901), 22.

BACCANI, GAETANO (1792–1867)
"G. B.," *Thieme-Becker, D.b.d.i., 5.*

BAGATTI-VALSECCHI, FAUSTO (1843–1914)
"F. B. V.," *D.b.d.i., 5.* Also see Milan.

BAGATTI-VALSECCHI, GIUSEPPE (1845–1934)
See Milan.

BALZARETTO, GIUSEPPE (1801–1874)
"G. B.," *Thieme-Becker, D.b.d.i., 5.*

BARABINO, CARLO FRANCESCO (1768–1835)
"C. F. B.," *Thieme-Becker, D.b.d.i., 5.*
Labò, Mario, "Carlo Barabino," *Emporium, 54* (1921), 207–23.

BARBIERI, GIUSEPPE (1777–1838)
"G. B.," *Thieme-Becker, D.b.d.i., 6.*
Barbieri, Giuseppe, *Cimitero della regia città di Verona . . . ,* Verona, 1833.

BASILE, ERNESTO (1857–1932)
"E. B.," *Enciclopedia italiana.*
Roberti, Salvatore Caronia, *Ernesto Basile e cinquant'anni di architettura in Sicilia,* Palermo, Ciuni, 1935.
Zevi, Bruno, "E. B.," *Metron, 37* (1950), 41.
Basile, Ernesto, *Studi e schizzi,* Turin, 1911.

BASILE, GIOVANNI BATTISTA FILIPPO (1825–1891)
"G. B. F. B.," *Thieme-Becker.*

BAZZANI, CESARE (1878–1939)
"C. B.," *Enciclopedia italiana.*
Bazzani, Cesare, *Concorso—Biblioteca Nazionale di Firenze,* Florence, 1903.

BELLI, PASQUALE (1752–1833)
"P. B.," *Thieme-Becker.*

BELTRAMI, LUCA (1854–1933)
"L. B.," *Thieme-Becker.*
Annoni, Ambrogio, "L. B.," *Metron, 37* (1950), 45 ff.
Mazzoni, Guido, *Bibliografia degli scritti di Luca Beltrami . . . ,* Milan, 1930.

BERLAM, RUGGIERO (1854–1920)
Budinis, Cornelio, "R. B.," *L'Architettura, 1* (1921–22), 263–75, 339–57.

BERTOTTI-SCAMOZZI, OTTAVIO (1719–1790)
"O. B-S.," *Thieme-Becker.*
Bertotti-Scamozzi, Ottavio, *Il Forestiero istruito . . . ,* Vicenza, 1761, 2nd ed. 1780.
——, *Le Fabbriche ed i disegni di Andrea Palladio,* 2 vols. Vicenza, 1776.

BIANCHI, PIETRO (1787–1849)
Venditti, Arnaldo, *Architettura neoclassica a Napoli,* Naples, n.d., c.1961.

BIANCHI, SALVATORE (1821–1884)
Callari, Luigi, *Storia dell'arte contemporanea,* Rome, 1909.

BOITO, CAMILLO (1836–1914)
Deon, B. A., *Camillo Boito,* Reggio Emilia, 1915.
——, *Camillo Boito,* Milan, 1916.
Grassi, Liliana, *Camillo Boito,* Milan, 1959.
Marangoni, Guido, "Artisti contemporanei: Camillo Boito," *Emporium, 28* (1908), 405–22.

BOLLATI, GIUSEPPE (1819–1869)
T. C. I., *Piemonte.*

BONSIGNORE, FERDINANDO (1767–1843)
"F. B.," *Thieme-Becker.*
D' Althan, Nino, *Gli Artisti italiani,* Turin, 1902, p. 64.

BRASINI, ARMANDO (b. 1879)
Orano, Paolo, *L'Urbe massima e l'architettura di A. Brasini,* Rome, 1917.

BRENTANO, GIUSEPPE (1862–1889)
"G. B.," *Thieme-Becker.*
Beltrami, Luca, *G. B.,* Milan, 1899.
Brentano, Giuseppe, *Concorso internazionale di II grado per la nuova facciata del Duomo di Milano,* Milan, 1888.
BROGGI, LUIGI (1851–1926)
"L. B.," *Thieme-Becker.*
De Gubernatis, Angelo, *Dizionario,* Florence, 1892, p. 576.
BRUNO, NICCOLÒ (—— d. 1899)
"N. B.," *Thieme-Becker.*
BUSIRI-VICI, ANDREA (1817–1911)
Busiri-Vici, Andrea, *Quarantatrè Anni di vita artistica; memorie storiche di un architetto,* Rome, 1891.

CACIALLI, GIUSEPPE (1770–1828)
"G. C.," *Thieme-Becker.*
Cacialli, Giuseppe, *Collezione dei disegni di nuove fabbriche e ornati fatti nella regia Villa del Poggio Imperiale . . . ,* Florence, 1823, also 1831.
——, *Raccolta di progetti architettonici ideati dall'architetto Giuseppe Cacialli e disegnati e incisi da Fabio Nuti e Carlo Chirici,* Florence, 1827.
CAGNOLA, LUIGI (1762–1833)
Brosio, V., "Nel primo centenario . . . del L. C. . . . ," *Emporium, 78* (1933), 94–101.
Della Chiesa, Angela, *L'Età neoclassica . . . ,* Como, 1959, pp. 63 ff.
Mezzanotte, Paolo, *L'Architettura di Luigi Cagnola,* Milan, 1930.
——, "L. C. architetto," *Architettura, 7* (1933), 337–56.
CALDERINI, GUGLIELMO (1837–1916)
"G. C.," *Thieme-Becker.*
Giampoli, Carlo, *Dizionario . . . ,* Naples, 1942, *1.*
Milani, Giovanni Battista, *Le Opere architettoniche di Guglielmo Calderini,* Milan, 1916.
CAMPANINI, ALFREDO (1873–1926)
Scheichenbaver, Mario, *Alfredo Campanini,* Milan, 1958.
CAMPORESE, GIUSEPPE (1763–1822)
"G. C.," *Thieme-Becker.*
CAMPORESE, PIETRO (1726–1781)
Tarchiani, Nello, *L'Architettura . . . ,* Florence, 1937, p. 11.
CAMPORESE, PIETRO, THE YOUNGER (1792–1873) "P. C.," *Thieme-Becker.*

CANEVARI, RAFFAELE (1825–1900)
"R. C.," *Thieme-Becker.*
CANINA, LUIGI (1795–1856)
Bendinelli, G., *L. Canina, le opere e i tempi,* Alessandria, 1953.
Canina, Luigi, *Le Nuove Fabbriche della Villa Borghese,* Rome, 1828.
——, *L'Architettura antica descritta . . . ,* 9 vols. Rome, 1834–44.
——, *L'Architettura greca,* Rome, 1827.
——, *Gli Edificj di Roma antica . . . ,* 6 vols. Rome, 1848–56.
CANONICA, LUIGI (1762–1844)
Della Chiesa, Angela, *L'Età neoclassica . . . ,* Como, 1959, pp. 63 ff.
CANTONI, SIMONE (1736–1818)
Alizari, F., *Professori del disegno in Liguria,* Genoa, 1864, *1.*
CARIMINI, LUCA (1830–1890)
Morpurgo, Vittorio, "Un Precursore: Luca Carimini, 1830–1890," *Architettura, 7* (1927–28), 193–211.
CATTANEO, RAFFAELE (1860–1889)
Cattaneo, Raffaele, *L'Architettura in Italia dal secolo VI al mille circa . . . ,* Venice, 1889.
Giavarini, Fortunato, *L'Architetto Raffaele Cattaneo,* Rovigo, 1941.
CEPPI, CARLO (1829–1921)
Midana, Arturo, "L'Architetto Conte Carlo Ceppi," *Atti . . . Società degli Ingegneri . . . in Torino,* n.s., *5* (Feb. 1951).
CERUTI, GIOVANNI (1842–1907)
De Gubernatis, A., *Dizionario . . . ,* Florence, 1892, p. 119.
CIPOLLA, ANTONIO (1823–1874)
Melani, A., *Architettura italiana . . . ,* Milan, 1910.
COLLEMARINI, EDOARDO (1864–1928)
Joseph, D., *Geschichte der Architektur in Italien,* Leipzig, 1907, p. 507.
CONCONI, LUIGI (1852–1917)
De Gubernatis, A., *Dizionario . . . ,* Florence, 1892.
Giollo, Raffaele, "L. C.," *Vita d'arte, 1* (1914), 136–44.
COPPEDÈ, GINO (1866–1927)
"G. C.," *Enciclopedia italiana.*

D'ANDRADE, ALFREDO (1843–1915)
Angelini, Luigi, "Alfredo d'Andrade," *Emporium, 43* (1916), 79–80.
Carandini, F., *La Rocca e il Borgo Medioevale eretti in Torino . . . ,* Ivrea, 1925.

Tarchiani, Nello, "D'Andrade," *Il Marzocco, 20* (Dec. 5, 1915).

D'ARONCO, RAIMONDO (1857–1932)
Nicoletti, Manfredi, *Raimondo d'Aronco,* Milan, 1955.

DE ANGELIS, GIULIO (1850–1906)
"G. de A.," *Thieme-Becker.*

DE FABRIS, EMILIO (1808–1883)
Callari, Luigi, *Storia dell'arte italiana contemporanea,* Rome, 1909.
De Gubernatis, A., *Dizionario . . . ,* Florence, 1892.
Gotti, Aurelio, "E. d. F.," *Italiani del secolo XIX . . . ,* Città di Castello, 1911.

DIEDO, ANTONIO (1772–1847)
Diedo, Antonio, *Fabbriche e disegni di Antonio Diedo . . . ,* Venice, 1846.
———, Cicognara, and Zanotto, *Descrizione delle fabbriche più cospicue di Venezia,* Venice, n.d.

FENOGLIO, PIETRO (b. 1865)
D'Althan, Nino, *Gli Artisti italiani . . . ,* Turin, 1902.

FICHERA, FRANCESCO (b. 1881)
Piacentini, Marcello, *Francesco Fichera,* Genoa, 1931.

FRANCO, GIACOMO (1818–1895)
Negrin, A. C., *Il Tempio di Lonigo e l'architetto Franco,* Vicenza, 1895.

FUGA, FERDINANDO (1699–1781)
Matthiae, Guglielmo, *Ferdinando Fuga e la sua opera romana,* Rome, n.d., c.1950.
Pane, Roberto, *Ferdinando Fuga,* Naples, 1956.

GHERARDESCO, ALESSANDRO (1779–1852)
Gherardesco, Alessandro, *La Casa di delizia . . . ,* Pisa, 1826.

GIOVANNONI, GUSTAVO (1873–1949)
"G. G.," *Enciclopedia italiana.*

GUERRA, ALFONSO (1845–1900)
Giannelli, *Artisti napoletani viventi . . . ,* 1916, p. 720.
Guerra, Alfonso and L. Ferrara, *Nuovo Palazzo della Borsa in Napoli,* Naples, 1909.

JAPELLI, GIUSEPPE (1783–1852)
Damerini, Gino, *Un Architetto veneziano dell'ottocento, Giuseppe Jappelli,* Venice, 1934.
Fiocco, Giuseppe, *G. Jappelli, architetto,* Padua, 1931.

Mantiglia, R. C., "Giuseppe Jappelli, Architetto," *L'Architettura, 1* (1955), 538–51.

JUVARRA, FILIPPO (1676–1735)
De Vecchi di Val Cismon, C. M., L. Rovere, V. Viale, and A. E. Brinckmann, *Filippo Juvarra,* Milan, Zucchi, 1937.
Telluccini, Augusto, *L'Arte dell'architetto Filippo Juvara* [sic] *in Piemonte,* Turin, 1926.

KOCH, GAETANO (1849–1910)
Piacentini, Pio, "Gaetano Koch," *Ann. Assoc. Cultori Architettura, 1908–09* (Rome, 1910), 134–43.

MACIACHINI, CARLO (1818–1899)
"Obituary," *Edilizia moderna, 8* (1899), 52.
Beltrami, Luca, *Il Cimitero monumentale di Milano,* Milan, 1889.

MANCINI, GIUSEPPE
Benelli, Sem, *L'Architettura di Giuseppe Mancini, schizzi e progetti,* Milan, n.d., c.1910.

MANFREDI, MANFREDO (1859–1927)
"Cronache," *Emporium, 67* (1928), 243–45.

MARCHIONNI, CARLO (1702–1786)
"C. M.," *Thieme-Becker, Enciclopedia italiana.*

MARVUGLIA, GIUSEPPE VENANZIO (1729–1814)
"G. V. M.," *Dizionario dei Siciliani illustri,* Palermo, 1939, pp. 317 ff.
Caracciolo, E., "Architettura dell'ottocento," *Metron, 7* (1952), 29–40.
Roberti, Salvatore Caronia, *Venanzio Marvuglia,* Palermo, 1934.

MASSARI, GIORGIO (1686–1766)
Moschini, V., "G. M. architetto veneto," *Dedalo, 12* (1932), 198–229.
Semenzato, Camillo, "Problemi di architettura veneta; Giorgio Massari," *Arte veneta* (1957), 151–61.

MATAS, NICOLA (1798–1872)
Matas, Nicola, *Dimostrazione del progetto per compiere . . . S. M. del Fiore . . . ,* Florence, 1843, 2nd ed. 1859.

MAZZANTI, RICCARDO (1850–1910)
De Gubernatis, A., *Dizionario . . . ,* Florence, 1892.

MELLA, EDOARDO ARBORIO (1808–1884)
D'Althan, Nino, *Gli Artisti italiani . . . ,* Turin, 1902.

MEMMO, ANDREA (1729–1793)
See Appendix A.
MENGONI, GIUSEPPE (1829–1877)
"Giuseppe Mengoni e la Galleria Vittorio
Emanuele di Milano," *Emporium, 39*
(1914), 393–98.
Ricci, G., *La Vita e le opere dell'architetto
Giuseppe Mengoni,* Bologna, 1930.
MEZZANOTTE, PAOLO (b. 1878)
"P. M.," *Thieme-Becker.*
Mezzanotte, Paolo, *L'Architettura di Luigi
Cagnola,* Milan, 1930.
MILANI, GIOVANNI BATTISTA (1876–1940)
"G. B. M.," *Enciclopedia italiana.*
MILIZIA, FRANCESCO (1725–1798)
See Appendix A.
MORELLI, COSIMO (1732–1812)
Gambetta, G., *C. M. architetto, 1732–
1812,* Imola, 1926.
Morelli, Cosimo, *Pianta e spaccato del
nuovo Teatro d'Imola,* Rome, 1780.
MORETTI, GAETANO (1860–1938)
Annoni, Ambrogio, "Tre architetti dell'
800," *Metron, 37* (1950), 42–43.
Beltrami, Luca, *Gaetano Moretti; costru-
zioni, concorsi, schizzi,* Milan, 1912.
Calzavara, Maurizio, "L'Architetto Gae-
tano Moretti," *Casabella,* no. 218 (1958),
pp. 69–83.

NICCOLINI, ANTONIO (1772–1850)
"A. N.," *Thieme-Becker, Enciclopedia
italiana.*
NOBILE, PIETRO (1774–1854)
Amodeo, Aurelio, "Un architetto neoclas-
sico a Trieste . . . ," *L'Architettura, 1*
(1955), 49–52, 378–84.
NOTTOLINI, LORENZO (1787–1851)
"L. N.," *Thieme-Becker.*

PALAGI, PELAGIO (1775–1860)
"P. P.," *Thieme-Becker.*
PALANTI, MARIO
Canotti, G., *Prima Esposizione personale
d'architettura . . . ,* Milan, 1917.
Palanti, Mario, *Architettura per tutti,* Mi-
lan, n.d., c.1940.
PAOLETTI, NICCOLÒ MARIA GASPARE
(1727–1813)
"G. P.," *Thieme-Becker.*
PETITI, ENRICO (1832–1898)
De Gubernatis, A., *Dizionario . . . ,* Flor-
ence, 1892.
PIACENTINI, PIO (1846–1928)
"P. P.," *Thieme-Becker.*

Callari, Luigi, *Storia dell'arte contempo-
ranea,* Rome, 1909, p. 127.
PIERMARINI, GIUSEPPE (1734–1808)
Boito, Camillo, *Giuseppe Piermarini, ar-
chitetto,* Milan, 1908.
Della Chiesa, Angela, *L'Età neoclassica
. . . ,* Como, 1959, pp. 51 ff.
Filippini, Enrico, *G. P. nella vita e nelle
opere,* Foligno, 1936.
PIRANESI, GIOVANNI BATTISTA (1720–
1778)
Foçillon, Henri, *Giovanni-Battista Pira-
nesi,* 2nd ed. Paris, 1928.
Mayor, A. Hyatt, *G. B. Piranesi,* New
York, 1952.
Parks, Robert O. and others, *Piranesi,*
Northampton, 1961.
Wittkower, Rudolf, "Piranesi's 'Parere su
l'architettura,'" *Journal of the Warburg
and Courtauld Institute, 2* (1938–39),
147 ff.
PIROVANO, ERNESTO (b. 1866)
"E. P.," *Thieme-Becker.*
Massarini, Tullo, *Le Ville Crespi,* Milan,
1905.
PISTRUCCI, CAMILLO (1856–1927)
"C. P.," *Thieme-Becker.*
De Gubernatis, A., *Dizionario . . . ,* Flor-
ence, 1892.
POCCIANTI, PASQUALE (1774–1858)
"P. P.," *Thieme-Becker.*
PODESTI, GIULIO (1857–1909)
"G. P.," *Thieme-Becker.*
POGGI, GIUSEPPE (1811–1901)
"G. P.," *Enciclopedia italiana.*
POLETTI, LUIGI (1792–1869)
"L. P.," *Thieme-Becker.*
POLLACK, LEOPOLD (1751–1806)
Della Chiesa, Angela, *L'Età neoclassica
. . . ,* Como, 1959, pp. 58 ff.
PRETI, FRANCESCO MARIA (1701–1774)
"F. M. P.," *Thieme-Becker.*
Favaro-Fabris, M., *L'Architetto F. M. P.
di Castelfranco . . . ,* Treviso, 1954.
Riccati, Giordano, ed., *Elementi di archi-
tettura del Signor Fr. M. Preti,* Venice,
1780.
PROMIS, CARLO (1808–1872)
"C. P.," *Enciclopedia italiana.*
Promis, Carlo, *Fabbriche moderne . . . ,*
Turin, 1875.
QUAGLIA, PIERO PAOLO (1856–1898)
Quaglia, Piero, *100 schizzi dei progetti pel
monumento a Vittorio Emanuele,* Rome,
1882.

——, *Quattro Chiacchiere* . . . , Rome, 1882.

——, *Palazzo di Giustizia, primo concorso,* Naples, 1884.

QUARENGHI, GIACOMO (1744–1817)
Della Chiesa, Angela, *L'Età neoclassica* . . . , Como, 1959, pp. 79 ff.
Isola, Maria Catelli, *Restauro di disegni di Giacomo Quarenghi,* Rome, 1963.
Quarenghi, Jacopo, *Fabbriche e disegni di G. Q.,* Milan, 1821, 2nd ed. Mantua, 1843–44.

RAGUZZINI, FILIPPO (c.1680–1771)
Rotili, Mario, *Filippo Raguzzini e il rococò romano,* Rome, n.d., c.1951.

RICATTI, GIORDANO (1709–1790)
"G. R.," *Thieme-Becker.*
Ricatti, Giordano, ed., *Elementi di architettura del Signor Fr. M. Preti,* Venice, 1780.

RUBBIANI, ALFONSO (1848–1913)
Malaguzzi-Valeri, F., *L'Architetti a Bologna,* Bologna, 1899.

RUSGA, LUIGI (1758–1822)
"L. R.," *Dictionary of Architecture, 6–7,* 83.

SABATINI, FRANCESCO (1722–1797)
"F. S.," *Dictionary of Architecture, 6–7,* 1.

SACCONI, GIUSEPPE (1854–1905)
Acciaresi, Primo, *Giuseppe Sacconi e l'opera sua massima,* Rome, 1911.
Morosini, Luigi, "Opera minore di G. S.," *L'Architettura, 1* (1921–22), 77.
Sapori, Francesco, *Il Vittoriano,* Rome, 1946.

SADA, CARLO (1809–1873)
"C. S.," *Thieme-Becker.*

SALVI, NICOLA (1697–1751)
Matthiae, Guglielmo, "Nicola Salvi minore," *Palladio,* n.s., *4* (1954), 161 ff.
Schiavo, A., *La Fontana di Trevi e le altre opere di Nicola Salvi,* Rome, 1956.

SANT'ELIA, ANTONIO (1888–1916)
Apollonio, Umbro, *Antonio Sant'Elia,* Milan, 1958.
Banham, Reyner, "Sant-Elia," *Architectural Review, 117* (1955), 295–301; *Architectural Review, 119* (1956), 343–44.
Caramel, Luciano, and Alberto Longatti, *Antonio Sant'Elia,* Como, 1962.
Mariani, Leonardo, "Disegni inediti di Sant'Elia," *L'Architettura, 1* (1955–56), 210–15, 704–05.

Marinetti, F. T., "Sant'Elia e la nuova architettura," *Mostra di opere* . . . , Como, 1929–30.
Sartoris, Alberto, *Sant'Elia e l'architettura,* Rome, 1944.

SANTI, LORENZO (1783–1839)
"L. S.," *Thieme-Becker.*
Santi, Lorenzo, *Progetti architettonici delli fratelli Santi* . . . , Rome, 1815.

SARTI, ANTONIO (1797–1880)
"A. S.," *Thieme-Becker.*

SCALA, ANDREA (1820–1892)
Callari, Luigi, *Storia dell'arte contemporanea,* Rome, 1909.

SCALFAROTTO, GIOVANNI ANTONIO (1700–1764)
"G. A. S.," *Thieme-Becker.*
See also Appendix A, 1752, 1762, 1770, and 1778.

SCHMIDT, FRIEDRICH VON (1825–1891)
"F. von S.," *Thieme-Becker.*

SELVA, GIANNANTONIO (1753–1819)
Bassi, Elena, *Giannantonio Selva, architetto veneziano,* Padua, 1936.

SELVATICO, PIETRO ESTENSE (1803–1880)
"P. S-E.," *Thieme-Becker.*
Selvatico, Pietro Estense, *Guida di Venezia e delle isole* . . . , Venice, 1852, etc.
——, *Scritti d'arte,* Florence, 1859.
——, *Sulla Architettura e sulla scultura in Venezia* . . . , Venice, 1847.

SFONDRINI, ACHILLE (1836–1900)
"A. S.," *Thieme-Becker.*

SIMONETTI, MICHELANGELO (1724–1781)
"M. S.," *Enciclopedia italiana.*

SOLI, GIUSEPPE MARIA (1745–1822)
"G. M. S.," *Dictionary of Architecture, 6–7,* 101–02.

SOMMARUGA, GIUSEPPE (1867–1917)
Angelina, Luigi, "Artisti contemporanei: Giuseppe Sommaruga," *Emporium, 46* (1917), 281–88.
Monneret de Villard, Ugo, *L'Architettura di Giuseppe Sommaruga,* Milan, 1908.
Sommaruga, Giuseppe, *Palazzo Castiglioni, Milano,* Milan, n.d., c.1903.

STACCHINI, ULISSE (b. 1871)
"U. S.," *Enciclopedia italiana.*

STERN, RAFFAELLO (1774–1820)
"R. S.," *Thieme-Becker.*
Stern, Raffaello, *Lezioni di architettura civile,* Rome, 1822.

TALUCCHI, GIUSEPPE (1782–1863)
"G. T.," *Thieme-Becker.*
Talucchi, V., *Brevi Cenni sulla vita e sulle*

opere dell'architetto G. M. Talucchi, Turin, 1917.
TEMANZA, TOMMASO (1705–1789)
Negri, F., *Notizie intorno alla persona e alle opere di T. T.,* Venice, 1830.
See also Appendix A, 1752, 1762.
TIRALI, ANDREA (c.1660–1737)
"A. T.," *Enciclopedia italiana.*
TIRELLI, GUIDO
Tirelli, Guido, *Palazzine e ville signorili,* Turin, 1923.
TREVES, MARCO (1814–1897)
"M. T.," *Thieme-Becker.*
TURCHINI, P.
Turchini, P., *Il Ferro lavorato—progetti originali* . . . , Turin, L'Artista Moderno, n.d., c.1910.

UGGERI, ANGELO (1788–   )
"A. U.," *Dictionary of Architecture, 8, 2.*
Uggeri, Angelo, *Della Basilica di S. Paolo* . . . , Rome, 1823, etc.
——, *Giornate pittoresche degli edifizi antichi di Roma,* 5 vols. Rome, 1800.
——, *Tivoli e Tusculum* . . . , 12 vols. Rome, 1800–19.

VALADIER, GIUSEPPE (1762–1839)
Ciampi, Ignazio, *Vita di G. V.,* Rome, 1870.
Schulze-Battman, Elfriede, *Valadier ein Klassizistescher Arkitect a Roms, 1767–1839,* Dresden, 1939.
Valadier, Giuseppe, *Architettura pratica,* Rome, 1828–39.
——, *Narrazione artistica dell'operato finora nel restauro dell'Arco di Tito,* Rome, 1822.
——, *Opere di architettura* . . . , Rome, 1833.
——, *Progetti architettonici,* Rome, 1807.
——, *Raccolta di diverse invenzioni,* Rome, 1796.
VALERI, ANTONIO (1648–1736)
Valeri, Ugo, *Antonio Valeri nella vita artistica dell '700 fra gli illustri architetti romani,* Rome, 1943.

VANTINI, RODOLFO (1791–1856)
"R. V.," *Thieme-Becker.*
VANVITELLI, CARLO (1739–1821)
"C. V.," *Thieme-Becker.*
VANVITELLI, LUIGI (1700–1773)
Chierici, Gino, *La Reggia di Caserta,* Rome, 1930.
Fichera, Francesco, *Luigi Vanvitelli,* Rome, 1937.
Mantonelli, G., *Vita e opere di L. V.,* Caserta, 1913.
Vanvitelli, Luigi, *Dichiarazione dei disegni del real Palazzo di Caserta,* Naples, 1756.
VESPIGNANI, FRANCESCO (1842–1899)
"F. V.," *Thieme-Becker.*
VESPIGNANI, VIRGILIO (1808–1882)
"V. V.," *Thieme-Becker.*
VINACCIA, GAETANO
Vinaccia, Gaetano, *Cottages,* Turin, n.d., c.1910.
VISENTINI, ANTONIO (1688–1782)
Visentini, Antonio, *Osservazioni di Antonio Visentini architetto veneto che servono di continuazione al trattato di Teofilo Gallacini,* Venice, 1771.
——, *Raccolta di schizzi,* Venice, 1735, 1742, 1761, 1777.
VITTONE, BERNARDO ANTONIO (1704/5–1770)
Olivero, Eugenio, *Le Opere di B.A.V. architetto piemontese del secolo XVIII,* Turin, 1920.
See Appendix A, 1760, 1766.
VOGHERA, LUIGI (b. 1788)
Voghera, Luigi, *Raccolta dei disegni dell' architetto Luigi Voghera,* Milan, 1842.

WINCKELMANN, JOHANN JOACHIM (1717–1768)
Justi, Carl, *Winckelmann und seine Zeitgenossen,* 3 vols. Leipzig, 1923.

ZANOIA, GIUSEPPE (1752–1817)
"G. Z.," *Thieme-Becker.*

Index

Italian buildings other than the antique are listed under cities. London and New York buildings are listed by name; all other buildings by name or location as they are identified in the text. For names of persons, the last element is usually the index reference. Dates, when obtainable, are given for architects and artists.